Great Ideas in Computer Science

Great Ideas in Computer Science

A Gentle Introduction

Alan W. Biermann

The MIT Press
Cambridge, Massachusetts
London, England

This book was set in Times Roman, Courier, and Helvetica by The MIT Press using computer disks provided by the author, and it was printed and bound in the United States of America.

Library of Congress Cataloging-in-Publication Data

Biermann, Alan W., 1939– *B+T APD 6-12-90*
   Great ideas in computer science: a gentle introduction / Alan W. Biermann.
     p. cm.
   Includes bibliographical references.
   ISBN 0-262-02302-4. — ISBN 0-262-52148-2 (pbk.)
   1. Computer science. I. Title.
QA76.B495 1990
004—dc20
                                                  89-13989
                                                   CIP

To my parents
David and Ruth Biermann

Contents

* Each section is labeled A, B, or C depending on whether it contains introductory, regular or optional
  material.

Preface

This is a book about computers—what they are, how they work, what they can do and what they cannot do. It is written for people who read about such topics as silicon chips or artificial intelligence and want to understand them, for people who need to have data processed on the job and want to know what can and cannot be done, and for people who see the proliferation of computers throughout society and ask about the meaning of it all. It is written for doctors, lawyers, preachers, teachers, managers, students, and all others who have a curiosity to learn about computing. It is also written for computer science students and professionals whose education may not have covered all of the important areas and who want to broaden themselves.

I was asked in 1985 to create a course in computer science for liberal arts students, and I decided that it was my job to present, as well as I could, the great intellectual achievements of the field. These are the "great ideas" that attract the attention of everyone who comes near and that, when collected together, comprise the heart of the field of computer science. I have spent considerable time in the succeeding years gathering together materials that capture these results.

What are the "great ideas" of computer science? The first and most important is the idea of the *algorithm*—a procedure or recipe that can be given to a person or machine for doing a job. The other great ideas revolve around this central one; they give methodologies for coding algorithms into machine readable form, and they describe what can be and what cannot be coded for machine execution. They show how concepts of everyday life can be meaningfully represented by electrical voltages and currents that are manipulated inside a machine, and they show how to build mechanisms to do these computations. They also show how to translate languages that people can use comfortably into languages that machines use so that the machine capabilites are accessible. They show how human-like reasoning processes can be programmed for machine execution, and they help us to understand what the ultimate capabilities of machines someday may become.

But it would seem that these great ideas are too complex and too technical to be understood by nonspecialists. Typically, a computer science major studies several years of mathematics and a long list of computer courses to learn these things, and we should not expect ordinary people to pick them up reading a single book. How can we meaningfully condense such extensive studies into a volume that many people can understand?

The answer is that the ideas must be reformulated in substantial ways, huge amounts of nonessential detail must be removed, and the vocabulary of the studies must be chosen carefully. Consider, for example, the traditional coverage of computer programming in a computer science curriculum. The student is taught all of the syntactic features of some programming language, numerous implementation details, and a variety of applications. We know that if we teach all of these things, there will be no time in the course for anything else. Students who want a broader view of the field than just programming will be frustrated. The treatment in this book teaches only a few of the features of Pascal, and all programs are restricted to those constructions. Most of the important lessons in programming can be taught within these limitations, and the reader's confusion from broad syntactic variety is eliminated. As another example, the traditional treatment of switching circuit design involves extensive study of Boolean algebra—equations, minimization, and circuit synthesis. But one can teach the most important ideas without any Boolean algebra at all. One can still address a design problem, write down a functional table for the target behavior, and create a nonminimal switching circuit to do the computation. The whole issue of circuit minimization that electrical engineers spend so much time on need not concern the general reader who simply wants to learn something about computers. Similar rather major revisions have been made to the traditional treatment of all computer topics. Thus we have Pascal without pointers, transistor theory without potential barriers, compilation without code optimization, computability theory without Turing machines, artificial intelligence without LISP, and so forth.

But all of these revisions have been made for a good reason. The goal is to give readers access to the essentials of the great ideas in one book. Readers learn to write a variety of programs in Pascal, design switching circuits, learn the essential mechanisms of transistor theory and their implementation in VLSI, study a variety of von Neumann and parallel architectures, hand simulate a compiler to see how it works, learn to classify various computations as tractable or intractable, gain an understanding of the concept of noncomputability, and come to grips with many of the important issues in artificial intelligence.

Of course, the presentation to nonspecialists must be done carefully in other ways as well. For example, it is important in the early chapters to introduce topics with motivating material. Each chapter on programming begins with a computational problem, and the lessons in programming are presented as a way of solving the problem. Also, much attention has been given to the choice of vocabulary. For example, computer scientists tend to use the word "move" in places where ordinary English speakers would say "copy." So the word "move" can cause confusion and has been banned from the book except where it is the only correct word. Dozens of other common vocabulary words have been similarly filtered where they might cause confusion, or they have been carefully defined when they are specifically required.

Another issue concerns the use of mathematical notations when the reader may not be experienced mathematically. The philosophy followed here is that such notations are essential to the study and that they must be included. The reason that a person reads a book in computer science is to study the field, and many of the things worth studying are notations. One of the great benefits of the study may be that a person who feels alien to formal notations, in fact, may become quite comfortable with them. The book introduces relatively few notations, explains them in considerable detail, and uses them repetitively so the reader can become comfortable with them.

Finally, one might ask whether the "great ideas" presented here are the same as those that would be chosen by other authors. In fact, while one would expect some variations in opinions, there is considerable agreement about what constitutes the field of computer science. The central themes presented here are probably the same as would be chosen by most experts. As an illustration, one can examine the "intellectual framework for the discipline of computing" as given by the Task Force on the Core of Computer Science: "Computing as a Discipline" by Peter J. Denning (Chairman), Douglas E. Comer, David Gries, Michael C. Mulder, Allen Tucker, A. Joe Turner, and Paul Young.* This report presents a view of the field and makes recommendations related to proper computer science education. Among the contributions of the report is a description of nine subareas that the authors propose cover the field. They are

1. Algorithms and data structures
2. Programming languages
3. Architecture
4. Numerical and symbolic computation
5. Operating systems
6. Software methodology and engineering
7. Database and information retrieval systems
8. Artificial intelligence and robotics
9. Human-computer communication

This book presents an introduction to most of the nine subareas. The notable exceptions are "operating systems" and some issues related to "human-computer communication." Space limitations prevented the inclusion of operating systems except that they are mentioned, and their function is briefly described in chapter 10. Human-computer communication via natural language is discussed but no mention of computer graphics is included. But except for these few omissions, the contents of this book are in agreement with the views of the committee.

Instructors of classes may find that this volume covers more material than they can fit into a single course. In this case, coverage can be limited, for example, to the first two thirds of the book with only one or two lectures allocated at the end for overviewing advanced topics. This yields a course on programming and a study of how computers work. Another way to accelerate the study is to cover the switching, transistor studies, and VLSI in a single lecture, and then to spend about half of the course on chapters 9 through 14. There is a third way to use the book that is

---

* Peter J. Denning (Chairman), Douglas E. Comer, David Gries, Michael C. Mulder, Allen Tucker, A. Joe Turner, and Paul R. Young, "Computing as a Discipline," *Communications of the ACM*, Volume 32, Number 1, January, 1989; also in *Computer*, Volume 22, Number 2, February, 1989.

applicable when students have already learned programming from another source. In this case, coverage can begin at chapter 5 and proceed to the end. I have used many variations of these strategies in my own course. I usually do not cover recursion or the C-ranked sections of the translation and noncomputability chapters because they are difficult for my students.

It is a pleasure to acknowledge the contributions of many individuals to the preparation of this book. I, first of all, am grateful to the Duke University Department of Computer Science which has given me an exciting environment and plenty of support for scholarly endeavors over the last fifteen years. I, secondly, would like to thank my several hundred students in this course who taught their instructor that he could not include all the things he wanted. They convinced me that I would have to remove much of the material that I dearly loved if any of it were to be understood, and they explained the problems with vocabulary: I might think I was using simple nontechnical vocabulary but the words I was using meant something else to them. This book is as much an accomplishment of these patient young people as it is of mine. I am especially appreciative of the efforts of Craig Singer who did a brilliant job as a Teaching Assistant over two years and Michael Hines and Jothy Rosenberg who taught the course other semesters. These people were sensitive to student difficulties and made excellent suggestions for improving the coverage. An early draft of the book was circulated for review among professors at other institutions during the 1987-88 academic year. I am very appreciative of many helpful comments by Shan Chi (Northwestern University), David Frisque (University of Michigan), Rhys Price Jones (Oberlin College), Emily Moore (Grinnel College), Richard E. Pattis (University of Washington), Harvey Lee Shapiro (Lewis and Clark College), Jill Smudski (at that time University of Pennsylvania), and eight anonymous reviewers. On the basis of these reviews and the classroom experiences, the book was reorganized and rewritten.

The new version of the book was brought to the classroom in the fall of 1988, and I would like to thank Ronnie Smith for contributing the excellent chapter on VLSI. I am again grateful to my students who filled out questionnaires on four occasions helping me find weak points in the explanations and to my Teaching Assistant, Albert Nigrin, for his help. I would also especially like to thank Elina Kaplan who spent countless hours on some of the early chapters finding ways to improve the presentation. Where simplicity and clarity occur in these chapters, much is owed to Elina. Many other individuals have contributed by reading chapters and making suggestions. These include Heidi Brubaker, Dania Egedi, Linda Fineman, Chris Gandy, Curry Guinn, Tim Gegg-Harrison, Barry Koster, Anselmo Lastra, Ken Lang, Albert Nigrin, Lorrie Tomek, Tom Truscott, and Doreen Yen. I am especially appreciative of errors found and suggestions made by David M. Gordon, Henry Greenside, Donald Loveland, and Charlie Martin. Many other friends have made suggestions and commented on the chapters.

The book has been given much of its personality by Matt Evans who created the cartoons at the beginnings of the chapters. I am extremely appreciative of his efforts. I am tremendously indebted to Ann Davis who typed the manuscript from my handwritten pages. Her diligence and accuracy greatly eased the burden of creating the book. I would also like to thank Marie Cunningham for typing some of the chapters and Denita Thomas for preparing the index. Barry Koster was kind enough to generate a large number of the figures, Eric Smith helped me on numerous occasions with library work, and Lorrie LeJeune of The MIT Press did the excellent job of typesetting. I would also like to express my heartfelt thanks to Robert Prior, Harry Stanton, and the other editors at The MIT Press who understood the dream of my book from the beginning and who have strongly supported my efforts. Finally, I would like to thank my wife, Alice, my daughter, Jennifer, and my son, David, for their enthusiasm and encouragement on this project.

Studying Academic Computer Science:
An Introduction

Rumors

Computers are the subject of many rumors, and we wonder what to believe. People say that computers in the future will do all clerical jobs and even replace some well-trained experts. They say computers are beginning to simulate the human mind, to create art, to prove theorems, to learn, and to make careful judgments. They say that computers will permeate every aspect of our jobs and private lives by managing communication, manipulating information, and providing entertainment. They say that even our political systems will be altered—that in previously closed societies, computers will bring universal communication that will threaten the existing order, and in free societies, they will bring increased monitoring and control. On the other hand, there are skeptics who point out that computer science has many limitations and that the impact of machines has been overemphasized.

Some of these rumors are correct and give us fair warning of things to come. Others may be somewhat fanciful, leading us to worry about the future more than is necessary. Still others point out questions that we may argue about for years without finding answers. Whatever the case, we can be sure that there are many important issues related to computers that are of vital importance, and they are worth trying to understand.

We should study computer science and address these concerns. We should get our hands on a machine and try to make it go. We should control the machine; we should play with it; we should harness it; and most important, we should try to understand it. We should try to build insights from our limited experiences that will illuminate answers to our questions. We should try to arm ourselves with understanding because the computer age is upon us.

This book is designed to help people understand computers and computer science. It begins with a study of programming in the belief that using, controlling, and manipulating machines is an essential avenue to understanding them. Then it takes the reader on a guided tour of the machine internals, exploring all of its essential functioning from the tiniest movements of electrons through semiconductors to the architecture of the machine and the software that drives it. Finally, the book explores the limitations of computing, the frontiers of the science as they are currently understood.

In short, the book attempts to give a thorough introduction to the field with an emphasis on the fundamental mechanisms that enable computers to work. It presents many of the "great ideas" of computer science, the intellectual paradigms that scientists use to understand the field. These ideas provide the tools to help the reader comprehend and live with machines in the modern world.

Studying Computer Science

Computer science is the study of recipes and ways to carry them out. A *recipe* is a procedure or method for doing something. The science studies kinds of recipes, the properties of recipes, languages for writing them down, methods for creating them, and the construction of machines that will carry them out. Of course, computer scientists want to distinguish themselves from chefs, so they have their own name for recipes—they call them *algorithms*. But we will save most of the technical jargon for later.

If we wish to understand computer science, then we must study recipes, or algorithms. The first problem relates to how to conceive of them and how to write them down. For example, one might want a recipe for treating a disease, for classifying birds on the basis of their characteristics, or for organizing a financial savings program. We need to study some example recipes to see how they are constructed, and then we need practice writing our own. We need experience in abstracting the essence of real-world situations and in organizing this knowledge into a sequence of steps for getting our tasks done.

Once we have devised a method for doing something, we wish to *code* it in a computer language in order to communicate our desires to the machine. Thus, it is necessary to learn a computer language and to learn to translate the steps of a recipe into commands that can be carried out by a machine. This book will introduce a language called *Pascal* which is easy to learn and quite satisfactory for our example programs.

The combination of creating the recipe and coding it into a computer language is called *programming*, and this is the subject of the first third of the book, chapters 1 to 5. These chapters give a variety of examples of problem types, their associated solution methods, and the Pascal code, the *program*, required to solve them. The final chapter in the sequence discusses the problems related to scaling up the lessons learned here to industrial sized programming projects.

While the completion of the programming chapters leads to an ability to create useful code, the resulting level of understanding will still fall short of our deeper goals. The programmer's view of a computer is that it is a magic box that efficiently executes commands, and the internal mechanisms may remain a mystery. However, as scholars of computer science, we must know something of these mechanisms so that we can comprehend why a machine acts as it does, what its limitations are, and what improvements can be expected. The second third of the book addresses the issue of how and why computers are able to compute.

Chapter 6 shows methods for designing electric circuits and how to employ these techniques to design computational mechanisms. For example, the reader is shown how to build a circuit for adding numbers. Modern machines are constructed using semiconductor technologies, and chapters 7 and 8 tell how semiconductor devices operate and how they are assembled to produce application circuits. Chapter 9 describes computer architecture and the organization of typical computers. Chapter 10 addresses the problem of translation of a high level computer language like Pascal into machine language, so that it can be run on the given architecture. An example at the end of chapter 10 traces the significant processing that occurs in the execution of a Pascal language statement from the translation to machine language, through the detailed operations of the computational circuits, to the migration of electrons through the semiconductors.

The final chapters of the book examine the limitations of computers and the frontiers of the science as it currently stands. Chapter 11 discusses problems related to program execution time and computations that require long processing times. Chapter 12 describes an attempt to speed up computers to do larger problems, the introduction of parallel architectures. Chapter 13 discusses the existence of so called *noncomputable* functions, and chapter 14 gives an introduction to the field of *artificial intelligence*.

An Approach for Nonmathematical Readers

A problem arises in the teaching of computer science in that the people who understand the field tend to speak their own language and use too much mathematical notation. The difficulties in communication lead the instructors to the conclusion that ordinary people are not able to understand the field. Thus, books and the university courses often skirt the central issues, and instead, teach the operation of software packages and the history and sociology of computing.

This book was written on the assumption that intelligent people can understand every fundamental issue of computer science if the preparation and explanation are adequate. No important topics have been omitted because of their difficulty. However, tremendous efforts were made to prune away unnecessary detail from the topics covered and to remove special vocabulary except where careful and complete definitions could be given.

Because casual readers may not wish to read all the chapters, the book is designed to encourage dabbling. Readers are encouraged to jump to any chapter at any time and read as much as is of interest. Of course, most chapters use some concepts gathered from earlier pages and where this occurs, understanding will be reduced. The programming chapters 1 through 4 are highly dependent on each other, and the architecture chapter (9) should be read before the translation chapter (10). Also, some of the advanced chapters (11 through 14) use concepts of programming from the early chapters (1 to 4). Except for these restrictions, the topics can probably be covered in any order without much sacrifice.

All of the chapter sections are classified as either A, B, or C again to encourage readers to taste much and devour only to the extent desired. Chapter sections labelled A include only introductory material and make few demands on the reader. One can get an overview of the book in a single evening by reading all the A sections. The B sections are the primary material of the book and may require substantial time and effort to read. The reader who completes the B material in a chapter will understand the major lessons on that topic and need feel no guilt about stopping at that point. The C material answers questions that careful readers may ask and supplements the main portions of the book.

Readings

For overview of computer science:

Brookshear, J. G., *Computer Science, An Overview,* Second Edition, Benjamin/Cummings Publishing Company, Menlo Park, California, 1988.

Goldschlager, L., and Lister, A., *Computer Science, A Modern Introduction*, Prentice-Hall, New York, 1988.

Schaffer, C., *Principles of Computer Science*, Prentice-Hall, Englewood Cliffs, New Jersey, 1988.

Pohl, I., and Shaw, A., *The Nature of Computation: An Introduction to Computer Science*, Computer Science Press, Rockville, Maryland, 1981.

For philosophical discussion:

Bolter, J. D., *Turing's Man,* University of North Carolina, Chapel Hill, North Carolina, 1984.

Great Ideas in Computer Science

1

An Introduction to Programming: Coding Decision Trees

Good News (A)*

In the old days before computers, if we wanted to do a job, we had to do the job. But with computers, one can do many jobs by simply writing down what is to be done. A machine can do the work. If we want to add up some numbers, search for a given fact, carefully format and print a document, distribute messages to colleagues, control an industrial process, or other tasks, we can write down a recipe for what is to be done and walk away while a machine obediently and tirelessly carries out our instructions. If we wish, the machine will continue working while we sleep or go on vacation or do other jobs. Our recipe could even be distributed to many computers, and they could all work together, carrying out the instructions. Even after we retire from this life, computers may still be employed to do the same jobs following the commands that we laid down.

The preparation and writing of such "recipes" is called *programming*, and it implements a kind of "work amplification" that is revolutionizing the society of man. It enables a single person to do a finite amount of work, the preparation of a computer program, and to achieve, with the help of computers, an unbounded number of results. Thus, our productivity is no longer simply a function of the number of people; it is a function of the number of people and the number of machines we have.

There is even more good news: computers are relatively inexpensive, and their costs are continuously decreasing. Machines with 64,000 word memories and 1 microsecond instruction times cost $1 million two decades ago, $100,000 a few years ago, and $1000 or $2000 now. For the cost of one month of a laborer's time, we can purchase a machine that can do some tasks faster than a thousand people working together. The power and importance of the computer revolution are clear.

We wish to study computer programming in this book so that we can experience the work amplification that computers make possible. We will study programming by learning fundamental information structures and processing techniques. We will do problem solving using these ideas and develop expertise in abstracting the essence of problem situations into machine code so that our jobs can be done for us automatically.

* Each section is labeled A, B, or C depending on whether it contains introductory, regular or optional material.

We will not study programming in the usual fashion, by learning the voluminous details of some particular programming language. We will not mention all rules for placement of the semicolons and commas, the most general form of every language construct, the number of characters allowed in variable names, the maximum allowed sizes of numbers or string lengths, or many other details. We wish to have all the fun of reading and writing simple programs while suffering as little as possible with syntactic precision and encyclopedic completeness. The chapters on programming in this book should be regarded as a guide for getting started, not as a comprehensive programming manual.

The programming examples and exercises use the programming language Pascal. However, we will use only a fraction of all of the features of Pascal in order to keep the language learning task under control. If all of Pascal were to be learned, there would be no time for the central theme of this book, the "great ideas" of computer science. Enough details are given here to enable readers to understand the example programs and to write similar programs as exercises. However, readers are advised to have a Pascal manual at hand for reference and study when they attempt more ambitious programs.

If we are to study programming, we must program something. It would be nice to write programs to embody some useful information processing structure. We would like to be able to do a variety of kinds of programs, and yet their structure should be simple enough to enable easy comprehension and coding by beginners. We also want to learn some important ideas that will be fundamental to more advanced studies. The first domain for programming for this book is thus *decision trees*. Decision trees can be used for classifying objects, for interviewing people, and many other tasks. First we will study decision trees, and then we will learn methods to write programs for them.

Decision Trees (B)

Suppose we wish to decide which book to recommend to a person who intends to get started in computer science. A good way to make the decision is to ask the person a series of questions and to arrive at the appropriate advice. The first question we might ask is whether a mathematical approach is to be used. We formulate a question and then indicate with arrows a direction to follow for the next question:

Book Recommendation
Decision Tree

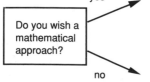

Then we decide what questions should be asked next, depending on the first answer:

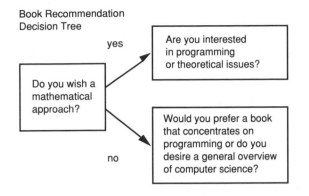

Let us assume that after asking two questions, it is possible to make the appropriate recommendation. Then the decision tree can be completed as follows:

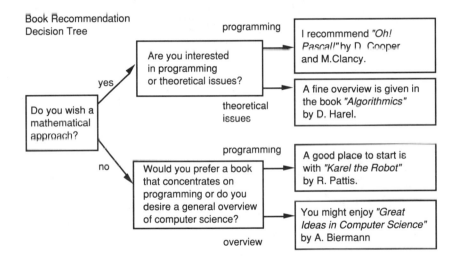

Following through the decision tree, it is possible to trace a sample interaction. Assuming the person is mathematically oriented and interested in theoretical issues, the path through the tree proceeds as follows:

Selecting a book to read in computer science:

Decision tree question: Do you wish a mathematical approach?

Response: yes

Decision tree question: Are you interested in programming or theoretical issues?

Response: theoretical issues

Decision tree advice: A fine overview is given in the book *Algorithmics* by D. Harel.

This tree contains only two sequential questions before arriving at its decision. But surely it is easy to envision a very large tree that asks many questions and recommends any of a wide variety of books at the end of the path. It is also clear that this type of tree can be used to give advice on almost any subject from medical treatment to fortune-telling. Here are some examples to illustrate the idea:

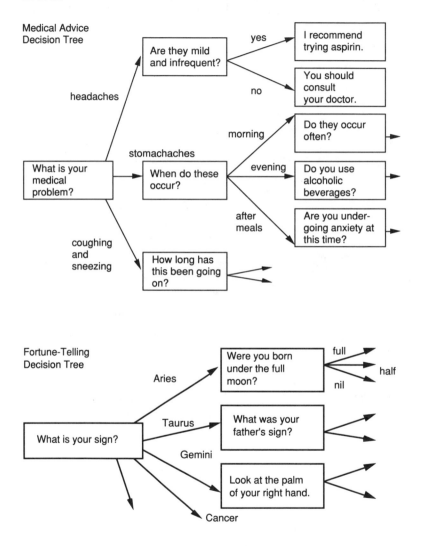

Decision trees can also be used to classify things. Suppose we have information on the characteristics of seagulls, and we wish to determine the exact classification of any specific gull. We could build a tree that might look like this:

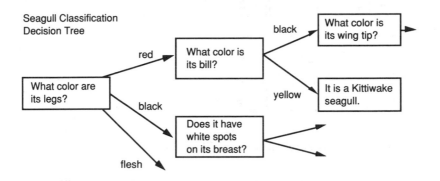

Seagull Classification
Decision Tree

We can even make a decision tree that will help us do our income tax. Here is how a tiny piece of it might look:

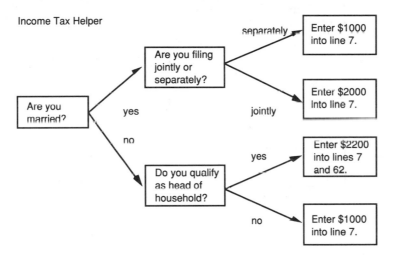

Income Tax Helper

Or what about a game-playing tree? This can be illustrated by the simple game Nim, which has the following rules. The first player can place one, two, or three Xs at the left end of a horizontal ladder; then the opponent can follow them with one, two, or three Os in the next sequential squares. This chain of moves repeats again and again, filling the ladder from left to right, with the winner being the one to place a mark in the last square. Here is an example of how a game might go if the ladder has seven squares.

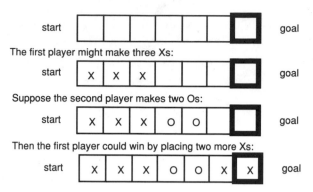

The first player might make three Xs:

Suppose the second player makes two Os:

Then the first player could win by placing two more Xs:

Here is a decision tree that will play the role of the second player for a Nim ladder of length seven:

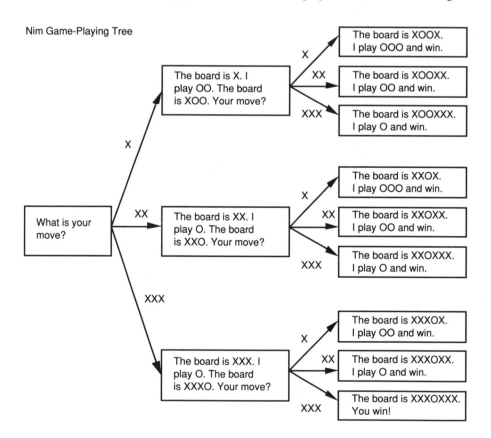

Ordinarily we think of trees as emerging from the ground and spreading their branches toward the sky. The trees in this chapter move from left to right so that they will be easier to program. The processing of the tree begins at the left-most box, or *root node*, and proceeds along a path toward the right. At each decision *node*, the user of the tree is asked a question, and the answer given serves to select the next branch to be followed. The path proceeds right until a final *leaf* node is encountered with no outward branches. This leaf node will contain a message giving the result of the sequence of decisions, and it will terminate processing.

Such decision trees are applicable to a multitude of information processing tasks, including advice giving, classification, instruction, and game-playing activities. Our task in this chapter will be to write programs that will contain these trees and automatically lead a person down the correct path and print the result. The ability to design and program these trees is a powerful skill with numerous applications.

Exercises

1. Complete one of the decision trees that is only partially specified in this section.

2. Design a complete decision tree that will play the part of the second player in Nim with a ladder of nine squares.

3. Specify a problem domain of interest to you, and design a decision tree to solve it.

Getting Started in Programming (B)

A *computer program* is a list of commands that can be carried out by a computer. It is a recipe of actions the machine is to perform, and it must be written in a language that the computer can understand. Most programs in this book will be written in the Pascal language, a popular and convenient language. Sometimes a program or part of a program is called *computer code*. We will use both terms in this book.

Here is an example program written in Pascal.

```
program FirstCode;
begin
writeln('   Great  Ideas   ');
writeln('        in        ');
writeln('Computer  Science');
readln;
end.
```

If we want these instructions carried out, we do what is called *running* or *executing* the program on a computer. In order to do this, it is necessary to have:

• a computer,

• a software system that enables your particular computer to process Pascal,

• a manual to help you get the machine turned on and running properly, and

• a knowledgeable instructor or friend.

Any computer is satisfactory if you can obtain a Pascal system for it, but two popular machines are the Apple Macintosh and the IBM Personal Computer. Every computer has its own machine language so you must always have a software system that can translate the language of choice, Pascal in this case, into that machine's language. The translator is a computer program called a *compiler,* which usually comes on a disk and can be bought at a computer store. The examples in this book have been written in Turbo Pascal, a dialect of the language developed by Borland International (at 4585 Scotts Valley Drive, Scotts Valley, California 95066). These programs have been written in Turbo Version 4.0 but will probably run on almost any version of Turbo Pascal since they use a small subset of the language. If you choose to use some other Pascal system, you may need help getting some of the programs to run because there are significant differences among the systems.

The manual is necessary because it will tell you which buttons to push on your computer to turn it on and to get your program typed in and running. Finally you need an instructor or friend to tell you what the manual did not. Computer science, like many disciplines, has an oral tradition, and some of the most important facts are passed only by word of mouth. You may be able to get along without the help, but learning is usually easier if it is there.

The procedure for starting the machine and typing in the first program is not much more difficult than learning to operate an electric typewriter. Students can usually achieve this in a few minutes and can immediately begin having the fun of computer programming. To get maximum benefit from this chapter, you should type in and run some of the programs given here and observe their behaviors. For instance, if the above sample is run, the following lines will be printed:

```
Great Ideas
      in
Computer Science
```

This program is very simple from some points of view, but there are many details related to its form and execution that must be understood from the beginning. These include the composition of the program in terms of statements, the order of execution of the statements, and their meaning and structure.

Program Form.

The primary parts of this program are its *header*, the keyword *begin,* a series of statements followed by semicolons, and the keyword *end* followed by a period. The header always must begin with the word *program,* and it includes a name for the program followed by a semicolon. Thus the first line,

```
program FirstCode;
```

tells the computer that this is a program with the name "FirstCode." The second line

```
begin
```

tells the computer that some programming statements follow. Next are four lines of code, each containing a program statement. The final line of the program is the marker telling the computer where the program ends.

```
end.
```

The Program	Comments
`program FirstCode;`	The program header.
`begin`	Indicator that code will follow.
`writeln('   Great Ideas   ');`	Statement followed by semicolon.
`writeln('      in       ');`	Statement followed by semicolon.
`writeln('Computer  Science');`	Statement followed by semicolon.
`readln;`	Statement followed by semicolon.
`end.`	Indicator that code has ended.

Statements.

A program statement is an individual command to the computer. It corresponds to an imperative sentence in English. It says to the computer, "You do this." The example program has four statements. The first one is this:

```
writeln('   Great Ideas   ')
```

It tells the computer to write the words "Great Ideas" on the screen. Some spaces are typed around these words because we would like to see those spaces when they are printed. (Literally, the instruction *writeln* means "write a line.") Each statement in a program usually is followed by a semicolon, so the statement will appear as follows:

```
writeln('   Great Ideas   ');
```

The second and third statements are also "write" statements.

The fourth statement instructs the computer to stop and wait for the computer user to type something. It says *readln,* or "read a line." This statement is not necessary for the program, but it serves the purpose of requiring the machine to stop and wait before doing anything else. Without the *readln* statement, typical Turbo Pascal systems would quickly write the three lines and exit to do another job before we have a chance to read what was written. In this book, most programs will include a *readln* statement before the final *end* statement to give you a chance to study the output messages before the program is terminated.

Thus, this program types three lines and halts, waiting for the user to type something. After the user types anything, usually just a single carriage return, the program exits.

Program Execution.

The computer functions by executing the statements in order. It executes the first statement, the second, and so forth. It always executes statements in order unless special statements require it to do something else.

Statement Meaning and Structure.

The particular statement

```
writeln('   Great Ideas   ');
```

has two parts: the command syntax for the machine and some data that the programmer has inserted:

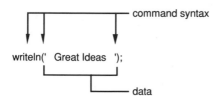

The command tells the machine to write whatever characters are between the quotation marks and then move its printer to the next line. If the program is being run on a video display terminal, the write command will put the characters on the screen in an area designated for writing.

When you type a program to the machine, all command syntax must be perfect. No typographical errors are allowed. None of the following programs will run properly because correct programming syntax has been violated:

```
program FirstCode;
begin
writein('   Great Ideas   ');
writeln('      in      ');
writeln('Computer  Science');
readln;
end.
```

(The first *writeln* is misspelled.)

```
program FirstCode;
begin
writeln('   Great Ideas   ');
writeln('      in      ')
writeln('Computer  Science');
```

```
readln;
end.
```

(There is a missing semicolon.)

```
program FirstCode;
begin
please writeln('   Great Ideas   ');
writeln('        in        ');
writeln('Computer  Science');
readln;
end.
```

("Please" is illegally used in this context.)

Most programming languages require perfect syntax, although a few allow some flexibility. Languages of the future will probably be less demanding.

If the command syntax is correct, the program will carry out the commands regardless of what is included as data. Thus the following program will execute normally.

```
program FirstCode;
begin
writeln('   Grit Iders      ');
writeln('        on        ');
writeln('C#7a-%%*        ');
readln;
end.
```

The machine has no basis on which to judge the correctness of the data and will obediently carry out the instructions without regard to what is being manipulated. The computer will do precisely what you say even though it may not be what you want.

One way a correct program can be modified without changing its correctness relates to its spacing. Spaces can be inserted at most places in a program without affecting its behavior. The following program is equivalent to the first one given above, though a blank line and many extraneous spaces have been inserted:

```
program
   FirstCode;
                    begin
   writeln
      ('   Great Ideas   ');
   writeln('        in        ');
            writeln('Computer  Science');
readln;            end.
```

Do not insert spaces in the middle of keywords such as *begin* or *end* or in names or data.

This section has presented a computer program to print three lines and halt. A careful understanding of this simple code is a huge step in the direction of understanding all computer programs. It is important to understand the form of the programs and the concept of the programming statement as the fundamental unit of command. Each statement specifies an action; the sequence of statements specifies a sequence of actions and the order of their execution. The formatting of each statement is precise and unforgiving except for the allowance of spacing between its parts.

Here is a program that performs another printing task:

```
program  SecondCode;
begin
writeln('****************************');
writeln('*                          *');
writeln('*        Decision Trees     *');
writeln('*                          *');
writeln('****************************');
readln;
end.
```

You should now be able to write a program that will print almost anything.

Exercises
1. Write a program that will print your name and address.

2. Write a program that will print the letters PEACE in block format.

```
PPPP    EEEEE      A          CCC    EEEE
P    P  E         AA        C    C   E
PPPP    EEE      A  A      C          EEE
P       E        AAAA       C    C   E
P       EEEE    A    A       CCC    EEEE
```

3. Draw a picture of a cottage in the woods with a path leading to the front door. Convert the picture to an array of characters as is done with the word PEACE above, and write a program to print it.

Reading and Storing Data (B)

The previous section introduced the concept of data—the information being manipulated by the program. In the previous examples, the data items were strings of characters that were being written out. Examples of such strings are "Computer Science", "**************", and "C#7a-

%%*". This section will show how to get your program to collect such data from the keyboard; it will read the keystrokes from typed input and store the data in the computer memory.

Before studying the read statement, however, it is necessary to be able to talk about locations in memory. Such locations are like pigeonholes with names where information can be stored and then retrieved when needed. For example, you might like to have a place in memory where a sequence of characters can be stored, and you might choose to name it "position1."

position1 [   ]

You can then store data in that location and use the data in various ways. You could instruct the machine to write the data in *position1* or move the data in *position1* to some other location.

The correct way to indicate in the Pascal language that such a memory location is to be set up is with the *var* declaration, as follows:

```
var
   position1:string;
```

This declaration tells the machine that a location is to be set up in memory called "position1," which can hold a string of characters. It is included in the program after the header. The name *position1* is called a *variable*.

Once such a memory location is set up, you can refer to it in other statements. The new statement to be studied has the form

```
readln(position1)
```

and it means

1. Receive the characters that are typed (ending with a carriage return).
2. Put this sequence of characters into the place named "position1." (These characters will also appear on the terminal screen as they are typed.)

Suppose that the machine executes the statement

```
readln(position1)
```

and that the user types the words "A Gentle Introduction" (but without the quotation marks and followed by a carriage return). Then the location named "position1" will receive the information as shown:

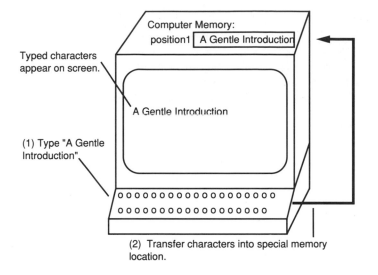

Typed characters appear on screen.

(1) Type "A Gentle Introduction".

(2) Transfer characters into special memory location.

Thus, a method for storing some information into the computer memory proceeds as follows. First, put in a declaration to create and name the desired memory location. Then include a *readln* statement to gather the keystrokes and enter them into that location. Finally, if you wish to check whether the data are there, include a write statement. Here is the complete program:

```
program  ReadData;
var
    position1  :string;
begin
readln(position1);
writeln(position1);
readln;
end.
```

Its operation proceeds by first waiting for some typed characters. Suppose you type

```
Very  Gentle
```

followed by a carriage return. This will be stored away in the location *position1*.

position1 | Very Gentle

Then the contents of *position1* will be printed on the screen. Finally, the program will wait for you to type one more thing, say a carriage return, and then exit.

Some Pascal systems require that the word *string* in the previous program be followed by an integer in parentheses telling the maximum length of the strings that may appear in this location.

For example, suppose the strings to be entered into the location *position1* are allowed to hold up to 100 characters. Then the declaration would be given as follows:

```
var
   position1:string[100];
```

Turbo Pascal assumes that the longest string will be 255 characters or fewer unless otherwise specified.

The program can be modified so that it will make more sense to the user. *Writeln* statements can be added to tell what is happening:

```
program ReadWriteDemo;
var
   position1:string;
begin
writeln('Please type in some data.');
readln(position1);
writeln('The data have been stored.');
writeln('Next the data will be printed.');
writeln(position1);
writeln('This completes the run.');
readln;
end.
```

Let us run this program to be sure that we understand it:

```
Please type in some data.          (computer message to user)
An Introduction                    (the user types the data)
The data have been stored.         (computer message to user)
Next the data will be printed.     (computer message to user)
An Introduction                    (the computer writes the data)
This completes the run.            (computer message to user)
(carriage return)                  (final user input)
```

Notice that two different forms of the *writeln* statement are being employed. If quotation marks are used, the characters between the quotes will be printed. Thus, in

```
writeln('position1')
```

the characters "position1" will be written (without the double quotation marks). But if there are no quotation marks, the processor will go to the memory location with the given name and write the contents of that location. Therefore, the statement

```
writeln(position1)
```

will print "An Introduction" if *position1* contains those characters.

If *writeln* is asked to print something not enclosed in quotation marks and not declared as a memory location, an error results, as in the case

```
writeln(An  Introduction)
```

A combination of input and output statements can be used to write a simple interactive progam. Here is an illustration. Can you tell what it does?

```
program  GetNameTown;
var
    PositionOfName,  PositionOfTown:string;
begin
writeln('Hi, tell me your name.');
readln(PositionOfName);
writeln('What town do you live in?');
readln(PositionOfTown);
writeln('Can you tell me something?');
writeln(PositionOfName);
writeln('How do you like living in');
writeln(PositionOfTown);
writeln('???');
end.
```

The names of the places in memory can be almost anything as long as they begin with an alphabetic letter, include only alphabetic and numeric characters, and are properly declared. For example, the names *A17* and *c8Zi* could be used:

```
program  GetNameTown;
var
    A17, c8Zi:string;
begin
writeln('Hi, tell me your name.');
readln(A17);
writeln('What town do you live in?');
readln(c8Zi);
writeln('Can you tell me something?');
writeln(A17);
writeln('How do you like living in');
writeln(c8Zi);
writeln('???');
end.
```

There are two rules to follow with names: First, they are not allowed to contain spaces. Second, there is a set of *reserved words* for your Pascal system that may not be used as names. Some examples of such words are *program, begin, end, if, else, and,* and, *or,* and you should consult your Pascal manual for the complete list.

Programmers commonly give a location the name of the object to be stored in that location. In this example, the two locations of interest could be *name* and *town* since they store, respectively, the name and town of a person. This makes the program most easily understood:

```pascal
program  GetNameTown;
var
    name, town: string;
begin
writeln('Hi, tell me your name.');
readln(name);
writeln('What town do you live in?');
readln(town);
writeln('Can you tell me something?');
writeln(name);
writeln('How do you like living in');
writeln(town);
writeln('???');
end.
```

An important fact is that storage positions should not be used until something is loaded into them, as is done by the input statements. Then they will continue to hold that information until they are reloaded, perhaps by other input statements. If they are reloaded, the earlier information is destroyed and lost forever. This is demonstrated by the following program. What does it do?

```pascal
program  LoadDemo;
var
    x, y: string;
begin
writeln('Input x.');
readln(x);
writeln('Input y.');
readln(y);
writeln('Contents of x and y.');
writeln(x);
writeln(y);

writeln('Input x.');
readln(x);                           *
```

```
writeln('Contents of x and y.');
writeln(x);
writeln(y);

writeln('Input  y.');
readln(y);                              **
writeln('Contents of x and y.');
writeln(x);
writeln(y);
end.
```

Here is an example of its behavior:

```
Input  x.                (printed message)
Jack                     (input to x)
Input  y.                (printed message)
Jill                     (input to y)
Contents of x and y.     (printed message)
Jack                     (contents of x)
Jill                     (contents of y)
Input  x.                (printed message)
Sam                      (input to x)
Contents of x and y.     (printed message)
Sam                      (contents of x)
Jill                     (contents of y)
Input  y.                (printed message)
Sally                    (input to y)
Contents of x and y.     (printed message)
Sam                      (contents of x)
Sally                    (contents of y)
```

The first two read statements of the program enter information into *x* and *y*. Next, *x* and *y* are printed. The statement marked by * reads into *x*, destroying its contents. When *x* and *y* are printed, the change can be seen. The statement marked by ** replaces the contents of *y*, and the final write statement shows the result.

This section has introduced several difficult concepts related to computer programming—the ideas of inputting data from the keyboard and its storage in the computer memory. Because of the subtlety of some of the ideas, you should study it carefully. The next section will introduce one more programming concept and show how to program decision trees.

Exercises

1. Write a program that reads your first and last names and then prints them out.

2. Write a program that will gather data from a prospective college student regarding academic background, standardized test scores, and so forth. Then the program should print the information in summary form for the college admissions office.

Programming Decision Trees (B)

Let us begin by programming the simplest possible tree, one with only one branching node:

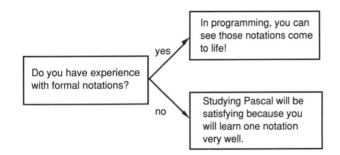

We learned in the previous sections how to make the machine print these kinds of messages and how to make it read the user's answers. But one additional feature is needed, the *if-then-else* statement, which will enable us to build the yes-no branch of the program.

The needed statement for the decision tree is typed on several lines and has the following form:

```
if answer = 'yes' then
        Pascal code A
else
        Pascal code B
```

Here *Pascal code A* and *Pascal code B* are sequences of Pascal statements. These sequences are called *compound statements* and are defined in the next paragraph. Assume that the program has executed

```
readln(answer)
```

where *answer* has been declared as a string location and that the program has stored either "yes" or "no" into *answer*. This code will execute *Pascal code A* if *answer* contains "yes" and *Pascal code B* otherwise.

Now we are able to write a computer program for this simple decision tree.

```
program FirstTree;
var
    answer: string;
begin
writeln('Do you have experience with formal notations?');
readln(answer);
if answer = 'yes' then
    begin
    writeln('In programming, you can see those notations');
    writeln('come to life!');
    end
else
    begin
    writeln('Studying Pascal will be satisfying because');
    writeln('you will learn one notation very well.');
    end;
readln;
end.
```

Notice that *Pascal code A* has become a four-line sequence as follows:

```
begin
writeln('In programming, you can see those notations');
writeln('come to life!');
end
```

It contains two *writeln* statements, which are preceded by the keyword *begin* and followed by the keyword *end*. The same is true for *Pascal code B*. In general, any sequence of statements contained between the keywords *begin* and *end* is called a *compound statement*; this is the format allowed in the positions called *Pascal code A* and *Pascal code B*. A variation of this rule will be mentioned in chapter 4. (Actually, this program has three compound statements in all—the two just mentioned and the main part of the program itself which also is a sequence of statements bounded by *begin* and *end*.)

Although this short program seems easy to understand, you should study it carefully. What would happen if you answered the initial question by typing "Yes, some," instead of "yes" or "no"? What would happen if you typed "Yes," instead of "yes."

Two extremely important issues are related to this program. The first concerns the indentation policy. Each line of code can be spaced in from the left margin any amount without affecting its execution. However, the readability of the program is enhanced tremendously by indenting the branch portions of each *if* statement. The eye is immediately drawn to the significant sections of code, and the flow of control in the program is easy to follow. You should write computer programs clearly in the same way that you would write in a natural language such as English or

Russian. If a careful indentation policy is ignored in writing a program, the offense is just as serious as the omission of section headings and paragraphs in a paper or article.

The other important issue relates to the placement of the semicolons. This book will follow the rules of placing semicolons (1) at the end of the header and the declaration, and (2) at the end of every statement within each compound statement.

In the earlier programs, this rule is easy to apply. They included only one compound statement— the main sequence of statements that are bracketed by *begin* and *end*. If we remember that *begin* and *end* are not themselves statements, the placement of semicolons is straightforward:

```
program ReadData;
var
    position1 :string;
begin
readln(position1);
writeln(position1);
readln;
end.
```

But the semicolons in FirstTree need careful attention. First, check that the header and declaration have semicolons. Next apply rule (2) to each statement in the main program disregarding the compound statements within the if-then-else construction (which are indented and are surrounded by *begin* and *end*). Finally, examine each indented compound statement and check that its contained statements are followed by semicolons. Consider first the main program, which begins and ends at the positions marked with Ms and the four associated statements marked with labels M1 through M4:

```
         program FirstTree;
         var
             answer: string;
{M}      begin
{M1}     writeln('Do you have experience with formal notations?');
{M2}     readln(answer);
{M3}     if answer = 'yes' then
             begin
             writeln('In programming, you can see those notations');
             writeln('come to life!');
             end
         else
             begin
             writeln('Studying Pascal will be satisfying because');
             writeln('you will learn one notation very well.');
             end;
{M4}     readln;
{M}      end.
```

All four statements begin at the same indentation level as their *begin-end* brackets. Each statement needs to end with a semicolon. But where are the ends? In three cases, the ends are at the right end of the line, but the *if-then-else* statement stretches over ten lines. Its end is the *end* that precedes the final *readln*. So rule (2) specifies that the positions marked *endM1*, *endM2*, *endM3*, and *endM4* require semicolons.

```
        program FirstTree;
        var
            answer: string;
{M}     begin
{M1}    writeln('Do you have experience with formal notations?'); {endM1}
{M2}    readln(answer);  {endM2}
{M3}    if answer = 'yes' then
            begin
            writeln('In programming, you can see those notations');
            writeln('come to life!');
            end
        else
            begin
            writeln('Studying Pascal will be satisfying because');
            writeln('you will learn one notation very well.');
            end;  {endM3}
{M4}    readln;  {endM4}
{M}     end.
```

Rule (2) also requires that each statement within the indented compound statements be terminated with a semicolon. For example, the compound statement surrounded by the *begin* and *end* keywords labeled with Ns is found to include two statements, N1 and N2. Their ends must have corresponding semicolons:

```
        program FirstTree;
        var
            answer: string;
{M}     begin
{M1}    writeln('Do you have experience with formal notations?'); {endM1}
{M2}    readln(answer);  {endM2}
{M3}    if answer = 'yes' then
{N}         begin
{N1}        writeln('In programming, you can see those notations'); {endN1}
{N2}        writeln('come to life!');  {endN2}
{N}         end
```

```
        else
            begin
            writeln('Studying Pascal will be satisfying because');
            writeln('you will learn one notation very well.');
            end;  {endM3}
{M4}    readln;  {endM4}
{M}     end.
```

Finally, examine the last compound statement to see that its two statements have semicolons. If you learn to follow these two rules rigorously, you will have no trouble with semicolons. But if you make mistakes in their application, your program will either not run at all or do unexpected things.

(If you read a standard Pascal manual, you will encounter a slightly different view of semicolons than that presented here. There semicolons are viewed as *separators* of statements within a compound statement. A compound statement is considered to be a sequence of statements between *begin* and *end*, and semicolons are placed between each pair of statements as follows where *s* stands for "statement":

```
begin s ; s ; s ; s end
```

When this is typed in the usual form for programs, it looks like this:

```
begin
s;
s;
s;
s
end
```

The last statement is not followed by a semicolon. This is sometimes confusing to students so this text uses the more uniform rule that every statement between the *begin* and *end* will be followed by a semicolon:

```
begin
s;
s;
s;
s;
end
```

The functioning of the programs is the same in both cases.)

Returning to decision trees, it turns out that all others are programmed similarly, but they may have more branches to keep track of. Let us program the book advice example. It begins very much like the previous one:

```
program BookAdvice;
var
    answer1: string;
begin
writeln('Do you wish a mathematical approach?');
readln(answer1);
if answer1 = 'yes' then
    Put code here to handle "yes" branch.
else
    Put code here to handle "no" branch. ;
readln;
end.
```

Next consider the code to handle the "yes" branch:

```
begin
writeln('Are you interested in programming');
writeln('or theoretical issues?');
readln(answer2);
if answer2 = 'programming' then
    begin
    writeln('I recommend "Oh, Pascal!" by');
    writeln('D. Cooper and M. Clancy.');
    end
else
    begin
    writeln('A fine overview is given in');
    writeln('the book "Algorithmics"');
    writeln('by D. Harel.');
    end;
end
```

Now we can insert the "yes" branch code into the appropriate position in the main program:

```pascal
program BookAdvice;
var
      answer1, answer2: string;
begin
writeln('Do you wish a mathematical approach?');
readln(answer1);
if answer1 = 'yes' then
   begin
   writeln('Are you interested in programming');
   writeln('or theoretical issues?');
   readln(answer2);
   if answer2 = 'programming' then
      begin
      writeln('I recommend "Oh, Pascal!" by');
      writeln('D. Cooper and M. Clancy.');
      end
   else
      begin
      writeln('A fine overview is given in');
      writeln('the book "Algorithmics"');
      writeln('by D. Harel.');
      end;
   end
else
      Put code here to handle "no" branch. ;
readln;
end.
```

Similarly, we can write the code for the "no" branch and insert it into the main program to make the code complete:

```pascal
program BookAdvice;
var
       answer1, answer2, answer3: string;
begin
writeln('Do you wish a mathematical approach?');
readln(answer1);
if answer1 = 'yes' then
    begin
    writeln('Are you interested in programming');
    writeln('or theoretical issues?');
    readln(answer2);
        if answer2 = 'programming' then
        begin
        writeln('I recommend "Oh, Pascal!" by');
        writeln('D. Cooper and M. Clancy.');
        end
    else
        begin
        writeln('A fine overview is given in');
        writeln('the book "Algorithmics"');
        writeln('by D. Harel.');
        end;
    end
else
    begin
    writeln('Would you prefer a book that');
    writeln('concentrates on programming or do you');
    writeln('desire a general overview of computer');
    writeln('science?');
    readln(answer3);
    if answer3 = 'programming' then
        begin
        writeln('A good place to start is with');
        writeln('"Karel the Robot" by R. Pattis.');
        end
    else
        begin
        writeln('You might enjoy "Great Ideas in');
        writeln('Computer Science" by A. Biermann');
        end;
    end;
readln;
end.
```

Different memory locations—*answer1*, *answer2*, or *answer3*—are used to store the different responses to questions. It is wise to keep these separated to avoid confusion in writing more complicated programs. Remember to declare all of these locations.

Another version of the *if* statement is useful in programming decision trees with more than two branches at some nodes:

```
if condition then
    compound statement
```

If the condition is satisfied, the associated compound statement will be executed. If it is not, this statement will cause nothing to happen, and the program will proceed as if the statement did not exist.

The seagull classification decision tree gives a good example of this kind of programming. The initial version of the code can be written as follows:

```
program SeagullClass;
var
    answer1: string;
begin
writeln('What color are its legs?');
readln(answer1);
if answer1 = 'red' then
    Code for the case of red legs. ;
if answer1 = 'black' then
    Code for the case of black legs. ;
if answer1 = 'flesh' then
    Code for the case of flesh legs. ;
if answer1 = 'green' then
    Code for the case of green legs. ;
end.
```

Continuing this program, the code for the individual cases can be filled in as follows:

```
program SeagullClass;
var
    answer1, answer2: string;
begin
writeln('What color are its legs?');
readln(answer1);
if answer1 = 'red' then
    begin
    writeln('What color is its bill?');
    readln(answer2);
```

```
    if answer2= 'black' then
      begin
      writeln('What color is its wing tip?');
      readln(answer3);
          More code.
      end;
    if answer2 = 'yellow' then
      begin
      writeln('It is a Kittiwake seagull.');
      end;
    end;
if answer1 = 'black' then
    Code for the case of black legs. ;
if answer1 = 'flesh' then
    Code for the case of flesh legs. ;
if answer1 = 'green' then
    Code for the case of green legs. ;
end.
```

All of the decision trees discussed (and any others) can be programmed similarly. The only programming constructions needed are *writeln, readln, if-then-else, if-then*, and the program header and declarations. But an objection to these programs is that they appear to be more complicated than is necessary. This is addressed in chapter 4 where the subroutine is introduced.

At this point, it would be helpful for you to run some of these programs on a machine and to try some new ones as well. But before running any program, check it extensively to make sure that it properly expresses your intent. There are two kinds of reexamination to carry out: First, execute the code by hand to check whether the statements actually do what they are intended to do; second, verify the syntax of the program to be sure it precisely follows the language rules.

Let us do these two kinds of checks on the BookAdvice program, beginning with the hand execution. The declaration at the beginning tells what memory locations must be maintained, so the hand calculation begins by writing these down.

```
answer1:
answer2:
answer3:
```

Then we start with the begin marker, read every line of code, and decide whether it is correct:

```
writeln('Do you wish a mathematical approach?');
```

After deciding that this is the correct first action, we go on to the second statement:

```
readln(answer1);
```

Is this correct, and is the answer being stored where we want it? Suppose the user types "no." Our hand simulation immediately records the result:

```
answer1: no
answer2:
answer3:
```

Moving to the next statement, we see that the test *answer1* = *'yes'* is made, and we must methodically look at the location *answer1* and see whether the test succeeds. In this case, it does not, and control will pass to the statement following the *else*. We must now confirm that this action is what we wanted. The hand simulation continues, with every program action being scrutinized carefully.

After all possible actions of the program are verified, we turn attention to the syntax of the code. Are all of the statements well formed according to the rules of the language? Are the semicolons placed properly? The program will not run unless every detail is correct.

The final check of the program concerns the spacing and line indentations. It is important that the program be clear and readable. Do the line indentations follow the policy that maximally displays the program's significant parts? Spacing will not affect what the program does, but we are careful to organize the code properly so that it is easy to understand.

Only after thorough and extensive rereading, revising, and repeated verification should a program be committed for translation and execution. Expert programmers know well that errors in programs can cause huge losses of time and other resources, and they wisely spend the great majority of their time in program preparation and hand verification.

Exercises

1. Program the income tax helper decision tree shown above.

2. Design a decision tree of interest to you. Write a program for your tree.

3. Write a program for the seven square Nim player described above.

Turbo Pascal Summary (C)

A study of the Pascal language is greatly simplified if a notation can be used to condense all of the previous discussions into a few precise rules. This section will introduce the notation and give the rules that specify all of the Pascal described in this chapter.

The first notation uses angle brackets around a name: <identifier>. This sequence of symbols "<identifier>" should be read as "an object called an 'identifier.'" The second notation is an arrow →, which in this context means "can be." Using these notations, one can give a rule:

```
<identifier>  →  a sequence of letters and/or digits that begins with a
                 letter
```

Translating this notation into English, one obtains: An object called an "identifier" can be a sequence of letters and/or digits that begins with a letter. Some examples of identifiers from this chapter are "ReadData" and "position1," and the notation can be used to specify them:

```
<identifier> -> ReadData
<identifier> -> position1
```

That is, an identifier can be the sequence of characters "ReadData" or the sequence "position1." Conceptually, identifiers are names given to objects such as programs or memory locations.

 Another kind of object is called the "string expression," and it also needs to be defined.

```
<string expression> -> <identifier>
<string expression> -> 'any string of printable characters '
```

Paraphrasing these rules, a "string expression" can be an identifier or any string of printable characters surrounded by single quotation marks. Some example string expressions from the chapter are:

```
<string expression> -> position1
<string expression> -> 'Do you wish a mathematical approach?'
```

String expressions are important because they are the things that can be printed.

 We also studied statements in the chapter, and these are represented as <statement>. Here are three forms introduced in the early sections:

```
<statement> -> writeln(<string expression>)
<statement> -> readln(<identifier>)
<statement> -> readln
```

The first of these rules states that a statement can be the sequence

```
writeln(<string expression>)
```

where <string expression> is defined above. For example, the two string expressions given above can be substituted here to obtain two legal statements.

```
writeln(position1)
writeln('Do you wish a mathematical approach?')
```

The two *readln* statements work in the same way.

 Once statements are defined, we can define a sequence of statements called a "compound statement":

```
<compound statement>  -> begin
                            a sequence of <statement>'s each followed by
                                                        a semicolon
                        end
```

An illustration of a compound statement from the chapter is:

```
<compound statement>   -> begin
                           readln(position1);
                           writeln(position1);
                           readln;
                           end
```

Some additional kinds of statements are the *if-then-else* and *if-then* forms.

```
<statement> -> if <boolean expression> then
                         <compound statement>
              else
                         <compound statement>
<statement> -> if <boolean expression> then
                         <compound statement>
```

The only "boolean expression" discussed so far is defined by

```
<boolean expression> -> <identifier> = <string expression>
```

An example boolean expression is

```
answer1 = 'yes'
```

and it can be used in an *if-then-else* form as with

```
<statement> -> if answer1 = 'yes' then
                   begin
                   writeln('In programming, you can see those
                                                  notations');
                   writeln('come to life!');
                   end
               else
                   begin
                   writeln('Learning Pascal will be satisfying
                                                  because');
                   writeln('you will learn one notation very well.');
                   end
```

We also studied "variable declaration" in the chapter, defined by the rules

```
<variable declaration> -> nothing
<variable declaration> -> var
                             list of <identifier>'s :<type>;
          <type> -> string
```

Thus a variable declaration may be "nothing"; that is, it may be omitted, or it may be the sequence *var* followed by a list of identifiers, colon, the type, and a semicolon. Here is a declaration from the chapter:

```
<variable declaration> -> var
                             answer1, answer2: string;
```

Finally, a definition of "program" is needed:

```
<program> ->program <identifier>;
          <variable declaration>
          <compound statement>.
```

This rule states that an object called a "program" is defined to be the following four things:

1. The header statement with the program name, an object called an "identifier," followed by a semicolon

2. The variable declaration

3. The body of statements of the program in the form of a compound statement

4. A period.

You can write a program if you know how to fill in the bracketed objects on the right-hand side: <identifier>, <variable declaration>, and <compound statement>. The earlier rules show how to do this.

In order to understand the usefulness of these rules, we will examine how they can *derive* a program in a sequence of steps. For the current purposes, the arrow —> should be read as "can be replaced by," and the derivation of the program will involve a sequence of replacements. The program to be derived will be *ReadData*:

```
program ReadData;
var
   position1: string;
begin
readln(position1);
writeln(position1);
readln;
end.
```

The process begins with the object <program>, and the above rules give the allowed substitutions for the creation of the target program. Beginning with the program rule, one obtains

```
<program> -> program <identifier>;
          <variable declaration>
          <compound statement>.
```

The identifier rule

```
<identifier> -> a sequence of letters and/or digits
                          that begins with a letter
```

tells us that <identifier> can be replaced in the program by any sequence of letters and/or digits that begins with a letter. The target program has the sequence *ReadData* in this location, and we know from the identifier rule that

```
<identifier> -> ReadData
```

This substitution is made into the program:

```
<program> -> program ReadData;
             <variable declaration>
             <compound statement>.
```

Next we note that the target program declares *position1* as a location for storing a string. Furthermore, the declaration rule makes it possible to generate the proper code:

```
<variable declaration> -> var
                             position1:string;
```

This substitution is made into the program:

```
<program> -> program ReadData;
             var
                 position1: string;
             <compound statement>.
```

The rule for compound statement makes it possible to generate a *begin,* any number of statements with semicolons, and an *end.* The target program has three statements, so this form should be used:

```
<compound statement> -> begin
                          <statement>;
                          <statement>;
                          <statement>;
                          end
```

This substitution leads to further development of the program:

```
<program> -> program ReadData;
            var
                  position1:  string;
            begin
            <statement>;
            <statement>;
            <statement>;
            end.
```

Finally the three rules

```
<statement> -> readln(position1)
<statement> -> writeln(position1)
<statement> -> readln
```

come from the general rules for statements. These can be applied to the program to complete the derivation:

```
<program> -> program ReadData;
            var
                  position1: string;
            begin
            readln(position1);
            writeln(position1);
            readln;
            end.
```

Notice that the rules have inserted every detail of the program correctly including the punctuation.

In summary, any program studied in this chapter can be similarly generated. Apply the syntax rules beginning with <program> until the final program is derived. Ordinarily we do not generate programs in this way, but we do study the rules with great care in order to learn the language better. If you are ever confused about exactly how to code something, these rules will state precisely the correct format.

A standard manual on Pascal provides a large number of rules beyond those given here—usually in the form of flowcharts with circles and arrows showing the allowed formats. This book uses only a fraction of the whole Pascal language and therefore includes relatively few syntactic rules.

Exercises

1. Use the syntax rules to generate two examples of each of the following kinds of objects: <identifier>, <string expression>, <statement>, <compound statement>, <boolean expression>, <variable declaration>, <program>.

2. Show how to generate the program *ReadWriteDemo* using the rules.

3. Show how to generate the program *FirstTree* using the rules.

Summary (B)

This chapter introduced the concept of the decision tree and its many applications to information processing. Then the concepts necessary for programming decision trees were covered, including the Pascal constructions for writing, reading, *if-then-else, if-then,* declarations, and programs. You should be able to use these ideas to design and program decision trees for numerous applications. A strategy introduced in chapter 4 will make it possible to simplify the coding of these trees so that larger ones can be more easily programmed.

Readings

For computer science overview:

Harel, D., *Algorithmics, The Spirit of Computing,* Addison-Wesley, Reading, 1987.

For programming:

Cooper, D., and Clancy, M., *Oh! Pascal!* , W. W. Norton, New York, 1982.

Dale, N. and Weems, C., *Pascal*, Second Edition, D. C. Heath and Co., Lexington, Massachusetts, 1987.

Jensen, K. and Wirth, N., *Pascal*, Third Edition, Springer-Verlag, New York, 1985.

Koffman, E. B., *Turbo Pascal: A Problem Solving Approach*, Addison-Wesley, Reading, Massachusetts, 1986.

Motil, J. M., *Programming Principles: An Introduction*, William C. Brown Publishers, Dubuque, Iowa, 1988.

Patterson, D. A., Kiser, D. S., and Smith, D. N., *Computing Unbound*, W. W. Norton, New York, 1989.

Pattis, R. E., *Karel the Robot: A Gentle Introduction to the Art of Programming*, John Wiley, New York ,1981.

Reges, S., *Building Pascal Programs*, Little, Brown Computer Science, Boston, Massachusetts, 1987.

Savitch, W. J., *TURBO Pascal, An Introduction to the Art and Science of Programming*, Second Edition, Benjamin/Cummings Publishing Company, Menlo Park, California, 1988.

Tremblay, J.-P., and Bunt, R. B., *Introduction to Computer Science*, Second Edition, McGraw-Hill, New York, 1989.

Turbo Pascal 4.0, Borland International, Scotts Valley, California, 1987.

Turbo Pascal for the Mac, Borland International, Scotts Valley, California, 1987.

2

Text Manipulation and Algorithm Design

What is Text Manipulation? (A)

"Something there is that doesn't love a wall."

Who wrote this line, where does it appear, and what was the context? We would like to be able to answer questions like this, but the required effort could be extreme. The only approach may be to collect a pile of books and hope that it will be found in one of them. We must begin with the first book, page through it carefully in our search, and then move through the rest of the books. Somewhere there may be an index that could lead us to the answer, but we cannot always expect to be so lucky.

Another way to solve this problem is to have our whole library stored on computer files and to let a machine do the work. If this line appears anywhere in any book, it will be straightforward for the machine to find it thousands of times faster than any human. This is an example of a *text manipulation* problem - the kind of calculation we will examine in this chapter. In particular, this is a *search* problem, and various other types of text manipulation will be considered.

Another example relates to spelling correction. Suppose you are about to submit a paper and wish to check that every word is correctly spelled. A pedantic methodology is to look up every word in a dictionary. Ordinarily this would be unthinkable drudgery, but if both the paper and the dictionary are stored in a machine (as they often are), it is not only possible but in some offices routine. Of course, if you have misspelled one word into another word in the dictionary as with "except" instead of "accept," the dictionary check will not catch the error, but another more complicated mechanism could. You need a computer program that will also check that each sentence is grammatically well formed, a difficult but not unapproachable calculation.

There are numerous examples of other interesting text manipulation problems, and one more, a kind of mathematical puzzle, will be given here. (Individuals not enthusiastic about such puzzles may skip forward to the next section.) Suppose there are two strings of symbols with the names *string1* and *string2*. Suppose further that there are five operations that modify these strings as follows:

Operation 1: Concatenate b to the right end of *string1* and bbabaa to the right end of *string2*. (Here "concatenate" means "join." Thus concatenating b to the right end of string cdce results in the new string cdceb.)

Operation 2: Concatenate ab to the right end of *string1* and abb to the right end of *string2*.

Operation 3: Concatenate abba to the right end of *string1* and ba to the right end of *string2*.

Operation 4: Concatenate aab to the right end of *string1* and bab to the right end of *string2*.

Operation 5: Concatenate bab to the right end of *string1* and a to the right end of *string2*.

These operations are summarized in the following table:

Operation	Concatenate to *string1*	Concatenate to *string2*
1	b	bbabaa
2	ab	abb
3	abba	ba
4	aab	bab
5	bab	a

The question is, assuming that *string1* and *string2* begin with no symbols, what sequence of one or more operations will result in the two strings being identical? Let us attempt to find a solution to this problem. We will begin by applying operator 1 to the empty strings:

string1 | b |

string2 | bbabaa |

This is a successful way to begin because the two strings are the same on the first symbol, and we can hope to find a way to apply other operators to make them identical throughout. Next we could apply operator 2:

string1 | bab |

string2 | bbabaaabb |

This was unsuccessful because the second and third symbols are different in the two strings. Operator 2 should not be applied here. But operator 1 could be applied a second time

string1 | bb |

string2 | bbabaabbabaa |

and then operator 2 could be tried:

string1 | bbab

string2 | bbabaabbabaaabb

This is a good start, but *string2* is becoming too long. Are there some operators that would enable *string1* to catch up and achieve equality? Maybe we should have started with a different operator. Or perhaps there is no solution.

This is an example of what is called the *Post correspondence problem*, and it has importance in computer science, as will be noted in chapter 13. For the purposes of the current study, it should be thought of as simply an interesting puzzle that computers can help us solve.

Thus this chapter will examine text manipulation problems. And, as in the previous chapter, we will also study some important concepts in computer science. These will include the idea of the *algorithm*, a recipe for doing something, and its design and coding into an executable program.

Algorithms and Program Design for Text Manipulation (*B*)

An *algorithm* is a method, procedure, or recipe for doing a job. It usually has *inputs*, objects that are to be used by the algorithm, and it always has *outputs*, which are the results of its action. The algorithm also must have a sequence of steps that show how the output is obtained. These steps must be well-defined actions provided by some mechanism at hand. Thus steps can be things like "move an object from one place to another" or "count the (finite) number of objects in a box." They cannot include operations such as "add up all of the integers in the universe" or "write a musical composition."

An algorithm does not specify who or what will carry out the steps. It is a method for doing something, and it could be carried out by a human or a machine. It may be written in a natural language such as English or a computer language. The field of computer science may be thought of as the study of algorithms and their automatic execution by machines.

When we study programming, we are studying the process of creating and coding algorithms. But it is important to separate the two processes and think clearly about each. The first involves the discovery of a method for doing a task and the second is concerned with translating that method into a computer language.

Consider the creation of an algorithm for exchanging the contents of two boxes. If we consider this problem for a moment, our brains call on programs hidden in our heads and tell us how to do it:

1. Move the contents of one box, say box 1, to a temporary storage place.

2. Move the contents of the other box, box 2, to box 1.

3. Move the objects in the temporary storage place into box 2.

(How such programs came into existence in our brains is a mystery.) After sufficient contemplation, we select a method for doing the task and write down the steps. The inputs to the algorithm are the two boxes with their given contents; the outputs are the same boxes with their contents exchanged.

Next we would like to use a computer language, say Pascal, to code this algorithm. There is no feature in Pascal to move objects as described in the steps, but there is a feature similar enough to be able to code the algorithm directly. This feature is called the *assignment* statement; it is written as

```
x := y
```

where *x* and *y* are the names of locations in memory. It means "destroy the contents of *x* and copy the contents of *y* into *x*." The main difference between "move" in the algorithm and "copy" is that "move" leaves nothing behind, and "copy" leaves everything behind. Moving objects from box 1 leaves box 1 empty; copying from box 1 leaves box 1 unchanged. Another important characteristic of the copy operation is that it destroys or covers up the objects in the destination location. Suppose *x* and *y* appear as follows:

x |abc |

y |efgh |

and *x* := *y* is carried out. That is, *y* is copied into *x*. Then the result destroys the contents of *x* and leaves two copies of the contents of *y*.

x |efgh |

y |efgh |

The three steps of the exchange algorithm can be coded using the assignment statement. Assume the inputs are *box1* and *box2* and that a temporary location for storing information is *temp*. The output is *box1* and *box2* with their contents exchanged:

```
temp:=box1;
box1:=box2;
box2:=temp;
```

Tracing the execution of this code on sample data, suppose the locations begin as shown:

box1 | abc | box2 | efgh | temp | |

Then the changes are easy to follow for the three statements:

```
temp := box1;
```

box1 | abc | box2 | efgh | temp | abc |

```
box1 := box2;
```

box1 [efgh]   box2 [efgh]   temp [abc]

```
box2 := temp;
```

box1 [efgh]   box2 [abc]   temp [abc]

The goal is achieved: the contents of *box1* and *box2* have been exchanged.

Here is the complete program for reading two strings, writing them, exchanging them, and then writing them again:

```
program Exchange;
var
    box1, box2, temp: string;
begin
readln(box1);
readln(box2);
writeln(box1,'      ',box2);
temp:=box1;
box1:=box2;
box2:=temp;
writeln(box1,'      ',box2);
readln;
end.
```

In this program the *writeln* statement is used to write three items: the contents of *box1*, the string containing a space, and the contents of *box2*.

In order to be sure that you understand program *Exchange*, run it on some sample inputs. Here is an example:

```
        Typed inputs:       Jack
                            Jill
        Machine responses:  Jack    Jill
                            Jill    Jack
```

Let us consider another problem, the acquisition of a person's name in the following dialogue:

Computer: `Tell me your first name.`
User: `Alan`
Computer: `Thank you, Alan. Tell me your last name.`
User: `Turing`
Computer: `Your full name is Alan Turing.`

The inputs to the algorithm for solving this problem are the user's two names, and the outputs are the three messages shown. Here are the required algorithmic steps.

1. Print "Tell me your first name."

2. Input a string of characters and store them.

3. Create a string beginning with "Thank you,"continuing with the characters that were typed in step 2, and ending with "Tell me your last name."

4. Print the string from step 3.

5. Input another string of characters.

6. Create the string "Your name full name is" followed by the string from step 2 followed by a space followed by the string from step 5 followed by the string "." .

7. Print the string from step 6.

Coding this algorithm is as easy as the previous one except that one new Turbo Pascal construction is needed, that for concatenation. In order to assemble the strings in steps 3 and 6, an operator is needed for gluing together strings. The operator is denoted by "+" and it concatenates two strings to produce a third. Thus the code

```
x  :=  'abc';
y  :=  'defg';
z  :=  x+y;
```

will put "abc" into *x*, "defg" into *y* and "abcdefg" into *z*. (This assumes that *x*, *y*, and *z* have been declared as strings.)

Using this operator, the seven steps may now be coded:

```
program  GetName;
var
    first, last,  message1, message2 :string;
begin
writeln('Tell  me  your  first  name.');
readln(first);
message1:='Thank you, ' + first + '. Tell  me  your  last  name.';
writeln(message1);
readln(last);
message2:='Your full  name is ' + first + '   ' + last + '.';
writeln(message2);
readln;
end.
```

This section has explained that programming can be separated into two distinct parts: the creation of the algorithm, which gives the method of solution, and the coding of the steps of the method. Each part can require substantial creativity, experience, and hard work. In addition, this section has introduced the assignment statement and concatenation operator and shown their application in some text manipulation problems.

Exercises

1. A program is to be written that reads a string of symbols and then prints two adjacent copies of that string. For example, if the program reads "algorithm", it will print "algorithmalgorithm". Design an algorithm to solve this problem. Remember one must create two copies of the input string and then put them together to obtain the output string. Then code the algorithm in Pascal.

2. Many regular nouns in English can be changed to their plural form by adding an "s" at the end. Write the algorithm that reads such nouns and prints their plural form. Write the code for the program.

3. Write an algorithm that interviews a person to obtain his or her address in the same fashion as the name acquisition program. Write the code.

4. Write an algorithm that does one step of the Post correspondence problem. It should input *string1* and *string2* and then ask the user which operator is to be applied. Finally it should apply the selected operator and print the new strings. The algorithm might look something like this:

1. Write "Input string1 and string2."
2. Read the strings.
3. Write "Which operator should be applied?"
4. Input 1,2,3,4, or 5.
5. If 1 was input then . . .
6. If 2 was input then . . .
ETC.
Then write a program to execute this algorithm.

5. Can you find a solution to the Post correspondence problem given in the introduction? Create another set of operations similar to those given and examine whether this version of the problem has a solution.

String and Integer Data Types(B)

A person asked to compute the following quantity may be confused:

```
423 + 51 = ?
```

Is the answer equal to 474, as might have been concluded before reading this chapter? Or is the answer 42351 which results from concatenating the two strings of symbols 423 and 51? The truth is that we must know whether the data objects 423 and 51 are to be regarded as integers or as strings. In the former case, the operation the "+" stands for the addition property that every schoolchild knows. In the latter case the symbols 423 are placed in sequence with 51.

We can conclude that data can be of various *types* and that the way they are processed depends on what types they are. This book will use three types—*string*, *integer*, and *real*—but Pascal and other languages have many other types as well. Thus it is necessary to tell the Pascal system which type is being used in each case so that it can compute the desired answers. Here is the program to read two strings, concatenate them, and print them:

```
program Concat;
var
    x, y, z: string;
begin
readln(x);
readln(y);
z := x + y;
writeln('z is  ',z);
readln;
end.
```

Here is the program to read two integers, add them up, and print the sum:

```
program Add;
var
    x, y, z: integer;
begin
readln(x);
readln(y);
z := x + y;
writeln('z is  ',z);
readln;
end.
```

Therefore it is very easy to declare the desired data type and to obtain the expected computation in each case. However, there is one rule that must always be followed in Pascal: each operator such as "+" functions properly only if it is given the correct types. If an illegal combination of types is presented to the operator, it will not be able to give a proper answer. Thus, "+" works correctly in these cases

```
(integer)  +(integer)  =(integer)
```

and

```
(string)  +(string)  =(string)
```

but there is no definition for the expression

```
(integer)  +(string)  =  ?
```

The following program will not function properly because it attempts to use "+" to operate on an illegal pair of objects:

```
program AddError;
var
    x: integer;
    y, z: string;
begin
readln(x);
readln(y);
z := x | y;
writeln('z  is  ',z);
readln;
end.
```

There are several other operators applicable to the integer type as well as addition. Some of them are multiplication "*", subtraction "-", and division "div". Also, there are additional forms that can be used in *if* statements, such as greater than ">" and less than "<" as in the following program which reads two integers and prints them out with the smallest one first:

```
program SmallestFirst;
var
    x, y: integer;
begin
writeln('Type  two  integers.');
readln(x);
readln(y);
writeln('In  order,  they  are');
if x > y then
    begin
     writeln(y,'  ',x);
    end
else
```

```
    begin
     writeln(x,' ',y);
    end;
readln;
end.
```

It is extremely important in the programs of this book for you to understand the difference between the various data types and to remember that each is always restricted to its own well-defined operations. Internally, the various data types are stored in different ways. Thus integers are stored as binary numbers (or a variant of them), as will be explained in Chapter 6. Strings are stored with one character in each of a sequence of memory cells. The following sections will give programs in which both string and integer data types are used.

Exercises

1. Design an algorithm that reads an integer and determines whether it is positive. If the integer is positive, it prints "positive," and otherwise it prints "not positive." Code the algorithm.

2. Design an algorithm that reads two integers and prints their sum, difference, product, and quotient. Code the algorithm.

3. Design an algorithm that reads three integers and prints them in order from smallest to largest. Code the algorithm.

More Text Manipulation(B)

Assignment and concatenation give methods for moving and gluing strings of symbols, but there are other operations that one might like to do. For example, how does one copy several characters out of the middle of a string? If a location contains the string "computer,"we would like to have a method to copy the letters "put" from its center. Ideally the operation should allow us to designate what string to copy characters from, where to begin copying, and how many characters to copy. Assuming that "computer" is stored in a location called *A1* and its three-character substring is to be moved into a location *A2* the image should be as shown:

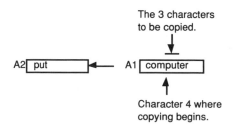

Turbo Pascal includes a convenient feature for doing this job— *copy*. It works as one might expect, and, in fact, the previous task is programmed with the following code:

```
A2 := copy(A1,4,3)
```

It means that characters are to be copied from *A1* starting at character number 4 and including a total of three characters. Those characters are to be copied into *A2*. In general, *copy(s,i,j)* means copy from string *s* starting at character number *i* and including a total of *j* characters. If *i* exceeds the length of string *s*, then a string of length zero will be copied.

Here are some more examples of the use of *copy*. If *x* contains "abcdefgh," then *y* will receive the string indicated:

Statement executed	New contents of y
y := copy(x,3,4)	cdef
y := copy(x,1,1)	a
y := copy(x,6,1)	f
y := copy(x,9,2)	(string of length zero)

Another useful Turbo Pascal feature—called *length*—finds the length of a string. You can find the length of string *x* by typing *length(x)*. Consider the following program:

```
program FindLength;
var
    x:  string;
    y:  integer;
begin
x := 'abcd';
y := length(x);
writeln(y);
readln;
end.
```

If this program is run, it will print the number 4. *x* has length 4, *length* will find it, and the second statement will load 4 into *y*. Note that *y* must be an integer.

What does the following program do?

```
program  FindIt;
var
    x,  y:  string;
begin
readln(x);
y := copy(x,length(x),1);
writeln(y);
readln;
end.
```

Suppose *FindIt* reads "abcd." Then *x* will receive this string. Then *length(x)* is 4, and *y* is loaded with *copy(x,4,1)*. So *y* receives "d," and this is printed. In general, this program will read a string and print the last character of the string. Thus we say *copy(x,length(x),1)* stands for the last character in *x*. Here are some more uses of *copy* and their meanings.

Expression	Meaning
copy(x,length(x)-1,1)	The second-to-last character in *x*
copy(x,length(x)-2,1)	The third-from-last character in *x*.
copy(x,length(x)-1,2)	The last two characters in *x*.
copy(x,1,1)	The first character in *x*.
copy(x,1,2)	The first two characters in *x*.
copy(x,1,length(x)-1)	All of *x* except the last character.
copy(x,2,length(x)-1)	All of *x* except the first character.
copy(x,2,length(x)-2)	*x* with its first and last characters removed.
copy(x,1,length(x) div 2)	The first half of *x*.

You should be able to analyze each of these expressions and see that the given meaning is correct.

You can use these substring features to write many interesting programs. Consider the problem of reading an English noun and printing its plural form. An examination of some sample nouns and their plural forms begins to lead to a theory of plural forms.

Nouns	Plural Forms
bird	birds
whale	whales
cow	cows
pony	ponies
bunny	bunnies
sheep	sheep
mouse	mice

Many nouns are made plural by adding an "s," as in the first three cases. However, some nouns end in "y" and should have the "y" replaced by "ies." Others follow neither rule and can be classed as special cases.

A way to design the pluralization algorithm is to have it check whether the incoming noun is a special case first. If it is special, find its plural form and stop. If it is not special, then it will follow one of the rules and the correct one can be applied.

1. Input a noun.

2. Check whether it is a known special case. If so, select its plural form, and mark the task done.

3. If the task is not done, check whether the noun ends in "y". (a) If so remove the "y" and add "ies". (b) Otherwise, add "s".

4. Print the plural form.

The program can then be coded using the string operations. We assume for brevity that the only known special cases are those in the table:

```
program Plurals;
var
    noun, plural, task: string;
begin
writeln('Input  a  noun.');
readln(noun);
task := 'not done';
if noun = 'mouse' then
    begin
     plural := 'mice';
     task := 'done';
    end;
if noun = 'sheep' then
    begin
     plural := 'sheep';
     task := 'done';
    end;
if task = 'not done' then
    begin
      if copy(noun,length(noun),1)='y' then
        begin
          plural :- copy(noun,1,length(noun)-1) + 'ies';
        end
    else
        begin
         plural := noun + 's';
        end;
    end;
writeln('The  plural  version  is  ',plural,'.');
readln;
end.
```

One more feature for string manipulation is needed to complete the examples in this chapter. It is the *position* feature, which finds the position of one string inside another. It is written as *pos*, and *pos(x,y)* means "find the position of the first character in the first occurrence of *x* in string *y*". If *x* is not in *y*, then *pos(x,y)* will give 0. Here are some sample evaluations.

x	y	pos(x,y)
cde	abcdef	3
de	abcdef	4
def	abcdef	4
aa	abcdef	0
bc	abcbcbc	2
cbc	abcbcbc	3
a	abcdef	1
abcd	abc	0

Exercises

1. Tell exactly what each program will do if the string *s1* that is read is 'cdef'. Where applicable, if an integer *i* is read, assume it is 3. Where a string *s2* is read, assume it is 'abcdefgh'. Then tell in simple English what the program does on inputs in general.

```
program  G1;
var
    s1:string;
begin
readln(s1);
s1 := s1 + 'aaaa';
writeln(s1);
readln;
end.

program G2;
var
    s1:string;
begin
readln(s1);
s1 := s1 + copy(s1,1,1);
writeln(s1);
readln;
end.

program G3;
var
   s1:string;
begin
readln(s1);
s1 := copy(s1,length(s1),1) + copy(s1,2,length(s1)-2) + copy(s1,1,1);
```

```
writeln(s1);
readln;
end.

program G4;
var
    s1:string;
    i:integer;
begin
readln(s1);
readln(i);
s1 := copy(s1,i,length(s1)-i+1);
writeln(s1);
readln;
end.

program G5;
var
    s1,s2:string;
    i:integer;
begin
readln(s1);
readln(s2);
i := pos(s1,s2);
s2 := copy(s2,i,length(s2)-i+1);
writeln(s2);
readln;
end.

program G6;
var
    s1:string;
    i:integer;
begin
readln(s1);
readln(i);
s1 := copy(s1,1,i-1)  +  '*'  +  copy(s1,i,length(s2)-i+1);
writeln(s1);
readln;
end.
```

2. Design an algorithm that reads a string and prints the string with its first and last characters removed. Write the Pascal code.

3. Design an algorithm that reads a string and a number. Then it prints the first part of the string, specifically the number of characters indicated by the number. Write the code.

4. Design an algorithm that reads a string and a number. Then it prints the last part of the string, the number of characters indicated by the number. Write the code.

5. Design an algorithm that reads two strings. If the first string is found to be a substring of the second, it outputs "yes"; otherwise it outputs "no." Write the code.

Programming Text-Editing Functions(B)

The following examples and exercises aim at constructing the parts of a text-editing program, which enables users to type text into a computer and to modify it or print it conveniently. We will design code for inserting and deleting text and for other simple operations. The next section will show how to combine these individual parts to produce a simple text-editing system.

This editor will use the concept of a *pointer*, which is an indicator of where changes are to be made. Suppose that we have the string "abcdaefgh" and wish to make a change just at the position of the second "a". We will set the pointer to that character:

```
abcdaefgh
    Δ
```

Suppose we decide to insert "bbb" at the position of that "a"; then we will do an insert command and type "bbb":

```
abcdbbbaefgh
    Δ
```

Now suppose that we wish to delete four characters starting at the position of the pointer; we will do a delete instruction and indicate four characters are to be deleted:

```
abcdefgh
    Δ
```

Here is how the actual dialogue will proceed to carry out these operations. The computer will indicate after each command the location of the pointer by typing a * immediately preceding the character being pointed to.

Computer: `Command:`

User: `i`   (This means "insert.")

Computer: `Insert what?`

User: `abcdaefgh`

Computer: `*abcdaefgh`

Computer: `Command:`

User: `p`   (This means "point.")

Computer: `Point to what?`

User: `aef`   (The pointer will mark the first

Computer: `abcd*aefgh`   character in the string typed.)

Computer: `Command:`

User: `i`   (Insert.)

Computer: `Insert what?`

User: `bbb`

Computer: `abcd*bbbaefgh`

Computer: `Command:`

User: `d`   (This means "delete.")

Computer: `Delete how many characters`

User: `4`

Computer: `abcd*efgh`

Computer: `Command:`

User: `p`   (Point)

Computer: `Point to what?`

User: `h`

Computer: `abcdefg^h`

Several individual routines must be written to insert, move the pointer, delete, and other operations. Let us examine the insert routine first. All of these considerations will assume the string of characters being manipulated is contained in a location called *text* and that an integer variable called *ptr* tells which character is being pointed to. Here is the algorithm:

1. Print "Insert what?"

2. Input a string and put it into *new*.

3. Construct the string of characters in *text* up to the position to the left of the pointer, followed by *new*, followed by the rest of the characters in *text*. Copy it into *text* .

4. Print *text*.

Next we write the code for insert. First translate expressions like "the string of characters in *text* up to the position to the left of the pointer" into Turbo Pascal. The *copy* feature provides the necessary mechanism:

English	Translation
the string of characters in *text* up to the position to the left of the pointer	`copy(text,1,ptr-1)`
the rest of the characters in *text*	`copy(text,ptr,length(text)-ptr+1`

Here is the code:

```
begin
writeln('Insert  what?');
readln(new);
text:=copy(text,1,ptr-1)  +  new  +  copy(text,ptr,length(text)-ptr+1);
writeln(text);
end
```

We can run this code and see that it performs the required insertion. However, when we compare its actions with those described in the editing example, we notice that the printed version of *text* is not quite correct. It does not print the text with the asterisk showing where the pointer is located. Let us revise the algorithm to create a "print form" for the data in *text*. This location will be called *pform* and it will be identical to *text* except that it will include an asterisk just to the left of the character being pointed to.

1. Print "Insert what?"

2. Input a string and put it into *new*.

3. Construct the string of characters in *text* up to the position to the left of the pointer followed by *new*, followed by the rest of the characters in *text*. Copy it into *text*.

4. Create a version of *text* that contains "*" immediately to the left of the character being pointed to. Put it into *pform*.

5. Print *pform*.

Here is the revised code:

```
begin
writeln('Insert  what?');
readln(new);
text:=copy(text,1,ptr-1)  +  new  +  copy(text,ptr,length(text)-ptr+1);
pform:=copy(text,1,ptr-1)  +  '*'  +  copy(text,ptr,length(text)-ptr+1);
writeln(pform);
end
```

This code preserves the concept that the text being manipulated always is in the location called *text*. Whenever a change is made, the new version is always loaded into *text*. The asterisk is not part of the text being manipulated, and it never appears in *text*. The location *pform* is the only place where an asterisk appears.

One can also consider programming the move pointer routine. The algorithm is straightforward:

1. Print "Point to what?"

2. Input a string and put it into *target*.

3. Put into the integer location called *ptr* the position of the first character of *target* in *text*. (This can be done with *ptr:=pos(target,text)*.)

4. Create a version of *text* which contains a "*" immediately preceding the character being pointed to. Put it into *pform*.

5. Print *pform*.

The coding of this algorithm is left as an exercise.

Exercises

1. Code the algorithm for setting the pointer as described above.

2. Design an algorithm for executing the delete operation described above. This algorithm should input the number of characters to be deleted and then remove the required number of characters starting at the pointer. Code the algorithm.

3. Design an algorithm for an operation called "change" that will be invoked using the code "c." This operation will read a number telling how many characters following the pointer are to be changed. Then it will read a string that is to be inserted in place of those characters. An example usage might be as follows assuming *pform* contains "abc*dafgh."

Computer? Command:

User: c

Computer: Change how many characters.

User: 2

Computer: To what?

User: rrrr

Computer: abc*rrrrfgh

Code the algorithm.

4. Sometimes it is useful to have a command "s" that will insert a space at the pointer position if one is needed. An example usage (assuming *pform* contains "abc*rrrrfgh") is:

Computer: Command:

User: s

Computer: abc* rrrrfgh

Design and code the algorithm.

Building the Editor Program (B)

There is a repetitive nature to the behavior needed for the editor program:

> input command
> carry out command
> input command
> carry out command
> input command
> carry out command
> - -
> (and so forth)

A program construction is needed to provide this cyclic action; it is called the *loop*, and its general action is indicated by the arrow.

```
 ┌──>input command
 │      carry out command
 └──────────────┘
```

The Pascal language offers a very easy way to program this loop. We simply mark the beginning of the code to be repeated with *while true do*:

```
while true do
    input command
    carry out command
```

The particular form "while true do" may seem like a strange way to ask for repetitions, but it will not seem so after some additional examples. Running this program will achieve the desired action, assuming the code for "input command" and "carry out command" is filled in properly. It will repetitively execute these commands without end.

There are two ways to stop a loop of this kind once it has begun. The first is to hit an "interrupt" key on the computer. Consult your computer manual or friend to find out how to stop a looping program. The other way is to change the *while* statement in a way that tells it when to stop (or "exit"). We will see how to do that later in this section.

The loop feature should be tested before it is used in the editor. Here it is in its simplest possible form:

```
program Repetition;
begin
while true do
   begin
    writeln('Begin the loop.');
    writeln('Here is some more.');
   end;
end.
```

Execution of this program yields the two indicated messages printed on your screen as fast as it can print them.

```
Begin the loop.
Here is some more.
Begin the loop.
Here is some more.
Begin the loop.
Here is some more.
   -   -

   -   -
```

Did you remember to ask someone how to stop this on your machine? Notice we follow an indentation policy with looping code similar to that established for *if-then* code. We also place *begin* and *end* markers around the indented code. Here is yet another program to try:

```
program  RepeatBs;
var
     position: string;
begin
position  .=  'A',
while true do
   begin
    position := position + 'B';
    writeln(position);
    end;
end.
```

Can you explain the behavior of this program? Each time the loop code is repeated, a string is created by the computation *position + 'B'*. Then this new string is placed into *position*.

Returning to the editor, we can be more precise about the behavior we seek. The dialogue of the previous section shows that a write statement *writeln('Command:')* must begin the code followed by an input statement to receive the user's command. Then if you type "i," the program should carry out the insert code developed in the previous section. If you type another command such as "p," "d," "c," or "s," the appropriate code should be executed. Here is the plan for the program:

> print the word "Command:"
> input the user's command
> if the user typed "i", then
> > carry out an insert operation
> if the user typed "p", then
> > do a pointer move operation
> if —

And here is some of the code.

```
writeln('Command;');
readln(command);
if command = 'i' then
   begin
   writeln('Insert  what?');
   readln(new);
   text := copy(text,1,ptr-1) + new + copy(text,ptr,length(text)-
      ptr+1);
   pform := copy(text,1,ptr-1) + '*' + copy(text,ptr,length(text)-
      ptr+1);
   writeln(pform);
   end;
if command = 'p' then
   put pointer code here ;
if command = 'd' then
   put delete code here ;
```

(*and so forth*)

But the program is not complete; some additions must be made. First, the loop instructions must be inserted. Also it is often helpful to write a message at the beginning and end of the program informing the user of the entrance and exit of the program. Another concern relates to the variables *text* and *ptr*, which should be given some initial values. All the instructions assume *text* contains something, so let us put a string of length zero into it. The string of length zero is represented by two single quotes typed next to each other. They also assume *ptr* always has a value. Let us put zero into it:

```
writeln('Enter  Editor.');
text := '';
ptr := 0;
while true do
   begin
   writeln('Command;');
   readln(command);
   if command = 'i' then
      begin
      writeln('Insert  what?');
      readln(new);
      text := copy(text,1,ptr-1) + new + copy(text,ptr,length(text)-
         ptr+1);
```

```
      pform  :=  copy(text,1,ptr-1)+'*'+copy(text,ptr,length(text)-
         ptr+1);
      writeln(pform);
      end;
   if command = 'p' then
      put pointer code here ;
   if command = 'd' then
      put delete code here ;

      (put other commands here )

   end;
writeln('Exit  Editor.');
readln;
end.
```

It is often quite helpful to write comments about a program in order to aid in its readability. These comments help the programmer to keep the various parts of the code in mind, and they are enormously useful to any other person who may use the code or need to revise it. Pascal offers a means for entering these comments. They need only be surrounded with curly brackets "{" and "}," and they can be placed anywhere in the code without affecting execution. When the computer runs the program, it never processes any of the characters nested within these brackets. Some detailed suggestions are given in chapter 4 related to where comments should be placed and what information they should contain. Here is another copy of the program with comments added to aid readability:

```
writeln('Enter  Editor.'); {This is the entrance message.        }
text := '';                 {text holds the text to be edited.    }
ptr := 0;                   {ptr gives the location to be modified. }
while true do
   begin
   writeln('Command;');
   readln(command);         {Read the editing command.}
   if command = 'i' then
      begin                 {This code implements an insert.}
      writeln('Insert  what?');
      readln(new);
      text := copy(text,1,ptr-1) + new + copy(text,ptr,length(text)-
         ptr+1);
      pform := copy(text,1,ptr-1) +'*'+copy(text,ptr,length(text)-
         ptr+1);
      writeln(pform);
      end;
```

```
   if command = 'p' then
       put pointer code here ;  {This code implements pointer move.}
   if command = 'd' then
       put delete code here ;    {This code implements a delete.}
       (put other commands here )
   end;
writeln('Exit  Editor.');          {This is the exit messaqe.}
readln;
end.
```

Counting all of the commands in the previous section with exercises, the editor now has five commands: i,p,d,c, and s. A final convenient addition will be the "q" command, "quit." It will cause the machine to exit the loop and end the run. What one really wants to say to the machine is this: "While ordinary commands like i, p, d, c, and s are being used, continue going around the loop; but if a 'q' is ever typed, halt." Or in other words, while the command is not "q", continue going around the loop. In Pascal, the test of whether the command is not "q" is written as *command<>'q'*. This test can be entered into the while loop statement to obtain the desired behavior, so the editor can be revised again to include this change:

```
writeln('Enter  Editor.');  {This  is  the  entrance  message.      }
text := '';                 {text holds the text to be edited.      }
ptr := 0;                   {ptr gives the location to be modified. }
command := '';              {command gives user's command           }
while command<>'q' do
   begin
   writeln('Command;');
   readln(command);                  {Read the editing command.}
   if command = 'i' then
       begin                 {This code implements an insert.}
       writeln('Insert  what?');
       readln(new);
       text := copy(text,1,ptr-1) + new + copy(text,ptr,length(text)-
           ptr+1);
       pform := copy(text,1,ptr-1) + '*' + copy(text,ptr,length(text)-
           ptr+1);
       writeln(pform);
       end;
   if command = 'p' then
       put pointer code here ; {This code implements pointer move.}
   if command = 'd' then
       put delete code here ;   {This code implements a delete.}
       (put other commands here )
   end;
```

```
writeln('Exit  Editor.');      {This  is  the  exit  message.}
roadln;
end.
```

The location *command* is initialized before entering the loop in the above program with the string of length zero. This is done so that when the test *command<>'q'* is made, it will have a value.

Exercises

1. Assemble the complete editor with the commands i,p,d,c,s, and q. Try it on your machine.

2. It is easy to forget the commands available on your editor or on any other computer program. A common practice is to include a command "help," which causes a message to be printed telling the user what the commands are. Program a "help" command, and add it to your editor. It should work as follows:

Computer: `Command:`

User: `help`

Computer: `The  available  commands  are`

           `c`   `change`

           `d`   `delete`

           `help`   `print  all  commands`

           `i`   `insert`

           `p`   `move  the  pointer`

           `q`   `quit`

           `s`   `add  a  space`

3. The editor still has some shortcomings. For example, if the string is "abcdabcd," the p command is unable to set the pointer to the last character. (Try it.) A second command "pl" that means "point to last character in a typed string" can be added to give more flexibility in setting the pointer. In the example, the "pl" command would be used as follows to set the pointer:

Computer: `Command:`

User: `pl`

Computer: `Point  to  last  of  what?`

User: `dabcd`

Computer: `abcdabc*d`

4. Run your editor on some examples to see how well it performs. Think of a command that will help you in manipulating the text, and add it to your editor.

5. In a previous section, code was designed to do a single step of the Post correspondence problem. Embed this code into a loop, and thus construct a program for doing any number of Post correspondence problem steps.

Building a Conversation Machine (C)

Some constructions introduced in this chapter can be employed in decision tree programs to achieve more interesting performance. Consider the following decision tree, which carries out a "conversation" with the user:

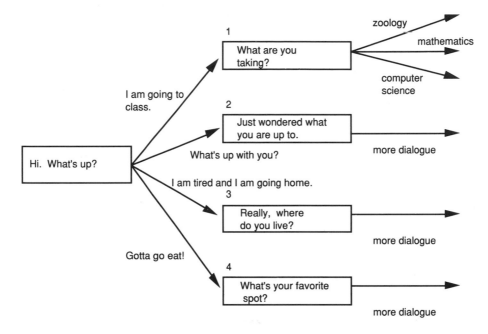

The trick to making this program work is to look for keywords in each user response. If the user says anything about "class," the program will go to node 1 and respond "What are you taking?" If the user mentions the word "eat," the program will respond, "What's your favorite spot?" If designed carefully, the program may be able to carry on a plausible conversation for some time.

Keywords are located using the *pos* feature. Thus if we wish to check whether "class" is in the user's sentence in *answer*, we use

```
if pos('class',answer) > 0 then
```

which says "find the position of 'class' in *answer* and if any position was found (greater than zero) then do the following."

Here is how to get started in the construction of such a program:

```
program  Conversation;
val
    answer1, answer2: string;
begin
writeln('Hi.  What  is  up?');
readln(answer1);
if  pos('class',answer1)  >  0  then
    begin
    answer1 := '#';
    writeln('What  are  you  taking?');
     readln(answer2);
        further  processing
    end;
if  pos('you',  answer1)  >  0  then
    begin
    answer1 := '#';
    writeln('Just  wondered  what  you  are  up  to.');
     readln(answer2);
        further  processing
    end;
if  pos('home', answer1)  >  0  then
    begin
    answer1 := '#';
     writeln('Really,  where  do  you  live?');
     readln(answer2);
        further  processing
    end;
if  pos('eat',answer1)  >  0  then
    begin
    answer1 := '#';
     writeln('What  is  your  favorite  spot?');
     readln(answer2);
        further  processing
    end;
readln;
end.
```

If one of the keywords — "class," "home," etc.— is found in the program, the user's answer is replaced by "#" to prevent a second reference to this answer. Without this change, the user's sentence could result in going down one path of the decision tree and then later following a second path. This would occur at the first node with the sentence, "I am going to class, and then I will eat."

A program of this type is pretentious because it appears to do something — understand English — it cannot really do. It provides interesting recreation and should be thought of as a kind of computer game. However, it cannot ethically be presented to serious users without a proper warning. In the chapter on artificial intelligence, we will describe some computer programs that do understand some simple kinds of English.

Exercise

1. Design a decision tree for some kind of conversational program. Write the program.

Turbo Pascal Summary (C)

Chapter 1 concluded with a discussion of the Turbo Pascal constructions used in that chapter and gave a set of rules describing them. Those rules will be repeated here with the additions needed for the constructions used in this chapter:

```
Program:
    <program>  -> program   <identifier>;
                  <variable  declaration>
                  <compound  statement>.
Variable  declaration:
    <variable  declaration>  -> nothing
    <variable  declaration>  -> var
                          a  sequence  of   <identifier:type>'s  each
                                  followed  by  a  semicolon
    <identifier:type>  -> <identifier  list>  :  <type>
    <identifier  list>  ->   a  list  of   <identifier>'s  separated  by
                                                        commas
Type:
    <type>  ->  string
    <type>  ->  integer
Compound  statement:
    <compound  statement>  -> begin
                                   a  sequence  of   <statement>  's
                                       each  followed  by  a  semicolon
                          end
Statement:
    <statement>  -> writeln(list  of   <expression>'s  separated  by
                               commas  )
    <statement>  ->  readln(<identifier>)
    <statement>  ->  readln
    <statement>  -> if   <boolean  expression>  then
                               <compound  statement>
                  else
                               <compound  statement>
```

```
      <statement> -> if   <boolean expression>   then
                              <compound statement>
      <statement> -> <identifier> := <expression>
      <statement> -> while <boolean expression> do
                              <compound statement>
Expression:
   <expression> -> <string expression>
   <expression> -> <integer expression>
String expression:
   <string expression> -> <identifier>
   <string expression> -> ' any string of printable characters
   <string expression> -> <string expression>+ <string expression>
   <string expression> ->
       copy(<string expression>,<integer expression>,<integer
                                              expression>)

Integer expression:
   <integer expression> ->  any integer
   <integer expression> -> <identifier>
   <integer expression> ->
                  <integer expression> <intop>   <integer expression>
   <integer expression>  > length(<string expression>)
   <integer expression> -> pos(<string expression>,<string
                                              expression>)
   <intop> ->  one of  +, *, -, or  div
Boolean expression:
   <boolean expression> -> <identifier> <comp> <expression>
   <boolean expression> -> true
   <comp> -> one of  >, <, >-, <=, =,  or  <>
Identifier:
   <identifier> -> a sequence of letters and/or digits
                            that begins with a letter
```

Summary (B)

This chapter introduced many new features related to text manipulation and showed how to combine them to build a simple text editor. It shows some of the mechanisms built into well known word processing systems and how they are constructed.

   The chapter also introduced some ideas related to good programming practice. The programmer is wise first to design the algorithm related to doing the appointed task and write down the steps in English or some other convenient language. As a separate step, the code should be prepared using a computer language.

The concept of "type" was introduced, and the two types were discussed. The first type, strings, can be input, printed, concatenated (+), cut into substrings (*copy*) , assigned (:=), measured for length (*length*), and searched (*pos*). The second type, integers, can be input, printed, assigned (:=), or operated on by integer operations (+,-,*,*div*).

The quotation at the beginning of the chapter is the first line of the poem "Mending Wall" by Robert Frost.

Readings

For programming:

Cooper, D., and Clancy, M., *Oh! Pascal!* , W. W. Norton, New York, 1982.

Dale, N. and Weems, C., *Pascal*, Second Edition, D. C. Heath and Co., Lexington, Massachu setts, 1987.

Jensen, K. and Wirth, N., *Pascal*, Third Edition, Springer-Verlag, New York, 1985.

Koffman, E. B., *Turbo Pascal: A Problem Solving Approach*, Addison-Wesley, Reading, Massachusetts, 1986.

Motil, J. M., *Programming Principles: An Introduction*, William C. Brown Publishers, Dubuque, Iowa, 1988.

Patterson, D. A., Kiser, D. S., and Smith, D. N., *Computing Unbound*, W. W. Norton, New York, 1989.

Pattis, R. E., *Karel the Robot: A Gentle Introduction to the Art of Programming,* John Wiley, New York ,1981.

Reges, S., *Building Pascal Programs*, Little, Brown Computer Science, Boston, Massachusetts, 1987.

Savitch, W. J., *TURBO Pascal, An Introduction to the Art and Science of Programming*, Second Edition, Benjamin/Cummings Publishing Company, Menlo Park, California, 1988.

Tremblay, J.-P., and Bunt, R. B., *Introduction to Computer Science,* Second Edition, McGraw-Hill, New York, 1989.

Turbo Pascal 4.0, Borland International, Scotts Valley, California, 1987.

Turbo Pascal for the Mac, Borland International, Scotts Valley, California, 1987.

3

Numerical Computation and a Study of Functions

Let Us Calculate Some Numbers (A)

How much would a young person have to save each month in order to save a million dollars in a lifetime? More specifically, suppose the person is twenty years old and wishes to achieve the goal by the age of sixty. Furthermore, suppose the person has a municipal bond program available that is tax free and pays an annual rate of 12 percent, compounded monthly. We could make a quick guess at the needed monthly payments by ignoring the interest and dividing a million dollars by the number of months (480). The answer is $2083.33 per month. But this guess is high because the regular compounding of interest makes a significant difference.

In order to find an accurate answer, we must do a very long and laborious computation. One way to do it would be to propose a monthly payment, and then for each of the 480 months, compute the interest on the existing account and add in the contribution for that month. After 480 repetitions of this computation, the total amount saved would be known for that level of payment. Then other payment levels could be tried until the right one is found. Another way to do this problem is to write a program and let a machine find the answer. This is the solution proposed in this chapter.

Another class of interesting tasks is the set of *optimization* problems where we try to find the best value for a parameter in some situation. As an illustration, suppose we wish to construct a cylinder made from 1000 square centimeters of tin, and we want to find the correct dimensions so that the cylinder has the largest possible volume. In our attempts to maximize volume, we might propose to build a very tall cylinder. But since the total amount of material is limited, this could lead to a very narrow shape. The cylinder might not hold much:

Next, we might propose that the cylinder should be very fat. The material limitation would this time result in a very short container. Again, the total volume might not be large:

Perhaps some intermediate level would be best with moderate height and moderate diameter:

Again, our computer will help us solve the problem and find the dimensions for the cylinder such that volume is maximized and the total material is exactly 1000 square centimeters. Simultaneously, we will learn a technique for solving optimization problems. (Readers who know calculus will have an analytical solution to this problem. However, our methodology is general and can be applied to problems that do not have such solutions.)

Having studied text processing in the previous chapters, we now will learn about numerical computation to round out our experience in computing. We will also continue to study new concepts in programming and problem solving.

Simple Calculations (B)

A new type of number is necessary for numerical computing. In earlier sections, integers were introduced, and they are useful for counting, for referencing specific characters in a string, and for other numbering situations. But this type of number has some severe limitations: it cannot take on fractional values as in 2 1/5, and the values must not be too large in the positive or negative direction. On many machines, an integer may not be larger than 32,767 or smaller than -32,768. On all machines, there will be similar limitations on the maximum and minimum values. In general computational applications, a type of number is needed that can take on fractional as well as very large and very small values.

The answer to this need is the *real* type, which represents numbers in two parts: the *significant digits* and an *exponent*. The number 177 might be represented as $1.77 * 10^2$ where 1.77 gives the significant digits and 2 is the exponent. The actual value of the number can always be retrieved from the representation ($1.77 * 10^2 = 1.77 * 100 = 177$) and the representation can be efficiently stored in the machine. This type of number solves the two problems of integers and still requires relatively little computer memory. It is used almost universally on modern computers. We will not discuss in detail exactly how the numbers are stored but will note that on typical desktop machines, the largest number may be around 10^{38}, the smallest number may be around 10^{-45}, and the number of significant digits may be about 7 or 8.

We can get started using this kind of number by doing a declaration:

```
var
    x, y, z: real;
```

This results in three locations for real numbers being set up in memory with the appropriate names:

```
x  ┌──────────────┐
y  ├──────────────┤
z  ├──────────────┤
   └──────────────┘
```

Then one can load a number into a location

```
x  :=  12.0
```

to obtain

```
x  ┌──────────────┐
   │   1.2 * 10¹   │
y  ├──────────────┤
z  ├──────────────┤
   └──────────────┘
```

x contains $1.2 * 10^1$

or add two numbers together putting the sum into memory,

```
y  :=  13.3  +  x
```

to obtain

```
x  ┌──────────────┐
   │   1.2 * 10¹   │
y  │  2.53 * 10¹  │
z  └──────────────┘
```

x contains $1.2 * 10^1$, y contains $2.53 * 10^1$

Or one can do a complicated calculation using addition (+), multiplication (*), subtraction (-), and division (/):

```
z  :=  (x + 17.2)  *  (121 - (y / x))
```

x contains $1.2 * 10^1$, y contains $2.53 * 10^1$, z contains $3.471637 * 10^3$

As a more practical example, consider the problem of computing the volume of a cylinder using the formula

$$V = \pi r^2 h$$

where V is the volume, π is a constant approximately equal to 3.14159, r is the radius of the cylinder base, and h is the height. In Pascal, this would be written as

$$V := 3.14159 * r * r * h$$

A computer program to compute the volume of a cylinder is easy to write. The algorithm is

> find the radius r
> find the height h
> calculate $V = \pi r^2 h$
> print the volume V

and the program is

```
program CylinderVolume;
var
    r, h, V: real;
begin
writeln('Give  the  cylinder  radius.');
readln(r);
writeln('Give  the  cylinder  height.');
readln(h);
V := 3.14159 * r * r * h;
writeln('The  volume  is  ',  V);
readln;
end.
```

(In most cases, I emphasize simplicity and clarity in this book and this sometimes leads to programs unnecessarily pedantic and long. A shorter version of the code is

```
program CylinderVolume;
var
    r, h: real;
begin
writeln('Give  the  cylinder  radius  and  height.');
readln(r,h);
writeln('The  volume  is  ',  3.14159 * r * r * h);
readln;
end.
)
```

As another example of a numerical calculation, write a formula for how much money a savings account will hold after receiving interest compounded once. If the interest is written as a decimal (e. g., 12 percent is denoted 0.12), then the new savings can be computed by adding the current savings to the earned interest.

newsavings = savings + (savings * interest)

In Pascal, you can perform the calculation on the right and store it back into the same location, *savings*:

```
savings := savings + (savings * interest)
```

Again, this can be embedded in a program to find the amount in an account after one interest period. The algorithm is

> find the original amount in the account
> find the interest rate as a decimal for the time period
> compute the new amount after one time period using the formula
> print the result

and the program is

```
program  FindSavings;
var
   savings,  interestrate:  real;
begin
writeln('Give  the  original  amount  in  the  account.');
readln(savings);
writeln('Give  the  interest  rate.');
readln(interestrate);
savings := savings + (savings * interestrate);
writeln('After  one  time  period,  the  amount  is',  savings:6:2);
readln;
end.
```

A demonstration of the program shows the form of the input and output numbers:

```
Give  the  original  amount  in  the  account.
100.00
Give  the  interest  rate.
0.09
After  one  time  period,  the  amount  is   109.00
```

The numbers may be typed in ordinary decimal form though they are to be stored in the computer as reals with a significant digits part and an exponent. The *writeln* statement requires that the number *savings* be printed in a field 6 places wide with two digits to the right of the decimal place: *savings:6:2*.

It is easy to write useful programs of this kind, but two hazards need to be mentioned. The first relates to the problem that the order of the arithmetic operations may be ambiguous. That is, if x =2, y =3, z =4 and we write

```
result := x + y * z
```

what will be loaded into *result*? The machine might add x to y (obtaining 5) and multiply by z to get 20. Or it might multiply y times z (obtaining 12) and then add x to get 14. Which will it do? Dramatically different answers occur in the two cases. In fact, Pascal and most other programming languages employ a precedence mechanism that requires, in ambiguous situations, that multiplication and division be done first followed by addition and subtraction:

> *Precedence order*
> multiplication, division
> addition, subtraction

Thus the second of the two results given is correct, 14.

In a series of computations of equal precedence, the computation moves from left to right. Thus, if $x = 6$, $y = 2$, and $z = 3$, then

```
result := x / y * z
```

will yield the computation $6 / 2 * 3 = 3 * 3 = 9$. It will not compute the value of $6 / 2 * 3 = 6 / 6$ = 1.

If precedence is a problem, the programmer should always force the order of actions to achieve his or her goals. Thus

```
result := (x + y) * z
```

will force the addition of x to y before multiplication by z.

```
result := x + (y * z)
```

will force the multiplication before the addition in case the programmer has forgotten the precedence order. While the fundamental principles have been given here, many more examples and detailed rules will appear in a programming manual, and it should be consulted as necessary.

The second hazard related to calculation with real numbers is that the machine will make errors. The simple numbers 1 and 3 can be stored in a machine precisely, so we can have confidence in their integrity. However, if we divide one by the other, the quotient is 0.333333. . . which is an infinite decimal expansion that will not fit in a computer register. So only an approximation to the correct answer is stored—the first half-dozen or so significant digits. For most purposes, this is not a concern because we need only a few places of accuracy. But in some complicated calculations, these errors can build up and greatly distort answers.

Consider the following program, which should read a number and print the same number:

```
program ErrorDemo;
var
    data, extra: real;
begin
readln(data);
readln(extra);
data := data + extra;
data := data - extra;
writeln(data:20:2);
readln;
end.
```

The only function of the program is to add a number called *extra* to *data* and then subtract it away again. One would hope that this program would read a value for *data* and then print out the same number. For small values of *extra* and ordinary data (like 100), the program will work correctly. However, if *extra* is large, the data will be destroyed. Here is a table showing the performance of this program on a particular computer:

data (input)	extra (input)	data (output)
100	100	100
100	1000	100
100	10000	100
100	100000	100
-	-	-
	.	-
100	1000000000000000000000	100
100	10000000000000000000000	96
100	100000000000000000000000	128
100	1000000000000000000000000	0
100	10000000000000000000000000	0

If the values of *data* and *extra* are moderate, than the program always gives the correct answer. But when *extra* is raised to a sufficiently large value, the value in *data* was altered in unpredictable ways. You can see what is happening by actually working through the details associated with the last line of the table. 10000000000000000000000000 added to 100 yields 10000000000000000000000100. But this sum is approximated by the number 10000000000000000000000000 because of the limited register size. Then when *extra* is subtracted away, the answer is 0.

Clearly such a computation in the middle of a formula to compute the strength of an aircraft wing or the trajectory of a spaceship could lead to random results, poor decisions, and loss of life. Thus specialists in numerical analysis must be in charge of large complicated and critical calculations. But for the purposes of this book, the computer will be quite accurate enough for the tasks being addressed, and the issue of numerical error will not be mentioned again. A book on numerical analysis will explain the characteristics of numerical computations.

Exercises

1. The volume of a sphere is $4/3\pi r^3$. Write a program that reads the value of the radius of a sphere and then computes its volume.

2. The temperature f in degrees Fahrenheit can be computed from the temperature c in degrees Celsius by the formula $f = 9/5\,c + 32$. Write a program that reads the temperature in degrees Celsius and returns the temperature in Fahrenheit.

3. Assume that $x = 6.0$, $y = 7.0$, and $z = 3.0$ are real numbers. What will be computed in each case?

(a) `result := x * y - x * z`
(b) `result := x * 20.0 / z + y`
(c) `result := (z * x / y) / x + y`

4. Run the program *ErrorDemo* given above for the case of *data* = 0.00001. How large must *extra* be before the value of *data* is altered in the computation?

Functions (B)

A *function* is an entity that receives inputs and yields outputs. An example of a function is the one that receives the name of a person and yields the name of his or her father. Usually functions have names and let us call this one F. If F receives the name Isaac, it will return the name of his father Abraham. If it receives Abel, it will return Adam. Other examples are the function that receives the name of a country and then returns its capital, and the function that receives the dimensions of a cylinder and returns its volume.

Five different methodologies will be used in this book to describe functions: English descriptions, mathematical notation, computer programs, tables, and graphs. Any technique that tells how to find the appropriate output for each given input is satisfactory for defining a function. These methodologies will be briefly described here.

The usual mathematical notation is to write the input in parentheses following the function name and the output after an "=" sign:

For the father function F, the examples are thus written:

> F(Isaac) = Abraham
> F(Abel) = Adam

In this chapter, we will be studying numerical functions that input and yield numbers. A simple example is the function that doubles its input and returns the answer. If it receives 3, it will output 6. If it receives 17, it will yield 34. Let us call this function d and write down these examples:

> d(3) = 6
> d(17) = 34

One can say that d of anything is twice that anything or

> d(anything) = 2 * anything

Mathematicians prefer to use the variable name x for "anything" and write

> d(x) = 2x

so this is the usual notation for describing the function that doubles.

Another numerical function is the one given for computing the volume of a cylinder. This one receives r and h and computes volume. If the function is named v, one would write

> $v(r,h) = \pi r^2 h$

and a program for computing this function is given above. Suppose its inputs are $r=2$ and $h=3$; then its output will be $3.14159 * 2^2 * 3 = 37.69908$.

Tables provide another way to represent a function. Suppose the double function d is defined to operate only on positive integers. Then it would be written as follows:

input	*output*
x	*d(x)*
1	2
2	4
3	6
4	8
5	10
6	12

The cylinder volume function needs a two-dimensional table to represent its value since it has two inputs:

v(r,h)	h 1	2	3	4	5	6
1	3.14	6.28	9.42	12.57	15.71	18.85
2	12.57	25.13	37.70	50.27	62.83	75.40
r 3	28.27	56.55	84.82	113.10	141.37	169.65
4	50.26	100.53	150.80	201.06	251.33	301.59
5	78.54	157.08	235.62	314.16	392.70	471.24
6	113.10	226.19	339.29	452.39	565.49	678.58

Finally, we can graph functions. Here is the double function:

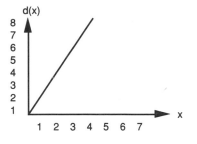

And here is the volume function with one graphical line for each value of *h*:

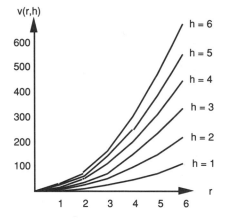

Exercise

1. Consider the function that computes the volume of a sphere from its radius. Show how the five given representations can be used to express this function.

Looping and a Study of Functions (B)

A good way to study functions is to build a program loop that calculates the value of the function repeatedly for many different input values. Suppose we wish to study the *d* function. We could execute the following code:

```
x := 1;
d := 2 * x;
writeln(x,d);
x := 2;
d := 2 * x;
```

```
writeln(x,d);
x := 3;
d := 2 * x;
writeln(x,d);
```

and so forth. This is the form of the loop:

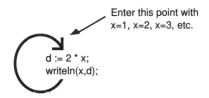

Enter this point with
x=1, x=2, x=3, etc.

d := 2 * x;
writeln(x,d);

Pascal offers a format for doing exactly this job:

```
x := 1.0;
while true do
    begin
    d := 2.0 * x;
    writeln(x,d);
    x := x + 1.0;
    end;
```

Conceptually this program sets *x* to 1 and then executes

```
d := 2.0 * x;
writeln(x,d);
```

Then it increases *x* by 1.0 and repeats:

```
d := 2.0 * x;
writeln(x,d);
```

This repeats for $x = 3$, $x = 4$, and so forth. Here is what is printed out:

```
1      2
2      4
3      6
4      8
5      10
6      12
-      -
-      -
```

As before, it is desirable to be able to stop the looping, and this is done by introducing a test in the *while* statement in place of *true*. Here is the complete program.

```
program Double;
var
    d, x: real;
begin
x := 1.0;
while x <= 10.0 do
    begin
    d := 2.0 * x;
    writeln(x:6:2,d:6:2);
    x := x + 1.0;
    end;
readln;
end.
```

The test $x <= 10.0$ means that x must be less than or equal to 10.0 in order for the loop body between the *begin* and *end* to be executed. The test is made just before the loop body is entered. If the test does not succeed because x is greater than 10, the loop body will be skipped and the statement following the *while* loop will be executed; thus *readln* will be the next action. Tracing all of the steps of this program, one can see its detailed operation:

instruction		x	d
x := 1.0		1.0	
(test) x <= 10.0	(yes)	1.0	
d := 2.0 * x		1.0	2.0
writeln		1.0	2.0
x := x + 1.0		2.0	2.0
(test) x <= 10.0	(yes)	2.0	2.0
d := 2.0 * x		2.0	4.0
writeln		2.0	4.0
x := x + 1.0		3.0	4.0
(test) x <= 10.0	(yes)	3.0	4.0
-		-	-
-		-	-
writeln		9.0	18.0
x := x + 1.0		10.0	18.0
(test) x <= 10.0	(yes)	10.0	18.0
d := 2.0 * x		10.0	20.0
writeln		10.0	20.0
x := x + 1.0		11.0	20.0
(test) x <= 10.0	(no)	11.0	20.0
readln			

Study the *Double* program with care because it illustrates the looping mechanism used in dozens of programs in the sections and chapters to come. A complete and detailed understanding of this code is essential to the comprehension of much later material.

It is now easy to approach the problem of finding the perfect dimensions for the cylinder described in the introduction. Its volume is $V = \pi r^2 h$, and its area is $A = 2\pi r^2 + 2\pi rh = 1000$. The second equation can be solved for h and substituted into the first equation to find the volume of the cylinder for each value of r, $V = 500r - \pi r^3$. Then a program can be written to compute V for each value of r from 1 to 10, and you can see how this volume changes:

```
program  CylinderVolumes;
var
    r,V: real;
begin
r := 1.0;
while r <= 10.0 do
    begin
    V := 500 * r - 3.14159 * r * r * r;
    writeln(r:8:2,V:8:2);
    r := r + 1.0;
    end;
readln;
end.
```

Running this program obtains the following values for r and V, which are graphed showing how V changes for each r:

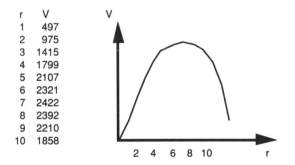

r	V
1	497
2	975
3	1415
4	1799
5	2107
6	2321
7	2422
8	2392
9	2210
10	1858

This graph makes it possible to confirm our suspicions at the beginning of this chapter. If the cylinder is extremely tall with a very small radius, the volume will be very small also. If the cylinder is very wide with a radius, say, larger than 10, the volume will not be large. In order to get the largest possible V, r should be set to an intermediate level, about 7. We will find a more exact value later. (Experts at differential calculus will have already found a more exact value using analytic methods but that is another story.) The cylinder of maximum volume looks approximately like this:

Let us next consider the interest problem. At the end of every month, the account will have the funds from the previous month (*savings*) plus the month's interest (*savings * monthint*) plus the new monthly payment (*payment*):

```
savings := savings + (savings * monthint) + payment
```

This calculation needs to be done on the last day of every month for the forty years (40 * 12 = 480 months). With the *while* loop, it is easy to write a program that will read a proposed monthly payment and compute the total forty-year savings.

> Algorithm:
>> find out monthly payment that is proposed
>> set savings = 0 and monthint = 0.01 (i.e. 0.12 per year)
>> for each of the 480 months compute:
>>> savings := savings + (savings * monthint) + payment
>> print amount of savings after 40 years

Program:
```
program Savings40Years;
var
    payment, savings, monthint, month: real;
begin
writeln('What payment do you propose?');
readln(payment);
savings := 0;
monthint := 0.01;
month := 1;
while month <= 480 do
    begin
    savings := savings + (savings * monthint) + payment;
    month := month + 1;
    end;
```

```
writeln(' Total savings after 40 years.', savings:10:2);
readln;
end.
```

Exercises

1. Type in the above program *Savings40Years* and see how much you will save if your monthly payments are $10. Is this enough to collect a million dollars? Try some other values until you find the correct one.

2. Use the methods of this chapter to find the lowest value that the function $f = x^2 - 5x + 4$ can have.

3. Use a program to compute $f = 1/3\ x^3 - 4x^2 + 15x + 3$ for values of x from 1 to 12. Graph the function.

Searching for The Best Value (B)

With some attention to detail, we can find a more accurate solution to the problem of maximizing the volume of the cylinder. The graph of the previous section would seem to indicate that r should be somewhat greater than 6. If r is exactly 6, the volume is

$$V = 500 * 6 - 3.14159 * 6^3 = 2321.42$$

Let us try $r = 6.01$, and see if the volume is larger:

$$V = 500 * (6.01) - 3.14159 * (6.01)^3 = 2323.02$$

So the theory is correct. Volume did increase when r was increased. Perhaps r should be increased again to 6.02:

$$V = 500 * (6.02) - 3.14159 * (6.02)^3 = 2324.61$$

Good! A strategy is to increase r repeatedly and see how many times V will continue to increase. If V ever gets smaller, stop. The previous value was the best. In fact, we can write a program to do this task.

Here is the method to be employed.

set r at some starting value
decide how much r should be increased each cycle
find V
increase r
find V
increase r
find V
increase r

———

——

if one ever notices that V got smaller, stop
the previous V was the best one found

Clearly the method is very repetitive and needs a loop.

> set r at some starting value
> decide how much r should be increased on each cycle
> find V
>
> increase r
> find V

if one ever notices that V got smaller, stop
the previous V was the best one found

Actually, the computer should be told to check, on every cycle through the loop, to see whether *V* is smaller than the previous *V*.

> set r at some starting value
> decide how much r should be increased on each cycle
> find V
>
> increase r
> find V
> if V is less than previous V, then stop

the previous V was the best one found

But in anticipation of putting this program into Pascal using a while loop, it is best to have the loop test at the beginning of the loop.

> set r at some starting value
> decide how much r should be increased on each cycle
> find V
>
> if V is less than previous V, then stop
> increase r
> find V

the previous V was the best one found

This algorithm has a bug in it. Notice its first four actions.

> set r at some starting value
> decide how much r should be increased on each cycle
> find V
> if V is less than previous V, then stop

But there is no previous *V*! This test is quite correct each time around the loop. But it makes no sense on the first encounter. The solution is to assume an initial value for the previous *V* which will make the loop work the first time. Assume that the previous *V* before entering the loop was zero.

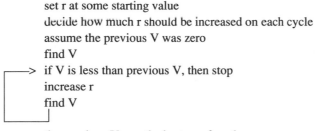

set r at some starting value
decide how much r should be increased on each cycle
assume the previous V was zero
find V
if V is less than previous V, then stop
increase r
find V

the previous V was the best one found

The algorithm is still not complete because the previous *V* is not systematically maintained. When *V* is computed each time around the loop, the previous value will be lost unless the program stores it. Thus a statement should be inserted just before the "find *V* " step that saves the current *V* into a place for the previous *V*.

set r at some starting value
decide how much r should be increased on each cycle
assume the previous V was zero
find V
if V is less than previous V, then stop
increase r
save V into a place called "previous V"
find V

the previous V was the best one found

This completes the design of the algorithm to find the largest value. The development of the loop required much care as is typical in most programming situations. We can now write the code.

```
program FindBest;
var
    r, V, previousV, increase: real;
begin
writeln('What  is  the  initial  value  of  r?');
readln(r);
writeln('How  much  should  r  be  increased  each  time?');
readln(increase);
previousV := 0;
V := 500 * r - 3.14159 * r * r * r;
while V >= previousV do
   begin
   r := r + increase;
   previousV := V;
```

```
   V := 500 * r - 3.14159 * r * r * r;
   writeln(r:10:2,V:10:2);
   end;
writeln('The  best  value  is  ',previousV:10:2);
readln;
end.
```

You should type this program into a machine and find a better solution to the cylinder maximization problem. Is it possible to find the best possible *r* accurate to three decimal places?

It could happen that this program will not find the best solution if the *V* curve has a strange shape as shown here.

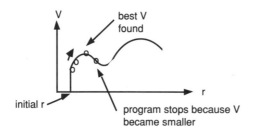

The program will increase *r* until *V* begins to decrease and will stop short of higher hill tops if they happen to exist. In the current example, this does not occur but in general one must investigate carefully to be sure the absolute maximum has been found.

This section has demonstrated a method to search for things with a computer. In our example, we were looking for the best possible value of *r* but in general, one can be looking for almost anything. The search method builds a loop that repeatedly checks for the desired item. The loop computation is continued until the searched item is found.

> (initialize computation)
> while item is not found do
>   (repetitive portion to get next item)
> print item found

Now we can solve the problem of finding the required payments to save a million dollars. In the previous section, we developed a program called *Savings40Years* to read the monthly payment and compute the forty year savings. But the real question was to find the needed monthly payment to achieve a million dollars. The searching strategy given above will work here. The algorithm should read the initial value for the variable called payment and then repeatedly increase payment computing forty year savings each time until the million dollar level is exceeded. Finally it should print the first payment that exceeded the goal.

> determine the initial value of payment
> find out the increment for this variable
> set the initial value of savings to zero
> while forty year savings is less than 1000000 do
>> increase the payment level
>> use Savings40Years program to compute 40 year savings
>> print payment

Here is the code:

```
program  MillionDollarAnswer;
var
    payment,  increase,  savings,  monthint,  month:  real;
begin
writeln('Payment  should  be  initialized  to  what?');
readln(payment);
writeln('How  much  should  payment  be  increased  each  time');
readln(increase);
savings :- 0;
while savings < 1000000 do
    begin
    payment := payment + increase;
    savings := 0;{This begins the calculation of 40 year savings.}
    monthint := 0.01;
    month :- 1;
    while month <= 480 do
        begin
        savings :- savings + (savings * monthint) | payment;
        month := month + 1;
        end;    {This completes the 40 year savings computation.}
    writeln(payment:15:2,savings:15:2);
    end;
writeln('The  sufficient  payment  level  is  ',  payment:10:2);
readln;
end.
```

A print statement has been included in the loop so that the progress of the calculation can be monitored. This is a complex program that you must study in detail to understand.

There are more efficient ways to solve this problem that will not be discussed here. One technique is to compute the forty year savings on a given payment level and then discover what fraction c of the goal is achieved. Then the correct answer can be found by dividing c into the payment level that was used.

Exercises

1. Find the dimensions, r and h, for a cylinder that has 1000 square centimeters of material and maximum volume. What is the maximum volume that is achieved? Give all answers accurate to three decimal places.

2. Suppose a person deposits $1000.00 into a bank account and then puts in monthly payments of $20.00 regularly for twenty years. Further suppose the bank pays an annual rate of 6 percent, compounded monthly. What will be the total savings at the end of the twenty years?

3. A person has the goal of saving $10,000.00 in ten years. They can obtain an annual interest rate of 12 percent, compounded monthly. Their plan is to initially deposit $1000.00 and then to make monthly payments for the rest of the ten years. How much should their monthly payments be?

4. Suppose we have two functions $f1 = 2x + 1/(x^3 + x^2)$ and $f2 = x^2 - 6x$. Write a program that will start x at some low value, say $x = 1$, where $f1$ is greater than $f2$ and increment x repeatedly while computing the values of $f1$ and $f2$ each time. The program loop should stop when $f1$ becomes less than $f2$. Find as well as you can what value of x is greater than 1 and makes $f1 = f2$.

5. Write a program that acts as a desk calculator. The program will have a command loop much like the editor program and will have a register that holds the number being manipulated. The commands will all operate by manipulating this register, clearing it, entering values into it, adding other numbers to it, and so forth. Here are the commands. Each command results in the indicated action, and then it prints the contents of the register to show its current status.

c   clear the register

e   enter a number into the register

a   add a number to the register

m multiply a number times the register

d   divide a number into the register

s   subtract a number from the register

h   help

Here is a sample interaction with the desired program:

```
Command:  e
17
Register  contents:  17
Command:  a
14
Register  contents:  31
Command:  c
Register  contents:  0
```

Storing Information in Arrays (B)

In order to encourage our person in the savings program, we might like to create an electronic savings table that would show the total amount of the savings at the end of each month. The person would be able to check the amount in the account for any month in the future assuming he or she makes all of the payments on time. This record can be constructed by creating an *array* in the computer memory which can hold all of the 480 entries in the proposed plan. In this section, we will study the concept of arrays, their utilization, and particularly their usefulness in the savings problem.

The first step in using an array is to create it in the memory with a declaration. The Pascal method for declaring an array involves the creation of a new type. Then the array is declared in the usual way with a *var* declaration. For the savings table, an array is needed which holds 480 real numbers so the new type will be given the name *realarray480*. The entries of the array will be numbered from 1 to 480, and the complete specification is as follows:

```
type
    realarray480  =  array[1..480]  of  real;
```

If the savings table array is to be given the name *table*, it is declared as

```
var
    table:   realarray480;
```

Each of the individual entries in this array will have its own name. The first is called *table[1]*, the second is *table[2]*, and so forth. Intuitively, the array should be envisioned as follows:

Before building the electronic savings table, let us study arrays and their manipulation with a few examples. Suppose we have an array called *A* of size 4, and we wish to put the number 10 into each entry. Here is a program to create *A* and make those entries.

```
Program  FirstArray;
type
    realarray4 = array[1..4] of real;
var
    A:  realarray4;
```

```
begin
A[1]  := 10;
A[2]  := 10;
A[3]  := 10;
A[4]  := 10;
end.
```

Another way to achieve the same result is to use a *while* loop.

```
Program  FirstArray;
type
    realarray4 = array[1..4] of real;
var
    A:  realarray4;
    i:  integer;
begin
i := 1;
while i <= 4 do
   begin
   A[i]  := 10;
   i := i + 1;
   end;
end.
```

Notice that the index *i* for the array must be declared as an integer.
   This program creates the array and then executes this sequence.

```
i := 1;
Is i <= 4 ? Yes.
A[1]  := 10;
i := 2;
Is i <= 4 ? Yes.
A[2]  := 10;
i := 3;
Is i <= 4 ? Yes.
A[3]  := 10;
i := 4;
Is i <= 4 ? Yes.
A[4]  := 10;
i := 5;
Is i <= 4 ? No.
```

By changing *i* repeatedly through the loop, the item in the array that is being referenced keeps changing as well.

Once some values exist in the array, we can print all those items.

```
i := 1;
while i <= 4 do
    begin
    writeln(A[i]);
    i := i + 1;
    end;
```

This will print

```
10
10
10
10
```

Here is a program that puts a sequence of integers into an integer array:

```
Program secondArray;
type
    integerarray4 = array[1..4] of integer;
var
    A:  integerarray4;
    i:  integer;
begin
i := 1;
while i <= 4 do
    begin
    A[i] := i + 10;
    i := i + 1;
    end;
i := 1;
while i <= 4 do
    begin
    writeln(A[i]);
    i := i + 1;
    end;
readln;
end.
```

This program will set *i* to 1 and then execute

```
A[1]  := 1+10
```

on the first loop repetition. So *A[1]* will receive 11. The other entries will receive 12, 13, 14 and the program will print

```
11
12
13
14
```

A slightly nicer format will be printed by this version:

```
Program  SecondArray;
type
    integerarray4 = array[1..4] of integer;
var
    A:  integerarray4;
    i:  integer;
begin
i := 1;            {The first loop fills the array.}
while i <= 4 do
    begin
    A[i] := i + 10;
    i := i + 1;
    end;
writeln('The  contents  of  A.');
writeln('Index     Value');
i := 1;          {The second loop prints the array.}
while i <= 4 do
    begin
    writeln(i,'      ',A[i]);
    i := i + 1;
    end;
readln;
end.
```

The output in this case will be:

```
The  contents  of  A:
Index        Value
1             11
2             12
3             13
4             14
```

This understanding of arrays makes it possible to build the electronic savings table. A small a ddition to the first compound interest program, *Savings40Years*, will create and fill up the need ed array.

```
program  FillSavingsTable;
type
    realarray480 = array[1..480] of real;
var
    table:  realarray480;
    payment,savings,  monthint:  real;
    month:integer;
begin
writeln('What  payment  do  you  propose?');
readln(payment);
savings := 0;
monthint := 0.01;
month := 1;
while month <= 480 do
    begin
    savings := savings + (savings * monthint) + payment;
    table[month] := savings;
    month := month + 1;
    end;
readln;
end.
```

The first time around the loop, *month* will have value 1. So *table[1]* will receive its appropriate entry, the amount of the savings. Each subsequent repetition will increase month by 1 and cause the next table entry to be made.

Code needs to be included to enable the saver to check the savings amount at any month's end. Let us design the program so that it works as follows:

Computer: What payment do you propose?
User: 10.00
Computer: Good, I have your forty year savings plan prepared.
Computer: What month do you wish to check?
User: 6
Computer: 61.52
Computer: What month do you wish to check?
User: 360
Computer: 34949.60
Computer: What month do you wish to check?
User: 0
Computer: This terminates the savings table program.

The computer allows the person to check the account level at any month and then conclude the session by asking for month 0.

Here is the algorithm for the query routine:

> ask "What month do you wish to check?"
> input the number of the month
> while month is greater than zero do
>> print the amount in the account for this month
>> ask "What month do you wish to check?"
>> input the number of the month

Here is the complete savings table program.

```
program SavingsTable;
type
    realarray480 = array[1..480] of real;
var
    table: realarray480;
    payment,savings, monthint: real;
    month:  integer;
begin

        {First make entries into table.}

writeln('What payment do you propose?');
readln(payment);
savings := 0;
monthint := 0.01;
month := 1;
```

```
while month <= 480 do
   begin
   savings := savings + (savings * monthint) + payment;
   table[month] := savings;
   month := month + 1;
   end;

      {Next enter the query routine.}
writeln('Good. I have your forty year savings plan prepared.');
writeln('What month do you wish to check?');
readln(month);
while month > 0 do
   begin
   writeln(table[month]:10:2);
   writeln('What month do you wish to check?');
   readln(month);
   end;
writeln('This terminates the savings table program.');
readln;
end.
```

Exercises

1. Write a program that has an array capable of holding ten integers. The program should ask the user to type a number and then store it into the array. Then it should ask the user for another number and store it, then another and store it, and so forth until all ten entries of the array arc full. Finally, the program should print the ten entries in the array.

2. Suppose a bank decides to give each of its customers a key number and then require that users give their number before computerized facilites are made available. Then a table must be stored in the computer indicating the key number for each customer so that the appropriate check can be made. Write a program that implements this scheme as follows. It will have two tables, one called *name* that holds the names of customers and one called *key* that holds their key numbers. The key numbers will be positive integers. For example, *name[1]* will hold the name of the first customer and *key[1]* will hold that person's key number. The program will first ask how many customers are to be stored with their key numbers. Then it will enable the user to input each name and associated key number. After it has stored these, it will enter a loop designed for customers. It will ask the customer for their name and key number. If it finds the name in the list and sees that the key number is correct, it will print the message "Welcome to the XYZ Bank Automated Teller." If it does not find the name and key number, it will print "Sorry, your name and key numbers are not approved for entry into this system."

3. A shortcoming with the system of problem 2 is that a computer expert might be able to find the table of secret key numbers, print them out, and use them in illegal ways. Let us revise the system so that if an expert found the table, he or she would still have considerable difficulty illegally

entering the system. Instead of giving each customer a key number, we will assign two integers which are prime numbers. The table will not store the key numbers because they will be known only to the customer. Our computer table will store only the *product* of the two numbers in the *key* array. When the customer is asked for their name, they will be asked to give two key numbers. Then the program will check that they are both positive and greater than 1, multiply them together, and note whether this product is in the table.

From the point of view of the customer, the system will work the same except that two key numbers will be required for entry. From the point of view of the bank, no one will be able to easily enter the customer's account even if they have the number in the *key* table. They will need to find two prime numbers that multiply to produce the number in *key*. If the number in *key* is large, this is not an easy problem.

Finding Sums, Minima, and Maxima (B)

Suppose the bank customer during a single month makes a series of bank deposits. Here we will ignore the issue of interest and assume a deposit was made on each of four weeks. Then we will ask what was the total of the deposits and what were the smallest and largest deposits. In answering these questions, we will examine general methods for accumulating quantities (sums, in this case) and for finding extreme elements (minima and maxima).

Begin by entering the amounts of the deposits:

```
program Deposit;
type
    realarray4 = array[1..4] of real;
var
    deposit: realarray4;
    i: integer;
begin
i := 1;
while i <= 4 do
    begin
    writeln('Enter  your  deposit.');
    readln(deposit[i]);
    i := i + 1;
    end;
readln;
end.
```

If the entered amounts are 6, 11, 9, 5, then the deposit array will appear as follows:

deposit[1]	6
deposit[2]	11
deposit[3]	9
deposit[4]	5

Next, develop a method for adding them up:

sum := 0
add deposit[1] to sum
add deposit[2] to sum
add deposit[3] to sum
add deposit[4] to sum

To add *deposit[1]* to *sum*, add the two quantities together

deposit[1] + sum

and put the result back into *sum*:

sum := deposit[1] + sum

The methodology becomes:

```
sum := 0
sum := deposit[1] + sum
sum := deposit[2] + sum
sum := deposit[3] + sum
sum := deposit[4] + sum
```

The loop is clear:

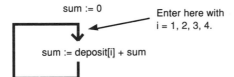

sum := 0

Enter here with
i = 1, 2, 3, 4.

sum := deposit[i] + sum

In Pascal, this is written as:

```
sum := 0;
i := 1;
while i <= 4 do
   begin
   sum := deposit[i] + sum;
   i := i + 1;
   end;
```

This program illustrates the format of the basic accumulator program:

initialize accumulator
initialize index
while there are more objects do
    let accumulator = object,operation,accumulator
    increment index

The accumulator can have any name, and the object and operation can have many forms. This basic format can be used to add up deposits as shown above or to do other similar tasks. Here are several examples of the usage of this basic format. The first is a program that adds up the numbers from 1 to *n*:

```
program SumN;
var
    i, n, sum: real;
begin
readln(n);
sum := 0;
i := 1;
while i <= n do
   begin
   sum := i + sum;
   i := i + 1;
   end;
writeln('The  sum  is  ',sum:8:2);
readln;
end.
```

Or you could multiply together the numbers from 1 to *n* and obtain *n* factorial:

```
program Factorial;
var
    i, n, product: real;
begin
readln(n);
product := 1;
i := 1;
while i <= n do
   begin
   product := i * product;
   i := i + 1;
   end;
writeln('The  factorial  is  ',product:8:2);
readln;
end.
```

Or you could accumulate a string of *n* As:

```
program Asequence;
var
    i, n: integer;
    asequence: string;
begin
readln(n);
asequence := '';  {Put empty string into asequence.}
i := 1;
while i <= n do
    begin
    asequence := 'A' + asequence;
    i := i + 1;
    end;
writeln('The A sequence is ',asequence);
readln;
end.
```

Another common task is to find the largest or smallest element in an array. Consider the issue of finding the largest deposit made during the month. Look at the first item, and temporarily store it as the largest seen so far. Then sequentially examine each later item looking for larger ones. If larger ones are found, they are copied into the "largest-so-far" slot. Here is the code to find the largest deposit:

```
largestsofar := deposit[1];
i := 2;
while i <= 4 do
    begin
    if deposit[i] > largestsofar then
        begin largestsofar := deposit[i];
        end;
    i := i +1;
    end;
writeln(largestsofar:8:2);
```

The general pattern for finding such extremes recurs often in programs:

> let extremesofar=first item
> initialize index
> while there are more objects to examine
>   if item is more extreme than extremesofar then
>   let extremesofar=item
>   increment index

This pattern can be used for finding the largest number, smallest number, numbers nearest some value, longest and shortest strings, and so forth.

Exercises

1. Write a program that reads ten strings and then prints the longest and shortest strings read. Then it prints a string that is the concatenation of all of the ten strings.

2. Write a program that reads an integer n and then prints a string of n Os.

3. Write a program that can draw a bar graph for the function $f = 1/4 \, x^2 + x + 2$ for the values of x from 1 to 10. For each value of x, it will build a string of Fs with length f using the method of exercise 2. Then it will print the value of x followed by the string. The program will do this for each value of x. The output should look something like this:

x	bar graph of f value
1	FFF
2	FFFF
3	FFFFF
-	- -

4. Use the idea of exercise 3 to build a general program for graphing any function.

Patterns in Programming (B)

By now you will have seen many programs and begun to notice patterns in the code. Programmers do not necessarily construct new programs from atomic language features. They often assemble familiar patterns or whole blocks of code adapted in appropriate ways to create new programs. The assembly of programs from larger pieces speeds the process of coding and increases the reliability of the product. These patterns will be called *code patterns* here, and an acquaintance with them will help you in the task of coding. This section will make some of these explicit as a review of previous studies and as an aid to future programming.

The first chapter examined decision trees where a question was asked at each node and, based on the answer, control was passed on to another node. Two formats for coding each node were presented, one for the case where there were two branches and the other for the case where there were many. Here are the node formats:

> Two branches.

            ask question
            input answer
            if one answer then
                execute next appropriate node
            else
                execute other appropriate node

        More than two branches.

            ask question
            input answer
            if answer=ans1 then
                execute node appropriate to ans1
            if answer=ans2 then
                execute node appropriate to ans2
            etc.

The construction of decision trees involved repeated nesting of such formats.

In chapter 2, a method for modifying the contents of a location was introduced. This is done with a single assignment statement of the form

```
location := location with some change
```

Thus you add a character A to the right end of string *s1* with

```
s1 := s1 + 'A'
```

and to the left end of *s1* with

```
s1 := 'A' + s1
```

You can remove the last character from *s1* with

```
s1 := copy(s1,1,length(s1)-1)
```

You can increase number *x* by 1 with

```
x := x + 1
```

and so forth.

Another code pattern that appeared in chapter 2 was the command control loop that enabled the user to request any action:

        while command is not 'q' do

```
ask for command
input command
if command = c1 then
    appropriate code
if command = c2 then
    appropriate code
─────
```

In this chapter, the simple loop for modifying all the numbers of an array was given:

```
set index to first item
while index is less than or equal to the number of entries do
    modify entry being indexed
    increment index
```

Also formats were given in earlier sections for searching for items and for accumulating and finding extreme values for a set of items.

Exercises

1. Find a code pattern that is used commonly in this book but that is not listed among the ones shown here.

2. Write a program for each code pattern of this section demonstrating its use.

Putting Things in a Row and a Special Characteristic of Functions (B)

A number of theoretical issues in computer science will be addressed in later chapters, and it is important to build the foundations along the way. In this section, we discuss an important concept; mathematicians call it *countability*, and this book calls it *putting things in a row*.

The fundamental idea concerns an unending chain of bins that extends off into infinity and the

question of whether there are enough bins to hold all the elements of a set of objects. We assume every bin is arbitrarily large so it can hold any individual regardless of its size. But the goal for a given set is to put each of its members in some bin in the chain. If we can succeed with a set, we will say we *put this set in a row*; mathematicians would say the set is *countable*.

The first set to consider is the set of positive integers, which can easily be put in a row. Put 1 in the first bin, 2 in the second, and so forth without end:

There are enough bins to hold every positive integer, and regardless of which integer is chosen, it will be somewhere in the chain. The set of positive and negative integers can also be put in a row, as follows:

Theoretically, the names of all human beings that have ever been born can also be put in a row

-1	1	-2	2	-3	3	-4

by placing the name of the lightest person at birth in bin 1, the second lightest in bin 2, and so forth. Where there are ties, they can be ordered on another dimension, such as the number of cells in their body. The set of all molecules in the universe can be arranged in a row by putting one molecule in bin 1, its closest neighbor in bin 2, its second closest neighbor in bin 3, and so forth. Again, a second dimension can be used to settle ties if necessary.

Consider the set of all finite strings of printable characters such as "computers," "#!-7," and "Let us go." This set can also be put in a row by putting the string of length zero in bin 1, and the strings of length one in bins $2,3,4,5,\ldots,n$ since we assume only a finite number of distinct characters. Next the strings of length two can be placed in bins $n+1$, $n+2$, ... etc., and so forth. This set of strings would thus contain all the words in any dictionary, all the sentences that could ever be written, all the books that ever have been or ever will be written, all the books that will *not* be written, and much more. This set can also be put in a row.

At this point, one might decide that some very large sets can be put in a row. Perhaps every set imaginable can be put in a row. It turns out that the functions that input a positive integer and yield a positive integer cannot be put in a row. No matter how one tries to squeeze them all into the bins, there will always be huge numbers more that will not fit. This is an important property with great implications for computer science. A demonstration that this is true appears in the next section, and a discussion of the significance of this fact is given in the chapter on noncomputability.

Exercises

1. Imagine a great two-dimensional checker board that goes on forever in all directions. Is the number of squares on the board countable? That is, can you find a way to put all of the squares in a row?

2. Imagine the set of all Pascal programs. Is it possible to put this set in a row?

Putting the Functions in a Row (C)

Let us begin putting the functions in a row and see where it leads us. We will consider only functions that accept positive integers as input and yield positive integers as output, and we will represent each function with its input-output table. Here is the beginning of the enumeration: The first function listed is the double function; the second calculates a simple polynomial; the

x	f(x)	x	f(x)	x	f(x)	x	f(x)
1	2	1	4	1	11	1	17
2	4	2	7	2	11	2	109
3	6	3	10	3	11	3	18
4	8	4	13	4	11	4	1
5	10	5	16	5	11	5	512
6	12	6	19	6	11	6	62
7	14	7	22	7	11	7	174
.	.	.	.	.	.	.	.
.	.	.	.	.	.	.	.

third always outputs 11 regardless of the input; and the fourth outputs a rather bizarre and unpredictable array of values. All are perfectly legitimate functions and are completely specified by their infinite tables.

Suppose next that an unboundedly patient and speedy being continues the task begun here and puts all the rest of the functions that exist in a row. Then the task will be complete, and we will have shown how to do yet another large set.

However, consider the function constructed as shown below. Its table is built as indicated. The first entry of the first function is incremented by one and put into its first output position. The second entry of the second function is incremented and put into its second output position. And, in general, for each $i = 1,2,3, \ldots$, the ith position in the ith table is incremented and put into the ith output position for the new function:

This new function is clearly as good as any other function. Its table is completely well specified.

New function.   The functions in a row.

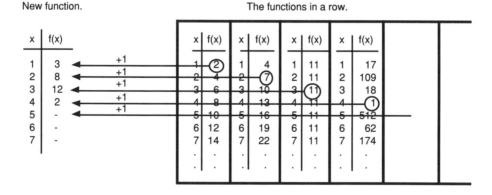

Therefore our unboundedly patient and speedy being must certainly have included it in one of the bins of the row. Let us try to find it. The new function is not in the first bin because it is different on the first entry. It is not in the second bin because it is different on the second entry. Wait a minute! It is different from the ith function in the ith position for all i. The new function is different from every function in the row and is thus not in any bin! So the "speedy being" did *not* put every function into the row.

It is easy to find millions of functions that were left out. Consider the functions constructed like the above new function except that 2 or 3 or something else is added to each entry. Consider the function that is built using the second output of the first function, the third output from the second function, and so forth. This function and all of its similar versions will also not be in the row.

The functions that have positive integers for inputs and outputs cannot be put into a row. Mathematicians say this set of functions is *uncountable*. All of the other sets discussed in the previous section are *countable*, but this one is not. Most other classes of functions are similarly uncountable, but none needs to be considered here. The fact that these functions cannot be put into a row is an extremely important fact for computer scientists (as will be discussed in the chapter on noncomputability).

Exercises

1. Describe various kinds of functions that will not be in the row of functions built in the above construction.

2. The set of infinite strings of printable characters cannot be put into a row. Show how the above argument can be modified to prove this fact.

3. Specify which of the following sets can be put in a row and which cannot be. Give a full explanation in each case.

   (a) The set of well-formed English sentences.

   (b) The set of functions that input a positive integer and output a positive integer and that each have the following property: for a given function, the output will be the same regardless of what the input is.

   (c) The set of decimal numbers that each have an infinite number of digits.

   (d) The set of all of the living creatures that have existed in the past or will exist in the future.

   (e) The set of all paths down an infinite tree constructed as follows: The root node has two branches below it of length 1 inch. At the end of each branch is a node with two more branches below it of length 1 inch. At the end of those branches are nodes with more branches without end.

Summary (B)

This chapter has undertaken the subject of numerical computation and its many aspects.

First, it was noted that integers are not adequate for general numerical computation because they cannot take on fractional or very large or small values. Then the real number type was introduced, and many examples were given showing its use.

Next, it was noted that numerical computation involves two possible hazards: First, the operators have a precedence that may cause an order of computation that is unexpected by the uninitiated and could yield undesired answers. Second, the computer will make mistakes when computing with real numbers. These mistakes are the round-off errors caused by the limited size of its registers. These errors are typically of little importance in textbook computations, but in some calculations, they can combine to undermine the integrity of the answer.

A fundamental concept of mathematics and computer science is that of the function. This idea was introduced, and five different methods were given for describing functions. Various programs for computing functions were given. You should be able to do a variety of additional examples. One class of functions was examined in the last two sections and shown to have the property that they cannot be "put into a row." This is an unusual property of a set and has implications discussed in chapter 13.

The chapter also examined looping programs and showed how to build them. Such programs can be used for studying the properties of a function by repeatedly evaluating the function on different inputs. For example, you might want to find the minimum or maximum values that a function could have. Looping programs can also be used to calculate complex functions such as the accumulation from the forty-year savings plan. The while-loop construction can be used for search. The test at the beginning of the while-loop must be designed to stop the repetitions when the searched-for item is found.

Experienced programmers will point out that there are other ways to code loops in Pascal. Thus the form

```
i := 1;
while i <= n do
    begin
    code
    i := i + 1;
    end;
```

can also be written as

```
for i := 1 to n do
    begin
    code
    end;
```

There is also a *repeat-until* construction similar to the *while* loop except that the test is at the end of the loop instead of the beginning.

These and many other features of Pascal are omitted from the current discussions because there are too many of them to include in a book with a far broader agenda. However, anyone who learns and is comfortable with them is encouraged to use them.

The chapter also introduced arrays for storing data and showed their use in various situations. Example programs illustrated ways to read, print, sum, and find the maximum or minimum values in arrays.

Finally, the concept of the "code pattern" was introduced with the recommendation that you look for and learn common patterns. Programming often proceeds by modifying and assembling these patterns of code rather than constructing things from atomic elements.

Readings

For programming:

Cooper, D., and Clancy, M., *Oh! Pascal!* , W. W. Norton, New York, 1982.

Dale, N. and Weems, C., *Pascal*, Second Edition, D. C. Heath and Co., Lexington, Massachusetts, 1987.

Jensen, K. and Wirth, N., *Pascal*, Third Edition, Springer-Verlag, New York, 1985.

Koffman, E. B., *Turbo Pascal: A Problem Solving Approach*, Addison-Wesley, Reading, Massachusetts, 1986.

Motil, J. M., *Programming Principles: An Introduction*, William C. Brown Publishers, Dubuque, Iowa, 1988.

Patterson, D. A., Kiser, D. S., and Smith, D. N., *Computing Unbound*, W. W. Norton, New York, 1989.

Pattis, R. E., *Karel the Robot: A Gentle Introduction to the Art of Programming*, John Wiley, New York ,1981.

Reges, S., *Building Pascal Programs*, Little, Brown Computer Science, Boston, Massachusetts, 1987.

Savitch, W. J., *TURBO Pascal, An Introduction to the Art and Science of Programming*, Second Edition, Benjamin/Cummings Publishing Company, Menlo Park, California, 1988.

Tremblay, J.-P., and Bunt, R. B., *Introduction to Computer Science*, Second Edition, McGraw-Hill, New York, 1989.

Turbo Pascal 4.0, Borland International, Scotts Valley, California, 1987.

Turbo Pascal for the Mac, Borland International, Scotts Valley, California, 1987

For numerical analysis:

Acton, F. S., *Numerical Methods That Work*, Harper and Row, New York, 1970.

Dahlquist, G., and Bjorck, A., *Numerical Methods*, Prentice-Hall, Englewood Cliffs, New Jersey, 1974.

Flannery, B. P., Teukolsky, S. A., and Vetterling, W. T., *Numerical Recipes in C: The Art of Scientific Computing*, Cambridge University Press, Cambridge, 1988.

4

Top-Down Programming, Subroutines, and a Database Application

Let Us Solve a Mystery (A)

As the afternoon sun faded on the village green, Chief Inspector Brown was just lighting his evening pipe when an urgent call came in from the Dunsmore Manor. It was from a terrified Miss Secrest, who had found Lord Peter Dunsmore collapsed on the drawing room floor. He was dead. The Lady Emily had gone to her chambers in shock, and the chief inspector was implored to hurry to the scene. This he did, and upon examining the body, proclaimed the cause of death: a lethal dose of poison administered within the last few hours.

The family and servants seemed too distraught to be questioned, but a quaint small computer terminal in the corner of the room gave access to some family data. The inspector sat down and began typing.

Who visited the manor today?

Machine response: Mr. Mason visited at 3:00 P.M.
The professor visited at 3:00 P.M.
Miss Secrest visited at 5:00 P.M.

Tell me about Mr. Mason.

Machine response: Mr. Mason has hobby tennis.
Mr. Mason visited at 3:00 P.M.
Mr. Mason is a chemist.

The inspector typed a long series of questions, slowly puffed his pipe, and finally arrived at a suspect. He was able to identify only one person who had all three prerequisites: an apparent motive, access to the poison, and a way of administering it to the victim.

Although we may want to know who committed the crime, as computer scientists, we are even more interested in knowing how the computer program works. In this chapter, we will study methodologies for creating larger programs than those of previous chapters, and one of them will be the question-answering program the inspector used. In the process, we will study the method of top-down programming, the use of subroutines, and techniques for keeping the greater complexity of large programs under control. The final sections of the chapter will illustrate the use of these methodologies for other example problems.

Top-Down Programming and the Database Program (B)

The central issue of computer science is the problem of complexity and how to deal with it. There are two important techniques for dealing with high complexity:

1. Represent the problem so that it can be dealt with easily.

2. Decompose the problem into simpler subtasks and then repeatedly decompose those subtasks until at the lowest level each remaining subtask is easy to comprehend. The solution to the whole problem is the assembly of all of the subtask solutions obtained in the decomposition.

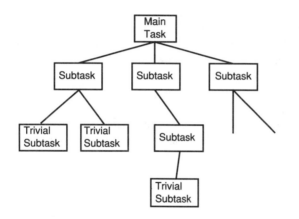

If each decomposition is simple and clearly correct and each lowest level subtask easy to code and also clearly correct, the complete program should be correct.

Let us now apply these ideas to creating the question-answering program the inspector used. A store of information such as that on the Dunsmore family is called a *database*. A program that stores such information and answers questions about it is called a *database program*. Our current task is to build one. However, the specifications implied by the discussion indicate that this program may become an immense undertaking. If we are to achieve success, we must find ways to reduce the problem complexity.

Thus our first task in addressing this problem is to seek a representation that is easy to comprehend and leads to the simplest possible program. As a first simplification, let us assume that the family information is stored as a set of facts represented by declarative sentences such as

        Mr. Mason visited at 3:00 P.M.
        Mr. Mason is a chemist.

Once this decision is made, we no longer need to grapple with the vague idea of "information," and the programmer's task is to settle on ways to store and retrieve sentences. We will further simplify by assuming that all questions can be answered by simply finding and presenting some of the stored sentences — those that answer the user's question. Thus if a user asks a question, the machine need only determine whether facts exist in the database to answer it and to print them out if they can be found. We will not consider the case where the program might be asked to infer some new fact that does not already explicitly exist in its database.

Having settled on a representation that clearly specifies what is meant by "information" and the nature of the information, we can begin to see the kinds of processing needed to solve the problem. The second step in dealing with complexity is to decompose the whole task into a set of easily approached subparts. We next turn our attention to discovering an acceptable decomposition.

The program will need two primary abilities: to read in facts and to answer questions related to them. We will construct the program with a command control loop and five commands:

f	find (this command will receive questions and print all of the relevant facts)
help	help (this command will list the five available commands)
i	input (this command will read facts)
p	print (this command will print all of the stored facts)
q	quit (this command will terminate program execution)

The initial version of the program will be

```
program Database;
var
    command: string;
begin
command := 'start';
while command <> 'q' do
    begin
    writeln('Command:');
    readln(command);
    if command = 'f' then
        find facts to answer a query;
    if command = 'help' then
        print the help message;
    if command = 'i' then
        input a fact;
    if command = 'p' then
        print all of the facts;
    end;
readln;
end.
```

Graphically, the database has been decomposed into a loop with five subtasks, two of them trivial:

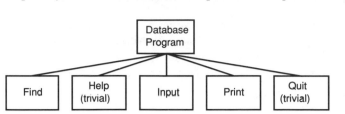

Next we examine the three nontrivial subtasks.

Consider the "input" routine. It will work as follows. First, a new place in memory will be located, and then the fact will be read and placed into that new position:

> Input routine:
>> find a new place in memory
>> read a new fact into that place

The "print" routine will also be easy:

> Print routine:
>> for each position in memory that has a fact,
>> print the contents

The "find" routine will first read the user's question. Then it will check each stored fact and print those facts that help to provide an answer to the question. For example, when the inspector requested general information regarding Mr. Mason, the program printed all of the stored facts mentioning him.

> Find routine:
>> read user's question
>> for each position in memory that has a fact,
>>> if that fact helps answer to the question, print it

The last part of the "find" routine seems complicated because we do not know when a fact "helps to answer the question." Let us decompose this process again and create a question-fact comparator. This routine will examine the question and the fact and report either "answer" or "no" depending on whether the fact partially answers the question or not. Using this routine, the "find" routine is now quite simple:

> Find routine:
>> read user's question
>> for each position in memory that has a fact,
>>> call the question-fact comparator
>>> if the comparator reports "answer" then
>>>> print the fact

Of course, the question-fact comparator may be a complex routine, but that is an issue to be examined later.

The database program has now evolved to this state:

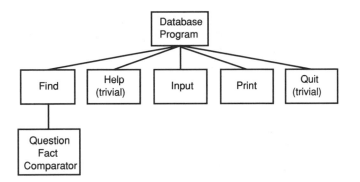

Once we have discovered a way to program the "question-fact comparator," the program will be reduced to a series of easy subtasks. You should review all of the parts and see that the seemingly complicated database program is effectively reduced to rather approachable subparts. Before considering these parts further, however, we must introduce subroutines to help with the decomposition process.

Exercise

1. Suppose a program is to read the names and backgrounds of a series of men and women and then pair them up, putting people of similar backgrounds together. The program should print out a listing of the couples. How should the data be represented? Show how to decompose this problem into a series of easily programmable subtasks.

Subroutines (B)

A *subroutine* is a sequence of programming statements. We always associate a name with a subroutine so that we can refer to it. In Pascal, subroutines are called *procedures*, and the two terms will be used interchangeably. Following is an example of a *subroutine definition* for a routine called *Byline*. The subroutine prints a message with an author's name and a line of hyphens above and below:

```
procedure Byline;
   begin
   writeln('----------------------------');
   writeln(' This program was written by ');
   writeln('    Lady Emily Dunsmore       ');
   writeln('----------------------------');
   end;
```

This subroutine does the job of printing the four lines shown. A programmer who wants those four lines printed need only include the statement

```
Byline
```

This statement *calls* the *Byline* procedure, which in turn, prints the four lines. Suppose that Lady Emily wrote the database program and decided that, each time it is used, it should begin by printing those four lines and end by printing them again. If her program had this appearance originally

```
program Database;
declarations
begin            { Beginning of the main program. }
    -   -   -

    -   -   -

    -   -   -
end.
```

the new version that begins and ends by printing her byline would look like this:

```
program Database;
declarations
begin            { Beginning of the main program. }
Byline;
    -   -   -

    -   -   -

    -   -   -
Byline;
end.
```

The newly added *Byline* statements are refered to as the *subroutine call* statements.

There is a problem with the new version: it does not include the definition of the procedure. This definition is placed following the other declarations in the program:

```
program Database;
declarations
procedure Byline;
   begin
   writeln('------------------------------');
   writeln(' This program was written by ');
   writeln('    Lady Emily Dunsmore        ');
   writeln('------------------------------');
   end;
```

```
begin              { Beginning of the main program. }
Byline;
    -    -    -
    -    -    -
    -    -    -
Byline;
end.
```

The program executes, as indicated in the figure below, the following sequence: The computation starts at the beginning of the main program after the *begin*. The first statement is *Byline*, which means go to the subroutine *Byline* and carry out the four print statements. After it is done, it will have finished the first call to *Byline*, and it will proceed to do the other parts of the database program. When it is finished, it will execute the second *Byline* statement, which again causes the system to go to the *Byline* subroutine. It will again execute those four print statements before halting.

In the following diagram, these events are graphed, with the thick lines indicating execution and the thin lines indicating jumps. The path shows the two procedure calls and the consequent jumps to the procedure body:

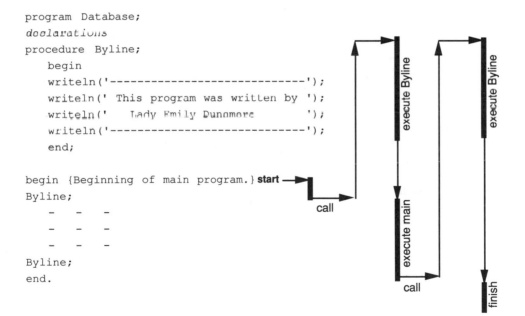

```
program Database;
declarations
procedure  Byline;
    begin
    writeln('-----------------------------');
    writeln(' This program was written by ');
    writeln('     Lady Emily Dunsmore        ');
    writeln('-----------------------------');
    end;

begin {Beginning of main program.} start
Byline;
    -    -    -
    -    -    -
    -    -    -
Byline;
end.
```

Subroutines are a tremendous help to programmers for two reasons. *First, they provide a means for avoiding typing the same lines again and again.* If the same task needs to be done twice, as in the above program, or many times, as in other programs, there is no need to type the same lines repeatedly. One types the code once in a subroutine definition, and in all other instances the code can be used by simply typing the name of the subroutine. Since the total program will be shorter, it will use less memory space inside the computer and will thus be less wasteful of resources. Because subroutines can be dozens of lines long and may be called often, the savings can be substantial.

The second reason that subroutines are useful is even more important than the first: *subroutines enable the programmer to isolate one task from another and thus help simplify problem solving.* For example, the programming problem for "find" in the database program may seem quite complex. The code is to receive a question from the user and then type all facts that contribute to the answer. But we simplify the problem greatly by separating away part of the job as a subroutine to be written later. We write code that receives the question and then, for each fact, uses a subroutine, the question-fact comparator, to check whether the fact is a part of the answer. If it is, our code will print it out:

> Find routine:
>> read user's question
>> for each position in memory that has a fact,
>>> call the question-fact comparator
>>> if the comparator reports "answer" then
>>>> print the fact

By pushing part of the task into the question-fact comparator subroutine, we can effectively write part of the code to solve the problem. Later we will concentrate our energies specifically on the subroutine. We have cut the problem into pieces and can hope that each part will be small enough to program easily.

It might be convenient to modify the *Byline* program so that it will print anyone's name, not simply Lady Emily's. Here is the appropriate change:

```
procedure Byline2(var name: string);
   begin
   writeln('----------------------------');
   writeln(' This program was written by ');
   writeln('     ', name);
   writeln('----------------------------');
   end;
```

The new variable *name* references the name that we wish to print, which could be any sequence of characters. The variable *name* is called a subroutine *parameter*, and it is identified as such when it is placed between parentheses in the subroutine definition after the subroutine name *Byline2*.

The variable *name* is very different from an ordinary variable in a program, such as *y* in

```
program Demo;
var
   y: string;
```

This is because *subroutine parameters declared as shown here are not assigned associated places in memory*. A subroutine parameter such as *name* refers to the place in memory created for some other variable as will be illustrated next.

Consider the execution of this program:

```
program  SecondSubroutine;
var
   n1, n2: string;
procedure  Byline2(var name: string);
   begin
   writeln('----------------------------');
   writeln(' This program was written by ');
   writeln('     ', name);
   writeln('----------------------------');
   end;
begin                    { Beginning of main program. }
n1 := 'Lord Dunsmore';
n2 := 'Miss Secrest';
Byline2(n2);
Byline2(n1);
end.
```

The variables *n1* and *n2* will have their associated locations in memory because they have been declared at the top of the program. But *name*, which is a subroutine parameter, will not. We will graphically represent these declared locations in the usual way but will indicate a parameter as an arrow that will point to some other entity:

```
program  SecondSubroutine;                    n1    [ Lord Dunsmore ]
var
   n1, n2: string;                            n2    [ Miss Secrest ]
procedure  Byline2(var name: string);
   begin
   writeln('----------------------------');   name ──────────▶  ?
   writeln(' This program was written by ');
   writeln('     ', name);
   writeln('----------------------------');
   end;
```

```
begin
n1 := 'Lord Dunsmore';
n2 := 'Miss Secrest';
Byline2(n2);
Byline2(n1);
end.
```

Now consider the execution of the program. The first and second statements of the main program will cause *n1* and *n2* to be loaded as shown. The third statement will cause control to pass to the subroutine. Notice that *n2* is the memory location referenced in the call statement. Here *n2* is called the subroutine *argument*, and it gives the memory location referred to by *name* in the subroutine:

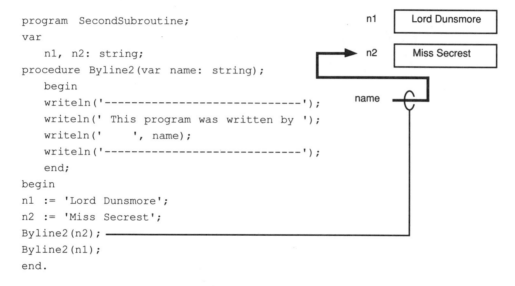

```
program  SecondSubroutine;
var
    n1, n2: string;
procedure Byline2(var name: string);
   begin
   writeln('-----------------------------');
   writeln(' This program was written by ');
   writeln('     ', name);
   writeln('-----------------------------');
   end;
begin
n1 := 'Lord Dunsmore';
n2 := 'Miss Secrest';
Byline2(n2);
Byline2(n1);
end.
```

So *name* and *n2* refer to the same memory location at this point in time. That is, the *Byline2* call statement has the function of linking the subroutine parameter *name* to the memory location *n2* at the time the subroutine is run.

After the subroutine has done its work and printed the byline message for Miss Secrest, the main routine will go on to its fourth statement, *Byline(n1)*. This time *name* is linked to *n1*, and Lord Dunsmore's name will be printed:

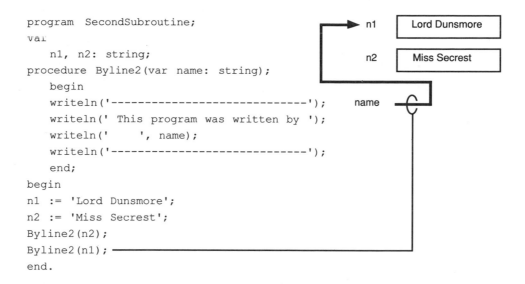

```
program  SecondSubroutine;
var
    n1, n2: string;
procedure Byline2(var name: string);
   begin
   writeln('---------------------------');
   writeln(' This program was written by ');
   writeln('     ', name);
   writeln('---------------------------');
   end;
begin
n1 := 'Lord Dunsmore';
n2 := 'Miss Secrest';
Byline2(n2);
Byline2(n1);
end.
```

To summarize, the parameters of a subroutine do not create new memory locations when they are declared as shown here. Rather, they refer to existing memory locations. These memory locations are linked to the subroutine parameters at the time of the subroutine call. The execution of the previous program will result in the following printout:

```
---------------------------
This program was written by
   Miss Secrest
---------------------------


---------------------------
This program was written by
   Lord Dunsmore
---------------------------
```

Let us reinforce these ideas by changing the program again. This time a subroutine will be included to read a person's name, and then the *Byline2* routine will print that name in the usual format:

```
program  ThirdSubroutine;
var
    n1: string;
```

```
procedure Byline2(var name: string);
   begin
   writeln('----------------------------');
   writeln(' This program was written by ');
   writeln('      ', name);
   writeln('----------------------------');
   end;

procedure GetName(var authorname: string);
   begin
   writeln('Type your name.');
   readln(authorname);
   end;

begin
GetName(n1);
Byline2(n1);
end.
```

Remember that *name* and *authorname* do not have associated memory locations. When *GetName* is called, it will link *authorname* to *n1* and the input name will be stored in *n1*. Then when *Byline2* is called, it will link *name* to *n1*, and the contents of *n1* will be printed.

Suppose this program is written erroneously without proper communication between the two procedures. That is, *GetName* and *Byline2* are called with two different arguments:

```
program  ThirdSubroutine1;
var
   n1, n2: string;
procedure Byline2(var name: string);
   begin
   writeln('----------------------------');
   writeln(' This program was written by ');
   writeln('      ', name);
   writeln('----------------------------');
   end;

procedure GetName(var authorname: string);
   begin
   writeln('Type your name.');
   readln(authorname);
   end;
```

```
begin
GetName(n1);
Byline2(n2);
end.
```

In this case, *GetName* will read the name and put it into *n1* as before. But notice that *Byline2* will print whatever is in *n2*. However, since *n2* has not been loaded, its content is unknown. *Byline2* may print almost anything.

Exercises

1. Write a procedure that prints your name. Write a program that calls the subroutine three times and thus prints your name three times.

2. Write a procedure called *Clip* that has two string parameters. It will receive a string in the first parameter, remove the first and last characters from the string, and then return the answer as the second parameter. Here is the main program:

```
Program Test;
var
    n1, n2: string;

procedure Clip(var s1,s2:string);
    - - -
    - - -
    end;
begin
writeln('Type a string.');
readln(n1);
Clip(n1,n2);
writeln('The clipped string is ',n2);
readln;
end.
```

Subroutines with Internal Variables (B)

Let us write another subroutine in order to study the case where a subroutine may need to have memory locations for its own internal use. Suppose, as a first example, a programmer is sketching a new piece of code and needs to compute factorial on several occasions. (The factorial of positive integer n is the product $1*2*3*.....*(n-1)*n$. Thus the factorial of 4 is $1*2*3*4 = 24$.)

```
(code)
—
z3 := the factorial of x
    - - -
```

```
y := the factorial of m
  - - -
num1 := the factorial of y
  - - -
```

Then a subroutine can be written that has two arguments: the answer resulting from the calculation and the input. If the name of the routine is *Factorial*, then the code can be written as follows:

```
(code)
  —
Factorial(z3,x);
  - - -
Factorial(y,m);
  - - -
Factorial(num1,y);
  - - -
```

The subroutine itself is straightforward to define using the accumulation pattern. Notice that the routine needs a memory location *i* to be used as a counter in the loop:

```
procedure  Factorial(var  out,n:integer);
    var
        i:  integer;
    begin
    out := 1;
    i := 1;
    while i <= n do
        begin
        out := i * out;
        i := i + 1;
        end;
    end;
```

In addition to the memory locations referenced by the parameters, this procedure also needs location *i* during the calculation. The declaration of *i* follows the procedure statement and has the same form as a declaration after a program statement. This declaration tells the machine to set up a properly named memory location to be used by this subroutine only during its execution. We will follow the policy here that *all variables in a subroutine will be either parameters of that subroutine or will be declared as variables in that subroutine*. Pascal allows variations from this rule, but they introduce numerous dangers.

The cause for confusion if this rule is not followed is easy to illustrate. Suppose one executes

```
i := 6;
writeln(i);
```

It seems reasonable to believe that a "6" will be printed. However, if

```
i := 6;
Factorial(r,s);
writeln(i);
```

is executed, one would again expect a "6" to be printed because there is no immediately visible reason why it should not. The goal should always to be to write obviously correct code with no subtle behaviors. Unfortunately, if *Factorial* does use *i* in some way without having its own declaration of *i*, the following sequence could occur: *i := 6;* would load "6" into *i* ; the routine *Factorial* could change *i* to some new value, say "10," and the *writeln* statement would print "10." Error! This is a very hard-to-find bug because *i* was changed in a separate, possibly distant place without any obvious indications. When this occurs, you can spend hours looking for the cause of the unexpected change in some location.

Thus, the rule to follow is that every variable in a subroutine should either be specified by subroutine parameters or by declarations in that routine. When it is, you can be sure that the subroutine can be inserted into a main program without affecting anything in the main program except items specifically listed in the parameter list. This will enable you to avoid a kind of programming error that is particularly bothersome to find.

Exercises

1. Write a procedure called *Checker* that reads an integer and prints "Okay" if the integer is greater than 0 and less than one 100. It should print "Not okay" otherwise. It should be called by the following program:

```
program Test1;
procedure Checker;
    - - -
    - - -
    end;
begin
Checker;
readln;
end.
```

When the program is run, it should work as follows:

> Machine: `Please type a number.`
> User: `17`
> Machine: `Okay`

2. Modify the program of exercise 1 so that the main program reads the integer and prints the result. The integer read should be passed to the procedure through the parameter list, and the string to be printed should be passed back to the main program through the parameter list. Here is the main routine:

```
program Test2;
var
    int:integer;
    str:string;

procedure Checker(var  i:integer;var  s:string);
        - - -
        - - -
        end;
begin
writeln('Please  type  a  number.');
readln(int);
Checker(int,str);
writeln(str);
readln;
end.
```

3. Write a procedure that has two arguments, an integer and a string. The procedure will check whether the integer is a prime number. If it is, it will return the string "Yes" in its second parameter. Otherwise it will return "No." Write a main routine to call your subroutine. It should read the number, call the subroutine, and then print the answer returned by the subroutine.

Note: A prime number is an integer greater than 1 which is not evenly divisible by any positive integers except 1 and itself. Thus 2, 3, 5, and 7 are prime numbers, but 4 is not because it is divisible by 2. In Pascal, we can check whether i divides j by checking whether $(j\ div\ i) * i$ equals j. If they are equal, then i divides j; otherwise it does not. The subroutine can do its job by having a while loop that checks whether i divides j for every i from 2 to j-1. If none is found, then j is prime.

4. Subroutines can be used to greatly simplify the decision trees of chapter 1. The strategy begins by coding the root of the decision tree into main program. Then every other node is given a name, and a procedure by that name does the processing of that node. Here is the main program for the book advice decision tree. Can you finish the program?

```
program  BookAdvice;
var
     answer1: string;

procedure  Math;
   Put code here to process the case of individuals
   who wish a mathematical approach.

procedure  Nonmath;
    Put code here to process the case of individuals
    who wish a nonmathematical approach.

begin
writeln('Do you wish a mathematical approach?');
readln(answer1);
if answer1 = 'yes' then
  begin
  Math;
  end
else
  begin
  Nonmath;
  end;
readln;
end.
```

5. Pick out a decision tree from chapter 1 with at least one long path of decisions. Show how subroutines simplify the code even when the tree is deeply nested.

Subroutines with Array Parameters (B)

Subroutines can have arrays as parameters using roughly the same methodology as for individual locations as described above. The syntax will be explained in the context of a program to add up a series of integers. We will create two procedures: *ReadArray* to read the integers and *AddArray* to add them. These routines will assume that the main program has declared *integerarray100* to be an array type as follows:

```
type
    integerarray100 = array[1..100] of integer;
```

Here is the *ReadArray* procedure:

```
procedure ReadArray(var  n:integer;var  B:integerarray100);
   var
       i:  integer;
   begin
   writeln('How  many  entries?');
   readln(n);
   i := 1;
   while i <= n do
      begin
      writeln('Input  entry.',i);
      readln(B[i]);
      i := i + 1;
      end;
   end;
```

The specification of the array *B* in the parameter list follows the same format as for other parameters, except that a declared rather than a basic type is used.

Suppose that this routine is called as

```
ReadArray(m,A)
```

where *A* has been declared as an array of type *integerarray100*, and *m* is an integer. Then *ReadArray* will go through its steps entering into *m* the number of entries to be read and entering into *A[1], A[2], A[3], . . . , A[m]* the integers that are read.

This same routine can be used again and again to read entries into other arrays, as with

```
ReadArray(Num,grades)
```

to read *Num* values into array *grades* or with

```
ReadArray(NN,DayTemperatures)
```

to read *NN* values into array *DayTemperatures*.

Next, the subroutine for summing the values in an array can be written:

```
procedure AddArray(var  n:  integer;var  C:integerarray100;
                                        var  answer:  integer);
   var
       i:  integer;
```

```
   begin
   answer := 0;
   i := 1;
   while i <= n do
      begin
      answer := C[i] + answer;
      i := i + 1;
      end;
   end;
```

Similarly, this routine can be used to add up the elements of all of the arrays mentioned previously:

```
AddArray(m,A,ans1);
AddArray(Num,grades,ans2);
AddArray(NN,DayTemperatures,ans3);
```

where the answers are placed into *ans1*, *ans2*, and *ans3*, respectively.

The following program uses these two procedures to read values into an array and then add them up:

```
program ReadAddArray,
type
    integerarray100 = array[1..100] of integer;
var
    n, answer: integer;
    A: integerarray100;

procedure ReadArray( . . . .);
    copy from above ;

procedure AddArray(. . . . );
    copy from above ;

begin
writeln('Read:');
ReadArray(n,A);
writeln('Add up.');
AddArray(n,A,answer);
writeln('The answer: ',answer);
readln;
end.
```

Exercises

1. Write a procedure *PrintArray(n,A)* similar to the *ReadArray* routine above. It should print the entries in array *A*.

2. Write a procedure *DoubleArray(n,A)* that doubles all of the entries in array *A*.

3. Write a procedure *CopyArray(n,A,B)* that copies all of the *n* entries in array A into array B.

4. Write a main routine that uses the above routines *ReadArray*, *DoubleArray*, *CopyArray*, and *PrintArray* to do the following:

    (a) It reads *n* values into array *XX*.
    (b) It prints the array *XX*.
    (c) Then it doubles the values in *XX* and prints them again.
    (d) Then it moves the values in *XX* to array *YY* and prints *YY*.
    (e) Finally, it doubles the values in *YY* and prints them again.

Your program should be very easy to write because it will contain no executable statements other than procedure calls. The procedures will do all of the work.

Subroutine Communication Examples (B)

Because communications with subroutines can be confusing, several examples of different types of communication will be included here. In each case, the subroutine will be named *double*, and it will double some real number. The interesting point will be how it gets its input and what it does once the number is doubled.

The first example is the case where there is no communication at all. The subroutine doubles an entry with nothing in it and does nothing with the result:

```
program communication1;
procedure double;
    var
        r1, r2: real;
    begin
    r2 := 2 * r1;
    end;
begin
double;
end.
```

We will have a graphical representation for each example; the following shows this case:

communication1

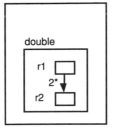

This unsuccessful program can be fixed by putting read and write statements into the subroutine:

```
program communication2;
procedure double;
    var
        r1, r2: real;
    begin
    readln(r1);
    r2 :- 2 * r1;
    writeln(r2);
    end;
begin
double;
end.
```

The picture now shows the information passing from the keyboard into the subroutine, where it is doubled and then printed:

communication2

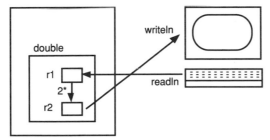

Next we could pass the information to the subroutine through the parameter list and then have the routine print its answer as before:

```
program communication3;
var
    num: real;
procedure double(var x: real);
    var
       r1, r2: real;
    begin
    r1 := x;
    r2 := 2 * r1;
    writeln(r2);
    end;
begin
readln(num);
double(num);
end.
```

communication3

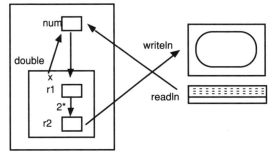

Also, we could modify the program to send its output back via the parameter list:

```
program communication4;
var
    num, ans: real;
procedure double(var x,y: real);
    var
       r2: real;
    begin
    r2 := 2 * x;
    y := r2;
    end;
begin
readln(num);
```

```
double(num,ans);
writeln(ans);
end.
```

communication4

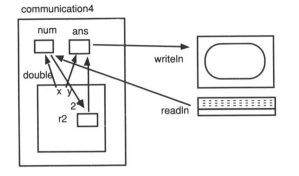

A shorter version omits the variable declared inside of the subroutine:

```
program  communication5;
var
    num, ans: real;
procedure double(var x,y: real);
    begin
    y := 2 * x;
    end;
begin
readln(num);
double(num,ans);
writeln(ans);
end.
```

communication5

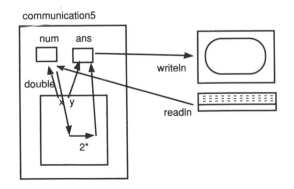

Finally, the subroutine can be revised to receive a number from the main routine and then return its answer to the same location:

```
program  communication6;
var
    num: real;
procedure double(var x: real);
    begin
    x := 2 * x;
    end;
begin
readln(num);
double(num);
writeln(num);
end.
```

communication6

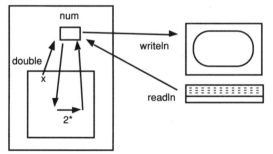

Exercise
1. Repeat the examples of this section except that the subroutine should add up a real array instead of doubling a location.

Storing and Printing Facts for the Database (B)

We now must develop a systematic plan for storing database facts of the kind given in the introduction:

> Mr. Mason is a chemist.
> The professor visited at 3:00 P.M.

It is important to notice that most of these facts are of the form

(noun phrase) (relationship) (noun phrase)

We will discover later that the question-answering task is made easier if we separate each fact into these three parts:

(Mr. Mason)(is)(a chemist.)
(The professor)(visited at)(3:00 P.M.)

We will call the first part *noun1* (for noun phrase 1), the second part *relation* (for relationship), the last part *noun2* (for noun phrase 2), and declare these as string variables. This strategy would store the first fact in Pascal with these statements:

```
noun1 := ' Mr. Mason';
relation := 'is';
noun2 := 'a chemist.';
```

In order to read a fact into these locations, you can use the statements:

```
readln (noun1);
readln (relation);
roadln (noun2);
```

Thus the fact should be typed in this form:

Mr. Mason
is
a chemist.

The separation of the statement onto three lines enables the program to divide the string of characters into three strings for the three sequential locations.

But the database program needs to store many facts, so the three locations should be expanded into arrays. This can be done with the following declaration which specifies that each array should hold 100 strings and each string may contain up to 30 characters:

```
type
   stringDB = string[30];              {All strings limited to length 30.}
   stringarray100 = array[1..100] of stringDB;{Only 100 facts allowed.}
var
   noun1A, relationA, noun2A: stringarray100;
```

noun1A[1]	Mr. Mason	relationA[1]	is	noun2A[1]	a chemist.
noun1A[2]	The professor	relationA[2]	visited at	noun2A[2]	3:00 PM.
- -			- -		- -
- -			- -		- -

Let us create a location called *last* that gives the position of the last fact in the tables. If only two facts are stored, then this location would be

last | 2 |

and if a place is needed for a new fact, we would increase *last* to 3 and put the new fact in position 3.

   Now it is possible to write rough draft code for the database input routine described above in English:

> Input routine.
>
> find a new place in memory
> read a new fact into that place

The code is

```
procedure  InputFact;
   begin
   writeln('Input a fact. Type three fields on sequential lines.');
   last := last + 1;
   readln(noun1A[last]);
   readln(relationA[last]);
   readln(noun2A[last]);
   end;
```

   This routine is correct except that its communication to the main program needs to be ensured. This is done with parameters. Here is the revised code:

```
procedure  InputFact(var  noun1A,relationA,noun2A:stringarray100;
                           var  last:integer);
   begin
   writeln('Input a fact. Type three fields on sequential lines.');
   last := last + 1;
   readln(noun1A[last]);
```

```
readln(relationA[last]);
readln(noun2A[last]);
end;
```

That is, *InputFact* places information into three arrays in the higher-level routine and updates the location of the last fact. (This routine assumes the arrays are large enough to store as many facts as the user will ever type. You might wish to revise the subroutine to print the message "Too many facts" if the user types more facts than can fit into the arrays.)

Similarly, we can write the print routine for the database program. We now have made much progress in building the database program. A way of storing the facts has been devised and it is straightforward to write subroutines to store facts and to print them. The only remaining task is to write the "find" routine which will enable the user to obtain the answers to questions.

Exercises

1. Write the print routine for the database program.

2. Revise *InputFact* so that if the user attempts to type more facts than there is room, the system will refuse to make the error and print the message, "Too many facts."

Representing Questions and Finding Their Answers (B)

Suppose a large number of facts are stored in the machine using the method of the previous section. The next problem to consider is how one who does not know those facts can access needed information. The problem will be approached very conservatively, and then a seemingly narrow technique will be expanded to become a powerful query-handling mechanism.

Suppose someone wishes to ask the question

> Is it true that Mr. Mason is a chemist?

What this question means is that the user wishes to know whether the fact

> (Mr. Mason)(is)(a chemist.)

is in the database. We will write code so that the system will ask the user for a query, and the user will type the fact he or she wishes to check for. Then the system will respond by typing that fact again if it is found.

Let us use the model begun in a previous section to write code to solve this simple problem. The version given above is

> Find routine:
>
> read user's question
> for each position in memory that has a fact,
>   call the question-fact comparator
>   if the comparator reports "answer" then
>   print the fact

We can now write the code for the find routine. Remember that the parameters can have any names and that they are not initially associated with any specific memory location. Only when the program is called are the parameters associated with memory locations. Here the arrays holding the facts are called *n1*, *r*, and *n2* in the parameter list, and they will eventually be referencing *noun1A*, *relationA*, and *noun2A*:

```
procedure Find(var n1,r,n2:stringarray100;var last:integer);
    var
        noun1, relation, noun2, result: stringDB;
        i: integer;
    begin
    writeln('Give the query. Type three fields on sequential lines.');
    readln(noun1);
    readln(relation);
    readln(noun2);
    writeln('THE RELATED FACTS:');
    i := 1;
    while i <= last do
        begin
        QFCompare(noun1,relation,noun2,n1[i],r[i],n2[i],result);
        if result = 'answer' then
            begin
            writeln(n1[i],' ',r[i],' ',n2[i]);
            end;
        i := i + 1;
        end;
    end;
```

The job of *QFCompare* is to return *result*="answer" if the query fact is identical to the given database fact. That is, one must check whether *noun1* = *n1[i]* and *relation* = *r[i]* and *noun2* = *n2[i]*. The routine is written with parameter names that make as much sense locally as possible regardless of how they may be used later. Here "Q" and "F" have the meaning "query" and "fact" to help make the procedure easily understandable:

```
procedure QFCompare(var Qnoun1,Qrel,Qnoun2, Fnoun1,Frel,
                                        Fnoun2,an:stringDB);
    begin
    if (Qnoun1 = Fnoun1)
            and (Qrel = Frel)
                and (Qnoun2 = Fnoun2) then
```

```
      begin
      an := 'answer';
      end
   else
      begin
      an := 'no';
      end;
   end;
```

This code will function as expected. If the user wishes to search for a given fact, that fact is typed as the query. If the fact is found, the system will print it:

```
Give the query. Type three fields on sequential lines.
Mr. Mason
is
a chemist.
THE RELATED FACTS:
Mr. Mason is a chemist.
```

We have developed the code to determine whether a given fact is in the database. If the fact is found, it is printed. If it is not found, the program will print nothing after the message "THE RELATED FACTS." However, this is not a very exciting capability and certainly would not be very helpful to the inspector. How is it possible to answer more interesting types of questions?

Suppose it is known that someone visited today at 3:00 P.M. but it is not known who. That is, we question whether any fact appears of the form

      (   ) (visited at)(3:00 P.M.)

and the answer to the question will be found in the first of the three fields. Therefore, the way to find the answer is to search the database and print any fact that matches on the second and third fields. A good way to type this question to the machine is

    ?
    visited at
    3:00 P.M.

where the question mark means "the user does not know this information." Here is a modification to the *QFCompare* routine to handle this query:

```
procedure QFCompare(var Qnoun1,Qrel,Qnoun2,
                            Fnoun1,Frel,Fnoun2,an:stringDB);

   begin
   if ((Qnoun1 = Fnoun1) or (Qnoun1 = '?'))
         and (Qrel = Frel)
            and (Qnoun2 = Fnoun2) then
```

```
      begin
      an := 'answer';
      end
   else
      begin
      an := 'no';
      end;
   end;
```

If the first field *Qnoun1* of the question is not "?," then the code will function as before. If *Qnoun1* is a "?," then the routine will return result *an* = "answer" whenever *Qrel* = *Frel* and *Qnoun2* = *Fnoun2* . Thus it will ignore the first field and print any fact that agrees on the second and third fields. Here is how it will look to the user:

```
      Give the query. Type three fields on sequential lines.
      ?
      visited at
      3:00 P.M.
      THE RELATED FACTS:
      The professor visited at 3:00 P.M.
```

Success! This program is clearly going to be of use to the inspector! Let us try another one:

```
      Give the query. Type three fields on sequential lines.
      ?
      has hobby
      tennis.
      THE RELATED FACTS:
      Lord Dunsmore has hobby tennis.
      Mr. Mason has hobby tennis.
```

This greatly improved system was achieved by allowing a question mark in the first field of any query. The question mark means that the user does not know what belongs in that field and the system should print all facts that match on the other two fields. The next obvious extension is to allow a question mark in any field. With this change, one may ask a huge variety of questions:

Question	Form for typed query
Mr. Mason visited at what time?	Mr. Mason visited at ?
What was Mr. Mason doing at 3:00 P.M.?	Mr. Mason ? 3:00 P.M.

Question	Form for typed query
Give me every fact about Mr. Mason.	Mr. Mason
	?
	?
	and
	?
	?
	Mr. Mason.
Who visited today and at what time?	?
	visited at
	?
What happened at 3:00 P.M.?	?
	?
	3:00 P.M.
Tell me everything you know.	?
	?
	?

This query system is now quite satisfactory for the inspector's use. He can easily ask any question required to find his prime suspect. In summary, this chapter began the seemingly awesome task of writing a program that would make it possible to store information and to answer almost any imaginable question about that information. The solution was found by formulating the task to be one of simply storing and retrieving facts and by discovering a powerful method for doing the retrieval. The coding effort was cut down to manageable proportions through a decomposition into subtasks, which were then implemented using subroutines.

Exercises

1. Show how to modify the *QFCompare* procedure to handle a question mark in every field.

2. Design a procedure called *FindAll* that receives one string from the user such as 'Mr. Mason' and then prints all facts that contain that string in any field. Thus in this case it would print facts such as

        Mr. Mason visited at 3:00 P.M.
        The Inspector is a customer of Mr. Mason.

Assembling the Database Program and Adding Comments (B)

Most of the work of coding the database program was completed in the previous sections. But one more addition needs to be made to finish the program in a professional manner. It is the inclusion of enough comment statements to document the code properly for anyone who may later wish to read it or change it. A properly commented program includes sufficient information regarding its input-output characteristics and method of operation to enable a reader of the code to use it, understand its functioning, and modify it if necessary. The program comments should also identify the author and give other nominal information such as the date and application.

Most of the programs in this book do not have many comments because the surrounding text includes the necessary information and the comments might distract attention from the code. In other situations, programs must stand alone without such explanatory material, and the programmer should carefully add the needed information to preserve their usefulness. Most industrial organizations have standards for their programmers specifying how code should be written and documented.

A reasonable policy for code documentation includes three kinds of comments:

1. The program header. This appears at the beginning of the program and includes (a) the programmer's name and other nominal information, (b) the input-output specification for the program, and (c) a brief description of how the code works.

2. Code block headers. Well-written code is always organized into "blocks" of self-consistent code that do well-defined tasks such as reading, sorting, or calculating. Each block should begin with enough comments to identify its purpose and its essential operation. Blocks usually are 5 to 20 lines in length and in many cases are organized as subroutines. In some cases, the author of a block may not be the same as the main author, and proper credit should be included in the header.

3. Line comments. You should write code that is so straightforward that its operation is obvious to any reader. But occasionally it is helpful to   add a short comment just to the right of a line of code to clarify its meaning. Comments are especially helpful at array declarations or at assignment statements where key computations occur.

Adherence to these standards should result in a completed program that can be read, used, or modified by any competent programmer. Here is the database program fully commented:

```
{                         Database Program                          }
{                       by Alan W. Biermann                         }
{                          January 1990                             }
{                                                                   }
{Inputs: In input mode (command i),"facts" are read in three fields- }
{   noun phrase, relationship, noun phrase. For example, "John is a  }
{   boy." is separated into three parts, "John," "is" and "a boy."   }
{   These parts are typed into the machine on three sequential lines: }
{                                                                   }
{       Input a fact. Type three fields on sequential lines.        }
{       John                                                        }
{       is                                                          }
{       a boy.                                                      }
{                                                                   }
```

```
{  In query mode (command f), queries are read in the same format as }
{  facts except that some fields may have a question mark instead of }
{  data.                                                             }
{                                                                    }
{Outputs: In query mode (command f), the program prints all fact    }
{  that  match the query on fields that do not have question marks.  }
{                                                                    }
{Method of operation: The facts are stored in three arrays called    }
{  noun1A, relationA, and noun2A. The ith fact has its first,        }
{  second, and third fields in the ith entries of, respectively,     }
{  noun1A, relationA, and noun2A. The program answers a query by     }
{  sequentially examining every stored fact and printing it if it    }
{  matches the query on the fields that do not contain a question    }
{  mark.                                                             }
{                                                                    }
{                                                                    }
program Database;
type
    stringDB = string[30];{All strings limited to length 30.        }
    stringarray100 = array[1..100] of stringDB;   {Only 100 facts
                                                     allowed.         }
var
    noun1A, relationA, noun2A: stringarray100; {Facts are stored in
                                                         these.  }
    command,noun1,relation,noun2:stringDB;
    last: integer;               {"last" tells how many facts are stored. }


procedure  InputFact(var  n1,r,n2:stringarray100;var  last:integer);
    { This procedure inputs a fact and inserts it into the database, }
    { which is stored in n1, r, and n2 as described. "last" tells    }
    { where in these arrays the last stored fact is placed.          }
    { The method of operation is to increase "last" by one and       }
    {insert the new fact into that position.                         }
    begin
    writeln('Input a fact. Type three fields on sequential lines.');
    last := last + 1;
    readln(n1[last]);
    readln(r[last]);
    readln(n2[last]);
    writeln('Total number of facts (not to exceed 100):',last);
    end;
```

```
procedure PrintFacts(var n1,r,n2:stringarray100;var last:integer);
{This procedure prints all of the database facts stored in n1, r, n2.}
        This code is left as an exercise. ;

procedure QFCompare(var Qnoun1,Qrel,Qnoun2,
                        Fnoun1,Frel,Fnoun2,an:stringDB);
{ This procedure is called "query-fact compare" or QFCompare and      }
{ it determines whether the query represented by the                  }
{ three strings Qnoun1, Qrel, Qnoun2, matches the fact represented    }
{ by strings Fnoun1, Frel, Fnoun2 on all fields that do not have a    }
{ question mark in the query.  If there is a match, then an           }
{ is loaded with "answer"; otherwise it is loaded with "no."          }

        Put code here as described above. ;

procedure Find(var n1,r,n2:stringarray100;var last:integer);
{ This procedure reads a query in the same format as a fact. However,}
{ some fields of the query may contain question marks. It examines    }
{ each fact in the database stored in n1, r, n2, and if QFCompare     }
{ reports result = "answer" for that fact, it prints that fact.       }

        Put code here as described above. ;

{ The main program begins here. It reads a command in the location    }
{ "command" and then calls the corresponding procedure.               }

begin
writeln('Entering  Database.');
last := 0;                           { The database begins with no facts.    }
command := 'start';
while command <> 'q' do
   begin
   writeln('Command:');
   readln(command);
   if command = 'help' then
      begin
      writeln('The  commands  are');
      writeln('  f     find facts which match query');
      writeln('  help   help');
      writeln('  i     input fact');
      writeln('  p     print facts');
```

```
            writeln('  q     quit');
            end;
   if command = 'i' then
        begin
        InputFact(noun1A,relationA,noun2A,last);
        end;
   if command = 'p' then
        begin
        PrintFacts(noun1A,relationA,noun2A,last);
        end;
   if command = 'f' then
        begin
        Find(noun1A,relationA,noun2A,last);
        end;
    end;
writeln('Exiting  database.');
readln;
end.
```

In this program, the *QFCompare* routine is declared before the *Find* routine because it is used in the *Find* routine. As the translator moves down the code, by the time it encounters the call to *QFCompare* inside *Find*, it should have already encountered the definition of *QFCompare*.

The above code can be shortened somewhat by following a rule allowed by Pascal. Whenever the form

```
        begin
        a single statement ;
        end
```

falls within an *if-then-else*, *if-then*, or *while* statement, it can be replaced by

```
        a single statement
```

Thus the *begin* and *end* are not needed if only one statement is being used. As an example, this rule can be applied to

```
        if command = 'i' then
          begin
          InputFact(noun1A,relationA,noun2A,last);
          end;
```

to obtain this equivalent and shorter code:

```
        if command = 'i' then
          InputFact(noun1A,relationA,noun2A,last);
```

This rule is not generally used in code presented here because it can cause confusion.

The time has finally come for us to discover the prime suspect for the murder mystery. Here is the database that the inspector used to draw his conclusion. Use the program to store the information and then type the necessary queries to find the prime suspect.

Lord Dunsmore is married to Lady Emily.

The gardener is married to the maid.

Poison can be gotten by a person for a blood relative.

Mr. Mason visited at 3:00 P.M.

A shared hobby causes friendship.

The gardener was recently dismissed by Lord Dunsmore.

Lord Dunsmore has hobby tennis.

The maid set tea on the table at 2:45 P.M.

Lord Secrest has hobby philosophy.

The gardener has hobby music.

Lord Dunsmore has rival Lord Secrest.

Mr. Mason is a chemist.

The Inspector is a customer of Mr. Mason.

Lord Secrest has daughter Miss Secrest.

The butler owes 10,000 pounds to Lord Dunsmore.

The butler helped serve lunch at 12:00.

The professor has hobby philosophy.

The professor visited at 3:00 P.M.

Lord Secrest is a customer of Mr. Mason.

The professor often brings gifts to Lady Emily.

Tea is always taken at 3:00 P.M.

Miss Secrest visited at 5:00 P.M.

Poison is sold by a chemist.

Lady Emily has hobby music.

Poison can be gotten by a person for a friend.

Mr. Mason has hobby philosophy.

Poison takes one hour to take effect.

The professor was once a suitor of Lady Emily.

The set of three-field facts in this problem is known as a *relation*. This technical definition of "relation" should not be confused with more ordinary uses of the word that may appear elsewhere in this book. The database system is referred to as a *relational database* system. Many such systems are in use in commercial applications, though often they are much more complex. It is quite common to have dozens of relations and dozens of fields in each relation.

One shortcoming of the database system described here is that it includes no inference system. Suppose as an illustration that "Jill is a sister of Nancy" and "Nancy is a sister of Barbara" are facts in the database. If the query appears requesting the sisters of Jill, one would like to have both Nancy and Barbara listed. However, the database of this chapter will not discover that Jill is a sister of Barbara. An inference is required of the form

"If X is a sister of Y and Y is a sister of Z, then X is a sister of Z."

No such inferential capabilities were programmed. Commercial database systems usually do include such features, and another programming system with such abilities is described at the end of chapter 10.

Exercises

1. Complete the assembly of the database program, and try it on a simple problem.

2. Which character in the story is most likely to have had a motive, access to the poison, and an opportunity to lace the lord's food? Can you reconstruct the events that probably led to the crime?

3. A problem with the database program is that it provides no method for deleting facts. A simple way to delete a fact is to replace all of its fields with an asterisk. Add a command to the system that requests the number of the fact to be deleted and then replaces its three fields with asterisks. Then change the print routine so that it skips over asterisks when they are encountered.

4. Write a delete program similar to the one described in exercise 3, but use a deletion procedure that is not so wasteful of space.

5. Prepare a database for the courses taught in a university department. The database should include such information as times the courses are taught, the instructors, and the associated prerequisites. Then a user should be able to obtain answers to such questions as

Which professors are teaching this semester?

Who is teaching Psychology 11?

What are the prerequisites to Psychology 207?

Are there any courses being taught at 4 P.M.?

6. Some relationships are called "symmetrical" because the order of the noun groups does not affect meaning. An example of such a relationship is sisterhood. If one can say

Julie is the sister of Ann.

then one can also say

Ann is the sister of Julie.

The database program does not account for this possibility and will thus answer some questions incorrectly. If the single fact

(Julie) (is the sister of) (Ann.)

is stored, it will not correctly answer the question, "Who is the sister of Julie?"

?
is the sister of
Julie.

Design a feature for the database program that can ask which relationships are symmetrical and then use this information to process queries that refer to them.

7. Solve some retrieval problems with the database program. Discover some of its shortcomings, and write code to correct them.

Another Application: The Towers of Hanoi Problem (B)

Another interesting problem that will be used for many examples in this book is called the Towers of Hanoi problem. This famous puzzle has a start position as shown with n disks of decreasing size piled on peg 1 of a three-peg system:

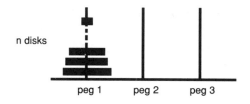

The puzzle requires that the stack of n disks be transferred to peg 3 by a sequence of individual disk moves from peg to peg and without ever putting any disk on top of a smaller disk. As an illustration, the $n = 2$ disk problem is solved by the following three-move sequence:

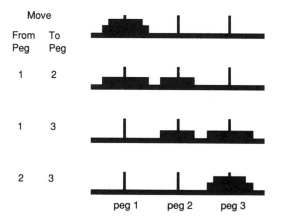

The first problem to be addressed is the representation of the pegs and the disks. The method will be to declare three arrays *peg1*, *peg2*, and *peg3* to represent the pegs and their "contents." For example, *peg1[1]* will hold the disk at the bottom of the *peg1* stack; *peg1[2]* will hold the second disk and so forth. The *n* disks will be represented by the integers 1,2,3, . . . ,*n*, with 1 representing the smallest disk and *n* the largest. A zero will represent the absence of any disks. This will make it possible to print the arrays so that they closely resemble the arrangement of the pegs and disks.

Thus, the initial position for the three-disk problem will be represented as

peg1[4]	0		peg2[4]	0		peg3[4]	0
peg1[3]	1		peg2[3]	0		peg3[3]	0
peg1[2]	2		peg2[2]	0		peg3[2]	0
peg1[1]	3		peg2[1]	0		peg3[1]	0
	peg1			peg2			peg3	

The program will enable the user to specify the "from-peg" and the "to-peg" for each move. It will then make the move and display the new configuration. Beginning at the above position, if the user specifies *frompeg* = 1 and *topeg* = 3, then the program will make the associated changes:

peg1[4]	0		peg2[4]	0		peg3[4]	0
peg1[3]	0		pog2[3]	0		peg3[3]	0
peg1[2]	2		peg2[2]	0		peg3[2]	0
peg1[1]	3		peg2[1]	0		peg3[1]	1
	peg1			peg2			peg3	

Notice that the position *peg1[3]* was changed to 0 and *peg3[1]* was changed to 1. This can be done with the statements

```
peg1[3] := 0;
peg3[1] := 1;
```

In general, these moves are easier to code if each peg has an associated location called *topi*, which tells where the lowest empty position is on that peg. Thus, if *peg1* has three disks, then *top1* will equal 4. If one disk is removed, *top1* will be lowcred to 3. *Topi* will always indicate where the next disk should be placed on its peg. With these additions, the initial state will look like this:

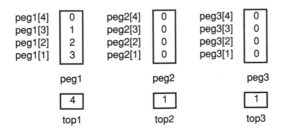

peg1[4]	0		peg2[4]	0		peg3[4]	0
peg1[3]	1		peg2[3]	0		peg3[3]	0
peg1[2]	2		peg2[2]	0		peg3[2]	0
peg1[1]	3		peg2[1]	0		peg3[1]	0
	peg1			peg2			peg3	
	4			1			1
	top1			top2			top3	

The code for moving a disk from *peg1* to *peg3*, using these variables, is thus written in English as

> lower top1
> move disk from 1 to 3
> raise top3

and in Pascal as

```
top1 := top1 - 1;
peg3[top3] := peg1[top1];
peg1[top1] := 0;
top3 := top3 + 1;
```

This will produce a new configuration:

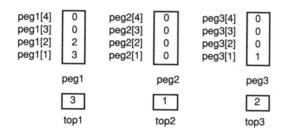

This discussion should be enough to enable you to get started programming the Towers of Hanoi problem. It will provide a source for many interesting examples in later sections.

Exercises

1. Write a program that requests a value for *n* and then displays the Towers of Hanoi problem representation described in the initial position with all *n* disks on *peg1*. Then the program should ask the user for the from-peg and to-peg, make the associated move, and print the new configuration. The user should be able to put in as many moves as desired. If the user reaches the goal with all disks on *peg3*, the program should print "Congratulations!" and halt.

2. Modify the program of problem 1 to check on each move whether the user is placing a disk on a smaller disk. If this is attempted, the program should print "Illegal Move!" and refuse to carry out the command.

3. Read the next section to learn how to represent the three pegs with only one array. Then simplify the code of problems 1 and 2 using this representation.

4. Find the solution to the Towers of Hanoi problem for *n* = 5.

A Program to Solve the Towers of Hanoi Problem (C)

Solving the Towers of Hanoi can require some thought and planning because a rather long series of moves is needed to achieve the goal. However, there exists a simple rule for always making the correct move, and this leads to a program for automatically generating the solution. This procedure will assume that n is odd, and the case where n is even will involve a small modification.

> move the smallest disk left one
> while the goal is not reached
> > make the only legal move that does not involve the smallest disk
> > move the smallest disk left one

The statement "move the smallest disk left one" means that if the disk is on *peg3*, it should be moved to *peg2*; if it is on *peg2*, it should be moved to *peg1*; if it is on *peg1*, it should be moved to *peg3* .

Try this method on several examples, where n is odd, and confirm that the rule is correct. If n is even, the same procedure works, but the word "left" should be changed to "right" in each case. Now we can proceed to write the program. The same programming methodology will be used as was explained earlier.

The solution method will be written in high level terms, and then the two techniques for reducing complexity will be applied: (1) find the best possible representation, and (2) break the task into smaller and smaller subtasks until each can be coded with relative ease.

Concerning technique 1, a modification of the notation of the previous section is helpful. Instead of using three arrays — *peg1*, *peg2*, and *peg3* — one two-dimensional array will be used: *peg*. The first index in the two-dimensional array will indicate the peg number, and the second will indicate the location on the peg. There will be a second array *top* that will contain the locations of the lowest empty positions on the pegs. Here is the new representation scheme:

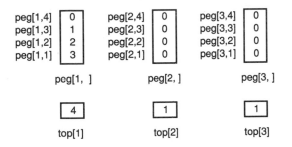

This new method presents a tremendous advantage because you can now write a single code segment referencing peg i rather than writing three pieces of code—one for each of pegs 1, 2, and 3. This idea will become clearer as the code is developed.

Concerning technique 2, the strategy for solving the problem can be expanded to give more detail:

> read n
> zero the arrays
> put n disks on peg1
> print arrays
> let frompeg = peg holding disk 1 and topeg = peg to left (right) of peg holding disk 1
> make move from frompeg to topeg
> print arrays
> while not all disks are on peg3
> >   let frompeg = peg holding smallest movable disk other than disk 1 and topeg=peg
> >   which is different from frompeg and peg holding smallest disk
> >   make move from frompeg to topeg
> >   print arrays
> >   let frompeg = peg holding disk 1 and topeg = peg to left (right) of peg holding
> >   disk 1
> >   make move from from peg to peg and print arrays

Here is the algorithm written in Pascal. Some subroutine calls are included where nontrivial tasks need to be defined later. A location called *positionsmallest* stores the number of the peg that holds the smallest disk:

```
program Hanoi;
{ A comment here should describe the function of this program, its }
{ inputs, outputs, and method of operation.                        }
type
    pegarray = array[1..3,1..10] of integer;
    toparray = array[1..3] of integer;
var
    peg:pegarray;
    top:toparray;
    n,frompeg,topeg,positionsmallest:integer;
procedure ZeroArray(var peg:pegarray;var n:integer);
    Code is left as an exercise. ;
procedure PutDisksOnPeg1(var peg:pegarray;var top:toparray;
        var positionsmallest,n:integer);
    Code is left as an exercise. ;
procedure PrintArray(var peg:pegarray;var n:integer);
    Code is left as an exercise. ;
procedure SmallestToWhere(var positionsmallest,n,
                    frompeg,topeg:integer);
    Code is left as an exercise. ;
```

```
procedure MakeMove(var peg:pegarray;var top:toparray;
      var frompeg, topeg:integer);
   Code is left as an exercise. ;
procedure DiskToWhere(var peg:pegarray; var top:toparray;
      var positionsmallest,frompeg, topeg: integer);
   Code is included below. ;

begin
writeln('How many disks?');
readln(n);
ZeroArray(peg,n);
PutDisksOnPeg1(peg,top,positionsmallest,n);    {Initialize data}
                                                {structures.}

PrintArray(peg,n);
SmallestToWhere(positionsmallest,n,frompeg,topeg);      {Move smallest.}
MakeMove(peg,top,frompeg,topeg);
PrintArray(peg,n);
while peg[3,n] = 0 do                                 {Begin loop.}
   begin
   DiskToWhere(peg,top,positionsmallest,frompeg,topeg); {Move other
                                                        {disk.}
   MakeMove(peg,top,frompeg,topeg);
   PrintArray(peg,n);
   SmallestToWhere(positionsmallest,n,frompeg,topeg);{Move  smallest.}
   MakeMove(peg,top,frompeg,topeg);
   PrintArray(peg,n);
   end;
writeln('End Execution.');
readln;
end.
```

The detailed code for most of the subroutines will not be included here. Rather, an explanation of the behavior of each will be given, and the completion of the subroutines is left as a series of exercises.

The procedure *ZeroArray (peg,n)* will place zeros in positions 1,2, . . . ,*n* for each of the three pegs.

The procedure *PutDisksOnPeg1(peg, top, positionsmallest, n)* will put the disks *n*, *n* -1, *n* -2, . . . , 1 on *peg1* with the largest disk on the bottom. The array *top* will be loaded to indicate the lowest empty position on each peg. *positionsmallest* will be set to 1, indicating that the position of the smallest disk is on *peg1*. If *PutDisksOnPeg1* is called with *n* =3, the result will be as shown in the previous figure.

The procedure *PrintArray(peg,n)* will print the array *peg*.

The procedure *SmallestToWhere(positionsmallest, n, frompeg, topeg)* finds a move for the smallest disk. It will set locations *frompeg* and *topeg* to indicate where the next move comes from and to where it should go. Then it will reset *positionsmallest* to equal *topeg*. If *n* is odd, the smallest disk should be moved left one as explained above. If *n* is even, the smallest disk should be moved right one. Assuming the position indicated above, if *SmallestToWhere(positionsmallest, n, frompeg, topeg)* is called, it will set *frompeg* = 1 and *topeg* = 3. It will also reset *positionsmallest* to 3.

The procedure *MakeMove (peg, top, frompeg, topeg)* will remove the disk from the top of the peg given by *frompeg* and place it on top of the peg designated by *topeg*. It will also decrement the integer giving the lowest empty position on the *frompeg* and increment that integer on the *topeg*. Assuming the position indicated above, *MakeMove (peg, top, 1,3)* will produce the following new configuration:

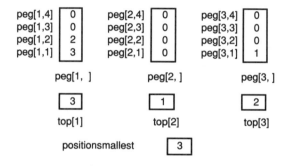

The procedure *DiskToWhere (peg, top, positionsmallest, frompeg, topeg)* will find the only legal move assuming that the smallest disk is not to be moved. Similarly to *SmallestToWhere*, this routine will indicate the source and destination pegs in locations *frompeg* and *topeg*. The routine will do its job by finding which pegs do not have the smallest disk and discovering which of these two should be the from-peg and which the to-peg. Assuming the position indicated above, *DiskToWhere* will find that pegs 1 and 2 do not contain the smallest disk. Furthermore, it will decide that the legal move is indicated by *frompeg* = 1 and *topeg* = 2. Here is the code:

```
procedure DiskToWhere(var peg:pegarray; var top:toparray;
    var positionsmallest, frompeg, topeg: integer);
{ Peg, top, positionsmallest, frompeg, and topeg are defined in the  }
{ text. This routine finds the only legal move assuming the          }
{ smallest disk is not to be moved. First the two pegs that do not    }
{ hold the smallest disk are found.They are called other1 and         }
{ other2. If one of them is empty, the disk is to be moved from the   }
{ other one to it. If neither is empty, the disk is to be moved       }
{ from the peg holding the smallest disk to the other peg.            }
```

```
var
    other1, other2: integer;       {Names of the other two pegs - those }
begin                         { that do not hold the smallest disk. }
other1 := positionsmallest + 1;   {Find a peg other than pos of }
                                                {smallest.}
other2 := positionsmallest + 2;   {Find a 2nd other than pos of
                                                {smallest.}
if other1 > 3 then                {If other1=4, set it to 1.}
    begin
    other1 := other1 - 3;
    end;
if other2 > 3 then                {If other2 > 3, subtract 3 from it.}
    begin
    other2 := other2 -3;
    end;
if top[other1] = 1 then           {If other1 peg is empty, then move}
    begin                   {  from other2 peg to other1 peg.      }
    frompeg := other2;
    topeg := other1;
    end
else
    begin
    if top[other2] = 1 then       {If other2 peg is empty, then      }
        begin                 { move from other1 peg to other2.    }
        frompeg := other1;
        topeg := other2;
        end
    else
        begin                     {If other1 has smallest disk, . . . }
        if peg[other1,top[other1]-1] < peg[other2,top[other2]-1] then
            begin
            frompeg := other1;     {Move from other1 to other2.     }
            topeg := other2;
            end
        else
            begin                 {else move from other2 to other1.  }
            frompeg := other2;
            topeg := other1;
            end;
        end;
    end;
end;
```

Exercises

1. Code the procedure *ZeroArray*.

2. Code the procedure *PutDisksOnPeg1*.

3. Code the procedure *PrintArray*.

4. Code the procedure *SmallestToWhere*.

5. Code the procedure *MakeMove*.

6. Assemble the program that solves the Towers of Hanoi problem. Run it on several values of *n*.

Recursion (C)

A major strategy for solving a problem is to divide it into parts, solve the parts, and then combine the solutions of the parts to obtain a solution to the whole problem. As an example, suppose we wish to compute the factorial of 5. It is 5*4*3*2*1 = 120. A way to do this calculation is to split it into the two parts—5 and 4*3*2*1— and calculate each part separately: 5 = 5 and 4*3*2*1 = 24. Then we can recombine the parts to obtain the answer: 5*24 = 120. This strategy can be represented with the following notation:

factorial(5) = 5 * factorial(4)

More generally, if *n* is greater than zero, one can write·

factorial(n) = n * factorial(n-1).

This is a very special calculation because it is circular in nature. The strategy for computing *factorial(n)* requires finding *factorial(n-1)* first. But how does one compute *factorial(n-1)*? The answer is that one must compute *factorial(n-2)* and so forth.

But the formula

factorial(n) = n * factorial(n-1)

fails if *n* = 0. In the case *n* = 0, we write

factorial(n) = 1.

In fact, the general definition of factorial is

factorial(n) =
   if n = 0 then
      1
   else
      n * factorial(n-1)

This is called a *recursive* calculation because the function being defined is used in the definition. Here is a general format for such calculations:

A method for doing computation C on data D to obtain result R.

if the calculation is trivial then
  do it and return the result R
else
  begin
  divide D into two parts D1 and D2
  do part of the calculation on D1 to obtain R1 (possibly using C)
  do part of the calculation on D2 to obtain R2 (possibly using C)
  combine R1 and R2 to obtain the result R
  end

This can be illustrated by showing how it works on factorial:

A method for computing the factorial of n to obtain result f.

if n = 0 then
  f := 1
else
  begin
  separate n into parts D1 = n and D2 — n-1
  do part of the calculation on D1 to obtain R1 := D1
  compute the factorial of D2 to obtain R2
  combine R1 and R2 to obtain f := R1 * R2
  end

Here is the factorial program:

```
procedure factorial(var n,f:integer);
   var
       D1,D2,R1,R2:integer;
   begin
   if n = 0 then
       f := 1
   else
       begin
       D1 := n;
       D2 := n-1;
       R1 := D1;
       factorial(D2,R2);
       f := R1 * R2;
       end;
   end;
```

This, of course, uses more data locations than are necessary. The program can be shortened to this:

```
procedure  factorial(var  n,f:integer);
    var
        i:integer;
    begin
    if n = 0 then
        f :- 1
    else
        begin
        i := n - 1;
        factorial(i,f);
        f := n * f;
        end;
    end;
```

(Note: If this program is run, it will overflow the integer variables for values of *n* that are not small.)

Recursion is a difficult concept to learn. But if you master it, you will discover that it makes many programs easy that otherwise might be very difficult to code correctly. Let us examine a method for sorting a list using recursion:

> A method for sorting a list L.
>
> if L has length 1 or less then
>   do nothing
> else
>   begin
>   choose a member x of L
>   let D1 be the members of L less than x
>   let D2 be the members of L greater than or equal to x
>   (but D2 does not contain x)
>   rearrange L so that D1 is to the left of x and D2 is to the
>   right of x
>   sort D1 to obtain R1
>   sort D2 to obtain R2
>   the final sorted list is R1 followed by x followed by R2
>   end

Suppose, as an illustration, the list 2,5,7,6,3,1,4 is to be sorted. The method of calculation chooses one member of the list—let us say the last one, 4—and moves the numbers less than 4 to the left end of the array and the numbers greater than 4 to the right: 2,3,1,4,5,7,6. Here we have $x = 4$, $D1$ = 2,3,1 and $D2$ = 5,7,6. Next $D1$ is sorted to obtain 1,2,3, and $D2$ is sorted to obtain 5,6,7. The final sorted list is $D1$ followed by x followed by $D2$: 1,2,3,4,5,6,7.

Here is the subroutine for this sorting algorithm. It is a famous sorting method and is known as *quicksort*. The routine *quicksort(ar,i,j)* sorts the integer array *ar* beginning at entry *i* and ending at entry *j*:

```
procedure  quicksort(var  ar:intarray;var  i,j:integer);
    var
        b1,e1,b2,e2:integer;  {b1 and e1 begin and end sublist D1.}
                              {b2 and e2 begin and end sublist D2.}
    begin
    if i < j then
        begin
        b1 := i;
        e2 := j;
        rearrange(ar,b1,e1,b2,e2);
        quicksort(ar,b1,e1);
        quicksort(ar,b2,e2);
        end;
    end;
```

There are many strategies for coding *rearrange*, and we will not discuss them here. The following is one Pascal version of this routine you may wish to study:

```
procedure  rearrange(var  ar: intarray;var  b1,e1,b2,e2:integer);
    var
        mover:string;
        i1,i2:integer;

    procedure  exchange(var  i,j:integer);
        var
            temp:integer;
        begin
        temp := i;
        i := j;
        j := temp;
        end;
```

```
begin
    i1 := b1;
    i2 := e2;
    mover := 'i1';
    while i1 < i2 do
        if mover = 'i1' then
            if ar[i1] > ar[i2] then
                begin
                exchange(ar[i1],ar[i2]);
                mover := 'i2';
                end
            else
                i1 := i1 + 1
        else
            if ar[i1] > ar[i2] then
                begin
                exchange(ar[i1],ar[i2]);
                mover := 'i1';
                end
            else
                i2 := i2 - 1;
    e1 := i1 - 1;
    b2 := i1 + 1;
end;
```

This procedure declaration should precede the declaration for *quicksort* so that references to *rearrange* in *quicksort* will be well defined when they are encountered. (*rearrange* differs slightly from our original definition, but its effect is the same.)

In conclusion, the method of dividing a problem into simpler parts and solving each separately was explored earlier in this chapter. In this section, the strategy for computing function C divides the data into parts, calculates partial results using C, and combines those results to obtain the final answer. The methodology is called recursion, and it is both subtle and powerful.

Exercises

1. Study the routine *rearrange* and explain how it works. Write a program that reads a series of integers and then uses the quicksort program to sort them.

2. The nth Fibonacci number is computed by adding the (n-1)th and the (n-2)th Fibonacci numbers. The first two are 0 and 1. Thus the Fibonacci numbers can be enumerated as 0,1,1,2,3,5,8,13,21, . . . Write a recursive program that reads a number N and then prints the Nth Fibonacci number. (Note that when this program is run, its execution time can be long if N is not small. Why is this? Program execution time will be studied more in chapter 11.)

3. The sum of n numbers in an array can be computed as follows: Add the first $n-1$ numbers, and then add that sum to the last number. Use this method to design and program a recursive procedure for adding an array.

4. Write a program that receives an array of values and then prints every arrangement (permutation) of those values. For example, if the program receives the array a,b,c, it will print out

a,b,c

a,c,b

b,a,c

b,c,a

c,a,b

c,b,a

Use a recursive strategy to solve this problem.

5. Design a recursive strategy for solving the Towers of Hanoi problem. Write the program.

Summary (B)

The central problem of computer science is the discovery of methods for managing complexity. The two techniques that have historically been most effective involve finding the best representation for the problem and then systematically decomposing it into simpler parts. These strategies appear to be universally applicable to all problem-solving situations, and their mastery seems fundamental to all education.

This chapter has illustrated both strategies in a series of examples. The first was the database problem, where the original statement of the task seemed to involve programming far beyond the grasp of novice programmers. Yet with careful structuring of the solution, a way was found to achieve the target behaviors with a single loop program and relatively little additional complexity. The Towers of Hanoi and sorting problems gave additional examples of the development of a representation and solution through problem decomposition.

Pascal and most other programming languages provide syntactic support to the decomposition process through the subroutine feature. A subroutine is a module of programming that solves a part of the total problem. Whenever the solution to any task seems complex, we section off parts of it into subroutines that will be written later. Each part of the solution should be cut down to such a proportion that it seems straightforward and obviously correct.

The use of the subroutine feature requires care in designing communication between the subroutine and its calling program. This communication is carried out through the parameter list. The higher-level program needs to have a job done on its data structures, and it calls the subroutine to do it. The subroutine references only the needed structures in the calling program through the parameter list. If the subroutine needs additional memory locations to do its work, it should have them declared internally.

The database program developed here introduces the concept of the relational database and shows how it organizes data. An excellent way to retrieve information from such a database is to search for data patterns where some but not all of the fields are specified. One of the shortcomings of the program studied here is its inability to do inferences when the needed facts are not explicitly in the memory. A later chapter will reexamine this shortcoming and describe a method for overcoming it.

This chapter completes the programming portion of the book. The Pascal features described in chapters 1 - 4 are sufficient to do almost any program. A description of the syntax used in these chapters appears in the Appendix. The Pascal language includes a long list of other features, but they are primarily embellishments of the constructions covered here: additional looping, branching, and subroutine constructions and additional data structure types and declaration facilities.

In the early days of computing, an interesting competition arose related to the power of computer languages. One researcher would show that his or her language could be used to compute every function that some other language could compute. Then someone else would show that the second language could compute everything that the first could. The implication was that neither language could compute anything more than the other; both were capable of computing the same class of functions. Such comparisons occurred many times with the same surprising result: *any nontrivial computer language that one can invent is apparently capable of computing no more and no fewer functions than all the other nontrivial programming languages.* This is known as the Church-Markov-Turing Thesis, and it applies to the part of Pascal described in this book. You have learned all the computational features needed to compute any function that can be programmed by any language yet invented. Additional features provide convenience but not increased computational capability.

The Church-Markov-Turing Thesis has even more profound implications. Consider the portion of the English language appropriate for discussing computation in very concrete terms. This widely used sublanguage includes such sentences as, "Find the largest number in this finite set that is prime" and "Sort the set of records on the fifth field." Let us call this portion of English *C-English* and think of it as just another programming language. As far as anyone can tell, the power of C-English is similar to any other programming language; it is capable of describing any calculation that any standard programming language can do and no more. The Church-Markov-Turing Thesis in its extended form thus asserts that *any computation that anyone can describe in concrete English (or any other natural language) can be computed by any modern programming language* , including the Pascal presented in this book. This thesis is embraced by most computer scientists, and it implies a kind of completeness to modern programming languages. It says that if you can describe a process in English, you can program it. Modern computer languages are powerful enough; no new languages will enable us to compute more functions than are now possible unless some currently unimaginable new paradigm for computing is created.

You should now be able to solve many problems of moderate size using the Pascal language. However, this is only a brief introduction to programming, and substantial additional study is needed in order to become an accomplished programmer. If you wish to become an expert, learn the rest of the Pascal features, as well as one or two other languages. Then you need to undertake an extensive study of data structures and the multitude of ways that can be used to represent data in computers. Associated with this study, learn to analyze the execution times of programs so that you can create efficient, as well as correct, programs. Also, you must learn methodologies for proving the correctness of programs, so that they can be guaranteed to meet the specifications that are claimed for them. Finally, you should gain experience applying all of these methodologies to the analysis and coding of a variety of problems.

Readings

For programming:

Bentley, J. L., *Writing Efficient Programs,* Prentice Hall, Englewood Cliffs, New Jersey, 1982.

For database systems:

Date, C. J., *An Introduction to Database Systems,* Fourth Edition, Addison-Wesley, Reading, Massachusetts, 1986.

Maier, D., *The Theory of Relational Databases*, Computer Science Press, Rockville, Maryland, 1986.

Ullman, J. D., *Principles of Database Systems,* Second Edition, Computer Science Press, Rockville Maryland, 1982.

For data structures:

Aho, A. V., Hopcroft, J. E., and Ullman J. D., *Data Structures and Algorithms,* Addison-Wesley, Menlo Park, California, 1983.

Horowitz, E. and Sahni, S., *Fundamentals of Computer Algorithms,* Computer Science Press, Rockville Maryland, 1987.

Knuth, D. E., *The Art of Computer Programming, Vol. 1, Fundamental Algorithms,* Second Edition, Addison-Wesley, Reading, Massachusetts, 1973.

Smith, H. F. *Data Structures, Form and Function,* Harcourt Brace Jovanovich, San Diego, 1987.

Tenenbaum, A. M. and Augenstein, M. J., *Data Structures Using Pascal,* Prentice-Hall, Englewood Cliffs, New Jersey, 1981.

Wirth, N., *Algorithms and Data Structures,* Prentice-Hall, Englewood Cliffs, New Jersey,1986.

2 MONTHS INTO 6 MONTH PROGRAMMING EFFORT

4 MONTHS INTO 6 MONTH PROGRAMMING EFFORT

6 MONTHS INTO THE PROGRAMMING EFFORT

5

Software Engineering

The Real World (A)

A recent honors graduate in computer science from a prestigious university, whom we shall call Brian, accepted an industrial programming job. Brian, an able programmer, had worked in that capacity in university laboratories during his student days and had earned a string of As in computer courses. He was accustomed to looking at a problem, sketching out a solution method, and accurately estimating both the size of the desired program and the amount of time needed to write and debug the code. For planning purposes, he was wise enough to multiply estimates by a factor of two to make sure he had "breathing room," and even then he sometimes found himself up late the night before the deadline getting things into perfect order. But he had a reputation for doing a good job, and he was usually on time.

After accepting employment at his new position, Brian was given a specification for a program and asked to develop a plan for getting it done. He followed his usual procedures and then went to his boss with a set of algorithms for the various subroutines, data structure descriptions, and a time schedule. He told his boss that he could finish the job in three months and described at length how he would do it. His boss, whom he respected immensely, listened carefully to the plan and studied the problem some himself. Then he made an announcement that astounded Brian: he assigned five programmers to the job and set the deadline for a year hence.

Brian went home that night confused and amazed. How, he wondered, can a company afford to spend such tremendous resources on this program? He believed that they should fire the five programmers and let him do it.

But Brian's boss had had plenty of experience in the industrial world, and he knew the difference between personal computing and industrial computing. He knew about standards that had to be met, interfaces that had to be negotiated, documentation that had to be written, and perhaps revised specifications that might be introduced from time to time. He had seen deadlines like Brian's set and then slipped. He had seen the number of programmers on a project doubled and later doubled again, and he had seen deadlines pushed back ever further. He had seen a system running except for a few bugs; but when those bugs were fixed, the changes introduced new bugs in an unending chain. He knew that entering into an industrial-scale programming project is a fiscally dangerous undertaking and that it should be done with care.

Such is the case for large-scale programming projects. Experiences that are gained with one or two people writing programs a few pages long do not extrapolate well into massive efforts. Extensive communications among programmers, requirements for documentation, the intrinsic complexities of large programs, and many other factors contribute to greatly reduced efficiency. Too many times large programming efforts have marched forward to produce a product that still has bugs, is many months late, and overruns the budget. Frederick Brooks in his book *The Mythical Man-Month* likens the world of industrial programming to the tar pits of old where "many great and powerful beasts have thrashed violently" only to become more and more entangled.

It is important to know that large-project programming is shockingly different from personal programming. It is important to understand the characteristics of such projects, the problems that can occur, and the remedies that can be tried. The following sections describe lessons that have been learned from large-scale projects, improved technologies that lead to better team effectiveness, and the life cycle of an industrial program.

Lessons Learned from Large-Scale Programming Projects (B)

The first lesson is that a *program* is much easier to produce than a *programming system*, which in turn is easier to produce than a *programming system product*. Brooks (in *The Mythical Man-Month*) has defined these three entities and estimated that each higher stage is at least three times more expensive to produce than the previous one. A *program* is the entity that students write in universities. Its specifications are given in a small document, and it computes the target behavior on a single machine and under the control of its author. A *programming system* involves a group of interacting components coordinated to do a central task. Each component must have carefully designed interfaces that match specifications with other components and may need to conform to other specifications. For example, components may have to meet restrictions related to size and speed. A *programming system product* must be documented thoroughly, usable in many environments, and robust in its operation. It must be sufficiently well described that its maintenance, revision, and operation can be carried on in the absence of the author.

The last class of entities is the most typical goal of an industrial project, and, by Brooks's estimate, is at least nine times as costly to produce as a simple program. In fact, this factor alone is nearly sufficient to account for the heavy investments that Brian's boss was prepared to make.

The second lesson is that programming is not necessarily an easily divisible task. If one is not to wait several years for Brian to produce a programming system product, more programmers will be needed. But these additional people will be communicating with each other and perhaps even arguing about how the design should proceed. They will have to develop precise specifications of the interfaces between their various parts of the code and may have to do additional work to meet these demands. Testing and debugging of the interacting modules may be more complex than for the more unified architecture that a single person would build. Thus the per person productivity for a multiperson effort usually will be lower than it would be for a single programmer. Halving the time required to finish a project requires more than doubling the number of programmers.

The more that programmers must interact with each other in order to do a job, the lower will be their productivity in terms of amount of code written. Brooks presents the following rough guidelines (by Joel Aron) for programmer productivity in terms of numbers of instructions written per programmer-year for design and coding activities (Brooks, chapter 8):

Numbers of interactions	Instructions per year
Very few interactions	10000
Some interactions	5000
Many interactions	1500

These figures roughly summarize the kinds of results that have been observed in various studies of programmer productivity. They can be off by a factor of two or more in some situations, but they give the order of magnitude for typical performance.

Programmers do not spend all of their time planning and writing code, so these figures may be high as an overall performance measure. Brooks (chapter 2) estimates that, in the course of a project, programmers spend roughly half their time in testing and debugging activities.

Therefore, the addition of programmers to speed up a project increases the complexity of the programming task and does not result in time improvements proportional to the number of added people. In fact, too many additional programmers can saturate the team and yield no improvement whatsoever. Most programming tasks require a certain minimum amount of time to reach maturity regardless of the number of programmers assigned.

Another effect observed in large projects is that large programs may be disproportionally more complex than smaller ones. That is, a larger program, say 500,000 lines of code, may require more than twice as much effort as a project of half that length. This effect may occur regardless of the number of programmers.

The combination of all of these effects sends average programmer productivity plummeting in a way that Brian could not be expected to appreciate. While he was able to write and debug comfortably 100 lines of code per day, the figures indicate, assuming 200 working days per year, that industrial programmers may code as few as 7 lines of code per day.

If Brian's original estimate had been used, probably he would have worked very hard for a month or two only to realize that he was not generating a product to meet the required standards. He would then have asked for additional programmers and a delayed deadline of perhaps two months. Next he would try to convince the new people that he had much of the task completed and would invest much effort in educating them to understand his theory of operation and his code. One way or another, they would finally get into the swing of the project, but the second deadline would be hard upon them. They would then ask for another slippage of the deadline. They also might ask for more programmers, who would also have to be trained and integrated into the effort.

Exercises

1. Assume that you are a manager and need to have a simple stand-alone program coded that will be approximately 500 instructions in length. How many programmers would you assign to the job, and when, based on figures given above, can you expect to have the program completed?

2. Suppose you are a manager and wish to have a programming system product coded that will be approximately 40,000 instructions in length. This, for example, might be the size of a compiler for a programming language. Assuming the above guidelines are applicable to your situation, how many programmers might you need in order to complete the job in three years? How would you revise your estimate if the time allotted were only two years? If your boss demanded that the program be completed within three months, how would you respond?

3. Repeat exercise 2 for the case where the target program will be approximately 200,000 instructions. This might be the length of an operating system for a moderate-sized machine.

4. What can you say about the amount of programming effort required for a large program such as a modern telephone switching system that could involve 10 million instructions? Assume that the time allowed for coding is four years.

Software Engineering Methodologies (B)

The tremendous cost of software has become a major concern of the computing industry. In the mid-1950s, software costs were less than 20 percent of total computing costs, but now they exceed 80 percent. This has led to a major emphasis on discovering ways to improve programming methodologies and to the birth of a new field, software engineering. The goal has been to change programming from a hit-or-miss, one-person-at-a-time operation to a sophisticated art and science where groups of people cooperatively work together to produce, reliably and efficiently, a worthy product. Three areas of software engineering will be discussed here: the development of strategies to improve the correctness of programs, the invention of new organizational schemes for programmers, and the creation of better programming tools.

Correctness. Beginning with program correctness, a system specification will often state the allowed error rates, and the product is required to stay within them. For example, the specification might require that the software system process inputs successfully at some high rate, say, 99.95 percent of the time. Software engineers enter into a project with the sobering knowledge that the ultimate product will be rejected if it does not achieve such a high level of reliability.

Therefore, the required strategy is to adopt a philosophy that brings correctness to the forefront of every designer's and coder's mind from the early stages of design to the day of product delivery. The philosophy asserts that correctness cannot be added as an afterthought but must be meticulously designed in at every stage. It disallows common attitudes that errors are natural and inevitable and asserts that errors exist in programs because people put them there. It asserts that correctness is a consequence of responsible programming practice and that no alternative should be contemplated. The generation of correct programs is important because the ultimate product must be correct and the cost of removing errors from running code can be tremendous.

Correctness considerations begin with the design of the program specifications—a careful, detailed, and exact description of every aspect of the product behavior. These specifications are to prescribe every detail that the external world will see but carefully avoid implying how the program will actually work. It is the job of the implementors to produce code that performs precisely as guaranteed in the program specifications. At these early stages, correctness must be carefully attended to since errors here will radiate into the product in unpredictable ways. Barry Boehm has estimated (in *Software Engineering Economics*, chapter 4) that specification errors repaired in the later stages of software development can cost as much as 100 times more to fix than if they were caught at specification time.

Next the system designers build a mental image of how the internals of the system will work and write specifications for the various modules proposed to do the job. Then smaller groups of programmers or individuals will be assigned these modules. Their task is to produce code with behaviors that are guaranteed to match the interface specifications. This means that programmers must have verification techniques for checking that the code advances through the proper steps and delivers precisely what is specified. These techniques usually involve studying each sequential statement, considering every possible situation that could arise, and showing that, in every case, the statement does the right thing. During the 1970s, methodologies evolved that enable a person to prove mathematically that a program achieves its specifications. However, such rigorous procedures are too expensive for most applications and are used only in rare situations where extreme measures are justified.

One of the most important innovations was the idea of top-down structured programming. It is an approach that encourages clear and systematic thinking about large programs and plays an essential role in the art of writing correct code. Before the days of structured programming, programming methodologies allowed the use of a "go to" statement that enabled the program control to jump from any point in a program to any other point. It was found that the use of such statements enabled for programmers to write code with a randomly organized flowchart that could be a nightmare to understand and debug. The elimination of the "go to" statement forces the programmer to use constructs with a more straightforward flow of control.

Another technology aimed at the correctness issue concerns the discovery of adequate test procedures for programs. Once a program has gone through the laborious design, coding, and verification procedures, it should be run on a carefully constructed set of inputs that will exercise every branch, activate every combination of submodules, and explore endpoints and extreme values. The hope is that every conceivable test will go smoothly, but where failures occur, the responsible individuals will be called upon to do the repair.

Organizational Schemes. The second area for improved programming methodology concerns the way the personnel are organized. Various innovations have evolved that encourage people to help each other and that attempt utilize the special talents of each.

A way to encourage good group dynamics in a programming environment is to break up the sense of ownership that programmers have in the code they have written. Consider, as an example, the case of a lone student in a classroom situation who has spent countless hours conceiving of the design, writing the code, and adding some much-loved special features. If later this program is said to be of poor quality or is discovered to have errors, the person justifiably will feel threatened or uncomfortable. In the environment of a programming team, the person could become protective, secretive, and defensive about the code when the goals of the group require openness and cooperation. A better model encourages so-called *egoless programming* where the code is considered to be a product of the group activity and where criticism and improvements from any member are always welcome. It may be that person A wrote the first draft, person B rewrote the code and got it running, and person C found some errors and made some improvements. All three individuals accept each other as both contributors and mistake makers, and the code is viewed as a separate entity that can be praised or criticized without threatening the individual. All team members want to get it right, and the best talents of each are aimed at the common goal.

Often an organization has programmers who are star performers, and a special arrangement is appropriate to utilize their talents properly. Unlike most other human activities where excellence involves being perhaps 20 percent above the norm, in programming the highest achiever may be ten times more productive than lesser contributors. Good management requires that such able people be freed to practice their trade and that others should gather around and do everything possible to help. This gives rise to the *chief programmer team*, which centers all activities around a single person.

The common organization for such a team begins with the *chief programmer* whose job is to conceive of the code, write it, debug it, and perhaps write the major documentation. The second most central individual is the *backup programmer*, who observes every action of the chief and knows the code and documentation. This person performs support activities such a verification of correctness, development of required subroutines, background research, and documentation. If the chief programmer becomes unavailable at any point, the backup must step in and keep things going forward without delays. A third major player is the *programming librarian*, who types, formats, stores, and retrieves code and documentation for the group. The team may also contain various other players who may be programming, testing, writing documentation, or doing other tasks. The chief programmer team idea has been used on numerous occasions, often breaking records for programmer productivity and for quality of the final product.

Programming Tools. The third field of software engineering discussed here is the area of software tools for productivity. The new image of a programmer is no longer a person with a pencil, paper, and a terminal nearby. Instead it centers on a large-screen workstation capable of displaying windows into a variety of facilities—libraries of code, a language editor, a run-time monitor, a debugging package, programming manuals, a theorem prover for verification activities, graphics subsystems, communications facilities to other programmers, and much more. The programmer then assembles code with the assistance of this collection of support systems, bringing in aid as needed.

In the ideal scenario with a modern environment, the programmer may write relatively little code. Instead, he or she will have an extensive knowledge of existing software and will attempt to find ways to assemble the target program from these pieces. A complete programming task might begin with the coder writing a top-level program to organize the computation. Then the person would peruse the code library for the correct subroutines to finish the programming job. In the future, it may be that the programmer will be able to check some menu items and have the routines automatically specialized to the application.

With the code assembled, the programmer might have a way to generate test data automatically, and then immediately run the code on the examples. If an error is observed, the programmer would study the code in one window, the data structures in another, the computation history in another, and so forth to try to determine the cause of failure. Later, with the code fixed and running, the person might signal, through computer mail, another team member of the accomplishment and send it to that person's machine for verification, modification, or use. Later he or she might receive the code back with comments and updates. Perhaps it would then be archived and indexed for later use.

Not all of the facilities mentioned here are in routine use in all programming organizations. But many of them are in use in many organizations, and the ideal situation approaches reality a little more each year.

Exercises

1. Select a program from an earlier chapter or from your own experience, and carry out a detailed study of its correctness:

(a) Write exact specifications for the class of legal inputs to the program. State explicitly every characteristic a legal input must have, including the lengths of allowed input strings, the number of significant digits and sizes of allowable numbers, and so forth. Give examples of legal and illegal inputs.

(b) Write complete and exacting specifications for the outputs of the program. Tell clearly what is to result in every possible computation that could result from inputs as specified in part a.

(c) Study every line of code and write down careful arguments to show that it will do the proper action assuming the input meets the specifications given. Show with your arguments that the collection of the statements, in fact, computes the outputs exactly as they have been given in part b. Be sure to check behaviors at endpoints where inputs may have length zero or otherwise stretch the performance of the program.

2. Study the topics covered in this section and suggest a field of software engineering that you believe should be studied but is not described here. What kinds of results do you think could be obtained if this field were undertaken?

The Program Life Cycle (B)

Software engineering does not restrict its vision to the program synthesis task. Economic investments with regard to a program begin early and may continue for many years after the program is written. This is because a program may have a long life cycle that substantially engages the organization at every stage. Decision making should account for this larger picture and attempt to optimize benefits for the long term. A system architecture optimized at the design stage but not amenable to later upgrade or maintenance will not be successful. A set of terminal specifications written to make programming easy but without regard to later training and usage requirements can lead to catastrophe. Thus the software engineer must keep the larger picture in mind at each stage to achieve a long-term success. We will briefly examine the life cycle of a typical software product with some of the concerns that appear at each stage.

Defining the Product. The first question to ask is: what need is to be addressed? The answer may be in terms of new information the client needs to compile, labor-intensive jobs that need to be automated, or the improvement of some already automated function. Whatever the goal, extensive interviews with the client and possibly market surveys need to be carried out to determine the nature of the problem.

Then automated solutions to the problem can be proposed in rough terms and measured against the originally stated need. Rough estimates can be made as to the cost and effectiveness of the solution, and judgments can be offered concerning their relative desirability. Sometimes an inexpensive prototype for a proposed system can be assembled and tested in the user environment to provide data regarding a proposed system's value. If one of the alternatives appears to be desirable, it can be selected, and the organization can begin steps toward its implementation.

Selecting the Programming Team. Assuming that the decision is to code a programming product to solve the problem, the organizers can begin choosing the members of the programming groups, making estimates as to the kind and numbers of people needed. As system specification and architecture develop, better estimates will become possible and more team members can be chosen.

Developing the Program Specification. Here the rough estimates of the earlier stages are made precise. An exact specification of the system's external characteristics is written down in a possibly voluminous document. In some cases, certain features of the ultimate product have not been decided. When this occurs, the required "hooks" are defined where later features can be inserted.

Designing the System Structure. The form of the system organization needs to be designed and the major data structures must be specified. At first the design will be sketched in rough form, but these ideas then must be solidified in another set of specifications. These working documents, which could be longer than the external specifications, will set forth the list of the subcomponents and their complete interface characteristics. Individual programming teams will be given these subcomponents as tasks and will have little guidance except what is stated in these documents.

Coding the System. Next the staff will write the program. Typically the implementation effort results in the discovery of errors or poor decisions at earlier stages, which must be corrected. Thus the original specifications and other working documents will be revised occasionally as the group changes its view of the whole project. If the original conception was good, changes will have only second-order effects, and the basic form of the architecture will remain.

Testing the Code. As individual parts of the system become operative, they can be tested to confirm that they meet the requirements given in the working documents. Many times special software is written to test system modules. Testing often results in revisions to the code but truly professional programmers can usually achieve early, if not immediate, convergence on acceptable performance. As larger subsystems come into existence, parts that were finished and tested earlier can be integrated into the whole.

Revision. As members of the group tend to mature in their conceptualization of a system, continuous improvements may be made in the system design. Even updates to the original system behavioral specifications will be made from time to time. This involves modifying documentation and rewriting parts of the code.

Documentation. All stages of the project require much documentation especially when many programmers are involved. In addition to the documentation of code, user manuals must be created for training, explanation of the principles of operation, installation, and maintenance. These documents will accompany the product into the user environment.

Delivery and Training. The product needs to reach the user and come into useful operation. This may involve sending project participants to the user organization to help with installation, early operation, and training of users.

Maintenance and Upgrade. Once a product is in field operation, the organization can expect to receive notification of errors in its behavior and requests for additional features. It is quite common for the vendor to keep a group of programmers working on the project for many years after its original development carrying on these maintenance and upgrade activities. Users can be sold contracts for such services so these efforts can be profitable ventures on their own.

Positioning for the Next Product. Success on one project engenders opportunities for others. A reputation gained by delivering one successful system can open the door to projects that complement the original one or lead to later follow-on projects.

Summarizing, the life cycle of a programming project includes many varied stages that can span a period of years. In order for a system to be successful, decision making must account for the whole life cycle and the best long-term interests of the project.

Exercise

1. Draw a flowchart for the enterprises in the program life cycle. Notice that they will not be linear as indicated above.

Summary (B)

Software engineering is the collection of disciplines that enable a group of people to build and maintain computer software systems. These include mathematical subfields that deal with program correctness and performance, numerous technologies related to programming languages and systems, some economics, and the psychology and sociology of team efforts.

The industrial programming of a software product is a substantially more ambitious undertaking than the construction of individual programs of the type students or laboratory workers may assemble. While isolated programmers may be able to assemble hundreds of lines of code per day to satisfy their own needs, programmers in an industrial project may produce on the average fewer than 10 lines of code in a programming systems product per day.

Numerous technologies have developed to aid the task of industrial programmers, including strategies for designing correctness into programs, methods for organizing programming groups, and automated systems for assembling code.

Readings

On software engineering:

Boehm, B. W., *Software Engineering Economics*, Prentice-Hall, Englewood Cliffs, New Jersey, 1981.

Brooks, F. P., Jr., *The Mythical Man-Month*, Addison-Wesley, Reading, Mass., 1975.

Mills, H. D., *Software Productivity*, Little, Brown, Boston, Mass., 1983.

Pressman, R. S., *Software Engineering: A Practitioner's Approach*, McGraw-Hill, New York, 1987.

Sommerville, I., *Software Engineering*, Addison-Wesley, Menlo Park, California, 1982.

On correctness:

Dijkstra, E. W., *A Discipline of Programming*, Prentice-Hall, Englewood Cliffs, New Jersey, 1976.

Gries, D., *The Science of Programming*, Springer-Verlag, New York, 1981.

McGowan, C. L., and Kelly, J. R., *Top-Down Structured Programming Techniques*, Petrocelli/Charter, New York, 1975.

Reynolds, J. C., *The Craft of Programming*, Prentice-Hall International, London, 1981.

On psychological issues:

Shneiderman, B., *Software Psychology*, Winthrop Publishers, Cambridge, Mass., 1980.

Weinberg, G. M., *The Psychology of Computer Programming*, Van Norstrand Reinhold, New York, 1971.

On programming environments:

Biggerstaff, T. J., *Systems Software Tools*, Prentice-Hall, Englewood Cliffs, New Jersey, 1986.

6

Electric Circuits

How Do Computers Work? (A)

In the previous chapters, we studied how to write Pascal programs. We learned to write code to input characters and numbers, to concatenate, to add and subtract, to modify iteratively, to print results, and so forth. But how does the machine behind the programming statements actually do these operations? How is it possible to make the computer receiving the statement

```
Z := X + Y;
```

actually find X and Y, add them, and put the result into the correct place? How does one organize electricity to make it calculate?

The purpose of this chapter and the next four is to answer these questions. In this chapter, we learn that program actions, such as the execution of the above statement, can be broken down into elementary *machine operations*. In typical processing, the Pascal statement is translated into *assembly language* and then converted to basic machine operations. Then electric circuitry executes these elementary operations:

Format	*Example*
Pascal Code	Z := X + Y;
|	|
| Translation	| Translation
|	|
V	V
Assembly Language Code	COPY AX,X
|	ADD AX,Y
|	COPY CN1,AX
|	COPY AX,CN1
| Translation	COPY Z,AX
|	|
|	| Translation
|	|
V	V

Machine Language Code   00101101
           | 01101010
           | - - - -
           | |
           V   V
Execution by Electric   Execution of codes
Circuitry   00101101, 01101010, . . .

For example, the statement

```
Z := X + Y;
```

may translate into something like this (as will be shown in chapter 10):

Get the quantity called X.   COPY AX,X
Get Y and add it to the first quantity.   ADD AX,Y
Store the result.   COPY CN1,AX
Take the result.   COPY AX,CN1
Put it into Z.   COPY Z,AX

The translator has the job of changing the input $Z := X + Y$; into an equivalent set of assembly language operations, here listed as as *COPY AX,Y,* etc. Then these operations are converted to binary codes such as 00101101, 01101010, . . . Finally basic electrical circuits can execute these binary codes in sequence to get the job done. (Note: The experienced reader will wonder why the statement compiles into five instructions instead of the expected three. The answer is that we are being consistent here with the compiler presented in chapter 10.)

   This chapter will show how those basic electrical circuits can be built to do the machine operations. The following chapters will show how those circuits are built with modern transistor and microelectronics technology. Chapters 9 and 10 will show how computers are organized and how the translation is done from the source language like Pascal into machine language. The complete set of studies will show all of the essential mechanisms involved in the execution of a program written in a language such as Pascal.

Computer Organization (B)

This chapter will show how to build electric circuits that do primitive machine operations such as adding two numbers. Computers are organized, as illustrated below, with circuits called registers that store information and circuits that calculate things to put into those registers. One special register, the *instruction register*, holds the code (like 00101101) telling what is to be done. Then circuitry deciphers the code and activates the circuit that will do the work, such as an arithmetic operation. This machine operation circuit then manipulates the data, which are stored in data registers, called $X_1, X_2, \ldots$ here:

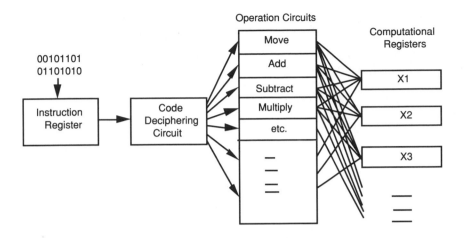

The computation in this example would proceed as follows: (1) Put the first instruction code (00101101) into the instruction register, (2) decipher it, and (3) call on the correct machine operation to do the job. Then load the next instruction code (01101010) and repeat the same actions. Continue loading and executing all sequential instructions until the task is complete.

Two kinds of circuits are needed in the construction of such a machine: the *storage circuits*, as illustrated above by the instruction and data registers, and the *function computation circuits*, as illustrated by the code decipher and machine operation circuits. The next portion of this chapter will study circuits for computing functions, and the last part of the chapter will examine circuits for storage.

Circuits for Computing Primitive Functions (B)

Our study of electric circuits begins with the simplest possible circuit—a battery connected to a light bulb:

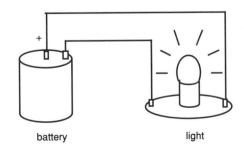

battery   light

If a battery is connected to a properly rated electric bulb as shown, the bulb will become illuminated. It is beyond the scope of this chapter to discuss the chemical and physical processes that create the electrical pressure within the battery and guide the electricity through the wires to light the bulb. We note only that batteries do exist, that they can force electric current through a wire, and that the current can light a bulb if it passes through.

Our view of a battery is that it is an electron pump where electrons are the tiny negatively charged particles that make up an electric current. The pump attempts to push the electrons out of the terminal marked minus (-) and to collect them from the terminal marked plus (+). Think of a battery as acting like a water pump with little whirling paddles grabbing electrons from the input path and pushing them out the output:

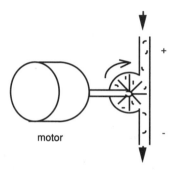

Think of the electric wires as pipes and the light bulb as a very thin pipe that turns a glowing white hot if the electrons are forced through at a fast enough pace. The total circuit then may be visualized as a simple loop with electrons flying around the circle at high speed under the pressure of relentless paddle blades, causing the thin part to glow brightly:

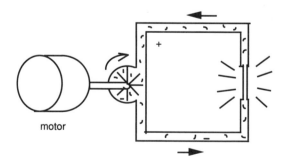

It is wise to have a symbolic form for such a circuit. It will be represented here as parallel lines for the battery and a circle with filament for the bulb:

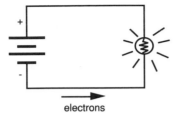

electrons

The electrons move from the shortest line on the battery symbol and proceed around the circuit back to the longer line on the battery symbol.

We can now modify this circuit to compute something. Specifically, we can insert a switch that acts like a water valve to turn the current off and on:

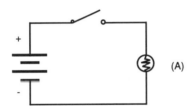

(A)

This modified circuit, if left alone in the state shown, will not carry an electric current and will not light the bulb. The electrons cannot travel around the loop because the conducting path at the top is broken. However, if a finger pushes the switch conductor down, the circuit is returned to the form discussed above, and the light will come on:

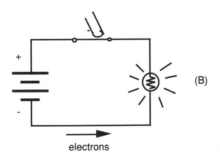

(B)

electrons

We will assume in this book that the switch is made of spring material and that it will bounce back to the position A if we remove the finger.

Next we wish to think of this circuit as a very simple computer. Suppose people are entering a room, and someone pushes the switch conductor down if the current person entering the room is tall. If a nontall person enters, the switch is not pushed down. We will say this circuit computes "tallness" in that the bulb will shine if the entering person is tall and will remain off otherwise. We do not address the issue of whose finger pushes the button at this time but concentrate on the resultant function.

We will also need a notation for representing such computations and will use the variable x_t to represent the property of tallness. If a person is tall, we will write $x_t = 1$; otherwise, we will say $x_t = 0$. We will then label the switch with the symbol x_t and note that the depressed position A corresponds to the assignment $x_t = 1$ and the released position B corresponds to $x_t = 0$. Variables that can take on only two values such as x_t are called *Boolean* variables.

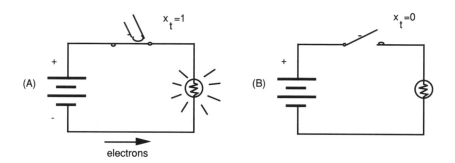

The circuit with a single switch is not a very exciting computer. We do such "computations" quite often when entering dark rooms and do not ordinarily think of them as such. A much more interesting computation is possible if we have two variables and thus two switches. Assume the people entering the room may be handsome as well as tall and consider the following circuit where x_t represents "tallness" and x_h represents "handsomeness":

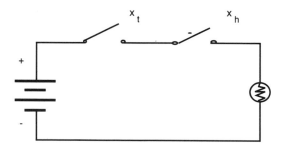

Clearly, the light will not shine in the position shown where $x_t = 0$ and $x_h = 0$. The electric current does not have a path to flow around the loop. Furthermore, if either switch is depressed individually ($x_t = 1, x_h = 0$ or $x_t = 0, x_h = 1$), the light will continue to remain off. Only if both switches x_t and x_h are depressed simultaneously will a current flow to light the bulb. The important word to note is "and"; if two switches are wired in series as shown, they compute the function

$f_{and}(x_t,x_h)$, which has value 1 if both x_t *and* x_h are 1 and value 0 otherwise.

x_t	x_h	$f_{and}(x_t,x_h)$
0	0	0
0	1	0
1	0	0
1	1	1

The "and" function is extremely important, as will be seen below. If two variables are written adjacent to each other as with $x_t x_h$, the convention in this book will be to say that they are connected by the function "and." That is, we will read $x_t x_h$ as "x_t and x_h" or $x_1 x_2 x_3$ as "x_1 and x_2 and x_3." Using this convention, we can write $f_{and}(x_t,x_h) = x_t x_h$, meaning that $f_{and}(x_t, x_h)$ has value 1 only when x_t and x_h both have value 1. As another example, suppose we write $f(x_1,x_2,x_3) = x_1 x_2 x_3$. Then $f(x_1,x_2,x_3)$ has value 1 only when all three of x_1 and x_2 and x_3 have value 1. Otherwise, $f(x_1,x_2,x_3)$ =0:

x_1	x_2	x_3	$f(x_1,x_2,x_3)$
0	0	0	0
0	0	1	0
0	1	0	0
0	1	1	0
1	0	0	0
1	0	1	0
1	1	0	0
1	1	1	1

If the above circuit had been wired differently, another interesting function would have been computed:

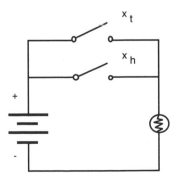

As before, in the configuration shown, there is no path for the electrons around the loop. However, if either switch x_t *or* x_h is depressed ($x_t=1, x_h=0$ or $x_t=0, x_h=1$), a path is provided for the electricity. If both switches are depressed ($x_t=1, x_h=1$), the electrons can flow through the bulb and through both switches back to the battery. This circuit thus computes the function $f_{or}(x_t, x_h)$, which has value 1 if either x_t or x_h is 1 or if both are 1:

x_t	x_h	$f_{or}(x_t, x_h)$
0	0	0
0	1	1
1	0	1
1	1	1

The notation for the "or" computation will be the plus sign "+" and so one can express $f_{or}(x_t, x_h)$ as $f_{or}(x_t, x_h) = x_t + x_h$. As another example, one could have a function $f(x_1, x_2, x_3) = x_1 + x_2 + x_3$ which has value 1 if at least one of x_1, x_2, or x_3 is 1:

x_1	x_2	x_3	$f(x_1, x_2, x_3)$
0	0	0	0
0	0	1	1
0	1	0	1
0	1	1	1
1	0	0	1
1	0	1	1
1	1	0	1
1	1	1	1

We have examined circuits for computing the "and" and "or" functions. One more type of circuit is needed to provide a rather general computation ability, the "not" circuit:

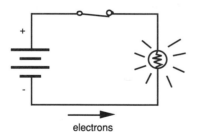

electrons

Here a new kind of switch is needed that will conduct electricity whenever the circuit is left alone. If a finger depresses the switch, the circuit is broken, and the flow stops:

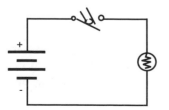

Assume a finger depresses the switch whenever a tall person enters the room. Then the bulb will light whenever it is *not* true that a tall person is entering the room. If x_t stands for tallness, we will continue the convention that $x_t = 1$ corresponds to pushing down on the switch. However, this time $x_t = 1$ will result in the bulb going off. We will use the notation x_t' to stand for the concept *not* tall. Let $f_{not}(x_t) = x_t'$ which has the following function table:

x_t	$f_{not}(x_t)$
0	1
1	0

The three functions "and," "or," and "not" can be combined to compute *any* function of binary variables. The following section will show how to do this, but it is first important to do a few problems.

Exercises

1. Suppose a circuit has two switches such that one is pushed if a person entering the room is tall and the other if the person is handsome. Find a circuit that will light a bulb if the entering person is tall but not handsome and will have the bulb off otherwise.

2. Suppose two switches are available; one is depressed if a person is older than 18, and the other is depressed if the person is accompanied by a parent. Draw a circuit that will light a bulb if the person can be admitted to a film rated R.

3. Suppose three switches are available. They are depressed, respectively, if a person (a) has received much money, (b) was robbed of everything, and (c) has a huge debt. Construct a circuit that will light a bulb if the person is rich.

4. Given the following circuit, fill in the table showing the function that it computes.

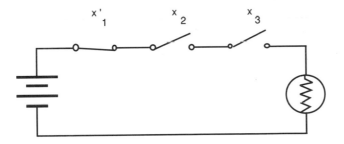

x_1	x_2	x_3	$f(x_1,x_2,x_3)$
0	0	0	?
0	0	1	?
0	1	0	?
0	1	1	?
1	0	0	?
1	0	1	?
1	1	0	?
1	1	1	?

Circuits for Computing Complex Functions (B)

Suppose the following circuit is given, and it is desired to determine what function f_1 it computes.

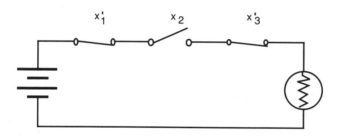

For example, if $x_1 =0$, $x_2 =0$, and $x_3 =0$, we see that none of the switches will be pushed down. Current will not flow because x_2 will not conduct, and the bulb will remain off. We conclude that $f_1(x_1,x_2,x_3) =0$. Trying another example, $x_1 =0$, $x_2 =0$, $x_3 =1$, we get the same result because both x_2 and x_3 will be nonconducting. Switch x_2 is normally nonconducting, and x_3 will not conduct because it is pushed down ($x_3 =1$). Continuing the analysis, the functional table emerges:

x_1	x_2	x_3	$f_1(x_1,x_2,x_3)$
0	0	0	0
0	0	1	0
0	1	0	1
0	1	1	0
1	0	0	0
1	0	1	0
1	1	0	0
1	1	1	0

The only situation that yields $f_1(x_1,x_2,x_3) =1$ is $x_1 =0$, $x_2 =1$, $x_3 =0$. Switches x_1 and x_3 are not pushed down, but x_2 is. The function is thus written as $f_1(x_1,x_2,x_3) =x_1'x_2x_3'$.

The way to see the relationship between the circuit and the table is to look at the table row where the output is 1. The inputs at this row are 0, 1, 0, and they are related to the switches in the circuit. An input of 0 corresponds to a normally closed switch (a not switch). An input of 1 corresponds to a normally open switch. Since the inputs are $x_1 = 0$, $x_2 = 1$, $x_3 = 0$ in that row with output 1, the circuit is built with switches normally closed, open, and closed, respectively, as shown.

Similarly another circuit can be analyzed that computes f_2 :

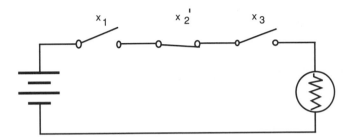

Its tabular function can be analyzed, and you can see a simple relationship between the circuit and the table:

x_1	x_2	x_3	$f_1(x_1,x_2,x_3)$
0	0	0	0
0	0	1	0
0	1	0	0
0	1	1	0
1	0	0	0
1	0	1	1
1	1	0	0
1	1	1	0

Again only one 1 appears in the table output, and it is easy to find: $f_2(x_1,x_2,x_3) = x_1 x_2' x_3$. Since the row in the table with a 1 output has the input 1, 0, 1, the circuit must have three sequential switches, which are normally open, closed, and open, respectively. Every similar circuit of three sequential switches will yield such a functional behavior with only a single 1 in the table output.

Now we can consider the "or" combination of these two circuits. It will yield a table with two outputs equal to 1 and a circuit with two series circuits:

x_1	x_2	x_3	$f_3(x_1,x_2,x_3)$
0	0	0	0
0	0	1	0
0	1	0	1
0	1	1	0
1	0	0	0

(table continues on page 186)

x_1	x_2	x_3	$f_3(x_1,x_2,x_3)$
1	0	1	1
1	1	0	0
1	1	1	0

$$f_3(x_1,x_2,x_3)=x_1'x_2x_3'+x_1x_2'x_3$$

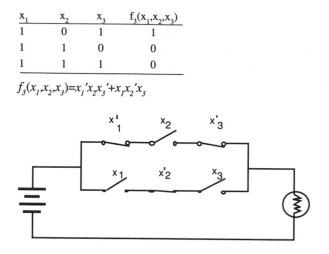

This circuit will light the bulb and thus yield $f_3(x_1,x_2,x_3)=1$ in just the cases $x_1=0$, $x_2=1$, and $x_3=0$ or $x_1=1$, $x_2=0$, and $x_3=1$.

For each line with a 1 output in the above table for f_3, there is a series of three switches in the resulting circuit. This makes it easy to create a circuit for a function with any number of 1s in its output. For example, consider f_4, which is similar to f_3 except that it has three 1s in its output:

x_1	x_2	x_3	$f_4(x_1,x_2,x_3)$
0	0	0	0
0	0	1	0
0	1	0	1
0	1	1	0
1	0	0	0
1	0	1	1
1	1	0	0
1	1	1	1

$$f_4(x_1,x_2,x_3)=x_1'x_2x_3'+x_1x_2'x_3+x_1x_2x_3$$

The associated circuit will have three sequences of three switches each. Can you write this circuit down?

You should now be able to write down a circuit for any binary function of any number of Boolean variables regardless of the number of 1s in the output. The circuit will light a bulb for any value of the input variables that yields a 1 output. As a final example, suppose the following function f is to be computed. The appropriate switching circuit is shown:

x_1	x_2	x_3	x_4	$f(x_1,x_2,x_3,x_4)$
0	0	0	0	0
0	0	0	1	0
0	0	1	0	0
0	0	1	1	0

(table continued from previous page)

x_1	x_2	x_3	x_4	$f(x_1,x_2,x_3,x_4)$
0	1	0	0	0
0	1	0	1	1
0	1	1	0	0
0	1	1	1	0
1	0	0	0	1
1	0	0	1	0
1	0	1	0	0
1	0	1	1	0
1	1	0	0	0
1	1	0	1	1
1	1	1	0	0
1	1	1	1	0

$$f(x_1,x_2,x_3,x_4)=x_1'x_2x_3'x_4 + x_1x_2'x_3'x_4' + x_1x_2x_3'x_4$$

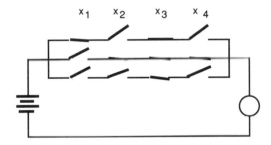

Exercises

1. Suppose that a, b, and c are integers such that the sum of a and b is c: $a + b = c$. Suppose x_a is a Boolean variable that has value 1 if a is an even integer and value 0 if a is odd. Suppose x_b is similarly defined for b. Design a circuit that will light a bulb if and only if c is even. Hint: Fill out the following table to determine the desired function:

x_a	x_b	$f(x_a,x_b)$
0	0	?
0	1	?
1	0	?
1	1	?

Then construct the desired circuit.

2. Repeat problem 1 except use the assumption that a times b is c.

3. A corporation has developed the following personnel classification scheme.

$x_m = 1$ if a person has management training
$x_m = 0$ otherwise

$x_s = 1$ if a person has sales skills
$x_s = 0$ otherwise

$x_t = 1$ if a person has a strong technical competence
$x_t = 0$ otherwise

The following table indicates the required qualifications for three job types: salesperson, manager, technical adviser.

x_m	x_s	x_t	Salesperson	Manager	Technical Adviser
0	0	0	0	0	0
0	0	1	0	0	1
0	1	0	1	0	0
0	1	1	1	0	0
1	0	0	0	0	0
1	0	1	1	0	1
1	1	0	1	0	0
1	1	1	1	1	0

Thus from line 2 of this table, if a person has no management training or sales skills but is technically competent, he or she may be used as a technical adviser. However, from line 4 if the person also has sales abilities, he or she should not be used as a technical advisor but should be moved to the sales department.

(a) Draw a circuit that will light a bulb if the person is qualified as a salesperson.
(b) Design a circuit to indicate management qualification.
(c) Repeat for technical adviser.

4. A computer is to be designed to operate an elevator in a two-story building where the stories are labeled 0 and 1. The system has four inputs as follows:

$x_0 = 1$ if the floor 0 elevator button is pushed
$x_0 = 0$ otherwise

$x_1 = 1$ if the floor 1 elevator button is pushed
$x_1 = 0$ otherwise

$x_e = 1$ if the elevator internal button is pushed
$x_e = 0$ otherwise

$x_f = 1$ if the elevator is at floor 1
$x_f = 0$ if the elevator is at floor 0

The elevator has three possible actions.

Action 1: Go to floor 1, open door, pause, close door.

Action 2: Go to floor 0, open door, pause, close door.

Action 3: Open door, pause, close door.

As elevator designers, we need to decide under what conditions each action is to be taken. Thus if the elevator is at floor 0 $(x_f=0)$ and the button at floor 1 is pushed $(x_1=1)$, we would like the elevator to rise to floor 1, open the door, pause, and close the door (action 1). (This assumes no one is pushing the floor 0 button or the internal button: $x_0=0$, $x_e=0$.) Similarly, it is necessary to specify every other possible situation and the appropriate action. The following table gives a reasonable specification:

x_0	x_1	x_e	x_f	Action 1	Action 2	Action 3
0	0	0	0	0	0	0
0	0	0	1	0	0	0
0	0	1	0	1	0	0
0	0	1	1	0	1	0
0	1	0	0	1	0	0
0	1	0	1	0	0	1
0	1	1	0	1	0	0
0	1	1	1	0	0	1
1	0	0	0	0	0	1
1	0	0	1	0	1	0
1	0	1	0	0	0	1
1	0	1	1	0	1	0
1	1	0	0	0	0	1
1	1	0	1	0	0	1
1	1	1	0	0	0	1
1	1	1	1	0	0	1

Design a circuit that will light a bulb whenever action 1 is required. Repeat for actions 2 and 3.

5.Find an electric circuit to compute the function

$$f(x_1,x_2,x_3,x_4) = x_1'x_2x_3'x_4 + x_1x_2'x_3'x_4 + x_1x_2x_3x_4'.$$

Relays (B)

But whose fingers are going to push all the switches in the previous section? In an ordinary calculation with a computer, thousands of switches get turned, and we know our own fingers do not do it. The answer is that other electrical circuits turn the switches. Thus it is necessary to study ways in which electricity can be made to turn switches. Two kinds of electrically operated switches will be examined in this book: *relays* which were the basis for early computers and telephone systems in the first half of the twentieth century and *transistors* which were introduced in the 1950s and have been used ever since. Relays will be introduced in this section and transistors will be described in the next chapter. (A third important kind of switch that was used in the 1940s and 1950s was the *vacuum tube*. It will not be discussed here.)

Relays are switches moved by electromagnets. Many children learn in school how to make electromagnets. A piece of insulated wire is wound around a nail many times. When the wire is connected to a battery, the nail becomes magnetic. If the wire is disconnected, most of the magnetism disappears:

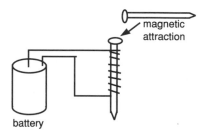

If the magnetic attraction from the electromagnet causes a switch to move, the electric current to the magnet will control the movement of the switch:

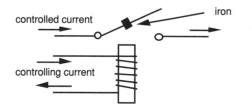

A piece of magnetic material, usually iron, must be attached to the electrical conductor of the switch. If the controlling current flows, it will magnetize the iron core in its coil and pull the movable switch iron downward closing the switch. If the controlling current is turned off, the magnetism disappears, and the switch spring action will return it to the "up" position.

Thus all of the switches in the previous sections could be moved by incoming electrical currents instead of by human hands. For example, you can repeat the circuit for f_3 given above assuming that electrical circuits control the switches. Suppose circuit 1 passes current whenever $x_1 = 1$ and ceases when $x_1 = 0$. Similarly circuits 2 and 3 are controlled by x_2 and x_3. Then f_3 is computed by this circuit:

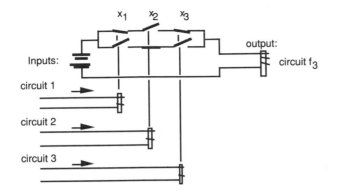

This circuit is shown symbolically. The vertical lines drawn downward from the switches show which switches will be pushed down by which magnets. In practical relays, the magnets are always extremely close to the switches in contrast to what appears here. Also notice that the light bulb has been replaced by the circuit output labelled "circuit f_3." Thus, if this output is connected to another electromagnet, that magnet will come on when $f_3(x_1, x_2, x_3) = 1$ and will turn off otherwise.

This means that the techniques are complete and sufficient to compute arbitrarily complicated functions. You can write down the functional table for any target behavior with any number of binary input variables. The associated circuit can then be constructed with its electrical inputs and outputs. The inputs may be the results of other calculations, and the outputs may feed into many other circuits. Any individual circuit will act like a subroutine to the whole calculation, and a large network of such circuits can perform huge tasks.

Exercises

1. Repeat the action 1 portion of the elevator problem assuming the inputs are provided by electrical currents and the output is a current to activate action 1. Fill in the following diagram to show all wires, relays, and batteries to drive the action 1 circuit.

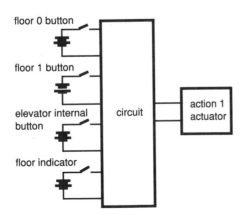

2. Suppose a three-floor elevator system is to be built similar to the one in exercise 4 of the previous section. Develop a complete design using the methodologies of this and previous sections.

Circuits for Storing Information (B)

The circuits of the previous sections have a severe shortcoming: they do not store information. If we put in an input, they will compute an output. If we stop the input, the output will return to its original value. Nothing is "remembered" about the previous input. We need another kind of circuit, one that will store information. This kind of circuit has the property that if you put in an input, the new output will come on, and *it will continue even if the input is removed*. This kind of circuit has memory. It is an essential part of all computers.

This chapter began with the assertion that two kinds of circuits are needed to build computers: circuits that compute functions and circuits that store information. The previous sections showed how to build the first kind of circuit; this section addresses the second.

The kind of information that needs to be stored might be the value of some binary variable such as x_t. This can be done with a relay by assigning the two positions of the switch to the two values for x_t. As an illustration, one could say that the switch "up" position will correspond to $x_t = 0$ and the "down" position to $x_t = 1$:

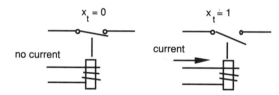

Unfortunately, the relay alone does not store information properly because if $x_t = 1$ and the input current is turned off, the value $x_t = 1$ will not be retained. The spring will pull the switch back to its original $x_t = 0$ position. A proper memory circuit will go to the position $x_t = 1$ if it is so adjusted and remain there even if its input current is turned off. The defining characteristic for memory is that an input sets the circuit state, and the circuit remains in that state even after the input is removed.

Thus an addition is needed so that the relay will stay in the $x_t = 1$ position even if there is no input current. The required improvement can be provided by adding a second relay below it and some wires, as shown:

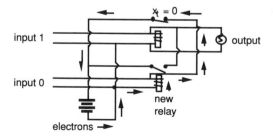

Here an electron current passes from the battery through the lower relay holding it in its "down" position, through the switch contacts of the upper relay, and back to the battery. This is the $x_t=0$ position which is represented with the output light off.

Consider the upper relay. It is turned off (with no current in its coil) in the $x_t=0$ position; its coil can receive current only from input 1 (which we assume is off) or from the lower relay contacts, which are also disconnected. There is no way for electrons to leave the negative side of the battery, find their way through the upper relay coil, and return to the positive side of the battery. In its turned off position, the spring holds the switch x_t in the "up" closed position.

Consider next what happens if current is forced on input 1 through the upper relay coil. That relay will turn on putting the system in the $x_t=1$ state. This will stop the current through the lower relay coil. It will also turn the output light on:

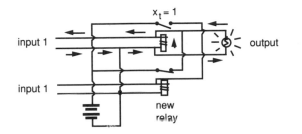

When the lower relay goes off, its contacts become closed, sending battery current through the output and through the upper relay coil. This means the upper relay is receiving current from two sources, the input 1 wires and the battery:

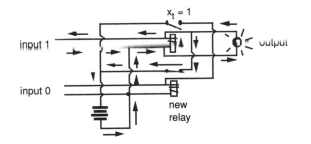

Therefore, if the input 1 current is removed, the circuit will remain in the $x_t=1$ position.

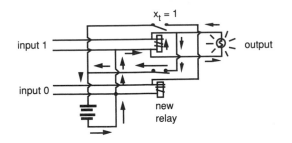

Since the circuit now retains its position at $x_t = 1$ when the input is removed, it is acting as a memory circuit.

If an input current is next applied to the input 0, this will turn the lower relay on again, returning the circuit to the configuration shown first.

In summary, this pair of relays working together can store the value of one binary variable (called x_t here). If current arrives from input 0, the circuit will switch to the $x_t = 0$ position and remain there even if the input is removed. If current arrives at input 1, it will switch to the $x_t = 1$ position and remain there. This type of circuit is called a *flip flop*.

All of these discussions are complicated, and it is helpful to develop a simple notation that captures the essence of the behavior. Our strategy will be to represent the two wires for input 0 with a single line and the two input wires for input 1 with another single line. Similarly, we will represent the two output wires with a single line. Then all of the wires and relays in the flip-flop will be represented by a box labeled with a 0 and a 1:

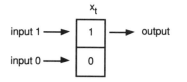

Think of an input signal to the 0 cell as forcing the flip-flop into the 0 state. An input to the 1 cell puts it in the 1 state which also yields a 1 output for x_t. A single flip-flop is said to hold 1 *bit* of information. It is a register that can hold a single binary digit — a 0 or a 1.

In most commercial computers, information is stored in *registers* that are often made up of, say, 16 or 32 such flip-flops. (They are thus called 16-bit or 32-bit registers, respectively.) Then information is coded into strings of 0s and 1s and stored in the flip-flops. This explains why computers use binary arithmetic rather than the decimal arithmetic. For example, the number 18 is expressed in 8 binary digits as 00010010 and can be loaded into an 8-bit register as follows:

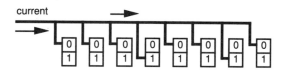

Exercises

1. Cut one of the wires in the flip-flop circuit and then repeat the explanation of its operation. Where does the circuit fail when the wire is omitted?

2. In the circuit given, indicate which relays are on (carrying current in their coils) and which are off in each situation.

   (a) With the circuit in the condition shown.

   (b) After switch A is closed.

   (c) After switch B is closed while keeping A closed.

   (d) After switch B is opened again while keeping A closed.

   (e) After A is also opened.

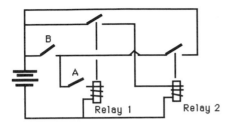

The Binary Number System (B)

Usually digital computer memory is made up of binary storage elements. The flip-flops of the previous section give an example of such elements, and later chapters will give other examples. So information must be coded into binary form. This section shows how nonnegative integers can be coded into binary numbers and manipulated.

We first examine the familiar decimal number system and notice its construction. The right-most digit tells how many 1s are in the number, the second digit tells how many 10s are in the number, and so forth. Thus 327 decimal has 7 1s plus 2 10s plus 3 100s. The binary number system functions similarly except that the sequential digits may only be 0s and 1s and they have this meaning:

Right-most digit	Number of 1s
Second from right-most digit	Number of 2s
Third from right-most digit	Number of 4s
Fourth from right-most digit	Number of 8s
Fifth from right-most digit	Number of 16s

And so forth.

This provides an easy way to convert any binary number to its decimal form. Simply write the binary digits in a column with the left-most digit at the top. Then add up the contributions of all digits as is shown below for the binary number 00010010:

$$0 * 128 = 0$$
$$0 * 64 = 0$$
$$0 * 32 = 0$$
$$1 * 16 = 16$$
$$0 * 8 = 0$$
$$0 * 4 = 0$$
$$1 * 2 = 2$$
$$0 * 1 = 0$$
$$18$$

The decimal form of 00010010 is 18.

A Pascal program to do this calculation is given here:

```
program BinaryToDecimal;
var
    length,base,decimal,bit,i:integer;
begin
writeln('Read the number of binary digits.');
readln(length);
base := 1;
i := 1; {First compute 2 to power (length-1)  putting result into
                                                        base.}
while i < length do
    begin
    base := base * 2;
    i := i + 1;
    end;
decimal := 0;
while base >=1 do {For each binary bit, add its contribution.}
    begin
    writeln('Input next binary digit.');
    readln(bit);
    decimal := decimal + base * bit;
    base := base div 2; {Set base to half of its previous value.}
    end;
writeln('The decimal value is ',decimal);
readln;
end.
```

The conversion from decimal to binary is equally as easy. To convert 18 into 8-bit binary, begin with the left-most binary digit. How many 128s are in 18? None, so the left-most digit is 0. How many 64s are in 18? None. The second digit is 0. Similarly, there are no 32s in 18 so the third digit is 0. How many 16s are in 18. One, so the next digit is 1, and we subtract away the 16 just found: 18-16 = 2. How many 8s are in 2. None, so 0 is next. How many 4s are in 2. None, so 0 is next. How many 2s are in 2. One, so choose the next digit to be 1 and subtract out 2: 2-2 = 0. How many 1s are in 0? None so the last digit is 0.

This calculation is better understood if it is kept in a tabular form as follows:

Number being considered	How many of these?	Resulting digit	
18	128	0	
18	64	0	
18	32	0	
18	16	1	(subtract from number)
2	8	0	

(table continued from previous page)

Number being considered	How many of these?	Resulting digit	
2	4	0	
2	2	1	(subtract from number)
0	1	0	

Once the binary number system is clear, you can study the manipulation of binary numbers. For example, how do you add the binary form of 5 to the binary form of 7? The process is identical to adding decimal numbers. The right-most digits are added and possibly a carry is added to the second from right-most column. Then that column is added, possibly leading to another carry, and so forth.

> 5 decimal is 0101 binary
> 7 decimal is 0111 binary

Adding the right-most column: $1+1 = 10$. (That is, adding 1 in binary to 1 in binary yields 2 in binary.) The result is 0 with a carry of 1:

```
carry         1
5        0 1 0 1
7        0 1 1 1
               0
```

Adding the second from right-most column, $1+0+1 = 10$. The result is 0 with a carry of 1:

```
carry       1 1
5        0 1 0 1
7        0 1 1 1
             0 0
```

Adding the third from right-most column yields $1+1+1 = 11$. The result is 1 with a 1 carry:

```
carry     1 1 1
5        0 1 0 1
7        0 1 1 1
           1 0 0
```

Adding the final column yields 1:

```
carry     1 1 1
5        0 1 0 1
7        0 1 1 1
         1 1 0 0
```

The answer is 1100 binary, which can be converted back to decimal to obtain 12.

Other operations on binary numbers can be carried out similarly to those on decimal numbers, but they need not be discussed further here.

Exercises

1. Convert decimal 77 to 8-bit binary form.

2. Convert decimal 101 to 8-bit binary form.

3. Find the decimal forms of the binary numbers 1010111 and 11110010.

4. Find the sum of the numbers in exercise 3 using binary addition.

5. Write a program that reads a decimal number and prints its binary equivalent.

6. A circuit is to be designed to input the binary form of one of the digits 0 to 9 and to present a digital display of the digits. The digital display is represented below as a seven line segment object where each line segment may be individually illuminated. Thus if the circuit inputs a binary 5, which is 0101, it will display the array shown where the darkened lights are the ones that are illuminated:

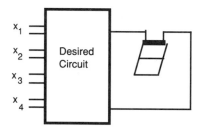

The digital display thus has seven linear light sources, and any of the ten digits can be presented by illuminating the correct ones. The table on the following page shows the digits and their associated displays.

Each of the seven lights of the digital display must have a switching circuit to turn it on for the appropriate inputs. For example, the middle light is always on except for the inputs 0000, 0001, and 0111.

Design a circuit that illuminates the top light of the display for all of the appropriate inputs. Clearly the driver for the complete digital display needs a seven such circuits.

Input in Binary Form

Digit	x_1	x_2	x_3	x_4	Display
0	0	0	0	0	
1	0	0	0	1	
2	0	0	1	0	
3	0	0	1	1	
4	0	1	0	0	
5	0	1	0	1	
6	0	1	1	0	
7	0	1	1	1	
8	1	0	0	0	
9	1	0	0	1	

A Circuit for Adding Numbers (B)

The combination of the function-computing capabilities of the early part of this chapter and the storage circuits of the latter part makes it possible to design any computing system. In order to show these capabilities, we will construct a part of a large digital computer, an integer adder for two registers.

Addition is a column-by-column operation, so we begin by examining a single column. The top register x_c in the column will hold the carry from any earlier calculation. The second and third registers x_1 and x_2 will hold digits to be added. The lowest register x_s will hold the sum of the column addition, and the carry will be transmitted to the next column to the left:

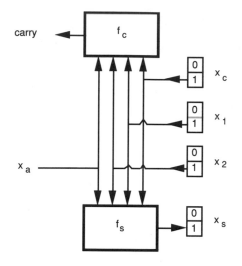

Two circuits are needed — one called f_s to compute the binary sum digit and the carry circuit f_c to compute the carry digit. The inputs to these functions are x_c, x_1, x_2, and a variable called x_a, which is 1 if the addition is to be performed and 0 otherwise. In other words, x_a serves as a switch to turn the adder off and on. The tables for the functions are easy to construct:

x_c	x_1	x_2	x_a	f_c	f_s
*	*	*	0	0	0
0	0	0	1	0	0
0	0	1	1	0	1
0	1	0	1	0	1
0	1	1	1	1	0
1	0	0	1	0	1
1	0	1	1	1	0
1	1	0	1	1	0
1	1	1	1	1	1

An asterisk * stands for any input. The first line of the table indicates that if the adder is turned off, x_a =0, the circuit outputs are f_c =0 and f_s =0. The circuits for f_c and f_s are easy to synthesize using the methods of this chapter.

If registers with many digits are to be added, then many copies of the above single-column adder will do the task as shown here. Two 4-bit registers x_1 and x_2 are to be added, leaving the sum in x_s:

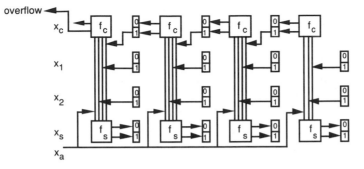

The final unanswered question for this section is how the x_a wire becomes activated. In a typical computer, there may be many instructions to operate on registers x_1 and x_2. There are often instructions to multiply, divide, subtract, move, shift, perform logic such as "and" and "or" operations, and much more. The addition circuitry is only a small part of the whole architecture, and means must be provided to turn it on when it is needed and to leave it inactive otherwise. The usual method of controlling such operations is to provide an *instruction register*, which controls operations in the other registers. An *operation code* is placed in the instruction register, and the action performed is determined by this code. In the current example, we might propose the following operations and their codes:

Operation	Code
Place zeros in registers x_1, x_2, x_s	0001
Copy x_1 into x_2	0010
Copy x_2 into x_1	0011
Add x_1 to x_2 putting the result into x_s	0100
Subtract x_1 from x_2 putting the result into x_s	0101
And so forth.	

The circuitry would be built to activate the appropriate operation depending on the code in the instruction register. For the codes given here, a 4-bit instruction register is needed. The required circuitry can be designed using the same methodology as applied elsewhere in this chapter. For example, the addition command needs to be invoked in the case where the instruction register holds 0100:

Instruction Register code	x_a
0000	0
0001	0
0010	0
0011	0
0100	1
0101	0
etc.	

A larger view of the computer design includes an instruction register with appropriate recognition or decoding circuitry to activate the individual operations. Executing a calculation involves sequentially loading a series of operation codes into this instruction register, which causes the operation to take place. This idea was introduced at the beginning of this chaper, and more details on machine architecture will be provided in later chapters.

Instruction Register

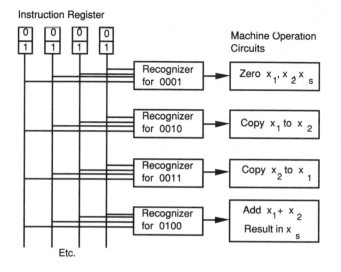

Exercises

1. Find circuits to compute the functions required in the adder, f_c and f_s.

2. Design a circuit similar to the one described in this section that loads into register x_2 a number one larger than the number in x_1. For example, if x_1 holds 1001 and this instruction is executed, the new value of x_2 will be 1010.

3. Design the recognizer (or decoder) for the 0100 instruction in the Instruction Register. If this circuit senses the 0100 code in this register, it outputs a 1. Otherwise, it outputs a 0.

4. If a computer has 100 different instructions, how big must the Instruction Register be?

Summary (B)

This chapter gives the fundamental principles needed to design a computer with relays, and the methodology is adequate to build machines of great complexity and functionality. It is designed to show the nontechnical reader how electric circuitry can be made to compute and introduces many ideas of universal importance in computing. Some of these ideas are the concept of circuit synthesis from table or algebraic specification, the concepts of function computing and information storage circuits and their total adequacy for the construction of any digital computer, the ideas of coding information into binary form and of the binary number system, and the concepts of machine operations, the appropriate circuitry, and the machine codes to drive such hardware.

Computer design is a refined and well-developed discipline, and much is necessarily omitted from this chapter. For example, switching circuit theorists place much emphasis on minimizing the number of switches required to implement a given function, yet this issue is not discussed here. Also many technologies have special characteristics that require new ideas and design methodologies. Many designs presented in this chapter are explained because they are easy to understand; they are not necessarily typical of actual modern machines. The fundamental concepts of the study are correct, but the implementation details are not necessarily representative of modern practice.

Readings

On switching circuit design:

Hill, F. J. and Peterson, G. R., *Introduction to Switching Theory and Logical Design*, Third Edition, John Wiley and Sons, Inc., New York, 1981.
Kohavi, Z., *Switching and Finite Automata*, Second Edition, McGraw-Hill, New York, 1978.
Mano, M. M., *Computer Logic Design*, Prentice-Hall, Englewood Cliffs, New Jersey, 1972.

7

Transistors

In Search of a Better Switch (A)

The last chapter showed how to use relays to build computer circuits. Relays are switches that can be turned off and on by an input electrical current that magnetizes an iron core and moves the switch conductor:

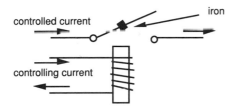

The problem with relays is that they are very large in dimensions, typically measuring most of an inch on each side; they are slow, being able to switch on and off possibly a few dozen times per second; and they require a lot of electrical power. In building computers, we want switches that are smaller than a period on this page, that turn on and off millions of times per second, and that use very little power. The fulfillment of these specifications comes from the transistor, one of the most astounding inventions in history of man and the subject of this chapter.

Transistors and their fabrication into Very Large Scale Integrated circuits (described in the next chapter) are *the* invention that has made modern computing possible. Without the ability to assemble machines with millions of fast switches in physically very small volumes, it would not be possible to build modern computers, from desktop machines to supercomputers. Many of the great accomplishments of modern science—the space program, the computerization of industry, the simulation of economic and physical systems, and more—are made possible by computers built from transistor technologies.

If we wish to build microscopic switches to control currents in tiny wires, it is necessary to understand the microscopic mechanisms that enable current to flow. The ability to comprehend these mechanisms leads to the ability to control them, specifically to turn them off and on. This chapter gives a lay introduction to the physics of electrons, the electron shells in atoms, and the processes of electrical conduction. Then it shows how these entities can be manipulated to build conductors that can be turned off and on.

Electron Shells and Electrical Conduction (B)

The atoms of the elements in nature organize themselves into rather orderly form. The protons and neutrons of the atom are collected together into a tightly bound mass, the *nucleus*. A nesting of *electron shells* surrounds the nucleus, with each sequentially larger shell being at a higher energy. That is, the electrons with the least amount of energy reside in the innermost shell, those with the next level of energy reside in the next level, and so forth. Electrons can exist only at the discrete energy levels of these shells.

fifth energy level, 50 electrons
fourth energy level, 32 electrons
third energy level, 18 electrons
second energy level, 8 electrons
lowest energy level, 2 electrons

nucleus

Each energy level is able to accommodate only a limited number of electrons. Each shell acts like an egg carton with only a limited number of slots for eggs. If there are only a few eggs or none in the carton, additional ones can be put into the available slots. But if all slots are full, no more can be forced in. Elements with only a few electrons will have those electrons in the lowest energy levels (assuming that there is little thermal or other energy to knock them into higher levels). Elements with more electrons will have their lowest levels filled and will have some electrons at higher energy levels. The following table lists a few elements and the electron population at each level:

Element	Atomic Number	Number of electrons at each energy level				
		1	2	3	4	(levels)
hydrogen	1	1				
helium	2	2				
lithium	3	2	1			
beryllium	4	2	2			
boron	5	2	3			
carbon	6	2	4			
nitrogen	7	2	5			

Element	Atomic Number	Number of electrons at each energy level				
		1	2	3	4	(levels)
oxygen	8	2	6			
fluorine	9	2	7			
neon	10	2	8			
sodium	11	2	8	1		
magnesium	12	2	8	2		
aluminum	13	2	8	3		
silicon	14	2	8	4		
phosphorus	15	2	8	5		
-	-	-				
-	-	-				
copper	29	2	8	18	1	

The atomic number gives the number of protons in the nucleus, and each proton has a positive charge equal to the negative charge of one electron. Thus, in order for the atom to be neutral (uncharged), there must be an equal number of protons and electrons.

Another important fact about the elements is that their properties are greatly affected by the number of electrons in the outermost populated shell. It is as if the world sees primarily this outermost shell as the atom is viewed from outside, and the inner characteristics tend to be obscured. The colors of elements, their electrical and heat conduction properties, their chemical bonding properties, and other characteristics seem to be dependent primarily on the number of electrons in the outermost shell. Thus, for example, elements with only one electron in their outermost populated shell, with the exception of hydrogen, tend to be metals, shiny to look at and good conductors of electricity and heat. Elements with completely full outermost shells tend to be poor electrical conductors and chemically inert.

Concerning metals with only one electron in the outermost shell, it appears that that electron is not tightly held to its own atom. In a solid made of such atoms, the outermost electrons are able to flow freely from atom to atom with the only constraint being that each atom must always have some electron in that shell (unless the material is charged electrically with a positive or negative charge). Thus, from the point of view of electrical properties, a solid copper bar looks like a lake of electrons suspended in the array of copper atoms. These electrons are the members of the outer shells of all the atoms, and they flow freely from atom to atom.

Our interest is in the property of electrical conductivity. If we hook our electron pump, a battery, to a metal (for example, a copper bar), then one would think we could move those electrons rather easily:

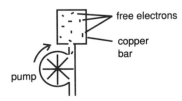

However, in the arrangement shown, little current will flow because as soon as a few electrons are pulled out of the bar, it will become positively charged: there will be more protons in the bar than electrons. Furthermore, the positive charge of those protons will be so strong as to hold on to the remaining electrons and not allow them to be pulled away by the pump.

The way to get a large current to flow through copper is to resupply the missing electrons at one end of the bar while pulling them out of the other end:

The symbolic form of this circuit is as follows:

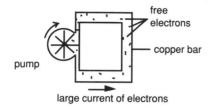

Such a connection leads to a large current and probably the early exhaustion of the battery.

Some other materials of interest are the semiconductors exemplified by silicon and germanium. These elements have four electrons in their outermost shells, and they are not necessarily good conductors. In fact, their atoms tend to arrange themselves into crystalline form—neat arrays with each atom sharing its outermost shell with four neighbors. This form is very stable, with each atom surrounded in its outermost shell by its own four electrons and one donated by each of its four neighbors. These eight electrons, which simultaneously surround each atom and are shared by nearby atoms, are held tightly between the atom cores. Hence no electrons are available for conduction:

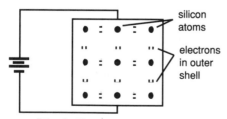

If a battery is applied, you will find that the electrons are bound to their local atoms, and little electrical current can be forced through. However, as will be seen in the next section, the electron structure can be manipulated to effect conduction. This is the breakthrough that makes it possible to build semiconductor switches.

Exercise

1. Study the table giving the electron structures of some elements and hypothesize which elements should have similar properties.

Engineering Conductivity (B)

The reason that semiconductor material in crystalline form does not conduct electricity is that there are no free electrons to move through the crystal. However, it is possible to insert some conduction electrons into the crystal, and this is the next key idea. Examining the chart of elements and their electron shells, we see that the entry after silicon is phosphorus, an element quite similar to silicon but with five electrons in its outermost shell. If we replace one of the silicon atoms in a silicon crystal with phosphorus, that phosphorus atom will fit in very nicely. It will resemble in most respects any other silicon atom and will even share four of its outermost electrons with its neighbors in the same way:

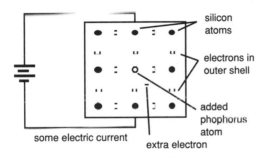

The fifth electron donated by phosphorus has no stable home, and it can be moved by an electromotive force. If phosphorus "impurities" of this kind are included in a silicon crystal even at a very low density, say several per million silicon atoms, enough conductor electrons are available to pass a significant current. The silicon crystal has been made into an electrical conductor by introducing phosphorus impurities. This crystal is called an *n-type* doped material because negative *carriers*, electrons, are added to achieve conductivity.

There are other ways to make crystalline silicon into a conductor. One common way is to introduce boron atoms, which contain only three electrons in the outer shell. These atoms, as with phosphorus, also settle into a silicon crystal much like silicon atoms except their outer shell lacks one electron. The unfilled electron position is called a *hole*, and it also provides a means for electrical conduction. The hole can easily migrate from atom to atom, causing a net movement of charge; a sufficient population of such holes, a few per million atoms, is enough to provide a path for electrical current. This type of crystal is called a *p-type* doped material, and the holes are also called *carriers*:

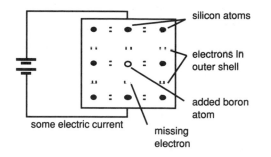

Breaking the balance in a silicon crystal with either too many or too few electrons can produce a conductor. The next step is to combine these two types of materials, n-doped and p-doped, to build a useful device.

Thus p-type silicon can be thought of as material with occasional holes here and there where electrons can fit, and n-type silicon is just the opposite, with extra electrons scattered around. If the two types of crystals are juxtaposed, some of the extra electrons on the n-side will fall across the boundary into holes on the p-side:

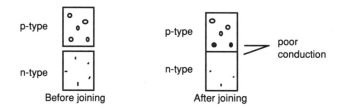

This means that the conducting mechanisms on both sides of the junction, the holes in the p-type material and the free electrons in the n-type material, are gone leaving a nonconducting region. We can test the conductivity by applying a battery as shown and will find little current flow. In fact, the battery will further reduce the effective number of carriers because it will add electrons to the holes at the top and remove electrons from the bottom:

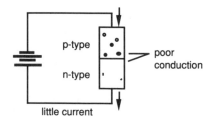

However, if the battery is reversed, a great change occurs. Now the electron carriers in the n-type material that were lost across the boundary will be replaced by the battery action. And the holes in the p-type material will be evacuated continuously again by the battery. A substantial electric current will flow because the carriers throughout both materials are replenished:

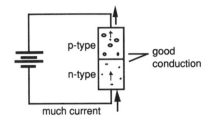

The surprising result is that a *pn-junction*, as this is called, acts like a one-way valve. If the battery action is in a direction to increase the loss of carriers at the junction, little current will flow. But if it acts to replenish the carriers on both sides, much current will flow. Electrons flow easily from the n-material to the p-material. They do not flow easily in the opposite direction.

A one-way electrical valve is called a *diode* and is a useful device in building many kinds of circuits. For example, in the early twentieth century, people found that diodes could be made by carefully inserting a metal probe into a quartz crystal, and this type of diode was a key component in the well known "crystal" radios. What those early experimenters did not know was that in probing around the quartz, they were seeking a region of crystal that had naturally formed with the proper levels of impurities to deliver diode junction behaviors.

But the goal of our current study is not yet achieved. We want to find a way to build a valve that will allow current in one circuit to control current in another circuit. The next section addresses this issue.

Exercise
1. What other elements might be used to provide p and n doping for silicon besides the ones already mentioned?

Transistors (B)

The next step is to build a three-level sandwich with two n-type regions separated by a p-type layer. For reasons that will become apparent, these three layers are called the *collector*, the *base*, and the *emitter*, respectively. Applying a small battery across the base-emitter junction will cause a current to flow as described in the previous section:

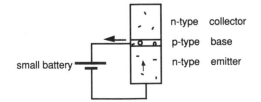

Electrons flow easily from n-type material to p-type material, enabling the current to move.

Next, let us turn off this "base current" and apply a larger battery across the whole device. What current will flow?

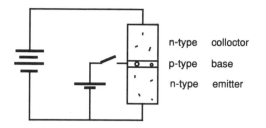

The electrons from the large battery will easily move across the junction from the emitter to the base. But those same electrons will have great difficulty moving from the base to the collector because this is a transition from p-type material to n-type material, so little or no current will flow. The upper junction is a diode that is turned off.

But if the small battery is reconnected and the base current is allowed to flow, many free carriers begin moving through the base-emitter junction again. Some of these carriers will *diffuse* across the base-collector junction and will allow it to pass current. So the base-collector junction, which was previously turned off, has begun to carry current. Furthermore, in a well designed device, most of the carriers flowing from the emitter will drift into the collector so a rather substantial current will flow. In summary, the small battery can produce a substantial current because it is pushing electrons through a pn-junction in the easy direction. This results in an abundance of carriers in the base that can easily drift into the collector region. The movement of electrons into the collector enables a large current to flow in the large battery.

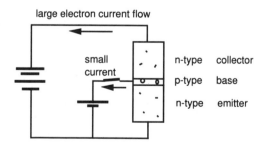

Thus the current flow in the small battery circuit controls the current of the large battery, and the desired switch has been constructed. This three-layer device is called a *transistor*. The transistor and its derivatives provide the millions of switches needed in modern computers. The following section shows how the transistor is used in switching circuits to solve problems of the kind addressed in chapter 6.

Exercise

1. This section has described the construction of a transistor made from a thin p-region sandwiched between two n-regions. This is called an *npn transistor*. You can also construct a *pnp transistor* in the obvious way. Draw a diagram and show how the batteries should be wired to obtain the same valve action described for npn transistors.

Building Computer Circuits with Transistors (C)

We now have seen how to build a switch by specially doping a silicon crystal. Electric current flowing in one circuit can turn on and off the current in another circuit. Our next concern is how to build computer circuits with such transistors.

The following diagram shows a computer circuit based on a transistor and two diodes. It has input circuits, x and y, shown as boxes at the left and one output f on the right. It has two batteries and some small resistors that slow the flow of current near the batteries and the transistor base. We will analyze the circuit and see that it does a useful calculation:

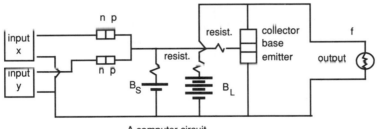

A computer circuit.

We will not be concerned about exactly what is in the input circuits except to note that they are other transistor circuits. Sometimes an input circuit will have a voltage of zero and will act as if it were a simple wire:

Input circuit when x = 0.

At other times, an input circuit will have a positive voltage and will act as a battery:

Input circuit when x = 1.

The analysis that follows will examine the behavior of the circuit assuming each input can have these two behaviors.

Let us begin by assuming that the two inputs are zero: $x = 0$ and $y = 0$. Then the small battery B_S will attempt to force electrons out its lower wire and collect them through its top wire. Those electrons will naturally flow on the easiest path, and they will have an easy route across the bottom to the left, through the input circuits, through the diode junctions in the easy direction from n to p, and back through a small resistor to the battery. Those electrons might also have a tendency to flow across the bottom to the right, through the transistor emitter-base junction, through two resistors, and back. But this route through two resistors and the transistor base is much harder in comparison to the other routes, and little current will flow in the transistor base. Therefore, the transistor will be turned off, and we will redraw the circuit as if the transistor does not exist to emphasize its nonconducting status:

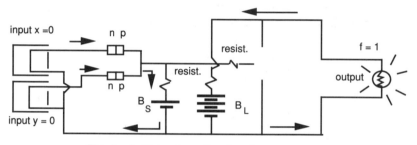

The circuit with inputs x = 0 and y = 0.

Notice the action of the large battery B_L in this situation. It also will attempt to force electrons out its lower wire and collect them at the top. These electrons will also follow the easiest available route, but in this case, with the transistor turned off, they will have only one path, and it is through the output. Therefore, we conclude the light is on and $f = 1$.

Summarizing, we have analyzed the case where $x = 0$ and $y = 0$ and concluded that $f = 1$.

Let us examine another case; assume $x = 1$ and $y = 0$. Here the x input will act like a battery and push the electrons from B_S in the opposite direction from which they were previously flowing. We will assume the x battery is the same size as B_S and will completely stop the current in the x input wire. The diode connected to the x input will stop conducting current, so we will display it as a separated wire. However, the y input will still continue as before, giving the electrons from B_S their easy path. The transistor base will still not carry current, and the transistor will remain off:

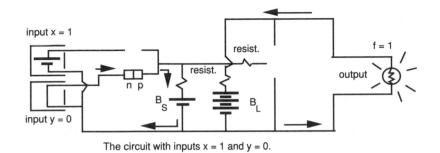

The circuit with inputs x = 1 and y = 0.

The output circuit will flow as before, and the circuit will still light the bulb, returning $f=1$. So, with $x=1$ and $y=0$, the output is still $f=1$. A similar situation occurs if $x=0$ and $y=1$. The result is $f=1$.

The final condition to check is where $x=1$ and $y=1$. Here both inputs will act as batteries and turn off flow through their respective diodes. Now the electrons from B_S will have no easy path to the left. Instead, they will suddenly begin to flow through the only available path. They will flow across the bottom to the right, through the transistor base, and back:

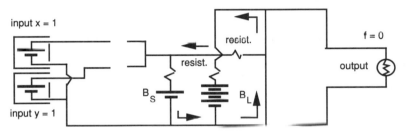

The circuit with inputs x = 1 and y = 1.

Now the transistor will turn on, and current will flow as if it were a straight wire. The electrons from B_L will have an easy path through the transistor, and the output light will go out. The circuit output in this case is zero; $f=0$.

This concludes the analysis of the circuit and enables you to fill in its functional table:

x	y	f
0	0	1
0	1	1
1	0	1
1	1	0

The circuit is called a *nor* circuit, and it is symbolized as follows:

It is the only building block needed for constructing all of the circuits of chapter 6.

   In order to see how useful *nor* circuits can be, we will build some of the circuits from chapter 6. The *not* circuit is constructed by redrawing the diagram of the above circuit with the *y* input wire removed. This new circuit will have the functional table for the *not* function:

x	f
0	1
1	0

It is symbolized as follows:

   Next we can build an *and* circuit for *x* and *y* by attaching a *not* to the output of the *nor* circuit.

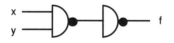

The functional diagram here is the same as for the *nor* circuit except that all outputs of $f = 0$ are changed to $f = 1$ and all outputs of $f = 1$ are changed to $f = 0$.

x	y	f
0	0	0
0	1	0
1	0	0
1	1	1

   Similarly, the *or* function can be computed by this combination:

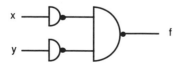

Its analysis is left as an exercise.

We began the section knowing the characteristics of the transistor but not knowing how to use it to build computing circuits. We now have seen how to wire a *nor* circuit that can be used to build all the circuits of the previous chapter and eventually all the circuits of a computer. However, the continuance of this study is properly a domain for electrical engineers and need not be carried further here.

Exercises

1. Show how to build a *not* circuit using a diode, a transistor, three resistors, and large and small batteries. Completely explain the operation of the circuit to prove that it computes the *not* function.

2. Show that the combination of *nor* and *not* circuits shown above for computing the *or* function actually does compute *or* correctly.

3. Suppose the following function is to be computed using the *nor* function. Show, using the simplified *nor* circuit symbol, how to assemble a group of circuits to compute the following function.

x	y	z	f
0	0	0	0
0	0	1	0
0	1	0	0
0	1	1	1
1	0	0	0
1	0	1	0
1	1	0	0
1	1	1	0

4. Repeat exercise 3 for the following function;

x	y	z	f
0	0	0	0
0	0	1	0
0	1	0	0
0	1	1	1
1	0	0	0
1	0	1	0
1	1	0	1
1	1	1	0

Summary (B)

The mechanical switches of chapter 6 can be used to build computers, but assemblies of millions of them would result in a machine of unwieldy proportions, with tremendous energy needs and a rather slow computation time. The prerequisite for building fast and efficient machines is a technology that reduces switch size to millionths of an inch and reduces switch execution time and power proportionally.

This chapter gives the essence of the idea: a semiconductor is used as the switch material, and current flow is turned on and off by controlling the availability of carriers. More specifically, the transistor is a three-layer device where the main circuit current passes through all three layers. No flow will occur unless there is a supply of electrical carriers in the middle layer, the base, and this supply is controlled by the input circuit. Therefore, the input circuit can control the current in the main circuit.

Once the theory of transistors is understood, there still remains the question of how to use them to build practical computing devices. The previous section showed a way to do this, and more techniques appear in the next chapter.

Readings

On semiconductor theory and atomic physics:

Clark, W. A., "From Electron Mobility to Logical Structure: A View of Integrated Circuits," *ACM Computing Surveys* 12, no. 3, September, 1980.

Malmstadt, H. V., Enke, C. G., and Toren, E. C., *Electronics for Scientists*, W. A. Benjamin, New York, 1963.

Microelectronics, A Scientific American Book, W. H. Freeman and Company, San Francisco, California, 1977.

Sproull, R. L., *Modern Physics*, Second Edition, John Wiley, New York, 1964.

Weidner, R. T., and Sells, R. L., *Elementary Modern Physics*, Allyn and Bacon, Boston, Massachusetts, 1960.

8

Very Large Scale Integrated Circuits*

Building Smaller and Faster Computers (A)

The previous chapter discussed the transistor, a device that facilitates the creation of faster, smaller, and more reliable switches, switches that are needed to build faster, smaller, and more reliable computers. However, more than just the development of the transistor was required to meet the needs for new computers. As computing technology developed, the list of applications to which people wished to apply computers grew. Furthermore, these applications required faster and faster computations. For example, the control system for a manned space flight must sometimes make virtually instantaneous decisions. Late decisions could lead to disastrous results. As another example, computer usage in weather prediction requires complex mathematical models. If the computer took 24 hours to perform the model calculations needed to obtain the one-day forecast, it would be too late to be of any use.

The time required for a "computation" in a transistor is the time required for the electric charge to move through the transistor. Thus, an important technique for speeding up computations is to make transistors smaller and pack them closer together, reducing the distance that the electric charge must travel during a computation. The speed at which electric charge can move is no faster than the speed of light, which is about 186,000 miles per second or about 300 million meters per second. Thus, the electrical charge can move through no more than 300 million meters of wire, circuits, and switches in a second. In reality, the electrical charge cannot be transferred through the conducting material at the speed of light. With current technology (late 1980s) the speed with which charge can travel through the conducting material, silicon "doped" with impurities, is only about 1/3000th the speed of light, or 100,000 meters per second. As a concrete example, consider the following. Suppose that we had to be able to do 1000 basic operations per second in a computer. A basic operation might be the addition or comparison of two numbers. Traveling at 1/3000th the speed of light, electric charge can travel over 328 feet in a thousandth of a second. Thus, in performing a basic operation, we can allow the electric charge to move through 328 feet of circuits, switches, and wires per basic operation. Modern computational requirements for computers

* This chapter was written by Ronnie Smith.

require the ability to perform at a much faster rate than 1000 basic operations per second. How far can the electric charge travel per basic operation and still be able to perform the basic operations quickly enough if we need to perform 1 million or 1 billion basic operations in a second? The table shown below gives the values.

Number of Basic Operations in a Second	Distance that Can Be Traveled by Electric Charge per Basic Operations (Speed Is 1/3000th the Speed of Light)
1 thousand	328 feet
1 million	3.9 inches
1 billion	0.004 inches

The values show that there are two ways to make computers faster: develop conducting materials for transistors that allow electric charge to pass through the transistors at a higher rate of speed or reduce the distance that the electric charge must travel during a basic operation. This is accomplished by reducing the size of the transistors and by packing the transistors and circuits closer together. This is the major goal of *very large scale integration* (VLSI).

VLSI is the capability to put thousands of transistors on an *integrated circuit* (IC). An IC consists of a small piece of silicon crystal, called a *chip*, that contains the various electrical components, primarily transistors, and their interconnections. The chip is encased in a metal or plastic package, and connections between ICs are made by external pins. The dimensions of a chip are normally less than 3 or 4 millimeters on each side, but the dimensions of an IC may be on the order of a few inches because of the need for many external pins and the need for heat dissipation from the chip. The flow of current through the transistors produces heat which must escape from the chip. Otherwise, overheating and failure of the transistors and electric circuits may occur. Shown below is an external view of an IC:

When ICs were first developed, very few transistors and thus very few switches could be placed on a chip. In recent years the technology of creating transistors has improved to the point that hundreds of thousands of transistors can be put in a single chip. Thus, among other things, VLSI technology has led to the development of smaller and smaller personal computers that sit on desks. These have much more computing power than the early computers that filled large rooms.

The evolution of VLSI has also resulted in techniques that greatly expedite the design and building of computers. The problem is that the use of transistors to make switches on a one-by-one basis is not a practical way to build a computer that is fast enough to perform desired calculations. One problem is that construction would take too long. Another problem involves the human designer of a computer. The designer would like to be able to think of the computer as a collection of *functional units*. A functional unit is a set of switches that performs a predefined task.

Two examples of functional units are an adder and a comparator. An adder adds numbers together; a comparator compares two numbers to see if they are equal or if one number is greater than the other. A designer's task is greatly eased by considering the computer as a collection of functional units rather than as a collection of switches. If the designer specifies a computer by its functional units, there should be a standard way of combining switches to make each functional unit. If all these switches and the needed connections between them could be manufactured simultaneously, it would reduce the time required to build the computer.

In VLSI technology all the switches and connections can be manufactured simultaneously. With VLSI technology, many functional units can be built or fabricated in just one or a few ICs. Furthermore, on those rare occasions when something goes wrong with some of the electrical components of a computer, repair can be accomplished by testing ICs rather than testing switch by switch. Since there are fewer ICs with VLSI technology, finding and repairing the source of trouble takes less time. Thus, VLSI facilitates quicker repair of computers as well.

VLSI has revolutionized and is still revolutionizing the computer industry. In this chapter we will look at the basic electrical concepts that make VLSI possible, including the introduction of a different type of transistor, the *field-effect* transistor, a current cornerstone of VLSI technology. In addition, we will show the basic steps in the fabrication of transistors used in VLSI and discuss some tools that make VLSI design accessible to even those with only basic knowledge about transistors. Finally, we will examine the outlook for future developments in VLSI.

Exercises

1. You are the vice-president of research and development for a semiconductor company. You must decide between two proposals for special research projects that are trying to develop faster transistors. Proposal 1 will lead to the development of transistors through which electric charge can travel at 250,000 meters/second, where the charge must travel a distance of $2.0 * 10^{-7}$ meters per transistor. Proposal 2 will lead to the development of transistors through which electric charge can travel at 150,000 meters/second, where the charge must travel a distance of $1.5 * 10^{-7}$ meters per transistor. The transistors developed will be used in a circuit requiring 100,000 transistors. Furthermore, the operation defined by the circuit must be performed more than 10.5 million times a second. Which research project will produce faster transistors? Would it achieve the desired speed of execution?

VLSI Technologies (B)

Different scientists have used different technologies to try to develop transistors of smaller and smaller dimensions. The kind of transistor that was described in the previous chapter is known as a *bipolar* transistor. The basic form of all bipolar transistors is the same. However, the ways in which scientists and engineers have tried to construct ICs using bipolar transistors have varied as the effort to put more and more transistors on an IC has progressed.

There is also another type of transistor known as the *field-effect* transistor. This kind of transistor has led to the more popular technologies for building VLSI circuits. This section will describe the field-effect transistor, as well as a technology utilizing field-effect transistors that is growing in popularity as the VLSI technology of choice. This is the *complementary metal oxide semiconductor* (CMOS) technology. ICs built using CMOS technology have many desirable properties. A particular feature that is very desirable is the low power consumption of CMOS ICs. Recall that electric current is required to drive electric circuits. This electric current requires power to be generated. Furthermore, this power usage gives off heat. For example, think about how hot a shining light bulb is. Now consider a computer chip where each of the thousands of transistors gave off as much heat as the one light bulb. When that is multiplied by the many chips needed for a computer, we see that it would be impossible to keep such a machine cool enough to be usable, and the power costs would be prohibitive as well. Thus, we see how important it is that as little power as possible is needed to drive the electric circuits. Electric circuits built using CMOS technology have very low power consumption relative to other VLSI technologies. In this section we will first discuss the limitations of bipolar transistors for VLSI. Then we will introduce field-effect transistors and CMOS technology that uses these transistors to build VLSI circuits.

Packing Bipolar Transistors
The goal of VLSI is to put millions of transistors onto one silicon chip. Recall from chapter 7 that a bipolar transistor looks like the following:

`- -` `- -`	n-type (collector)
`o o`	p-type (base)
`- -` `- -`	n-type (emitter)

where n-type silicon has extra electrons and the p-type silicon has extra holes. How would you go about putting multiple transistors on one silicon chip? A representative way is shown in the following side view of a silicon chip (the sizes are not to scale):

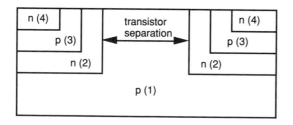

The basic steps are as follows (the numbers in the figure refer to the step number when the corresponding area was made):

1.The entire chip is made into p-type silicon by introducing impurities (boron atoms).

2. Separate n-type islands within the silicon are created for each transistor by introducing phosphorus atoms into portions of the silicon. These islands are known as isolation islands. They become the collectors for each transistor. These isolation islands must be separated by what is called the *transistor separation*. Recall that current flow through a transistor occurs when the flowing electrons diffuse across the base-collector junction. Similarly, if the separation between the collectors of the two transistors is not great enough, a current flow in one of the transistors will diffuse through the separating p-type material into the other transistor, destroying the electrical integrity of the transistors. Thus, we see that there is a minimum distance by which two transistors must be separated.

3.Within these islands p-type silicon is made. This becomes the base.

4.Finally, n-type silicon is introduced within the p-type area. This becomes the emitter.

A more detailed discussion on the creation of specific areas of n and p-type material within a silicon chip is given in the section on fabrication. The problem with packing bipolar transistors is the isolation islands. There must be a sufficient separation of these in order to prevent electric current from leaking between the transistors. This space that must be used for separation is wasted silicon and acts as a fundamental limit on the number of transistors that can be packed on a chip. This limiting factor led to the study of the use of another kind of transistor, the field-effect transistor, for use in building VLSI ICs.

Field-effect Transistors

The development of the field-effect transistor was based on the concept of an electric field. To introduce the idea of an electric field, we note that a property of electrically charged objects is that particles of opposite charge attract and particles of like charge repel. Thus, if we have two electrons, denoted ⊖, in an isolated environment, they will act to repel each other:

(direction of movement) ◀—— ⊖   ⊖ ——▶ (direction of movement)

However, if we have an electron and a positively charged particle, a proton, denoted ⊕, they will act to attract each other:

direction of
movement
⊖—▶   ◀—⊕

It is said that a charged particle is surrounded by an *electric field*, and that any other charged particles that come within that field are affected by the electric force of the field.

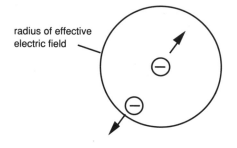

Thus, if an electron is positioned within the electric field of another electron, the force of the electric field of the first electron will repel the second electron (and similarly, the force of the electric field of the second electron will repel the first electron).

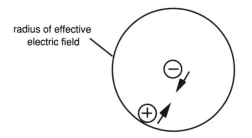

However, if a proton is positioned within the electric field of the electron, the force of the electric field will pull the proton toward the electron:

The major way in which the field-effect transistor differs from a bipolar transistor can best be illustrated by looking at a comparative picture of the two transistors:

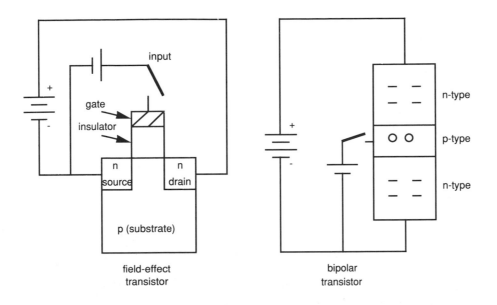

field-effect
transistor

bipolar
transistor

The key difference is that there is not a direct connection between the small battery circuit, or circuit input, and the p-type material in the field-effect transistor. An *insulator*, a type of material that prohibits conduction of current, lies between the gate and the p-type material, the *substrate* of the field-effect transistor. The gate is the conducting material connected to the circuit input, and the substrate is the large body of silicon material in which the transistors are made. If there were a direct connection of the circuit input to the substrate, it would be a bipolar transistor.

A field-effect transistor operates as follows: when the circuit input is off, there is no conduction between the two n-type areas of the transistor—the *source* and the *drain*. However, when the circuit input is on, the gate becomes positively charged. Thus, it is surrounded by an electric field. Although the gate is insulated from the p-type substrate, its electric field exerts a force on the protons at the top of the substrate, acting to push them away from the top of the transistor:

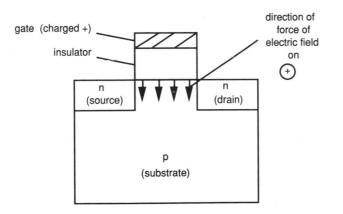

Consequently, at the top of the substrate, an *inversion layer* is created. This inversion layer has a majority of electrons, and as a result current flows from the source to the drain:

```
                    ┌──────────┐
                    │   gate   │
                    ├──────────┤
                    │ insulator│
        ┌───────────┤          ├───────────┐
        │     n     │   ───►   │     n     │
        │  (source) ├ - - - - -┤  (drain)  │
        │           │ current  │           │
        └───────────┤  flow    ├───────────┘
        │                                  │
        │              p                   │
        │          (substrate)             │
        │                                  │
        └──────────────────────────────────┘
```

Thus, again we have the desired circuit, that is, the current flow in the circuit input controls the current of the large battery. This description is meant to illustrate the basic process. Several important technical details have been omitted.

The key advantage of field-effect transistors over bipolar transistors for VLSI is that no isolation islands are needed. Recall that isolation islands were required in order to create multiple transistors on a silicon chip when using bipolar transistors. These islands had to be large enough to contain the base and emitter for the transistor. However, in the field-effect transistor, no isolation islands are needed. The n-type regions for the source and drain can be smaller than the n-type region for the collector in the bipolar transistor, a substantial size reduction. Thus, more field-effect transistors can be put on a silicon chip of fixed size than bipolar transistors. This is illustrated in the following comparative side view:

s - source
d - drain

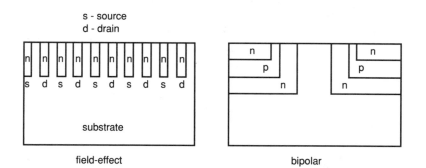

field-effect   bipolar

No isolation islands are needed because there is no direct connection to the substrate material. Thus, the substrate does not become charged everywhere. Only at the inversion layer between the source and the drain of a transistor does a majority of electrons appear. Between the source of one transistor and the drain of the adjacent transistor, there is no inversion layer and hence less danger of electron flow. There still must be a minimum separation distance between the transistors, but it is much smaller than the transistor separation required with bipolar transistors because the danger of current leakage is less.

CMOS Technology

In recent years CMOS technology has grown in usefulness. In CMOS technology both n-mos and p-mos transistors are used on the same silicon chip. We have already seen what an n-mos transistor looks like—the source and drain are n-type material and the substrate is p-type material with the current, consisting of negatively charged particles, flowing from source to drain when the input circuit is on. A p-mos transistor is just the opposite (side view shown below):

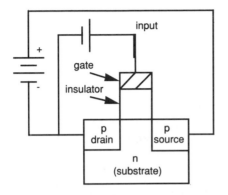

Here the source and drain are p-type material, and the substrate is n-type material. When the input circuit is on, no flow from source to drain occurs. However, when the input circuit is off, the gate is negatively charged. Consequently the electric field created pushes electrons away from the top of the substrate. This creates an inversion layer at the top of the substrate of positively charged particles, causing a flow of negatively charged particles from drain to source because there are excess holes, the positively charged particles, in the inversion layer. The negatively charged particles move from left to right, from hole to hole. This is equivalent to saying the holes move or flow from right to left or from source to drain. Thus, for the p-mos transistor, we consider the flow to be a flow of holes:

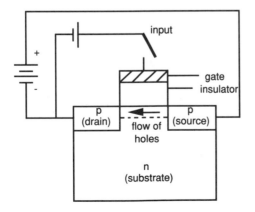

Symbolically, we represent an n-mos transistor as

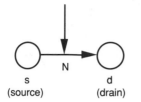

s   d
(source)   (drain)

and a p-mos transistor as

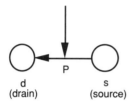

d   s
(drain)   (source)

The main advantages of using CMOS technology are the following:

1. Transistors can be made as small as electrically feasible without affecting the basic properties of performance.

2. Symmetry of design in constructing computer circuits.

3. Low power consumption.

It is beyond the scope of this book to describe the technical characteristics of CMOS technology that allow transistors to be made as small as possible or to describe a technique that can be used to design any type of circuit with CMOS technology. We will discuss why CMOS circuits have low power consumption within the context of the following simple example: the "not" circuit. For an input of 1, the not circuit produces an output of 0, and for an input of 0, the not circuit produces an output of 1. An inverter has the following function table:

x	f(x)
0	1
1	0

Symbolically, the CMOS circuit that computes "not" (called an inverter) looks like the following:

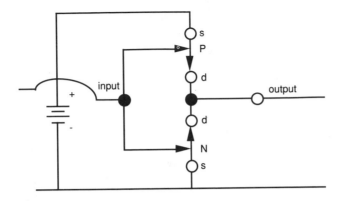

s and d denote source and drain respectively. The top transistor is the p-mos transistor, and the bottom transistor is the n-mos transistor. The circuit behaves in the following manner:

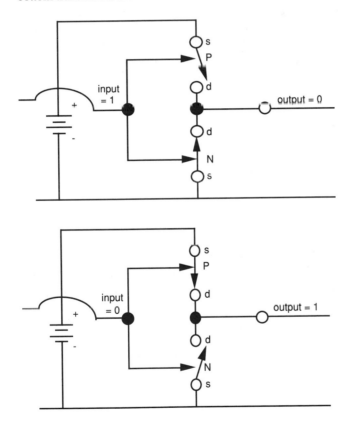

In the top drawing, the input is 1. When the input is 1 (high), there is no charge flow in the p-mos transistor. Thus, the output is connected to the - end of the battery, and the output is 0. The opposite occurs when the input is 0; there is no flow in the n-mos transistor; the output is connected to the + end of the battery; and the output is 1. The important point is the following: *in neither case is there a current flow through the large battery*. Thus, power usage is much less than in a bipolar circuit. The only power consumption is some small leakage that naturally occurs in such circuits, as well as a small flow through the battery when the output changes from 0 to 1 or from 1 to 0. Regardless, this feature of low power consumption, hence less heat, makes CMOS technology very desirable in the construction of VLSI circuits.

A Comparison of Bipolar and Field-Effect Transistors

We first discussed bipolar transistors, the first type of transistor developed. Limitations on packing bipolar transistors led to the development of an alternative transistor, the field-effect transistor, as a technology for packing transistors closer together. We looked at a particular VLSI technology, CMOS technology, that is representative of the VLSI technologies using field-effect transistors and has its own particular advantages. Other types of VLSI technologies that use just n-mos or p-mos transistors have also been developed. We should note that CMOS technology has less of an advantage over bipolar technologies for VLSI applications in terms of space utilization than VLSI technologies that exclusively use n-mos or exclusively use p-mos transistors. This is because of the need for an extra well of n-type material to act as the substrate for the p-mos transistor as shown in the side view below:

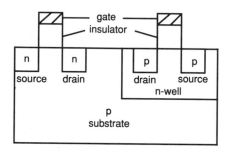

However, the advantages of CMOS—design symmetry, low power consumption, and the ability to make the transistors as small as electrically feasible, compensate for the less efficient space utilization in many applications. Despite the many advantages of field-effect transistors, they are not better than bipolar transistors in all situations. Researchers are still working on making bipolar transistors smaller, for they do have an advantage over field-effect transistors in terms of speed of individual transistors. Thus, we see that both types of transistors are applicable to VLSI. Now we will look at how transistors are actually created or fabricated onto a silicon chip.

Exercises

1. Complete the truth table for the following CMOS circuits:

   (a) circuit 1

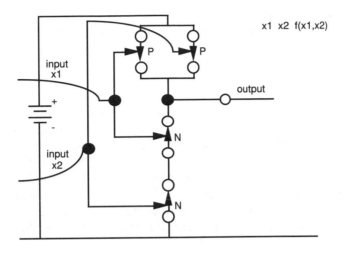

x1 x2 f(x1,x2)

   (b) circuit 2

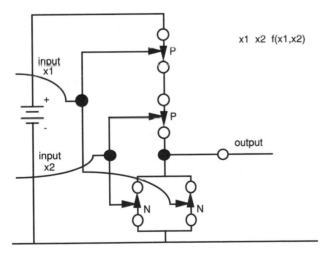

x1 x2 f(x1,x2)

Fabrication (B)

In the previous section we looked at CMOS technology, a technology used in building VLSI circuits. In this section we will discuss *fabrication*—how transistors are actually made. This discussion will focus on one common method of fabrication for field-effect transistors, but it is not the only one that has been developed. First, we will look at the basic materials and techniques used in fabrication. Then we will see how these materials and techniques are used to fabricate transistors.

Basic Materials and Techniques

The material from which transistors are formed is silicon. Silicon has four electrons in its outer shell and acts as a semiconductor. Through the introduction of phosphorus or boron atoms, known as *dopants*, the silicon can be made into a conducting material, either n-doped or p-doped material. Initially, fabrication begins with a wafer or disk of pure silicon from 75 mm to 150 mm (3 to 6 inches) in diameter and less than 1 mm thick. These wafers are cut from single crystal silicon. The silicon wafers are n-doped or p-doped depending on the type of material to be used for the substrate. Fabrication of transistors consists of creating appropriately doped regions within the wafer together with the addition of the necessary insulation and gate material. Several chips can be obtained from each wafer.

In order to get properly functioning transistors, the various regions of doped material must be precisely sized and placed. To be able to do this requires what is called *selective diffusion*. The steps in selective diffusion are the following:

1. Through chemical and physical processes, grow a material on top of the silicon wafer. This material must prevent dopants from penetrating into the silicon underneath it. This material is called the *barrier*.

2. Remove the barrier, but not the underlying silicon, over a precisely defined region where a dopant must be added to the silicon.

3. Subject the silicon to the dopant, creating the desired region in the exposed silicon. The silicon still underneath the barrier will not receive the dopant because of the barrier.

Scientists learned that *silicon dioxide* (SiO_2), could function as a barrier in the fabrication. SiO_2 is grown on top of the silicon wafers by heating silicon wafers in an oxidizing environment such as oxygen or water vapor. The heating causes the silicon to react chemically with the oxygen, creating SiO_2. This causes some of the silicon at the top of the silicon wafer to be changed into SiO_2. However, since SiO_2 has twice the volume of silicon, the effect is that the SiO_2 is grown on top of the silicon, as illustrated below:

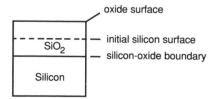

SiO$_2$ can be removed by acid. Thus, SiO$_2$ can be removed selectively by exposing it to acid after coating the portion to remain with an acid-resistant coating. This coating is normally a photosensitive material called *photoresist*. The procedure used is to cover *all* of the SiO$_2$ with photoresist and then remove the photoresist that covers the SiO$_2$ to be eliminated. Photoresist is removed when it is exposed to ultraviolet light. Thus, if we expose only the portion of the photoresist to be removed to the ultraviolet light, the desired portion of the photoresist will be removed, exposing the part of the SiO$_2$ to be removed. Controlling the exposure of the photoresist to ultraviolet light is achieved by covering the photoresist with a glass mask coated with an opaque material that does not allow ultraviolet rays to penetrate. The portion of the glass mask that will cover the photoresist and SiO$_2$ to be removed is not coated with the opaque material, creating a *mask pattern*. When the mask is placed over the silicon wafer and exposed to ultraviolet light, the ultraviolet light penetrates the glass mask through the area of the mask pattern and removes the photoresist underneath it:

ultraviolet light

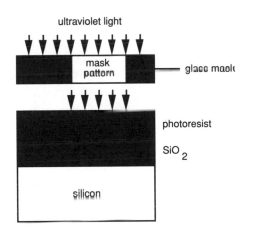

glass mask

photoresist

SiO$_2$

silicon

RESULT

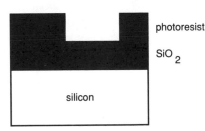

photoresist

SiO$_2$

silicon

Now the desired area of SiO$_2$ can be removed by acid, with the remaining photoresist protecting the rest of the SiO$_2$. This is known as the *etching process*. Then the remainder of the photoresist can be removed, yielding the desired exposure of the original silicon, as shown below:

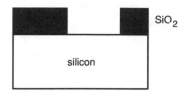

A three-dimensional view of this process of selective removal is shown below:

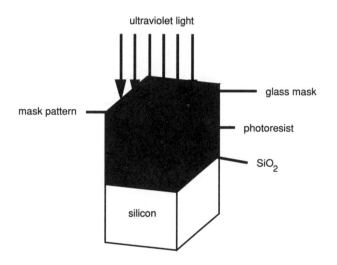

RESULT AFTER EXPOSURE TO ULTRAVIOLET LIGHT

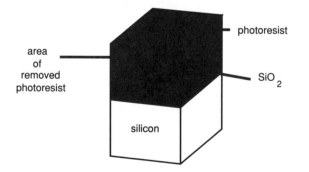

RESULT AFTER PERFORMING SELECTIVE REMOVAL

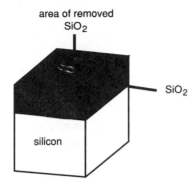

From this we see that the key step in the fabrication of a transistor is the creation of the mask pattern on the glass mask. These patterns define regions of the silicon wafer that will be doped with the appropriate material in order to create the different components of the transistor.

One other basic material used in the fabrication process is *polysilicon*, silicon that is not organized in crystalline form. It is created when silicon is deposited on SiO_2. Polysilicon is the material out of which the *gate* of a CMOS transistor is made. Recall that the gate is connected to the input of the transistor. The biggest advantage to using polysilicon for the gate is that it can be used as a mask that allows for more precise definition of the source and the drain of the transistor, as we shall see.

Fabrication Example

We assume that the silicon wafer was initially doped with p-type material and that the SiO_2 that covered the silicon region where the transistor will go has been etched away:

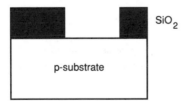

The next step is to grow another thin layer of SiO_2 on top of the silicon where the transistor will be placed. This will be called the *thin oxide*. This will ultimately be the insulator between the gate and the p-type substrate. The original layer of SiO_2 is called the *field oxide*:

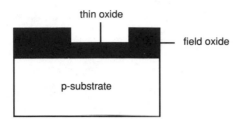

After the thin oxide is added, the wafer is covered by polysilicon. By a process similar to the etching process that removed the SiO_2, the polysilicon not needed is etched away, leaving the gate:

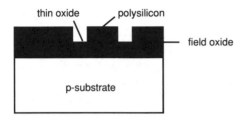

This is followed by the etching away of the thin oxide except for that covered and protected by the gate:

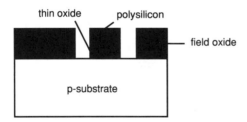

Now the silicon wafer can be exposed to the dopant, creating the source and drain. The polysilicon gate masks the substrate underneath it, ensuring that the source and drain are separate regions:

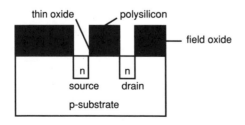

Completing fabrication of the transistor requires that metal contacts be added to the gate, source, drain, and substrate. These are used for the necessary electrical connections to the transistor. The method by which the metal and metal contacts are added to the transistor is similar to the method used to create the various regions of the transistor.

Exercise

1. Recall the use of glass masks to remove a selected portion of photoresist in order to remove a selected portion of SiO_2. Starting from

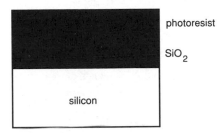

what would be the glass mask required to achieve the following removals of photoresist (and consequently SiO_2)?

(a)

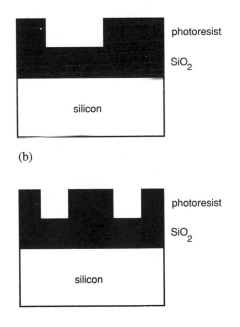

(b)

Design (C)

In previous sections we have presented a representative technology used for VLSI circuits and discussed how transistors using this technology can be fabricated. Now we turn to the question of design. How can we use this technology to build circuits for computers? In chapter 6 we looked at the basic issues of how to define circuits for computing primitive functions, the most important of which are "and," "or," and "not." Chapter 7 showed how to use transistors to compute these functions. However, the question remains, how do we go from pencil and paper drawings to the creation of transistors that can compute these functions? Other interesting questions include the following:

1.Recall that one of the characteristics of a bipolar transistor is that a small current can be used to drive a large current. How can we do the same thing with field-effect transistors?

2.There is a delay from the time the input signal reaches the gate to the time when current starts to flow in the transistor. How do we make the delay as small as possible (and consequently make the computer as fast as possible)?

3.Recall that a goal of VLSI technology is to pack as much computing power into as small a space as possible. How small can these transistors be made without affecting their reliability?

The goal of this section is to answer these questions. First, we will discuss the answers to these questions. The factors addressed in these questions are called *design parameters*. That is, current gain, transistor delay, and transistor size can be varied according to the relative sizes of certain components of the transistor. This allows designers to control performance characteristics of the transistors and consequently control performance characteristics of the associated circuit. The second part of this section will deal with the crucial issue of how designers can provide specifications for transistors and circuits that can be translated into directions for fabrication. Large computers require millions of circuits. If it took 10 minutes to design each of one million circuits, it would require one person nearly 20 years to design all these circuits (without stopping). Among the great developments within VLSI technology are the methods developed for designing transistors for VLSI fabrication. We shall examine this more carefully in the second part of this section.

Design Parameters

In order to understand how the relative sizes of transistor components can affect various characteristics of the transistor, we need to look at a top view of a transistor:

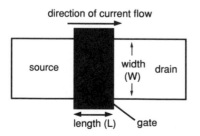

In this picture are shown two key dimensions of transistor design. The first is the *length* (L) of the channel. Recall that the region under the gate is the substrate material that electrically separates the source and drain. Under the gate is created the inversion layer that causes current flow when the appropriate input signal reaches the gate (1 for an n-mos transistor, 0 for a p-mos transistor). This area in the substrate where the inversion layer is created and the current flows is called the *channel*. Thus, the length is the distance the current must flow through the channel. The *width* (W) of the channel is given in the picture by the vertical distance from the bottom to the top of the region containing the source and drain. The gate overhangs the transistor to provide protection against short circuits. Thus, the width of the channel is always slightly less than the dimension of the gate in the same direction. However, we see that the length and width of the channel are closely related to the length and width of the gate.

Now we are ready to show how the length and width of the channel affect current gain and delay. It is far beyond the scope of this book to provide all of the technical explanation about the cause of these effects, but an intuitive discussion can be provided.

Current Gain

For current gain we have the following picture:

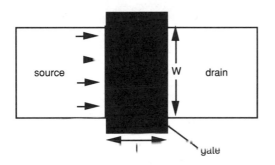

Current gain is caused when a larger current flows from the source to the drain than originally flowed into the source. This is analogous to the additional flow from the emitter to the collector in a bipolar transistor. Current gain is desirable because the output of one circuit may be used as an input to several other circuits. The extra current is needed to be able to provide the input to many circuits. When the width of the channel is greater, more area is available for current to flow from source to drain. When the channel length is smaller, the current must travel less distance from source to drain; more current will flow completely through the channel into the drain. We see that the amount of current gain is proportional to width over length (*W/L*). This can be viewed from the picture in the following way. Highlighted within the picture are fixed-size rectangles. Each rectangle gives the same amount of current gain. Thus, when the ratio *W/L* increases, the number of rectangles in the channel increases, and the gain increases:

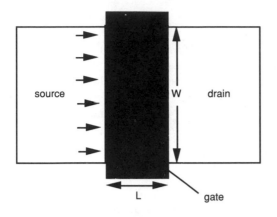

Similarly, when *W/L* decreases, the number of rectangles in the channel decreases, and the gain decreases:

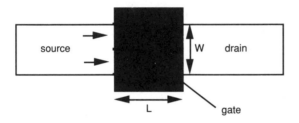

Transistor Delay

Transistor delay is the time the current flow takes to reach from source to drain after the triggering input signal has been received. It is a function of two electrical properties of materials, *resistance* and *capacitance*.

Resistance is a property of all materials. As its name implies, it is the extent to which a current flow is resisted in a material. As resistance to current flow increases, the delay increases. The primary resistance in a transistor is the channel resistance. The key parameters in determining this resistance are the same as for current gain, channel width (*W*) and length (*L*). For reference we again show a simple top-level view of a transistor. Recall that the channel is under the gate:

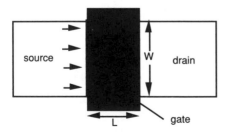

When the length increases, the distance the current must travel through the channel increases. Thus, the resistance increases. When the width increases, more room is available for current to flow in the channel. Consequently, the resistance decreases. Thus, resistance is proportional to the ratio of the length to the width (L/W). An equivalent viewpoint is that resistance is inversely proportional to W/L. When W increases while L is fixed, resistance decreases and delay reduces. We have also seen that when W increases while L is fixed, current gain increases. Thus, it would seem that if we make the width of the transistor grow without bound, we will have transistors with virtually no delay and infinite current gain.

This is not practical, however, and there are mitigating factors. One problem is that we want small transistors so that we can have smaller computers that use less power and produce less heat. The other problem is that resistance is not the only contributing factor to delay. Another major factor is capacitance, the ability of a material to hold an electric charge. For a transistor, the main source of capacitance is the gate. An increase in the capacitance of the gate causes an increase in transistor delay because the electric charge that the gate holds due to its capacitance slows the flow of the current through the channel. The capacitance of a material is proportional to the area of the material. In the case of the gate, $area = L * W$. Thus, we see that while increasing W with L fixed reduces resistance, it also increases the area of the gate, increasing its capacitance. The effect on transistor delay depends on the magnitude of the change and the kind of material used for the gate and channel. Thus, there is a trade-off on the dimensions of the channel. Relative to a fixed L, increasing W reduces resistance but increases capacitance. The sizing of transistors must be made with this consideration in mind. Furthermore, there are other factors that affect transistor delay, although resistance and capacitance are the most important. Now we will look more carefully at the issue of optimal transistor size.

Transistor Sizing

We have just seen how the size dimensions of the transistor channel and the gate can have contradictory effects on the performance characteristics of the transistor. Increasing channel width while leaving channel length fixed increases current gain but has an unknown effect on transistor delay because it decreases resistance while increasing capacitance. Furthermore, it also increases transistor size. However, if we reduce the channel length in the same proportion as we increase the channel width, then the area of the gate over the channel will remain constant and capacitance will not increase. For example, if the channel width is increased by a factor of 2, and channel length is reduced by a factor of 2, the area remains the same:

$$New\ Area = (2*W)*(L/2) = L*W = Original\ Area$$

However, the ratio of width to length increases (to $4 * W/L$ from W/L) and thus resistance decreases. Therefore, we have both an increase in current gain and a reduction in transistor delay. Unfortunately, there is a limit to improving transistor performance by increasing channel width and reducing channel length by the same proportions. The constraining feature is that there is a limit to how small the channel length can be made. The channel separates the source from the drain, and the source and drain must be separated by a minimal distance to prevent a short circuit.

That is, if the source and drain are too close together, current will travel from the source to the drain regardless of the input on the gate, rendering the transistor useless.

For the CMOS technology that we have studied, it turns out that making transistors as small as possible is as desirable as any other choice of sizing. In particular, it offers the potential for packing the most computing power into the smallest area. The limiting factors in reducing the size of transistors include the need for protection against short circuits and that as the dimensions get smaller, certain factors that affect performance and can be ignored in larger transistors must be taken into consideration in smaller transistors. A discussion of all these factors is beyond the technical scope of the chapter. Another important limiting factor is the precision of the fabrication process. Tolerances in the placing of the various components of a transistor must be allowed. The overhang of the gate over the channel is an example of such a tolerance. Recall that the gate acts as a mask over the channel when the dopants are added to create the source and drain. This overhang provides a necessary safety margin to ensure that the channel is protected from the dopants. This overhang also increases the size of a transistor. As precision in fabrication improves, tolerances can be reduced, and transistor sizes can be reduced.

Current technology can produce transistors whose sizes are on the order of *microns*. A micron is one one-millionth of a meter (1 million microns = 1 meter). To get an idea of how small this is, consider the following: With current technology, transistors can be made that occupy less than 100 square microns of area. Let us assume that we have transistors that occupy 100 square microns. This includes sufficient area to isolate the transistors electrically. In the following block, 1 square inch of area,

over 6 million of these transistors can be placed! In a real circuit, fewer transistors could be placed in this block because of the room required for wires to make the various connections among the circuits of which the transistors are a part, but even in a very inefficient case, there would still be room for over a half-million transistors together with all the necessary interconnections. The actual number of transistors that can be placed in a block with an area of 1 square inch depends on the type of circuit and the interconnections required between transistors, as well as the precision of fabrication and the technology used. This provides a dramatic example of the extent to which VLSI technology has led to the packing of more and more transistors, the building block of computers, into smaller and smaller spaces.

Design Styles

We are now ready to discuss the process by which transistors are actually designed. The improvement in design techniques for VLSI technology has been as important to the growth in the use of VLSI circuits as have been improvements in the technologies and the fabrication techniques. In this section we will discuss the evolution of design techniques that has caused the accessibility of VLSI design for all areas of computer science.

Mask Layout

The most important fact to remember is that *all design techniques must allow for the design specification to be translatable into the masks needed for fabrication.* Recall from our discussion of fabrication that masks are used at each step of the process to specify the various components of the transistor. Thus, from a design there must be a way to obtain the masks needed for fabricating the transistor. Originally design was performed by manual specification of mask sizes. This was an incredibly time-consuming and error-prone method. One particularly significant problem was that it was hard to ensure that the masks specified would produce the desired circuit without actually fabricating the circuit and testing to see if it worked, a cost-prohibitive operation, especially if the process was unreliable. Another problem was that these masks could become obsolete when improvements in the technology allowed for smaller transistors and consequently a change in the masks and mask sizes that were needed. Still another concern was the need to remember all the rules pertaining to minimal size of components and minimal separation of components. These also changed as technologies and fabrication precision improved.

Symbolic Layouts

Designers needed a method of design that allowed them to specify what was needed in the way that they originally thought about the problem. Designers do not think about masks; they think about circuits. The idea of *symbolic layouts* allows designers to specify their designs in terms of circuits. An example of a symbolic layout is the following symbolic layout of a CMOS inverter (recall the symbolic CMOS inverter circuit in the section on CMOS technology):

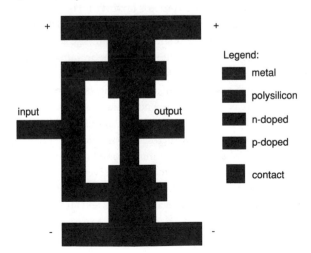

This layout assumes that the underlying p-type substrate and the n-type well within it that contains the p-mos transistor are automatically provided. Each of the different types of material is designated by a different symbol. On color terminals, the materials are represented by different colors. Similarly, the region where two materials overlap is normally represented by a different symbol or color representing the combination of the materials. Designers can specify circuit designs using these symbolic methods. The designers control the size of the transistors by the size of the various materials in their graphic design. These graphic displays can be represented in the computer and stored as files that can be processed by programs that can determine automatically the sequence of masks needed to fabricate the circuit.

By symbolically designing the circuit, designers avoid the problem of not being able to validate that the circuit performs the proper computation without first fabricating the circuit. This can be done by computer programs that can simulate the performance of a circuit based on the symbolic layout. Designers can run a simulation on the symbolic layout to see if the fabricated chip will work. Of course, fabricated chips might still not perform as desired, but the probability of their correct performance increases greatly. By another key idea, these designs avoid the problem of becoming obsolete as technologies and fabrication techniques improve. This idea is the usage of an *abstract unit of measure*. Instead of letting a particular distance in a symbolic layout represent a fixed distance in a real unit of measure, say 75 microns, a particular distance will represent a fixed distance in an abstract unit of measure called *lambda*(λ). Each different technology will then specify the real distance that 1λ unit corresponds to in their technology. Thus, a design can remain valid as technologies improve and transistor sizes get smaller. For example, ten years ago, a length of 1λ might have equaled 750 microns for a technology, but today for an improved version of that technology, $1\lambda = 3$ microns. The same design can be used for fabricating a circuit in either technology. Furthermore, designers do not have to worry about the changing electrical constraints on minimal sizes of components or on minimal separations between components. With the advent of the abstract unit of measure came design rules that gave these electrical constraints also in this abstract unit. For example, the minimum length of a gate (and hence the minimal separation of the source and drain) would be 2λ. Thus, a design that satisfies all constraints will still satisfy the constraints even when the technology changes or the fabrication process improves. The developers of new or improved technologies can define the appropriate equality between 1λ and the real unit of measure of their technology. Symbolic layouts and the related idea of an abstract unit of measurement have revolutionized computer design. Graduate students taking an introductory class in VLSI can design adders in a couple of days after only a few weeks of class.

Another consequence of symbolic layouts and the associated descriptive files that represent these layouts is the idea of *standard cells*. Standard cells define the fundamental circuits that are used as the building blocks of the larger units of the computer. For example, circuits to compute the primitive functions of "and," "or," and "not" could be defined symbolically and the information saved in files. These cells could then be included in more complicated circuits, allowing designers to use these circuits without having to define them themselves. This can be done to build standard layouts for more and more complicated circuits such as adders and comparators. Designers can then take these predefined adders and comparators and all the many other functional units required and put them together to design a computer. Standard cells provide another revolutionary method for faster, more reliable design.

In this discussion of design we have ignored many issues, the most important of which is a trade-off associated with using standard cells and more abstract approaches to design than using mask layouts. As design gets more and more abstract, the designs tend to waste more space on the silicon, and fewer transistors can be put on the chip. Also, by using such ideas as standard cells, one gives up the goal of optimizing the performance of every transistor. However, the performance of circuits designed with these more abstract techniques is still excellent, and the reduction in the time it takes to have a fabricated circuit from the moment design begins is substantial. The idea of a symbolic layout has provided the impetus for the explosion in the use of VLSI circuits.

Exercise

1. This exercise is designed to show how many flip-flops can be placed on a silicon chip with an area of 1 square inch, as well as to show the usefulness of the symbolic unit of measure λ. The following is a top view of a transistor with the minimum size requirements indicated:

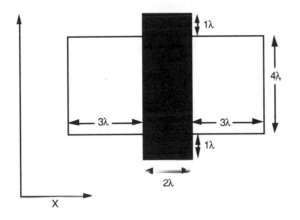

Furthermore, there must be a minimal separation of 4λ between transistors in both the x and y direction for electrical integrity and for wire connections.

Six transistors are required in CMOS technology to build one flip-flop. If in our technology, $1\lambda = 1.5$ microns (a reasonable value for late 1980s technology), how many flip-flops can be placed on a silicon chip with surface area of 1 square inch (recall 1 micron = 1 one-millionth of a meter)?

What if $1\lambda = 1$ micron? or $1\lambda = 0.5$ microns?

Future Prospects for VLSI (A)

VLSI technology has revolutionized the design and fabrication of electric circuits, the building blocks for computers. Many researchers feel that we have only scratched the surface of the possible advances in technology and fabrication. For example, researchers are investigating the possible use of a new material, gallium arsenide, instead of silicon, as the base material for transistors. Transistors fabricated in gallium arsenide are much faster than transistors fabricated in silicon but are still much more expensive. Researchers are also investigating the use of lasers in the fabrication process. It is predicted that by 1995 VLSI chips containing 100 million memory cells will be possible and that VLSI chips that compute some type of logical function will be able to contain 10 million transistors. The potential future reductions in transistor size may lead to desk-top computers with the computing power of present-day machines of much greater size by the turn of the century.

Another realm where huge advances are still possible is in the area of design. Symbolic layouts have greatly facilitated circuit design, but not all designers are just designing circuits. The ability to perform VLSI design at an even higher level would lead to an even greater usage of VLSI technology in constructing ICs for all types of applications. People interested in designing computers or computer chips for specific applications are interested in a higher level of detail than the behavior of a circuit. For example, the designers of a computerized air traffic controller do not think about circuits. They think about planes, velocities, locations, and priorities. The designers of an air traffic controller would like to be able to specify the computations required in terms of planes, velocities, locations, and priorities rather than in terms of circuits and have a computer program automatically translate their specification into circuits and ultimately the mask specifications needed for the fabrication process. Research into the development of languages that could be used to specify the computations of a system that could be automatically translated into the fabrication of computer chips is still in an early stage. The biggest problem is the design of automatic methods for placing transistors onto a silicon chip that are not largely wasteful of space. If this and other problems with these specification languages could be surmounted, there would be an even greater explosion in the usage of VLSI technology than has been seen yet. It would then be almost as easy to design a special computer chip for a particular application as it would be to write a program for the application on a general-purpose computer. For applications where speed is critical, the general-purpose computer would become obsolete.

In summary, VLSI technology is a great idea that is revolutionizing the computer industry and computer science and will continue to do so for many years.

Readings

Frensley, W.R.,"Gallium Arsenide Transistors," *Scientific American*.257(2), August 1987, 80–87.

Mead, C. and Conway L., *Introduction to VLSI Systems*, Addison-Wesley, Reading, Massachusetts, 1980.

Meindl, J.D., "Chips for Advanced Computing," *Scientific American* 257(4), October 1987, 78–88.

Weste, N.H.E. and Eshragian, K., *Principles of CMOS VLSI Design*, Addison-Wesley, Reading, Massachusetts, 1985.

9

Machine Architecture

Let Us Build a Computer (A)

We now have learned how to build simple circuits that compute functions and store information. The next task is to study the assembly of such circuits into a computer.

Most computer architectures that have been built up to the present day have two major subparts, the machine *central processing unit (CPU)* and the *memory*. The CPU executes the calculations and thus has *computational registers* wired to do the arithmetic operations and other manipulations on data. It contains the Instruction Register introduced in chapter 6, and its associated decoding circuitry. It contains all the mechanisms for retrieving instructions to be executed, sequencing them through the Instruction Register, and getting the individual instructions executed.

The memory has no ability to compute anything. It is simply a huge array of very low-cost registers where information can be stored when needed. The registers are numbered, usually from 0 to *n*, where each location may hold perhaps 8, 16, or some other number of bits, and the values of *n* may be large, say, from 32,767 to many millions.

The central processor needs two kinds of information that are stored in the memory: its own instructions and the data that it works on. Its instructions are stored in the memory as a sequence of binary coded machine instructions, and they are sequentially brought into the central processor for execution. The resulting computations utilize the other kind of information stored in the memory, the data. These data contain the character sequences and the numbers that the user wants to manipulate to obtain the desired answers.

A typical instruction for the machine in this chapter is *COPY AX,X* as will be described in a later section. When such an instruction is stored in the memory or in a register, it is usually coded as a binary number such as 0010111000010100. However, we will not use these binary codes in the discussions but will write *COPY AX,X* * where the surrounding asterisks indicate that the instruction has been translated into binary code. That is, *COPY AX,X* is an instruction to the machine, and **COPY AX,X ** represents its binary code:

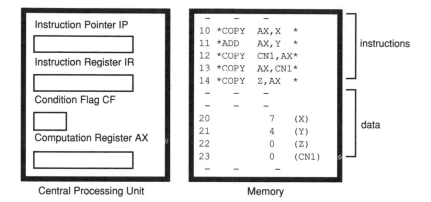

Instruction Pointer IP	10 *COPY AX,X *
	11 *ADD AX,Y *
Instruction Register IR	12 *COPY CN1,AX*
	13 *COPY AX,CN1*
Condition Flag CF	14 *COPY Z,AX *

CPU box contains: Instruction Pointer IP, Instruction Register IR, Condition Flag CF, Computation Register AX.

Memory contains instructions:
```
-   -    -
10  *COPY  AX,X   *
11  *ADD   AX,Y   *
12  *COPY  CN1,AX*
13  *COPY  AX,CN1*
14  *COPY  Z,AX   *
-   -    -
-   -    -
20         7    (X)
21         4    (Y)
22         0    (Z)
23         0    (CN1)
-   -    -
```
instructions (10–14), data (20–23).

Central Processing Unit   Memory

The computation involves continuously bringing into the CPU data items, which are then combined and modified according to the instructions and returned to the memory.

A huge variety of digital machines exists in today's world, and it is not important to enumerate them here. There are machines with only one computational register in the CPU and a few instructions. There are also machines with dozens of such registers and hundreds of instructions. An example architecture is the CPU for the IBM Personal Computer, which uses the Intel 8088 VLSI chip as its central processor. It has 12 registers and 92 instructions, which do a variety of arithmetic, logical, and character operations. This processor performs primitive internal operations at the rate of one every 210 nanoseconds (.000000210 second). Many basic instructions require two such cycles, and a few complex instructions require many such cycles. For example, 16-bit division requires 206 cycles.

Another way of varying the architecture is to have several copies of the CPU-memory configuration shown above. This is called a *parallel architecture*, and it enables the programmer to divide a computation into several different parts, which can all be worked on simultaneously. Parallel architectures and their uses are described in chapter 12.

Regardless of the details, most digital computers use the same fundamental mechanisms, and our understanding will be sufficient if we can comprehend the workings of only a very simple machine. The machine described here will have only one register for manipulating data and only 12 instructions. It is called the *P88 Machine*, which stands for "part of an Intel 8088." Its instructions are nearly identical to some of the instructions of the Intel 8088 for the sake of achieving some degree of realism. A programmer for a real Intel 8088 needs to learn to use 12 computational registers instead of one and 92 instructions instead of 12.

An Example Architecture: the P88 Machine (B)

The P88 computer contains the components shown below: an Instruction Pointer Register IP, an Instruction Register IR, a Condition Flag CF, the Computational Register AX, and the memory.

The functioning of the computer proceeds by repeatedly executing the following two steps:

Repeat without end:

1. (Fetch) Find the instruction in memory at the address given by IP and put that instruction into IR. Increment IP to give the address of the next instruction.

2. (Execute) Execute the instruction in IR.

These two steps comprise what is called the fetch-execute cycle, and they can best be understood by going over an illustration. Suppose that the machine instruction codes

```
*COPY  AX,X    *
*ADD   AX,Y    *
*COPY  CN1,AX*
*COPY  AX,CN1*
*COPY  Z,AX    *
```

reside in the memory at locations 10 through 14 and that the machine is about to execute these codes. Then the address (10) of the first such code *COPY AX,X* will be in IP:

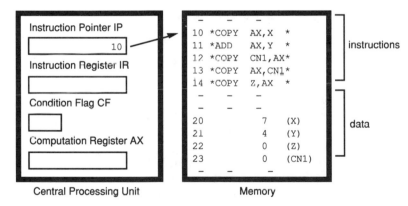

The first step of the fetch-execute cycle involves loading IR from the location given by IP. Then IP is incremented to give the address of the next instruction:

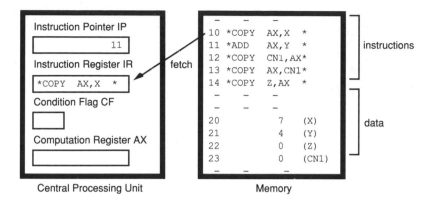

The second step is the execute cycle, which carries out the instruction in the Instruction Register IR. In this case, *COPY AX,X * is executed. As is explained below, the contents of memory location *X* will be copied into the register *AX* . The circuitry doing this task is that explained in chapter 6, the instruction decoding and execution (D&E) circuits:

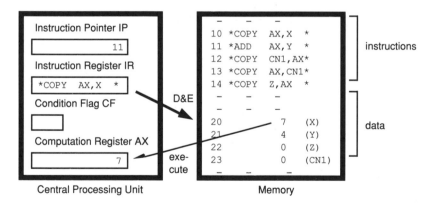

The fetch-execute cycle continues without stopping. On the next cycle, the instruction is fetched from location 11 in the memory. This is an add instruction, *ADD AX,Y *. It adds the contents of memory location *Y* to the contents of register *AX* and leaves the result in register *AX* . Here is the result of this fetch and execute:

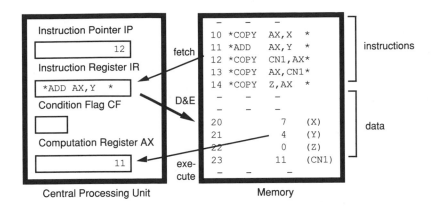

Another pass through the fetch-execute results in the third instruction's being executed. This instruction causes the contents of the A*X* register to be copied into the memory location *CN1*:

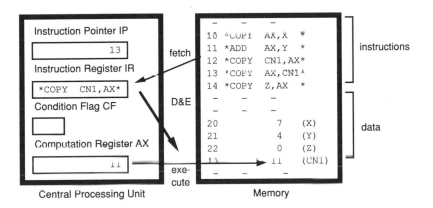

Thus the machine sequentially loads the string of commands in memory and carries them out. Occasionally a "jump" instruction will load a new value into IP, which begins a new sequence of commands. For example, in the above case, it is possible that some instruction would cause 10 to be loaded into IP again and result in another execution of this sequence.

The fundamental operation of every digital computer is built around the fetch-execute cycle as described here. This is, in fact, the only thing that modern computers are designed to do—to fetch instructions and execute them. There is no need to be impressed with the intelligence of any modern computer, no matter how large, with its blinking lights, complex displays, and many workers huddled over their terminals. *The giant machine is doing nothing more than fetching instructions and executing them. It never has in the past, cannot now, and never in the future will be able to do more or less than this!*

Exercises

1. Trace the execution of the final two instructions in the above example—those instructions in memory locations 13 and 14. Show every detail of the fetch-execute cycle.

2. In the example above, the instruction pointer IP increases one on each cycle and will apparently soon reach 20. An error will occur if it does. Explain the nature of the error. What instruction must be included after location 14 but before location 20 to avoid this error?

Programming the P88 Machine (B)

The P88 has 12 instructions, as shown below. Each individual instruction is simple in its operation, as described by its *action* entry. Thus, the first instruction is called a "copy" and is written *COPY AX,mem* where *mem* refers to a location in memory. If this instruction is executed, the contents of the memory at location *mem* is copied into register *AX*. Another copy instruction *COPY mem,AX* copies the contents of *AX* to memory location *mem*. As an illustration, one can use these two instructions to move data from memory location *A* to memory location *B*.

```
COPY AX,A
COPY B,AX
```

Here are the instructions.

Instruction	Format	Action
copy from mem	COPY AX,mem	AX := mem
copy to mem	COPY mem,AX	mem := AX
add	ADD AX,mem	AX := AX+mem
subtract	SUB AX,mem	AX := AX-mem
multiply	MUL AX,mem	AX := AX*mem
divide	DIV AX,mem	AX := AX/mem
compare	CMP AX,mem	If AX < mem then
		CF := B
		else
		CF := NB
jump	JMP lab1	Go to the instruction
		with label lab1.
jump if not below	JNB lab1	Go to the instruction
		with label lab1 if
		CF=NB. Otherwise go
		to next instruction.
jump if below	JB lab1	Go to the instruction
		with label lab1 if
		CF=B. Otherwise go to
		the next instruction.

```
input              IN  AX           Input an integer
                                       into register AX.
output             OUT AX           Output an integer
                                       from register AX.
```

The P88 has four arithmetic instructions—*ADD*, *SUB*, *MUL*, and *DIV*—which perform their respective operations on *AX* and a memory location and leave the result in *AX* . Thus *ADD AX,B* adds the contents of memory location *B* to *AX* and leaves the result in *AX*.

It also has instructions for reading and printing integers, *IN* and *OUT*. These instructions can be used for writing some P88 programs. Here is a P88 program for reading an integer into register *AX* and then printing it:

```
IN   AX
OUT  AX
```

Or one could read an integer, square it, and print the result:

```
IN   AX
COPY M1,AX
MUL  AX,M1
OUT  AX
```

As another example, one could read two numbers, divide the first by the second, and print the result:

```
IN   AX
COPY A,AX
IN   AX
COPY B,AX
COPY AX,A
DIV  AX,B
OUT  AX
```

Another type of instruction is the "jump," which loads a new address into IP and causes the machine to jump to an instruction that is not next in sequence. As an example, consider the following program, which adds the number in memory location *A* to *AX* repeatedly:

```
L1   ADD     AX,A
     JMP     L1
```

This program adds *A* to *AX*, and then the next instruction causes a jump to the instruction labeled *L1*. Here *A* is again added to *AX*. Then the jump instruction sends the machine back to *L1* again and so forth. This program loops forever, adding *A* to *AX* an unlimited number of times.

Of course, it is usually preferred to write a loop that will halt after an appropriate number of repetitions. This is done with the combination of the "compare" and conditional jump instructions, *JB* and *JNB*. An example of this type of program is the following code, which prints the numbers from 1 to 10 before exiting. This program assumes the numbers 0,1, and 10 appear in memory locations *M0*, *M1*, and *M10*.

```
        COPY     AX,M0
L1      ADD      AX,M1
        OUT      AX
        CMP      AX,M10
        JB       L1
```

The compare instruction loads *B* into register CF if *AX* is less than (below) *M10*. The "jump if below" instruction jumps to *L1* if CF is *B*, that is, if *AX* is below *M10*. A paraphrase of this program shows its method of operation.

```
        Put 0 into AX.
L1      Add 1 to AX.
        Print the contents of AX.
        Check whether AX is less than 10.
        If it is, go to L1.
```

Another example of a program that uses the compare and jump commands is the following, which reads a number and changes its sign if it is negative. This program thus computes what is called the "absolute value" in mathematics:

```
        IN   AX
        COPY M1,AX
        SUB  AX,M1
        CMP  AX,M1
        JB   NEXT
        SUB  AX,M1
        COPY M1,AX
NEXT    COPY AX,M1
        OUT  AX
```

The final example will be a program to add a series of nonnegative numbers. If a negative number is read at any time, the program prints the sum of all nonnegative numbers read and exits:

```
          IN   AX
          COPY M1,AX
          SUB  AX,M1
          COPY ZERO,AX
          COPY SUM,AX
          COPY AX,M1
LOOP      CMP  AX,ZERO
          JB   FIN
          ADD  AX,SUM
          COPY SUM,AX
          IN   AX
          JMP  LOOP
FIN       COPY AX,SUM
          OUT  AX
```

The language of machine instructions written in symbolic form as described here—*COPY, ADD, CMP*, etc.—is called *assembly language*. This type of language was heavily used during the 1940s and 1950s before higher-level programming languages like FORTRAN, PL/I, and Pascal were available. Each instruction in assembly language can be directly translated into a binary code, the machine language, denoted in this chapter by instructions surrounded by asterisks. The machine language instructions can be loaded into the IR register and executed as explained here and in chapter 6.

Exercises

1. Explain what function the following program computes:

```
          IN AX
          COPY M1,AX
          SUB  AX,M1
          CMP  AX,M1
          JB LAB1
          OUT AX
          JMP LAB2
LAB1      COPY AX,M1
          DIV  AX,M1
          OUT AX
LAB2      END
```

2. Write an assembly language program that reads two integers and prints the larger one.

3. Write an assembly language program that reads two integers—a small integer followed by a larger one. Then it prints all of the integers between but not including them.

4. A programmer noticed that a machine was running more slowly each day and wondered why. Furthermore, it acted erratically from time to time. She studied the code running in the machine, and after considerable effort, found the following code that she could identify as being of unknown origin:

```
V1        JMP        BEGIN
ZERO      0
ONE       1
TEN       0
FIFTY     50
LENGTH    33
COUNT     0
N1        0
BEGIN     COPY       AX,RANDOM
          COPY       N1,AX
          DIV        AX,TEN
          MUL        AX,TEN
          SUB        AX,N1
          CMP        AX,ZERO
          JB         EXIT
          COPY       AX,ZERO
          COPY       COUNT,AX
LOOP1     COPY       CX,RANDOM
          COPY       AX,COUNT
          CMP        AX,FIFTY
          JNB        EXIT
          COPY       BX,ZERO
LOOP2     CMP        BX,LENGTH
          JNB        NEXT
          COPY       AX,V1+c(BX)
          COPY       c(CX),AX
          ADD        BX,ONE
          ADD        CX,ONE
          JMP        LOOP2
```

```
NEXT        COPY        AX,COUNT
            ADD         AX,ONE
            COPY        COUNT,AX
            JMP         LOOP1
EXIT
```

In fact, the programmer had found a computer virus, and your job is to analyze it to discover how it works. This is a program that might be inserted into a computer system by an unfriendly person. It sits quietly in the middle of any program that it is inserted into until the right moment. Then it springs into action and duplicates itself many times around the machine memory.

Can you answer the following questions about the virus: How does it make the decision to go into action? How does it hide when it is not doing anything? What mechanism does it use to duplicate itself? How many times does it duplicate itself? Why does the virus cause the machine to seem to slow down? Why does it cause the system to act erratically sometimes? What should the programmer do to get rid of this virus? What problem does this virus have in carrying out its destructive job, and how can it be improved?

The virus uses some features of the P88 machine not discussed before. It references a location called *RANDOM*, which contains a random number. Every time that location is referenced, it gives a different random number. Two additional registers are assumed: they are called *BX* and *CX*. The notation *c(CX)* refers to the memory location with the address equal to the number in *CX*. Thus, If register *CX* contains 100, then *COPY c(CX), AX* will put the contents of *AX* into location 100 in memory. The expression *V1+c(BX)* refers to the memory location found by starting at location *V1* at the beginning of the program and counting *BX* locations beyond it.

Summary (B)

This chapter describes the classic architecture of the great majority of digital computers. They have a CPU that runs the fetch-execute cycle on sequences of instructions, and these instructions are stored in memory with the data of the computation. This is called the *von Neumann* architecture, and the only common deviations from it are the parallel machines described in chapter 12.

This chapter completes another link in the chain of concepts required to understand how computers work. At the lowest level are the transistors, the valves that control electric current flow. Above them are the electric circuits, which we can design to compute functions and store information. Such circuits can be organized to do useful tasks such as add numbers or manipulate characters. Binary coded machine language instructions are used to activate the appropriate computational circuits, and such instructions are sequenced through the Instruction Register IR in order to do a nontrivial calculation. The binary coded machine instructions are actually translations of symbolic assembly language instructions, which are much more convenient for humans to read. This assembly language, its binary coded form, and its execution on a machine have been the topic of this chapter.

The final and highest level set of concepts in the chain relates to the translation of a high-level language such as Pascal into assembly language. This study will complete the chain and will be the topic for the next chapter.

Looking at this chain in the other direction, you can trace the processing of a Pascal statement from its entry into the computer to the detailed switching of electrical currents inside of the machine. Consider, for example, the statement

```
Z := (X + Y)
```

and all of the resulting processing. It is translated into assembly language and then into machine language. These instructions are sequenced through the Instruction Register which gets the job done. *X* is brought in from memory, *Y* is added to it, and the result is placed in *Z*:

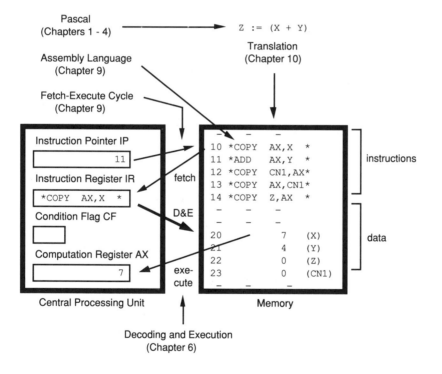

Readings

On computer architecture and assembly language programming:

Gear, C. W., *Computer Organization and Programming*, McGraw-Hill, New York, 1974.

Hwang, K., and Briggs, F. A., *Computer Architecture and Parallel Processing*, McGraw-Hill, New York,1984.

Levy, H. M., and Eckhouse, R. H., Jr., *Computer Programming and Architecture*, Digital Equipment Corporation, Bedford, Mass., 1980.

Mano, M. M., *Computer Systems Architecture,* Prentice-Hall, Englewood Cliffs, New Jersey, 1976.

Scanlon, L. J., *IBM PC and XT Assembly Language, A Guide for Programmers,* Brady Communications Company, New York, 1985.

Stone, H. S., *High-Performance Computer Architecture*, Addison-Wesley, Reading, Mass., 1987.

10

Language Translation

Enabling the Computer to Understand Pascal (A)

The vehicle of all communication is language, and history abounds with the story of languages. Language behavior is a primary characteristic that differentiates humans from other animals, and a huge multiplicity of languages has developed over the millennia. The advent of computers has brought an additional large collection of them

But most languages have no meaning to us unless we can translate them into familiar terms. So translation is a process of great importance to people and machines We wish to understand and use many languages, and the process of translation can give us access to them.

Computer scientists are experts at some kinds of language translation, and a powerful technology has developed for doing this task. This chapter will introduce the methodology, a general technique applicable to many translation problems, and will thus familiarize you with another "great idea" of the field. The methodology has been quite successful on computer languages and can handle small subsets of natural languages as described in chapter 14.

Our concern here is the translation of a higher-level programming language, like Pascal, into a lower level language, assembly language or machine language. Machines do not "understand" such higher level languages but they do understand machine language or, with the help of a very simple translator, assembly language. For example, we ask how the Pascal statement

```
Z := (X + Y)
```

is translated into the following assembly language code, which correctly expresses the desired meaning:

```
COPY AX,X
ADD AX,Y
COPY CN1,AX
COPY AX,CN1
COPY Z,AX
```

If we can understand the mechanisms that do this simple translation, we will understand fundamental processes of translation applicable in almost any domain. (Note: The assembly language translation shown here is not of minimal length, and you can probably find a shorter program to do the same job. Automatic translators have the task of producing correct translations, but they do not always produce optimum ones as is the case here.)

This chapter will introduce some fundamental ideas related to the theory of languages and to translation. Then it will show how to assemble these ideas to build a translator for a small part of Pascal, and it will give many examples of translation.

Syntactic Production Rules (B)

Language is embodied in sequences of symbols. In order to understand language, we must have a mathematics for sequences of symbols. This mathematics will show how to generate and analyze such sequences and will supply the necessary mechanisms for doing translation.

The first idea is that of the *production rule*. Such rules were introduced in the last section of chapter 1, and additional rules were added in later chapters to describe Pascal language syntax. These rules will be discussed in more detail here and provide the basis for our translation mechanisms. Conceptually a production rule changes a given object or set of objects into something else—a different object or set of objects. An example of a production rule from chapter 1 is

```
<identifier> ->   a sequence of letters and/or digits
                  that begins with a letter
```

which will be written in a modified form here as

```
R1: <i> -->   a sequence of letters and/or digits
       j      that begins with a letter
```

This rule has been given the name R1 and means "change $<i>_j$ into a sequence of letters and/or digits that begins with a letter." The term <identifier> from previous chapters has been shortened to <i> and given a subscript j. Each time R1 is used, j will have a specific value, and a specific alphabetic string will be used. An example *instantiation* of R1 is

```
<i>  -> ABLE
   7
```

which means "change $<i>_7$ into *ABLE*." We will be studying *syntactic production rules* like R1, which convert symbols, like $<i>_7$, into strings of symbols like *ABLE*. All of these rules will be simplifications of the rules given previously for a much larger fraction of Pascal than will be considered in this chapter.

Once we have a rule, we can then *apply* the rule to modify some string. For example, suppose we have the string $(<i>_7 + <i>_{19})$. Let us use this version of R1 to change this string:

```
(<i>  + <i>  )
    7      19
```

The rule $\langle i \rangle_7 \rightarrow ABLE$ says that $\langle i \rangle_7$ can be changed to *ABLE* so the result will be

```
(ABLE  +  <i>19)
```

Since the form $(\langle i \rangle_7 + \langle i \rangle_{19})$ has been changed to $(ABLE + \langle i \rangle_{19})$, we can write

```
(<i>7  +  <i>19)  ->  (ABLE  +  <i>19)
```

The $\langle i \rangle_7$ in the first form has been replaced by *ABLE* as shown in the second form. If we wish to apply R1 again, we could use the following instantiation

```
<i>19  ->  BAKER
```

to obtain

```
(ABLE  +  <i>19)   ->  (ABLE + BAKER)
```

In these rules, $\langle i \rangle_j$ stands for "identifier name," and the string of symbols generated by $\langle i \rangle_j$ will be an identifier name.

It also may be desirable to apply rules to other things besides $\langle i \rangle_j$'s. R2 is another useful rule; it enables us to convert $\langle e \rangle_i$ into $\langle i \rangle_j$:

```
R2:   <e>i  ->  <i>j
```

For example, using the version $\langle e \rangle_3 \rightarrow \langle i \rangle_7$ plus the R1 rule given above, we have

```
<e>3  ->  <i>7  ->  ABLE
```

The asterisk * is used to indicate that any number of rule applications has occurred. Thus, the above two-step derivation could be written

```
<e>3  -*->  ABLE
```

In these rules, $\langle e \rangle_i$ stands for "expression" or "arithmetic expression," as defined in previous chapters.

None of this looks like it has much to do with Pascal. But rule R3 introduces a familiar construction, the assignment statement:

```
R3:   <s>k  ->   <i>j  :=  <e>i
```

This rule says that $\langle s \rangle_k$ can be replaced by " $\langle i \rangle_j := \langle e \rangle_i$". But the real meaning of the rule is that a legal statement $\langle s \rangle_k$ in Pascal is the sequence of symbols " $\langle i \rangle_j := \langle e \rangle_i$," where $\langle i \rangle_j$ is an identifier name and $<e>_i$ is an arithmetic expression. Using the combination of rules R1 to R3, you can generate legal assignment statements. As an illustration, consider the generation of the Pascal statement

```
X := Y
```

Derivation	Rules
$<s>_1$	R3: $<s>_1 \rightarrow <i>_2 := <e>_3$
$<i>_2 := <e>_3$	R1: $<i>_2 \rightarrow X$
$X := <e>_3$	R2: $<e>_3 \rightarrow <i>_4$
$X := <i>_4$	R1: $<i>_4 \rightarrow Y$
$X := Y$	

In this derivation, we begin with $<s>_1$, which means we wish to generate a statement in Pascal. Then we use a case of rule R3 to convert $<s>_1$ to something else, namely "$<i>_2 := <e>_3$." The conversion is done with the rule $<s>_1 \rightarrow <i>_2 := <e>_3$. Next we wish to change the $<i>_2$ to X, and this is done with R1 of the form $<i>_2 \rightarrow X$. The result of this change appears on the third line of the derivation: $X := <e>_3$. Finally, rule R2 is used to convert $<e>_3$ to $<i>_4$, and rule R1 is used to convert $<i>_4$ to Y.

Only two more rules are needed for our examples, R4 and R5, which make it possible to handle some complex arithmetic expressions:

R4: $<e>_i \rightarrow (<e>_j + <e>_k)$
R5: $<e>_i \rightarrow (<e>_j * <e>_k)$

This set of five rules makes up a gr*ammar* for some assignment statements in Pascal and is sufficient to provide many interesting examples for this chapter. They are simplifications of rules introduced in earlier chapters. A few sample derivations appear here:

Derivation	Rules
$<s>_1$	R3: $<s>_1 \rightarrow <i>_2 := <e>_3$
$<i>_2 := <e>_3$	R1: $<i>_2 \rightarrow Y$
$Y := <e>_3$	R4: $<e>_3 \rightarrow (<e>_4 + <e>_5)$
$Y := (<e>_4 + <e>_5)$	R2: $<e>_4 \rightarrow <i>_6$
$Y := (<i>_6 + <e>_5)$	R1: $<i>_6 \rightarrow XX$
$Y := (XX + <e>_5)$	R2: $<e>_5 \rightarrow <i>_7$
$Y := (XX + <i>_7)$	R1: $<i>_7 \rightarrow YY$
$Y := (XX + YY)$	

The following shows the generation of a more deeply nested arithmetic expression:

Derivation	Rules
$<s>_1$	R3: $<s>_1 \rightarrow <i>_2 := <e>_3$
$<i>_2 := <e>_3$	R1: $<i>_2 \rightarrow SUM$
$SUM := <e>_3$	R4: $<e>_3 \rightarrow (<e>_4 + <e>_5)$
$SUM := (<e>_4 + <e>_5)$	R5: $<e>_4 \rightarrow (<e>_7 * <e>_8)$

Derivation	Rules
SUM := ((<e>$_7$ * <e>$_8$) + <e>$_5$)	R2: <e>$_7$ -> <i>$_9$
SUM := ((<i>$_9$ * <e>$_8$) + <e>$_5$)	R1: <i>$_9$ -> X
SUM := ((X * <e>$_8$) + <e>$_5$)	R2: <e>$_8$ -> <i>$_{10}$
SUM := ((X * <i>$_{10}$) + <e>$_5$)	R1: <i>$_{10}$ -> C
SUM := ((X * C) + <e>$_5$)	R2: <e>$_5$ -> <i>$_{11}$
SUM := ((X * C) + <i>$_{11}$)	R1: <i>$_{11}$ -> SUM
SUM := ((X * C) + SUM)	

Of course, any nesting of multiplication and addition can be generated in the arithmetic expressions:

```
<s>  -*-> Y := ((XX * YY) + (XY * (YX + XXX)))
   1
```

A question arises in all of these derivations concerning how the indexes are determined. For example, if we have the string

```
X := (Y + <e> )
               6
```

and wish to apply the rule <e>$_i$ -> (<e>$_j$ + <e>$_k$), what method should be used to determine i, j, and k? The answer is that the index on the left-hand side is determined by the symbol to be replaced. For example, the symbol <e>$_6$ is to be replaced in the statement so the left side of the rule must be <e>$_6$: <e>$_6$ -> (<e>$_j$ | <e>$_k$). The indexes on the right-hand side can be anything as long as they are different from any indexes used previously in this derivation. Suppose that 8 and 9 have not been used. Then we can set $j = 8$ and $k = 9$ to obtain the form <e>$_6$ -> (<e>$_8$ + <e>$_9$). Applying this rule in the above statement then results in

```
X := (Y + (<e>  + <e> ))
               8      9
```

Once a grammar has been established for a language (or, as in our case, part of a language), the grammar can be used for either *generation* of the language or *analysis* (or understanding) of it. The above examples illustrate generation; a person wanting to "say something" in Pascal begins with the decision to "say" a statement and then generates the thing to be said.

```
<s>  -> <i>  := <e>  -> X := <e>  ->   . . .   -> X := (Y * X)
   1       2       3            3
```

Each application of a rule further specifies what is to be said until the statement is completely defined. But the rules can also be applied in reverse to analyze or understand a statement. Thus given

```
X := (Y * X),
```

you can use R1 to discover where the identifiers are:

$$\langle i \rangle_1 := (\langle i \rangle_2 * \langle i \rangle_3)$$

Then rules R2 and R5 uncover the structure of the right-hand side:

$$\langle i \rangle_1 := \langle e \rangle_4$$

Finally, R3 tells us that a complete statement has been made:

$$\langle s \rangle_0$$

So the same rules that were used in generation can be used backward to disassemble, analyze, and understand a Pascal statement.

Analogous processes probably account for the human's processing of English. Presumably humans have something like a grammar in their brains and generation proceeds by applying the rules to create well-formed utterances. A person might decide to assert a declarative sentence

(declarative sentence)

and a grammar could indicate that such sentences have subjects and predicates:

(subject) (predicate)

Further rules could enable these symbols to be replaced by actual words:

The boy went to town.

Understanding would involve the reverse process, finding the parts of speech of the spoken words, finding how they assemble to become sentence constituents such as subjects and predicates, and ultimately, finding the structure of the complete sentence. This is discussed more in chapter 14.

This section has addressed the issue of the syntax of language. We have examined mechanisms for generating or analyzing the strings of symbols that make up language. The next section concerns itself with the semantics of language. There we will study the concept of "meaning" and show how meaning is associated with the utterances of language, the syntactic strings of symbols.

Exercises

1. Apply the given rules to $\langle s \rangle_1$ to generate strings of symbols.

    (a) Rules R3, R1, R2, R1.

    (b) Rules R3, R1, R5, R2, R1, R2, R1.

    (c) Rules R3, R1, R4, R2, R1, R5, R2, R1, R2, R1.

2. Use the rules given above, R1 through R5, to generate each of the following strings of symbols

starting from $<i>_1$ or $<s>_1$:

(a) YXY

(b) JACK

(c) X := Y

(d) X := (X * X)

(e) YYY := (Y * (X + X))

(f) XX := ((X + XX) * Y)

(g) X := ((Y * Y) + (X * X))

3. What new rules are needed to be able to generate the following statement?

SUM := FACT - X

Use your new rules to show the complete generation of this statement.

4. Build a grammar that can generate all of the following sentences.

The boy knows the girl.

This girl knows that boy.

That boy knows this boy.

Jack knows that boy.

Jill knows Jack.

Jack knows Jill.

etc.

Semantics (B)

For the purposes of this discussion, the *meaning* of a sentence or statement in a language will be defined to be its translation into another language. The language being translated will be called the *source language*, and this language is translated into the *object language*. The source language is presumably not usable by the recipient while the object language is. The source language being considered in this section is the set of Pascal statements that can be generated by rules R1 to R5. The object language is the P88 assembly language defined in chapter 9. This object language is satisfactory for specifying the meaning of Pascal statements because its own meaning is well defined.

The symbols $<i>_j$, $<e>_j$, and $<s>_j$ on the left sides of the grammar rules R1 to R5 are called *grammar variables*, and the grammar semantics will assign meaning to them. Each rule will have two parts—the syntactic part given in the previous section and the semantic part, which is a function that computes the meaning or translation associated with the rule. Suppose that in a given grammar, the rule "$<i>_1$ -> homme" appears. If we were building a translator from the unknown language to English, the meaning of the symbol "homme" might be "man." So we would associate with the rule "$<i>_1$ -> homme", the semantic function $M(<i>_1)$ = "man"; the meaning of $<i>_1$ is "man."

Syntax   Semantics

R: `<i>`$_1$ `-> homme`   `M(<i>`$_1$`) = man`

Then if we were to analyze the string

```
XXXX  YYYY  homme  ZZZZ,
```

one step of the analysis would be to use R backward to find a new version of the string

```
XXXX  YYYY  <i>₁ ZZZZ
```

and to invoke the semantics of R to note that the meaning of `<i>`$_1$ is "man." A proper analysis of the complete utterance would result in the translation of all portions so that a well-formed English sentence would result.

Our study of semantics will proceed by examining each of the five rules from the previous section and attaching the appropriate semantic rules to them. The result will be a translator for the class of Pascal statements that they represent.

What should be the meaning associated with the simplest rule R1?

```
R1:  <i>ⱼ -> a sequence of letters and/or digits
            that begins with a letter
```

That is, if a variable is called X in the source language, what name should it have in the object language? Let us make things as easy as possible and let the variable have the same name in both languages:

```
R1:   <i>ⱼ -> w               M(<i>ᵢ) = w
```

where w is some identifier string. Thus, we might have the following instantiation of R1:

```
<i>₉ -> ABLE               M(<i>₉)= ABLE
```

Next we consider the semantics associated with R2. The left-hand variable `<e>`$_i$ has two parts to its meaning representation, $M(<e>_i)$ and $code(<e>_i)$. Intuitively, the arithmetic expression `<e>`$_i$ will have a name $M(<e>_i)$ and some lines of assembly language code, $code(<e>_i)$:

```
R2:   <e>ᵢ -> <i>ⱼ           M(<e>ᵢ)= M(<i>ⱼ)
                            code (<e>ᵢ) = nothing
```

Thus as an example, if `<e>`$_1$ `-*->` $ABLE$, then $M(<e>_1) = ABLE$ and $code(<e>_1)$ is a list of instructions (code) of length zero.

Rule R3 provides the first interesting semantics. If $<s>_k$ generates a Pascal statement, then $code(<s>_k)$ will give its translation in terms of P88 assembly language.

```
R3:   <s>  -> <i>  := <e>      code (<s> ) =   code  (<e> )
          k       j       i               k                i
                                          COPY  AX,M(<e> )
                                                        i
                                          COPY  M(<i> ),AX
                                                     j
```

Thus $code(<s>_k)$ is the list of all instructions in $code(<e>_i)$ followed by the two *COPY* instructions shown.

Notice that this chapter follows a particular notational convention. Fragments of code are typed as similarly indented sequential lines of programming. Such fragments should be regarded as units even though they are spread across several lines. In the above definition, $code(<s>_k)$ is defined as

```
code  (<s> ) =    code  (<e> )
           k                 i
                  COPY  AX,M(<e> )
                              i
                  COPY  M(<i> ),AX
                             j
```

The convention requires that the three lines of code

```
code  (<e> )
           i
COPY  AX,M(<e> )
              i
COPY  M(<i> ),AX
           j
```

be considered as a single unit. Thus, the definition states that $code(<s>_k)$ is the three lines of code given, not just the single line $code(<e>_i)$. This convention is followed throughout this chapter.

To illustrate the use of the rules R1 to R3 with their semantic components, let us do a complete translation of the statement

```
X  :=  Y
```

into assembly language. From the previous section, it is clear that the sequence of rules R3, R1, R2, R1 is sufficient to derive the source statement. So we write down the complete derivation that will determine the semantic rules required to find the translation. This derivation is identical to the one carried out in the previous section except that the semantic portion of each rule is written down beside the syntactic portion. However, we have not yet done anything with these semantic portions:

Derivation	Rules	
$\langle s\rangle_1$	R3: $\langle s\rangle_1 \rightarrow \langle i\rangle_2 := \langle e\rangle_3$	$code\,(\langle s\rangle_1) = \quad code\,(\langle e\rangle_3)$ $COPY\ AX,M(\langle e\rangle_3)$ $COPY\ \ M(\langle i\rangle_2),AX$
$\langle i\rangle_2 := \langle e\rangle_3$ $X := \langle e\rangle_3$	R1: $\langle i\rangle_2 \rightarrow X$ R2: $\langle e\rangle_3 \rightarrow \langle i\rangle_4$	$M(\langle i\rangle_2) = X$ $M(\langle e\rangle_3) = M(\langle i\rangle_4)$ $code\,(\langle e\rangle_3) = nothing$
$X := \langle i\rangle_4$ $X := Y$	R1: $\langle i\rangle_4 \rightarrow Y$	$M(\langle i\rangle_4) = Y$

The first two columns in this table are taken from the previous section on syntax. The third column is new; it gives the semantic portion of each of the rules used. The exciting thing about this third column is that it gives us a direct way to find the translation.

The translation of statement $\langle s\rangle_1$ is found by evaluating $code\,(\langle s\rangle_1)$ using the rules in the third column. From the first line in the above table we find:

$$code\ (\langle s\rangle_1)\ =\quad code\ (\langle e\rangle_3) \qquad by\ R3$$
$$COPY\ AX,M(\langle e\rangle_3)$$
$$COPY\ M(\langle i\rangle_2),AX$$

This is almost a satisfactory translation except that some terms are unknown. For example, $M(\langle i\rangle_2)$ is unknown, but the second line in the table gives its value: $M(\langle i\rangle_2) = X$. Let us substitute this value:

$$code\ (\langle s\rangle_1) =\quad code\ (\langle e\rangle_3) \qquad by\ R1$$
$$COPY\ AX,\ M(\langle e\rangle_3)$$
$$COPY\ X,AX$$

There are other unknown entries in the code. What are $code(\langle e\rangle_3)$ and $M(\langle e\rangle_3)$? The answers are given in the third line of the table. $code(\langle e\rangle_3)$ is nothing, and $M(\langle e\rangle_3) = M(\langle i\rangle_4)$, so these can also be substituted in the code.

$$code\ (\langle s\rangle_1)\ =\quad COPY\ AX,M(\langle i\rangle_4) \qquad by\ R2$$
$$COPY\ X,AX$$

Finally, we wonder what the value of $M(\langle i\rangle_4)$ is. This is given by the fourth line in the table to be $M(\langle i\rangle_4) = Y$, and it should also be entered:

$$code\ (\langle s\rangle_1)\ =\quad COPY\ AX,Y \qquad by\ R1$$
$$COPY\ X,AX$$

The translation rules thus assert that the meaning of $X := Y$ in Pascal is

```
COPY AX,Y
COPY X,AX
```

in P88 assembly language. The Pascal statement says "find the value in Y and put it into X". The translation says the same thing in P88 assembly language: "Copy Y into AX and then copy AX into X." This example is worthy of careful study because it demonstrates all the essential mechanisms of the translator without undue complexity.

In summary, the input to the translation process was the following:

Translation Input:
```
X := Y
```

The rules R1, R2, and R3 were applied as indicated, resulting in the following semantic relationships, which are column 3 in the above table.

Semantic Rules:
```
code(<s>₁)  =     code(<e>₃)
                  COPY AX,M(<e>₃)
                  COPY  M(<i>₂),AX
M(<i>₂) = X
M(<e>₃)  =  M(<i>₄)
code(<e>₃)  =  nothing
M(<i>₄)  =  Y
```

Finally, $code(<s>_1)$ was evaluated using these rules.

Translation Output:
```
COPY AX,Y
COPY X,AX
```

But more interesting translations will be possible only if semantics is available for our last two rules, R4 and R5.

```
R4:   <e>ᵢ -> (<e>ⱼ + <e>ₖ)    M(<e>ᵢ)  =  createname
                               code(<e>ᵢ)  =  code (<e>ⱼ)
                                                code (<e>ₖ)
                                                COPY AX,M(<e>ⱼ)
                                                ADD  AX,M(<e>ₖ)
                                                COPY M(<e>ᵢ),AX
```

```
R5:   <e>_i -> (<e>_j * <e>_k)      M(<e>_i) = createname
                                    code(<e>_i) =  code  (<e>_j)
                                                   code  (<e>_k)
                                                   COPY AX,M(<e>_j)
                                                   MUL  AX,M(<e>_k)
                                                   COPY M(<e>_i),AX
```

These semantic rules use the function *createname* that creates a name that has not been used elsewhere. Thus, if one encounters $M(<e>_7) = createname$, the system might create the name *CN1* and assign it: $M(<e>_7) = CN1$. If later one encounters, say, $M(<e>_9) = createname$, the result might be $M(<e>_9) = CN2$.

Examining the code semantics for the addition rule R4, you can see that the code segments for $<e>_j$ and $<e>_k$ are expanded to determine the value of these arithmetic expressions. Then the results are added into the register *AX* by two P88 instructions and finally stored away to be used by a later calculation. An analogous thing happens with the rule R5.

The usage of these two rules is demonstrated in the following two derivations. The first is the translation of

```
Z := (X + Y)
```

Derivation	Rules	
$<s>_1$	R3: $<s>_1 \rightarrow <i>_2 := <e>_3$	code $(<s>_1) =$ code$(<e>_3)$ COPY AX,M(<e>_3) COPY M(<i>_2),AX
$<i>_2 := <e>_3$ $Z := <e>_3$	R1: $<i>_2 \rightarrow Z$ R4: $<e>_3 \rightarrow (<e>_4 + <e>_5)$	M(<i>_2) = Z M(<e>_3) = CN1 code(<e>_3)= code (<e>_4) code (<e>_5) COPY AX,M(<e>_4) ADD AX,M(<e>_5) COPY M(<e>_3),AX
$Z := (<e>_4 + <e>_5)$	R2: $<e>_4 \rightarrow <i>_6$	M(<e>_4) = M(<i>_6) code(<e>_4) = *nothing*
$Z := (<i>_6 + <e>_5)$ $Z := (X + <e>_5)$	R1: $<i>_6 \rightarrow X$ R2: $<e>_5 \rightarrow <i>_7$	M(<i>_6) = X M(<e>_5) = M(<i>_7) code(<e>_5) = *nothing*
$Z := (X + <i>_7)$ $Z := (X + Y)$	R1: $<i>_7 \rightarrow Y$	M(<i>_7) = Y

Again, the meaning of the original Pascal statement can be determined by expanding the above semantics formulas to determine the value of *code*($<s>_1$):

```
code (<s>_1)   =   code  (<e>_3)        by R3  (line 1 of table)
                   COPY AX,M(<e>_3)
                   COPY M(<i>_2),AX
```

```
code (<s>₁)  =   code (<e>₃)           by R1  (line 2 of table)
                 COPY AX,M(<e>₃)
                 COPY Z,AX

             =   code (<e>₄)           by R4  (line 3 of table)
                 code (<e>₅)
                 COPY AX,M(<e>₄)
                 ADD  AX,M(<e>₅)
                 COPY CN1,AX
                 COPY AX,CN1
                 COPY Z,AX

             =   code (<e>₅)           by R2  (line 4 of table)
                 COPY AX,M(<i>₆)
                 ADD  AX,M(<e>₅)
                 COPY CN1,AX
                 COPY AX,CN1
                 COPY Z,AX

             =   code (<e>₅)           by R1  (line 5 of table)
                 COPY AX,X
                 ADD  AX,M(<e>₅)
                 COPY CN1,AX
                 COPY AX,CN1
                 COPY Z,AX

             =   COPY AX,X             by R2  (line 6 of table)
                 ADD  AX,M(<i>₇)
                 COPY CN1,AX
                 COPY AX,CN1
                 COPY Z,AX

             =   COPY AX,X             by R1  (line 7 of table)
                 ADD  AX,Y
                 COPY CN1,AX
                 COPY AX,CN1
                 COPY Z,AX
```

This completes the translation of the original statement. The whole computation can be summarized as follows:

Translation Input:
```
Z := (X + Y)
```

Semantics Rules:
```
(given by column 3 of syntax-semantics table)
```

Translation Output:

```
COPY  AX,X
ADD   AX,Y
COPY  CN1,AX
COPY  AX,CN1
COPY  Z,AX
```

Translators often produce nonminimal code as has occurred in this example. Code segments of this kind can be optimized by numerous well-known techniques, but such studies are beyond the scope of this book.

The last example of this section demonstrates the translation of a more complicated arithmetic expression:

```
U1 := (X + (Y * Z))
```

Derivation	Rules	

$<s>_1$	R3: $<s>_1 \to <i>_2 := <e>_3$	code $(<s>_1)$
		= code $(<e>_3)$
		  COPY AX,M$(<e>_3)$
		  COPY M$(<i>_2)$,AX

$<i>_2 := <e>_3$
 U1 := $<e>_3$
	R1: $<i>_2 \to$ U1
	R4: $<e>_3 \to (<e>_4 + <e>_5)$
		M$(<i>_2)$ = U1
		M$(<e>_3)$ = CN1
		code$(<e>_3)$
		= code $(<e>_4)$
		  code $(<e>_5)$
		  COPY AX,M$(<e>_4)$
		  ADD AX,M$(<e>_5)$
		  COPY M$(<e>_3)$,AX

U1 := $(<e>_4 + <e>_5)$	R2: $<e>_4 \to <i>_6$	M$(<e>_4)$ = M$(<i>_6)$ code$(<e>_4)$ = *nothing*

U1 := $(<i>_6 + <e>_5)$
 U1 := $(X + <e>_5)$
	R1: $<i>_6 \to$ X
	R5: $<e>_5 \to (<e>_7 * <e>_8)$
		M$(<i>_6)$ = X
		M$(<e>_5)$ = CN2
		code$(<e>_5)$
		= code$(<e>_7)$
		  code$(<e>_8)$
		  COPY AX,M$(<e>_7)$
		  MUL AX,M$(<e>_8)$
		  COPY CN2,AX

U1 := $(X + (<e>_7 * <e>_8))$	R2: $<e>_7 \to <i>_9$	M$(<e>_7)$ = M$(<i>_9)$ code$(<e>_7)$ = *nothing*
U1 := $(X + (<i>_9 * <e>_8))$ U1 := $(X + (Y * <e>_8))$	R1: $<i>_9 \to$ Y R2: $<e>_8 \to <i>_{10}$	M$(<i>_9)$ = Y M$(<e>_8)$ = M$(<i>_{10})$ code$(<e>_8)$ = *nothing*
U1 := $(X + (Y * <i>_{10}))$ U1 := $(X + (Y * Z))$	R1: $<i>_{10} \to$ Z	M$(<i>_{10})$ = Z

The translation is found by expanding *code*$(<s>_1)$.

```
code(<s>₁)  = code  (<e>₃)              by R3 (line 1 of table)
              COPY  AX,M(<e>₃)
              COPY  M(<i>₂),AX

            = code  (<e>₃)              by R1 (line 2)
              COPY  AX,M(<e>₃)
              COPY  U1,AX

            = code  (<e>₄)              by R4 (line 3)
              code  (<e>₅)
              COPY  AX,M(<e>₄)
              ADD   AX,M(<e>₅)
              COPY  CN1,AX
              COPY  AX,CN1
              COPY  U1,AX

            = code  (<e>₅)              by R2 (line 4)
              COPY  AX,M(<i>₆)
              ADD   AX,M(<e>₅)
              COPY  CN1,AX
              COPY  AX,CN1
              COPY  U1,AX

            = code  (<e>₅)              by R1 (line 5)
              COPY  AX,X
              ADD   AX,M(<e>₅)
              COPY  CN1,AX
              COPY  AX,CN1
              COPY  U1,AX

            = code(<e>₇)                by R5 (line 6)
              code  (<e>₈)
              COPY  AX,M(<e>₇)
              MUL   AX,M(<e>₈)
              COPY  CN2,AX
              COPY  AX,X
              ADD   AX,CN2
              COPY  CN1,AX
              COPY  AX,CN1
              COPY  U1,AX

            = code(<e>₈)                by R2 (line 7)
              COPY  AX,M(<i>₉)
              MUL   AX,M(<e>₈)
              COPY  CN2,AX
              COPY  AX,X
```

```
          ADD  AX,CN2
          COPY CN1,AX
          COPY AX,CN1
          COPY U1,AX
```

$= \text{code}(<e>_8)$ by R1 (line 8)
```
          COPY AX,Y
          MUL  AX,M(<e>8)
          COPY CN2,AX
          COPY AX,X
          ADD  AX,CN2
          COPY CN1,AX
          COPY AX,CN1
          COPY U1,AX
```

$= $ COPY AX,Y   by R2 (line 9)
```
          MUL  AX,M(<i>10)
          COPY CN2,AX
          COPY AX,X
          ADD  AX,CN2
          COPY CN1,AX
          COPY AX,CN1
          COPY U1,AX
```

$= $ COPY AX,Y   by R1 (line 10)
```
          MUL  AX,Z
          COPY CN2,AX
          COPY AX,X
          ADD  AX,CN2
          COPY CN1,AX
          COPY AX,CN1
          COPY U1,AX
```

This completes the description of the translator for a small class of Pascal assignment statements. The system uses the syntactic portions of the rules to find the structure of the unknown statement. The semantic portions of the rules are functions that compute portions of the meaning. The expansion of these functions and their combination provides the final translation. This general methodology is quite satisfactory for handling many translation problems and is the basis for numerous existing translators.

A program can be written to do all of the translation steps shown above for a complete programming language such as Pascal. Such a program is called a *compiler*. Many have been written for the various programming languages that have been developed. The following section gives several more translation rules for the compilation of simple looping programs. These rules show how the methodology of this chapter can be extended to handle larger programming constructions.

Exercises

1. Use rules R1 through R5 to translate the following statement into assembly language:

   ```
   ABLE := (C * BAKER)
   ```

2. Use rules R1 through R5 to translate the following statement into assembly language:

   ```
   I := (I + ONE)
   ```

3. Use rules R1 through R5 to translate the following statement into assembly language:

   ```
   X := ((T * U) * V)
   ```

4. Use rules R1 through R5 to translate the following statement into assembly language:

   ```
   TOTAL :=  ((C1 * MAX) + (C2 * MIN))
   ```

5. Examine very carefully the translations given in this section for the statements $Z := (X + Y)$ and $U1 := (X + (Y * Z))$. Can you write assembly language code that will do the same task but with fewer instructions? Can you make a rough estimate of how much shorter minimal assembly language programs are on the average than programs output by the translator? Can you guess how much faster optimal assembly language programs will be than computer generated ones?

The Translation of Looping Programs (C)

The previous sections gave a general approach to the design of translators. This section adds no new ideas to the theory but provides additional examples of rules and shows how larger code segments can be translated.

Two more rules are needed to enable translation of a sequence of statements rather than a single statement:

$$R6: \quad <q>_i \; ->\;<s>_j \; ; \qquad code\,(<q>_i) \; = \; code\,(<s>_j)$$
$$<q>_k \qquad\qquad\qquad code\,(<q>_k)$$
$$R7: \quad <q>_i \; ->\;<s>_j \; ; \qquad code\,(<q>_i) \; = \; code\,(<s>_j)$$

Here $<q>_i$ stands for a "sequence" of statements. To see how these rules work, apply R6 several times in a row to $<q>_1$:

Derivation	Rules		
$<q>_1$	R6: $<q>_1 ->$	$<s>_2$;	$code\,(<q>_1) = code\,(<s>_2)$
		$<q>_3$	$code\,(<q>_3)$
$<s>_2$;	R6: $<q>_3 ->$	$<s>_4$;	$code\,(<q>_3) = code\,(<s>_4)$
$<q>_3$		$<q>_5$	$code\,(<q>_5)$
$<s>_2$;	R6: $<q>_5 ->$	$<s>_6$;	$code\,(<q>_5) = code\,(<s>_6)$
$<s>_4$;		$<q>_7$	$code\,(<q>_7)$
$<q>_5$			
$<s>_2$;			
$<s>_4$;			
$<s>_6$;			
$<q>_7$			

Three applications of R6 produce a sequence of three statements, $<s>_2$, $<s>_4$, $<s>_6$, each followed by a semicolon. Then you can apply R7 once to add a final statement to the sequence:

Derivation	Rules
$<s>_2$; $<s>_4$; $<s>_6$; $<q>_7$	R7: $<q>_7 \rightarrow <s>_8$; code($<q>_7$) = code($<s>_8$)
$<s>_2$; $<s>_4$; $<s>_6$; $<s>_8$;	

Then the semantics rules can be applied to determine codes for the four statements $<s>_2$, $<s>_4$, $<s>_6$, $<s>_8$:

```
code  (<q>₁) =  code  (<s>₂)     by first R6
               code  (<q>₃)
            =  code  (<s>₂)     by second R6
               code  (<s>₄)
               code  (<q>₅)
            =  code  (<s>₂)     by third R6
               code  (<s>₄)
               code  (<s>₆)
               code  (<q>₇)
            =  code  (<s>₂)     by R7
               code  (<s>₄)
               code  (<s>₆)
               code  (<s>₈)
```

The result is as expected. The translation of $<s>_2$, $<s>_4$, $<s>_6$, $<s>_8$ is

```
=  code  (<s>₂)
   code  (<s>₄)
   code  (<s>₆)
   code  (<s>₈)
```

But Pascal always embeds statement sequences between the keywords *begin* and *end* to form a *compound statement*. A rule is needed for this:

```
R8:   <c>ᵢ ->  begin        code(<c>ᵢ)  =  code(<q>ⱼ)
               <q>ⱼ
               end
```

Using this rule with the others, you can then show that

```
<c>  -*->    begin
   0
                <s>  ;
                   2
                <s>  ;
                   4
                <s>  ;
                   6
                <s>  ;
                   8
             end
```

and the semantics rules are the same as in the previous example.

Summarizing, if a compound statement of n sequential statements is to be translated, rule R8 should be used once, followed by rule R6 $n-1$ times and R7 once. This will give n statements whose translation will be n code segments. Illustrating this idea, suppose the following short program is to be compiled.

```
begin
X := Y;
Z := (X + Y);
U1 := (X + (Y * Z));
end
```

These individual statements were translated in the previous section, so those details can be omitted.

Derivation	Rules	
$<c>_0$	R8: $<c>_0 \rightarrow$ begin $<q>_1$ end	code $(<c>_0)$ = code $(<q>_1)$
begin $<q>_1$ end	R6: $<q>_1 \rightarrow$ $<s>_2$; $<q>_3$	code $(<q>_1)$ = code $(<s>_2)$ code $(<q>_3)$
begin $<s>_2$; $<q>_3$ end	R6: $<q>_3 \rightarrow$ $<s>_4$; $<q>_5$	code $(<q>_3)$ = code $(<s>_4)$ code $(<q>_5)$
begin $<s>_2$; $<s>_4$; $<q>_5$ end	R7: $<q>_5 \rightarrow$ $<s>_6$;	code $(<q>_5)$ = code $(<s>_6)$
begin $<s>_2$; $<s>_4$; $<s>_6$; end		

And you can show that

```
code  (<c>_0) = code  (<s>_2)
                 code  (<s>_4)
                 code  (<s>_6)
```

where

```
<s>_2  -*-> X := Y
<s>_4  -*-> Z := (X + Y)
<s>_6  -*-> U1 := (X + (Y * Z))
```

and $code(<s>_2)$, $code(<s>_4)$, and $code(<s>_6)$ were computed in the previous section. Substituting the results of previous sections, we obtain

```
code  (<c>_0)   = COPY  AX,Y
                  COPY X,AX
                  COPY AX,X
                  ADD  AX,Y
                  COPY  CN1,AX
                  COPY AX,CN1
                  COPY Z,AX
                  COPY AX,Y
                  MUL AX,Z
                  COPY  CN2,AX
                  COPY AX,X
                  ADD  AX,CN2
                  COPY  CN1,AX
                  COPY AX,CN1
                  COPY U1,AX
```

(This code is not precisely what is generated by the rules because we did not use new names *CNi* for each new assignment statement as it was generated. This detail does not affect the computation so will not be discussed here.)

The final rule to be examined in this chapter will make it possible to do looping programs:

```
R9: <s>_i -> while <i>_j <  <e>_k  do    M(<s>_i)  = createname
                 <c>_h                    M'(<s>_i) = createname

                          code(<s>_i)  = M(<s>_i)      code(<e>_k)
                                                       COPY AX,M(<i>_j)
                                                       CMP AX,M(<e>_k)
                                                       JNB M'(<s>_i)
                                                       code(<c>_h)
                                                       JMP M(<s>_i)
                                         M'(<s>_i)     NO-OP
```

This rule translates loops that have a single test in them, $<i>_j < <e>_k$. One new assembly language instruction, *NO-OP*, appears in the code. It means "no operation" and is included only because a place is needed to put the label $M'(<s>_i)$.

Let us collect together all of the rules for the translator in one place:

Name	Syntax	Semantics
R1:	$<i>_j \rightarrow$ w where w = *a sequence* *of letters and/or digits* *that begins with a letter*	$M(<i>_j)$ = w
R2:	$<e>_i \rightarrow <i>_j$	$M(<e>_i) = M(<i>_j)$ code $(<e>_i) = $ *nothing*
R3:	$<s>_k \rightarrow <i>_j := <e>_i$	code $(<s>_k) = $ code $(<e>_i)$ COPY AX,M($<e>_i$) COPY M($<i>_j$),AX
R4:	$<e>_i \rightarrow (<e>_j + <e>_k)$	$M(<e>_i)$ = createname code$(<e>_i) = $ code $(<e>_j)$ code $(<e>_k)$ COPY AX,M($<e>_j$) ADD AX,M($<e>_k$) COPY M($<e>_i$),AX
R5:	$<e>_i \rightarrow (<e>_j * <e>_k)$	$M(<e>_i)$ = createname code$(<e>_i) = $ code $(<e>_j)$ code $(<e>_k)$ COPY AX,M($<e>_j$) MUL AX,M($<e>_k$) COPY M($<e>_i$),AX
R6:	$<q>_i \rightarrow <s>_j$; $<q>_k$	code'$(<q>_i) = $ code$(<s>_j)$ code$(<q>_k)$
R7:	$<q>_i \rightarrow <s>_j$;	code $(<q>_i) = $ code$(<s>_j)$
R8:	$<c>_i \rightarrow$ begin $<q>_j$ end	code $(<c>_i) = $ code$(<q>_j)$
R9:	$<s>_i \rightarrow$ while $<i>_j < <e>_k$ do $<c>_h$	$M(<s>_i)$ = createname $M'(<s>_i)$ = createname code$(<s>_i) = $ $\quad M(<s>_i)$ code$(<e>_k)$ $\qquad$ COPY AX,M($<i>_j$) $\qquad$ CMP AX,M($<e>_k$) $\qquad$ JNB M'$(<s>_i)$ $\qquad$ code$(<c>_h)$ $\qquad$ JMP M$(<s>_i)$ $\quad M'(<s>_i)$ NO-OP

The use of these rules is illustrated in the translation of a program to compute factorial. This program computes $1 * 2 * 3 * \ldots * N$ and leaves the result in *FACT*. Thus, if $N = 5$, it will compute $FACT = 1 * 2 * 3 * 4 * 5 = 120$. The process of translating variable declarations will not be considered here, but it will be assumed that *I*, *FACT*, *N* and *ONE* have been declared as integers, that *ONE* contains a 1, and that *N* contains the argument for the calculation:

```
begin
I := ONE;
FACT := ONE;
while I < (N + ONE) do
      begin
      FACT := (FACT * I);
      I := (I + ONE);
      end;
end
```

The compilation of this program using rules R1 to R9 follows. Some steps are omitted:

Derivation	Rules		

$<c>_0$	$<c>_0 \rightarrow$ begin
	     $<q>_1$
	     end
		code $(<c>_0)$ =	code $(<q>_1)$

begin
$<q>_1$
end
	$<q>_1 -*-> \; <s>_2$;
	          $<s>_4$;
	          $<s>_6$;
		code $(<q>_1)$ =	code $(<s>_2)$
			code $(<s>_4)$
			code $(<s>_6)$

begin $<s>_2$; $<s>_4$; $<s>_6$; end	$<s>_2 -*-> \; I := ONE$	code $(<s>_2)$ =	COPY AX,ONE COPY I,AX
begin I := ONE; $<s>_4$; $<s>_6$; end	$<s>_4 -*-> \; FACT := ONE$	code $(<s>_4)$ =	COPY AX,ONE COPY FACT,AX
begin I := ONE; FACT := ONE; $<s>_6$; end	$<s>_6 -*-> \;$ while $<i>_7 < \; <e>_8$ do $<c>_9$	code (s_6) = CN6	$M(s_6)$ = CN6 $M'(s_6)$ = CN7 code (e_8) COPY AX,M $(<i>_7)$ CMP AX,M $(<e>_8)$
			JNB CN7 code $(<c>_9)$ JMP CN6
		CN7	NO-OP

Derivation	Rules

```
begin                <i>₇ -*-> I              M(<i>₇) = I
I:= ONE;
FACT := ONE;
while <i>₇ <  <e>₈  do
    <c>₉;
end
```

$$<e>_8 \ -*-> \ (N + ONE) \qquad M(<e>_8) = CN8$$

```
                                             code (<e>₈) =    COPY AX,N
                                                              ADD  AX,ONE
                                                              COPY CN8,AX
begin                <c>₉  -*-> begin         code(<c>₉) =    code(<s>₁₀)
I := ONE;                      <s>₁₀ ;                        code(<s>₁₁)
FACT := ONE;                   <s>₁₁ ;
while  I <  (N + ONE)  do   end
    <c>₉;
end

begin                <s>₁₀ -*-> FACT := (FACT * I)
I := ONE;
FACT := ONE;                                 code (<s₁₀>) =   COPY AX,FACT
while  I <  (N + ONE)   do                                    MUL  AX,I
    begin                                                     COPY CN9,AX
    <s>₁₀;                                                    COPY AX,CN9
    <s>₁₁;                                                    COPY FACT,AX
    end;
end

begin                <s>₁₁ -*->  I := (I + ONE)
I := ONE;
FACT := ONE;                                 code (<s>₁₁) =   COPY AX,I
while  I <  (N + ONE)   do                                    ADD  AX,ONE
    begin                                                     COPY CN10,AX
    FACT := (FACT * I);                                       COPY AX,CN10
    <s>₁₁;                                                    COPY  I,AX
    end;
end

begin
I := ONE;
FACT := ONE;
while  I <  (N + ONE)   do
    begin
    FACT := (FACT * I);
    I := (I + ONE);
    end;
end
```

Applying the semantics rules obtains the final translation.

```
code (<c>₀) =          COPY  AX,ONE
                       COPY  I,AX
                       COPY  AX,ONE
                       COPY  FACT,AX
            CN6        COPY  AX,N
                       ADD  AX,ONE
                       COPY  CN8,AX
                       COPY  AX,I
                       CMP  AX,CN8
                       JNB  CN7
                       COPY  AX,FACT
                       MUL  AX,I
                       COPY  CN9,AX
                       COPY  AX,CN9
                       COPY  FACT,AX
                       COPY  AX,I
                       ADD  AX,ONE
                       COPY  CN10,AX
                       COPY  AX,CN10
                       COPY  I,AX
                       JMP  CN6
            CN7        N0-OP
```

Comparing the source language program with its translation, it is easy to see the tremendous gains in clarity and simplicity that come from using the higher-level language.

Exercises

1. Fill in the details for the translation of the factorial program.

2. Show how the rules R1 to R9 can be used to compute the translation of the following program. Assume that *ZERO* and *ONE* are integers that are initialized at 0 and 1, respectively. Assume that *N* is a nonnegative integer and *X* is an integer; both have been initialized as data items, perhaps from read statements:

```
begin
J := ZERO;
POWER := ONE;
while J < N do
      begin
      POWER := (POWER * X);
      J := (J + ONE);
      end;
end
```

What does this program compute?

3. Write a Pascal program that is within the generative scope of rules R1 to R9. Use the rules to find its translation.

4. Design an if-then construction and create a rule R10 to translate it. Write a program using your if-then construction, and show how it can be translated using rules R1 to R9 with your new rule R10.

Programming Languages (B)

Once compiler design became understood during the 1950s and 1960s, it was relatively easy to invent new higher-level languages and write compilers for them. In the years since, hundreds of computer languages have been developed.

A few well-known computer languages will be mentioned briefly here to give a glimpse of the rest of the programming world. We will examine the code required to add a column of numbers in each case for ease in making comparisons. The initializations and declarations in the programs are omitted in order to place emphasis on the lines of code that execute the addition.

The place to begin is with the language of this book, Pascal. Assume that an array A has been declared to hold the numbers to be added. The location SUM stores the sum of the numbers, and I indexes through the array:

```
SUM := 0;
I := 1;
while I <= N do
     begin
     SUM := A[I] + SUM;
     I : I | 1,
     end;
```

The for-loop feature of Pascal, not described in this book, makes it possible to write this in shorter form:

```
SUM := 0;
for I := 1 to N do
     SUM := A[I] + SUM;
```

Pascal has been adopted widely and is known for its clarity and simplicity. One of its significant features is the ability to declare a variety of different kinds of data structures. (This is another feature not mentioned in this book.)

The earliest compiled language to come into wide use was FORTRAN, which was developed in the 1950s. Variations of this language continue to be popular today, and the compilers have become refined and efficient. Here is the FORTRAN code to add the column of numbers:

```
           SUM = 0
           do 100   I = 1,N,1
           SUM = A[I] + SUM
100        continue
```

Notice various differences with Pascal, including punctuation and formating. The second line of code is a looping statement, which says "do all of the statements from here to the statement label 100 for the values of I from 1 to N incrementing 1 each time." FORTRAN was developed before structured programming evolved, and programmers were forced to rely on statement labels and "go to" statements for program control. More recent versions of FORTRAN have included the features for structured programming.

A later development was "programming language one," or PL/I. This language is famous for its large number of automatic features and its syntactic variety. For example, in most languages if I and R are declared to be integer and real, respectively, then one cannot do the assignments $I := R$ and $R := I$ because of type incompatibilities. However, PL/I allows such intermixing of types and automatically does conversions. PL/I is a structured language with many resemblances to Pascal as is evident from its code:

```
SUM = 0;
I = 1;
do while (I <= N);
    SUM = A(I) +  SUM;
    I = I + 1;
    end;
```

A problem with PL/I, however, is that its many features result in an immensely complicated compiler and possibly slow execution times.

A very popular language in current use is C, which has features that give the programmer rather exact control over the details of the computation. It is thus often used by professional programmers in systems programming work. Here is the column sum program:

```
SUM = 0;
I = 1;
while (I <= N)
      {SUM = A[I] + SUM;
       I++};
```

The while statement loops through all of the statements between the brackets {}. The $I++$ statement causes I to increment by one.

Another popular language in recent years is BASIC, which is widely used on personal computers. However, this language is in disfavor with many computer scientists because of its reliance on the "go to" statement for control and the weakness of its subroutine feature. A recent and dramatic upgrade of the language was completed in the mid-1980s, and this change eliminated many of the original problems. The new language is called True Basic. Here is its column sum code:

```
let SUM = 0
let I = 1
do while I <= N
     let SUM = A(I) + SUM
     let I = I + 1
loop
```

After this short look at five different languages, you may begin to believe that they all are the same except for punctuation and formatting. In fact, these and most other popular languages (ALGOL, COBOL, ADA, etc.) are in the same family, and their similarities enable programmers to move from one to the other with relative ease. A competent programmer with one language can usually begin writing simple programs in another after a single day of study. Competence in the new language will come usually within a few weeks. Of course, for the initiated, the differences in these languages become noticeable. In a particular environment, one of these languages may be far more desirable than the others because of some feature—perhaps its fast execution, its ease of interface with other languages, its allowed data structure forms, or some other capability.

But there are also some important languages that do not fall into the same family as Pascal. APL is one such language; it features a large number of single symbol operators that are designed to manipulate arrays. The column sum program is written in APL as

```
SUM   <- +/A
```

which means, "add up the numbers in array A, putting the result into SUM." Larger programs can be created by assembling a sequence of operators. Here is a program to compute prime numbers:

```
PRIMES N    (2=+/[1]0=(⌐N)o.|⌐N)/⌐N
```

The powerful operators of the language enable a programmer to obtain a lot of computation with just a few symbols. The programs, however, are typically somewhat difficult to read.

Another well-known language outside the Pascal family is LISP, a language designed for symbolic rather than numerical computation. Its constructs are designed to make it easy to build and manipulate complicated structures such as trees. It uses recursion heavily for control in the manner explained in the section on recursion in chapter 4. It is sometimes useful for quickly assembling a prototype program in a situation where execution time may not be critical. The column sum program can be written in LISP as follows:

```
f(A) = (cond ((atom A) 0)
             (T (plus (car A) (f (cdr A))))))
```

Here is a paraphrase of this program, which adds up the list *A*:

f(A) =   on the condition that A has length 0, return 0

             otherwise, add the first entry of A to

                       f(A with first entry removed) and return the answer

The explanation for recursive computations of this type appears near the end of chapter 4.

    Another important language is Prolog, which uses a declarative style rather than an imperative form for programs. Note that all of the languages discussed elsewhere in this book and almost all languages in regular use are imperative in nature. The programs are of the form

```
Do this.
Do that.
Do something else.
   etc.
```

Thus, the programmer uses the program to tell the machine what to do. Prolog programs are of the form

```
This is a fact.
That is a fact.
Something else is a fact.
   etc.
```

Here the programmer does not use the program to tell the machine how to do a calculation. The program merely states facts, and the machine automatically finds the facts needed to answer a question.

    Here is an example of a usage of Prolog. We will state four facts regarding height relationships:

```
fact(jill, tallerthan, sally).
fact(sally, tallerthan, renee).
fact(renee, tallerthan, nancy).
fact(nancy, tallerthan, mary).
```

Then we ask questions such as, "Who is taller than Mary?" Here is how the question is asked:

```
fact(X, tallerthan, mary).
```

The system will respond with X = nancy. Or we could ask, "Who is taller than who?"

```
fact(X, tallerthan, Y).
```

The machine will respond:

```
X = jill, Y = sally
X = sally, Y = renee
X = renee, Y = nancy
X = nancy, Y = mary
```

Actually this feature acts exactly like the database program of chapter 4. It even has the shortcoming that the database program had: it does not infer information not explicitly given in the facts.

But Prolog allows much more powerful assertions. We can also state generalized facts of the following type:

```
fact(X, tallerthan, Z) :- fact(X, tallerthan, Y),
                                   fact(Y, tallerthan, Z).
```

This should be read as "X is taller than Z if X is taller than Y and Y is taller than Z." Using the previous four facts and this one, let us again ask the question, "Who is taller than Mary?"

```
fact(X, tallerthan, mary).
```

This time the system will use all of the original information plus the generalized fact to infer new facts:

```
X = nancy
X = renee
X = sally
X = jill
```

Thus the Prolog system uses the total of the facts given to assemble the answer even though the programmer has not explicitly indicated how to do the computation. It has done a kind of inference that our database program could not do, and this property makes it an extremely important kind of language.

A programming language of this type is quite different from Pascal and other languages in ordinary computations. Here is a Prolog program to add a list of numbers:

```
f(0,[ ]).
f(S,[X|Y]) :- f(Z,Y), S is X + Z.
```

The first fact says, "f associates 0 with the list with no entries." The second fact says, "f associates S with a list beginning with X and ending with a list Y of other entries if f associates Z with Y and S is X + Z."

In other words, the sum S is found by adding up everything Y but the first entry X in the list $[X/Y]$ to obtain Z. Then X is added to Z to obtain the result S. This is another recursive program that can be understood only if recursion (chapter 4) is understood. But we can demonstrate how to use it to add numbers. We type the following,

```
f(X,[7,3,9,2]).
```

and the system will respond $X = 21$.

Many languages are available to computer scientists, and an experienced programmer must choose which to use in a given application. Some languages resemble Pascal in form but have special characteristics that may make them better or worse than Pascal in one situation or another. But other languages are dramatically different, and they have correspondingly different strengths and weaknesses.

Exercises

1. Make up a table with a column for each of the eight languages discussed here. Fill in the table as well as you are able giving the following information for each language: form of assignment statements, punctuation for statement termination, form of looping construction, the addition operator, length of the sample code in number of characters, strengths, and weaknesses.

2. Study the section on recursion, and then show how the LISP program for addition works. *(atom A)* is true if A is a list of length zero. The function *(car A)* returns the first entry of list A, and the function *(cdr A)* returns A with its first entry removed.

3. Study the section on recursion in chapter 4, and analyze the Prolog program for addition. The notation $L = [X/Y]$ means that L is a list of objects where X is the first entry on the list and Y is the list containing the rest of the entries of L.

Some Pragmatics of Computing (B)

As we conclude the portion of the book on hardware and software, it is important to mention some issues that are not discussed elsewhere. This book assumes that you have access to a computer and its manuals and are doing exercises along the way. Thus some practical concerns are not discussed and are left to be learned through these experiences. However, a few concepts and some vocabulary will be reviewed here in case they are not otherwise clear.

The two main parts of the computer are the central processing unit (CPU) and the memory. The CPU has the job of executing instructions that do such things as bring in data from the memory, manipulate them, and store them back into the memory. There are usually a hundred or more instructions for a CPU, and they are typically designed to process a fixed amount of data in each operation. That is, there will be some number N, and each CPU instruction will copy or manipulate N bits of data. For many early microcomputers, N was 8 or 16, but more recently, most have N of 32. Many large mainframe machines process 32 or 64 bits per operation, but a variety of other sizes have been built.

Memory is usually constructed with magnetic medium rather than with flip-flops, as described in chapter 6. That is, a 0 or 1 is stored by magnetizing a tiny area of ferrous material rather than by setting switches. The size of a memory is ordinarily measured in bytes where 1 byte equals 8 bits. This is a convenient size because most coding schemes allocate 1 byte per character. Thus, a 1 million byte memory can hold 1 million characters. Typical machines may have a few tens of thousands (K) of bytes up to several million bytes (several *megabytes*). For example, a machine with 32,000 bytes of memory will be said to have a 32K memory. A machine with 2 million bytes will be said to have 2 megabytes of memory.

When a program or a set of data is not being used, it is typically stored on a *disk*. These disks are coated with a ferrous material and hold information using magnetization as does an ordinary tape recorder. A *disk drive* spins the disk and either reads information from or stores information on the disk surfaces. A *floppy disk* is a disk made of a thin plastic material that can be carried around with its stored information and inserted into the machine's *floppy disk drive* if the information, programs or data, is needed. A *hard disk* is a high-precision disk permanently mounted in a closed case. A floppy disk can store possibly a few hundred K bytes of memory. Hard disks can store from a few dozen megabytes to many thousands of megabytes.

The information on a disk is organized into packages called *files*. A file contains either a program or a set of data and is moved around in the computer as a unit in the same way that an envelope of pages might be handed around an office. A file can be stored on a disk, it can be brought into the computer memory, it can be modified in the machine, it can be stored back on the disk, or it can be printed.

In the early days of computing, the computer operator had many tasks, such as checking whether the customer was an approved user for the machine, loading the user's program, loading a translator for the program, running the translation, loading the data, and turning on the printer. Soon people discovered that it is possible to write a program to do all of these functions, and such a program is called an *operating system (OS)*. The OS enables the user to tell the machine which of these many jobs is to be done, and it then directs the machine to do it. In a typical interactive session, the OS might ask the user to type a keyword before it will allow further computation. Once the user has done this, he or she might ask the OS to bring in the file containing the editor program from disk. Next, the user might type a program and request the OS to store the program as a file on the disk. The user could ask the OS to display the directory and confirm that the program has been stored. Later, the OS might be called on to compile the program, run it, print results, and so forth. The command language for the OS is sometimes called *job control language*.

Large computers can be connected to many user terminals at one time. In this case, the users *timeshare* the machine; they all may have resident tasks in the machine memory or on disks, and they may all simultaneously be using the machine. The machine operates by servicing one user's job, then the next, then the next, and so forth until it returns to the first user again. It is usually so fast that no individual notices any delays, and all can enjoy the power of a large machine. It will appear to each user that he or she has complete control of the machine. However, if too many users log in at any given time or if the ones who are logged on require very much computation, the machine will get behind, and all users will notice unpleasant slowdowns. The operating system for a timesharing machine must be extremely complicated in order to keep track of all of the users, their programs, the availability of memory, the printing devices, and so forth.

This overview is extremely brief; you are advised to read more adequate descriptions of these facilities associated with your own machine.

Summary (B)

This chapter has explained a methodology for translating one language to another. Translation rules are described that build a linkage between the two languages. Each rule has two parts—a syntactic part and a semantic part. The syntactic parts of the rules are used to discover the form of a sentence in the source language; one finds a way to generate the source language sentence from an initial symbol such as $<s>_1$, and the rules needed to do the generation indicate the parts of the source statement. For example, the discovery that the multiplication rule R5 is needed at a particular point to generate a Pascal statement is an indication that a multiplication is to be done, and the rule discovers what is to be multiplied.

Once it is known which syntactic rules generate the source statement, the structure of that statement is known, and its translation can be determined. This is done by the semantic portions of the rules that were used in the syntactic analysis. Straightforward substitution and combination of these semantics definitions yields the result, the translation in the object language. All of these ideas are demonstrated in the first several sections by the rules R1 to R5, which can be used to translate some Pascal assignment statements to assembly language. In a later section, rules R6 to R9 were introduced, showing how to translate complete code segments, including some loops into assembly language.

A translation program from a source language such as Pascal to a lower-level language such as P88 assembly language is called a *compiler*. The compiler is composed of all of the translation rules, code to use the rules to do the syntactic and semantic analyses, and many other routines to optimize the code, send messages to the user, and so forth.

Another way to use a computer language on a computer, besides compiling it, is to use an *interpreter* for it. Interpreters are programs that execute a source language program without any initial translation. From the user's point of view, they may seem to function in the same way as compilers, although their execution time will be slower. Their principles of operation are beyond the scope of this book.

This chapter completes the section of the book that traces the mechanisms of a computer hardware and software system from the program at the highest level through the architecture of the machine to the switching circuits and the electron flows at the very lowest level. A review of the chapters is worthwhile to collect together the total view. We will summarize by once again tracing all processing for the single Pascal statement

```
Z  :=  (X + Y)
```

Using the rules R1 through R5 of this chapter, this statement is translated or compiled into equivalent assembly language:

```
COPY AX,X
ADD  AX,Y
COPY CN1,AX
COPY AX,CN1
COPY Z,AX
```

These instructions are then translated in a process called assembly into a set of binary codes, which we have written as

```
*   COPY AX,X      *
*   ADD  AX,Y      *
*   COPY CN1,AX    *
*   COPY AX,CN1    *
*   COPY Z,AX      *
```

but which really look something like this:

```
0010101010011001
0100000101101100
-  -  -
-  -  -
0010101000101001
```

These are loaded into the memory of the machine and when they are used, the Instruction Pointer gives their location. Chapter 9 catalogs the events associated with their execution.

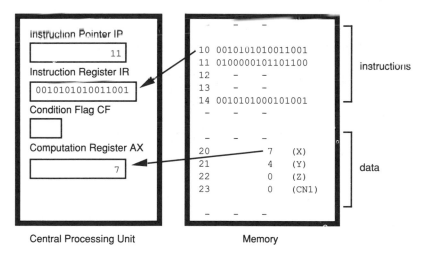

Central Processing Unit   Memory

At a more detailed level, you can examine the ways that the commands are decoded and carried out. Each instruction is decoded as explained at the end of chapter 6, and circuits of the type examined there are used to do the calculation. For example, the second instruction in the example is an *add* instruction, and a complete circuit for adding was given:

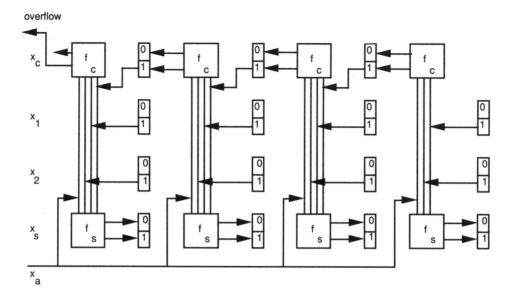

The machine must contain such circuits for all machine instructions, add, copy, multiply, and so forth.

But how do these circuits work? They are made up of many tiny switching circuits constructed from semiconductors as described in chapters 7 and 8. Here is an example:

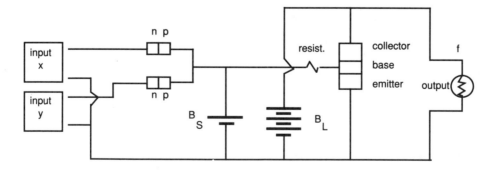

A computer circuit.

The transistor is turned on by supplying carriers to its base region and turned off by removing them.

Finally, hundreds of thousands of such circuits are packed on a silicon chip using microscopic doping and etching processes. The batteries that are shown are replaced by a single power source, which sends wires to all of the individual circuits.

Readings

On translation and compilers:

Aho, A. V., Sethi, R., and Ullman, J. D., *Compilers: Principles, Techniques, and Tools,* Addison-Wesley, Menlo Park, California, 1986.

Borat, R., *Understanding and Writing Compilers,* Macmillan, London, 1978.

Gries, D., *Compiler Construction for Digital Computers*, John Wiley, New York, 1971.

On programming languages:

MacLennan, B. J., *Principles of Programming Languages: Design, Evaluation, and Implementation,* Holt, Rinehart and Winston, New York, 1983.

Pratt, T. W., *Programming Languages,* Prentice-Hall, Englewood Cliffs, New Jersey, 1984.

Sammet, J. E., *Programming Languages: History and Fundamentals,* Prentice-Hall, Englewood Cliffs, New Jersey, 1969.

Tucker, A. B., *Programming Languages,* Second Edition, McGraw-Hill, New York, 1986.

On APL:

Iverson, K. E., *A Programming Language,* John Wiley and Sons, New York, 1962.

On LISP:

Friedman, D. P., and Felleisen, M., *The Little LISPer,* The MIT Press, Cambridge, Massachusetts, 1987.

Steele, G. L. Jr., *Common LISP: The Language*, Digital Press, Burlington, Massachusetts, 1984.

Weissman, C., *LISP 1.5 Primer*, Dickenson, Belmont, California, 1967.

On Prolog:

Clocksin, W. F. and Mellish, C. S., *Programming in PROLOG,* Second Edition, Springer-Verlag, New York, 1984.

Sterling, L. and Shapiro, E., *The Art of Prolog,* The MIT Press, Cambridge, Massachusetts, 1986.

11

Program Execution Time

On the Limitations of Computer Science (A)

In the first four chapters of this book, we studied programming. After one has a reasonable degree of experience in programming, it is quite common to become confident in one's ability to code absolutely anything. Programmers will often announce, "If you tell me what you want done, I can code it for you." At the end of chapter 4, we discussed the Church-Markov-Turing Thesis, which hypothesizes that any procedure that can be precisely explained can be coded in any standard programming language.

It therefore may come as a surprise to learn that computer scientists are not able to compute everything they want. There are very many calculations that would be extremely useful but in fact cannot be done. This chapter and the ones that follow will examine a number of problems that are either hard or impossible for modern computer scientists to solve. We will examine the current limitations of the field, the topic areas for much research.

There are three major reasons that many useful calculations cannot be done:

1. The execution time of the program may be too long. Instead of simply running the program and reading the answer after a few seconds or minutes, the program may require a year or even a century or more to find the answer. This may happen even though the fastest and most modern computer is used.

2. The problem may be what computer scientists call *noncomputable*. There are problems that no computer program can solve using current technologies or any technologies that can be foreseen. Many of these problems are of great practical interest and seem to form an impenetrable blockage to certain kinds of progress.

3. We may not know how to write the program to solve the problem. There are many problems that could conceivably be solved with present-day machines and languages, but methods are not known for solving them. Many of these are problems in the field of artificial intelligence, questions related to how to make machines "understand" language, visual data, and other concepts, how to make machines learn, and other tasks.

These three topics related to the limitations of computer science are the concern of this and later chapters. In this chapter, we will study the execution time of programs and limitation 1. In the next chapter, we will examine parallel machine architectures that make it possible to speed up some computations. Chapter 13 will present the fundamental facts related to noncomputability and will give examples of important problems that are unsolvable by any known method. Chapter 14 will give an overview of the field of artificial intelligence, a study of problems that may be solvable but in many cases are beyond our abilities.

Program Execution Time (A)

Ideally a computation happens quickly. We would like to type the input to the machine, wait for no more than a few seconds, and then see the answer printed. Most of the programs examined in this book run this satisfactorily, and in a learning environment, it is not obvious that the execution time of programs can become a problem. But in the real world of industry, government, and research laboratories, program execution time is a matter of great concern. The quantity of data that needs to be processed can become astronomical, and even the fastest machines can require hours, days, or even years to complete given tasks.

It is no longer satisfactory simply to write a program and run it until the job is done. It becomes important to understand timing considerations for programs and to be able to predict how much time specific calculations will require before they are attempted. Before the Internal Revenue Service attempts to sort the social security numbers of taxpayers, it is important to know how many hours, months, or years of computer time may be needed to do the job. Before a power company attempts to compute the most efficient routing of power lines around a region, it is advisable to estimate how many hours, months, or years of machine time will be expended. The cost of the calculation may be so high as to be prohibitive, forcing managers to look for alternative ways to manage their data and make their decisions.

This chapter will examine the execution times of some programs and estimate how long they would require to handle some rather large blocks of data. The concept of a *tractable* computation will be introduced; this is a calculation that can usually be completed on even large blocks of data within "reasonable" amounts of time. Then some *intractable* calculations will be introduced that can require astounding amounts of computation for almost any problem beyond the most trivial examples. The conclusion of the study will be that computations divide themselves roughly into two classes: those that can be done with reasonable expenditures of time and those that cannot be realistically completed except for rather small examples. Since problems in both classes are quite common in practical situations, these limitations are of substantial importance.

Tractable Computations (B)

For the moment, a *tractable computation* should be understood intuitively to be a calculation that can be done within a reasonable amount of time, even if large amounts of data are to be processed. A more precise definition of this term will be given later in this section.

We will begin the study by examining a particular computation— the task of collecting the names of all people with a specified height and weight. We assume three arrays are given —*name*, *height*, and *weight* —which hold in position *i*, respectively, the name, height, and weight for a particular person. Suppose the arrays contain information for six people; they might look as follows:

name		height		weight	
1	John Jones	1	67	1	120
2	Sue Black	2	67	2	131
3	Bill Smith	3	73	3	166
4	Frank Doe	4	68	4	140
5	Jean White	5	67	5	131
6	Nancy Blike	6	71	6	162

In other words, John Jones has a height of 67 inches and a weight of 120 pounds, and the other five persons have the associated heights and weights as shown. The program will store these arrays and then receive two pieces of information—a target height and a target weight. The program will then print the names of all people who have this target height and weight. A sample execution of the program would begin by first reading in all the entries in the arrays as shown above. Then it would proceed as follows:

```
Computer:   Give the target height.
User:       67
Computer:   Give the target weight.
User:       131
Computer:   The list of persons with the specified height and weight is:
            Sue Black
            Jean White
            End of search.
```

Let us examine a program written to do this task:

```
program PersonSearch;
type
    stringarray100 = array[1..100] of string;
    realarray100 = array[1..100] of real;
var
    name:stringarray100;
    height,weight:realarray100;
    n,i:integer;
    targetheight, targetweight: real;
```

```
begin
{ Put code here to enter data into the arrays. }
{ Assume that entries 1 to n have been          }
{ filled with data in the three arrays.         }
writeln('Give the target height.');
readln(targetheight);
writeln('Give the target weight.');
readln(targetweight);
writeln('The list of persons with specified height and weight is:');
i := 1;
while i <= n do
   begin
   if (targetheight = height[i]) and (targetweight = weight[i]) then
       writeln(name[i]);
   i := i + 1;
   end;
writeln('End of search.');
readln;
end.
```

This program is capable of holding the information for up to 100 people. Throughout this chapter, the symbol n will be used to measure the size of the task being undertaken. In this example, n will represent the number of people whose records must be examined. For the above example, $n=6$ and for the given program, n may not exceed 100 unless the declarations are changed.

The loop in the program examines sequentially *weight[1]* and *height[1]*, then *weight[2]* and *height[2]*, and so forth, printing out the associated name whenever the examined values both equal the target values.

The execution time for the program has two parts: the part required to fill the arrays and type in the target values and the part required to perform the looping computation. We will consider only the second portion; it is that part of the execution where the search through the data takes place. Thus we are measuring the time required to examine the records of n people to find all cases that meet the two requirements. We are measuring the amount of time elapsed between the printing of the two messages:

"The list of persons with specified height and weight is:" and
"End of search."

A version of this program was entered into a computer, and measurements were made of its search times. It was assumed that the number of persons might equal the number of students in a small university—up to 10,000 people. The results showed that this is a very inexpensive calculation even for this large number of people:

Number of people, n	Execution time in seconds, t
2500	1.275
5000	2.550
7500	3.825
10,000	5.100

Ten thousand people can be checked in about 5 seconds on this particular machine!

These values can be graphed showing that they form a straight line, and algebraic methods can be used to find an equation for the line. In fact, the execution time in seconds for the program will be represented by t, and in this case, one can show that

$$t = 5.1 * 10^{-4} * n.$$

You should check to see that if values of n from the table are entered into this equation, then the associated times t in the table will be computed. Checking the second entry in the table, where $n=5000$,

$$t = 5.1 * 10^{-4} * 5000 = 2.55$$

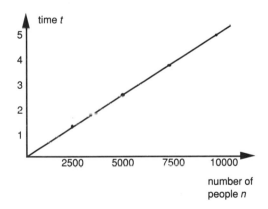

It is often difficult to find formulas to compute execution times as was done here. But if they can be found they are very useful. For example, one might ask how long it would take to run this program on the total population of the United States. As a rough approximation, assume $n = 300$ million, and the execution time can be computed to be 153,000 seconds or 42.5 hours. This program can search the whole population of the United States in just a couple of days. It is a good example of an easily tractable computation. (In this example, we have ignored the problem of how to fit the records of so many people onto a single computer. We only address the issue of execution time here, the most severe constraint in most situations.)

Let us examine another computation, the process of sorting numbers into ascending order. That is, suppose an array A has values as shown:

	A
1	47
2	12
3	46
4	10
5	41
6	33
7	44
8	86

How long does it take a computer to put these numbers into order?

	A
1	10
2	12
3	33
4	41
5	44
6	46
7	47
8	86

We studied in chapter 4 a program called "quicksort" that can do this task and can examine its running time here. Again, considering populations of people of the size of a small university, a quicksort program was run for values of n up to 10,000. The following table gives the values obtained.

Number of people n	Execution time in seconds, t
2500	59.261
5000	129.021
7500	202.745
10,000	279.042

Assuming that sorting names is roughly as time-consuming as sorting numbers, one could use this type of program to alphabetize the names of the students at a university of size 10,000. The required time would be slightly over 4 minutes. This is another example of a tractable computation.

These values also can be graphed as shown below, but the result is not quite a straight line. However, you can still use algebraic techniques (not discussed in this book) to obtain an approximate formula for execution time in seconds:

$$t = 2.1 * 10^{-3} * n * \log_2 n$$

The function $log_2 n$ commonly occurs in algebra and computer science. Some of its values are given here:

n	$log_2 n$
1	0
2	1
4	2
8	3
16	4
32	5
2,500	11.2877
5,000	12.2877
7,500	12.8727
10,000	13.2877

You can check that the formula agrees with the values in the table. Thus, at $n = 5000$,

$$t = 2.1 * 10^{-3} * 5000 * 12.2877 = 129.021.$$

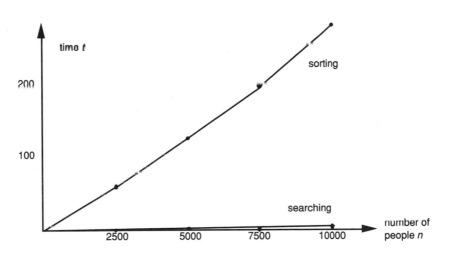

The graph shows the run time for both sorting and searching. Sorting is clearly far more expensive than searching, but it is still classified as tractable.

Again, it is possible to calculate the cost of running this program on a huge population, say that of the United States. Using the fact that if $n = 300$ million, then $log_2 n = 28.1604$, the formula gives the sorting time as 205.34 days. This is a long time, but remember that the size of the job is huge. If the Internal Revenue Service wants to do this calculation, they will presumably use large computers rather than a desktop model, and such machines might run ten or more times faster than our formula would suggest. So the calculation probably could be reduced to a couple of weeks. Thus we conclude that sorting is another example of a tractable computation. (This is why the Internal Revenue Service is able to match income statements from corporations to individual income tax returns. They sort the statements on the individual names or social security numbers and then check to see that those individuals reported the income.)

We are now able to give a more precise definition of tractability; this is the definition used by most computer scientists. A computation will be called *tractable* if its timing formula is a polynomial on n (and possibly $log_2 n$). Such polynomials are sums of terms of the form $a * n^b$ or $a * n^b * (log_2 n)^c$ where a, b, and c are fixed numbers. For example, the following formulas give timings for tractable computations:

$$t = 3 * n^2$$

$$t = 4 * n^3 + 16 * n^2 + 7 * n + 8$$

$$t = 4 * n^2 * log_2 n + 3 * n$$

$$t = 17 * (log_2 n)^2 + n$$

You should check that the execution times for the above search and sort programs do have the required form and thus qualify officially as tractable computations.

In contrast to tractable computations, there are intractable ones. This can happen if the timing formula includes an n in the exponent. As an example,

$$t = 6^n$$

is a formula that does not conform to the definition in the previous paragraph. In this case, t increases in a profoundly different manner than in tractable situations and at a much faster rate as n is increased. The next section will give an example of an intractable computation.

Exercises

1. Run the following program for various values of n. Graph its execution time versus n. The formula for execution time should have this form:

$$t = C_0 + C_1 n$$

What values do the constants have for this program on your computer? How long would it take your program to count to 300 million?

```
program E1;
var
    i,n:integer;
begin
readln(n);
i := 1;
while i <= n do
   begin
   writeln(i);
   i := i + 1;
   end;
writeln('done');
readln;
end.
```

2. Repeat exercise 1 for the following program. The execution time equation should have this form:

$$t = C_0 + C_1 n^2$$

```
program E2;
var
    i,j,k,n:integer;
begin
readln(n);
i := 1;
j := 1;
while j <= n do
    begin
    k := 1;
    while k <= n do
        begin
        writeln(i);
        i := i + 1;
        k := k + 1;
        end;
    j := j + 1;
    end;
writeln('done');
readln;
end.
```

3. The program of exercise 2 was constructed by nesting a loop inside of another loop. Revise that program to have three nested loops instead of two and find a formula for its execution time.

4. The program to find all individuals of specified height and weight will run faster if the data in the arrays are organized in a special way. Can you find that way and show how to revise the program to run faster? Can you find a formula for its execution time and estimate the time required to process all of the people of the United States?

Intractable Computations (B)

A computation is called *intractable* if its execution time increases with increasing *n* faster than any polynomial of the form described in the previous section. An example of an intractable computation is the solution to the Towers of Hanoi problem described in chapter 4. In that chapter, you may have tested the given program on towers with three, four, or five disks, and the issue of computation time may not have seemed to be critical. The program apparently solved the problem immediately. In this section, we will measure a Towers of Hanoi program and see that its execution time increases quickly as *n* increases.

Following the method of the previous section, let us run the program for several values of n and find a function that will estimate the run time. Before doing the test, it is necessary to appropriately increase the size of the arrays, and one should remove the print statements to speed up the computation as much as possible. We will run the program on the usual values and graph the observed timings:

Number of disks, n	Execution time in seconds, t
2,500	?
5,000	?
7,500	?
10,000	?

Strangely, the measurement is not successful, and the program apparently runs forever when started on these values. What is wrong? Perhaps the program will not work if n is large. Or it may be that the Towers of Hanoi problem has no solution for these values of n.

In fact, there is a solution, and the program will solve it even for these large n, but the execution time is large. Let us run the program on some small values of n and see how fast the run time grows:

Number of disks, n	Execution time in seconds, t
1	less than 1 second
2	less than 1 second
3	less than 1 second
4	less than 1 second
5	less than 1 second
6	less than 1 second
7	less than 1 second
8	1
9	3
10	6

For these values, the program completes the task rather quickly. But for larger n, the real trend becomes apparent:

n	t
11	11
12	23
13	45
14	90
15	180
16	360

Adding these data to the graph of the previous section, it is clear that a new phenomenon is occurring. The time to complete the task at $n = 16$ is greater than it was for sorting at $n = 10,000$. Furthermore, it is climbing on a line that is nearly straight up!

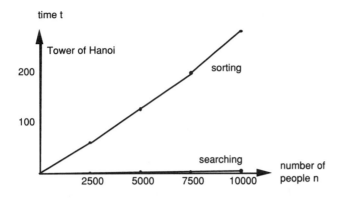

We can find a formula to estimate the timing in seconds for this program.

$$t = 5.49 * 10^{-3} * 2^n$$

Then we can evaluate t for increasing values of n and see what computer scientists mean when they call something "intractable":

n	t (approximate)
5	0.17 seconds
10	5.62 seconds
15	3.00 minutes
20	1.60 hours
25	2.13 days
30	68.23 days
35	5.98 years
40	191.30 years
45	6120.94 years
50	195,870 years
55	6,267,840 years
60	200,571,000 years
65	6,418,270,000 years
70	205,385,000,000 years

The time required to do 35 disks is several years, to do 40 disks is several centuries, and to do 45 disks is a period longer than all of recorded history. Physicists say that the sun will burn out in a few billion years; so the machine would not be able to do 65 disks unless it were moved to a different solar system. The history of the universe since the "big bang", as theorized by cosmologists, is a mere 15 billion or so years, not enough to time to do even 70 disks.

In contrast with the examples of the previous section where the calculations were completed for n of 10000 or even 300,000,000, with the current example n may not exceed even a few dozen. There is no comparison between the run times of tractable problems and the computation discussed here.

One might propose that future technology will be able to circumvent the problem of intractability. Large numbers of faster machines all working together may someday make it possible to handle even the problem discussed here for large n. Unfortunately, there is little hope that technology will help much for such problems. Suppose a rather substantial improvement in machines enabled them to run a thousand times faster. Suppose furthermore that a way were found to break the problem into small parts so that a thousand such machines could work in parallel on the solution. Even with this 1 million-fold increase in effort, it would be possible to solve problems with only 20 more disks than is currently possible in a given amount of time. The system still could do just a few dozen disks.

Finally, the question arises concerning the importance of this result. How many managers of contemporary industry really want to utilize a machine to solve the Towers of Hanoi problem for many disks? Probably none, but this is an easy example to understand, and it demonstrates all of the significant characteristics of some truly important practical problems. The next section will describe several of them.

Exercise

1. Type the following program and test it on your machine. Run it on some short strings of length 2 or 3. Draw a graph of execution time versus string length n. Can you find a formula for its execution time? (You will have difficulty reading the code unless you have read the section on recursion in chapter 4.)

```
{A program to list all the orderings (permutations)               }
{    of a set of characters.                                       }
{Input: A string of characters.                                    }
{Output: A set of strings giving every possible reordering of the  }
{    characters in the original string. For example, if the input  }
{    is abc, the the output will be abc, acb, bac, bca, cab, cba.  }
{Method of operation:  The program maintains two strings, original }
{    and target. Original begins by holding the original string and }
{    as the target string is constructed, characters are moved from }
{    original to target. The program makes every possible choice for }
{    what character should be in the first position, then every     }
{    possible choice from the characters left for the second        }
{    position, etc.                                                 }

program P1;
var
    permstring,blank:string;

procedure permutation(var target,original:string);
    {This routine finds all rearrangements of the characters in    }
    {original, and concatenates them to right end of the string    }
    {in target.                                                    }
```

```
    var
        i:integer;
        target1,original1:string;
    begin
    if length(original)=0 then          {If original has no characters,  }
        writeln(target)                  {then print target.             }
    else
        begin                            {Otherwise, for each i move the  }
        i:=1;                            {ith character of original to    }
        while i<=length(original) do {right end of target and do a     }
            begin                        {a recursive call.              }
            target1:=target + original[i];
            original1:=copy(original,1,i-1)
                            + copy(original,i+1,length(original)-i);
            permutation(target1,original1);
            i:=i+1;
            end;
        end;
    end;

begin                                    {Begin the main program.        }
writeln('Input a string of characters.');
readln(permstring);                      {Read the original string.      }
blank:='';
writeln('The set of permutations:');
permutation(blank,permstring);           {Find all orderings.            }
writeln('Done.');
readln;
end.
```

Some Practical Problems with Very Expensive Solutions (B)

We will examine three problems in this section that appear to be as computationally expensive as the Towers of Hanoi and have numerous applications in scientific and industrial endeavors. The problems address the issues of finding minimum cost paths on a flat plane, the most efficient coverage of an area with odd shaped parts, and the discovery of the best choice in a decision making environment.

Finding the Minimum Cost Path.

Suppose a traveling salesman wishes to visit a series of cities, beginning at his home city, driving to visit each of the other cities exactly once, and then returning home. Suppose further that there are a total of six cities, as shown below. The question is: Which route should he follow in order to achieve the shortest possible trip?

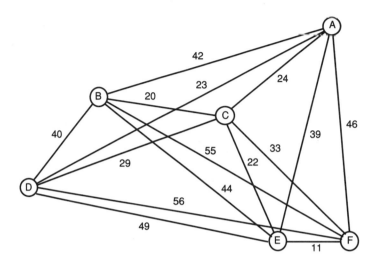

An example route might start at city A and then proceed sequentially to cities B, C, D, E, F, and back to A. The distance traveled is easy to compute.

From A to B	42
From B to C	20
From C to D	29
From D to E	49
From E to F	11
From F to A	46
Total	197

But is this the shortest possible distance? Perhaps some other route would be better. The goal is to find it.

One way to find the shortest route is to find all routes, compute their lengths, and then select the optimum one. Here are a few of the routes that might be tried and their respective lengths.

Route	Length
AECDBFA	231
ACBDEFA	190
ABFEDCA	210
AEFDCBA	197
AFDECBA	235

The minimum one found here has a length of 190, and there may be even shorter paths. For problems with n cities, if n is greater than 2 then there are

$$s = ((n-1)*(n-2)* \ldots *1)/2$$

different such paths. So for $n = 6$ cities, one must check

$$s = (5*4*3*2*1)/2 = 60$$

different paths to solve the problem.

Clearly this calculation for n cities is extremely expensive if no better solution method is found. This is called the *traveling salesman problem*, and it has been studied by many scholars over the past three decades. Some substantially better algorithms have been discovered, but even the best yield only intractable calculations. The details of such methodologies are beyond the scope of this book. However, if we were to write a program to implement any such procedure that is known, the time chart would look very similar to the one for the Towers of Hanoi. Some problems have been solved for cases where $n = 50$ cities or more, but the amount of computer time can be large. Problems where n ranges in the thousands are completely out of the question as they were with the Towers of Hanoi.

One can hope that a more efficient solution may be invented some day. There may be a clever technique to find the best path very quickly; the world needs only to have the proper person find it. As an illustration, one could propose that the following algorithm will always obtain the shortest path through the cities:

1. Select a city randomly.

2. From the current city, choose the shortest path leading out to a city that has not yet been visited. Follow that path to the next city. If there are still unvisited cities, repeat step 2 again.

3. Connect the final city back to the home city.

Following this algorithm, we might start at city E and note that the nearest unvisited city is F. From F, the nearest unvisited city is C; from C the nearest unvisited city is B; and so forth. This calculation is very fast, but, unfortunately, it does not find the best route. All other fast algorithms that have been tried also fail to find the best solution. Many times they do find answers that are good enough for most purposes.

The traveling salesman problem is of considerable economic importance because such shortest-path solutions are needed for setting up truck routes, electric power distribution systems, and many other applications. Furthermore, it has been shown that if a fast method for doing this calculation could be found, many other seemingly intractable problems would become tractable. (The traveling salesman problem is a member of the class of so called *NP-complete* problems that all appear to require exponential time. But it has been shown that if any member of the class could be solved in tractable time, then all members of the class could be solved in tractable time.)

Finding the Best Coverage of an Area.

Suppose an area of specified size is to be covered as completely as possible with a set of odd-shaped objects:

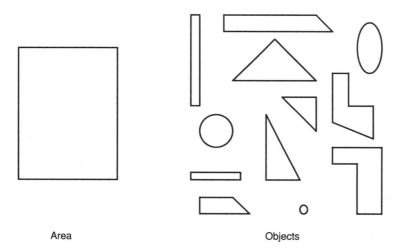

Area   Objects

Any of the available objects may be used, and they may be rotated in any way. The goal is to pack them into the limited space in such a way as to minimize the amount of uncovered space:

Area   Unused objects

The problem is to find which objects to use and how they are to be fit together to achieve the best fit.

The naive solution is reminiscent of the method proposed for the traveling salesman problem: try every set of objects and try them in every orientation. This problem also has been studied extensively and many improvements are known to the very slow "try-everything" approach. However, the best-known results again have execution times similar to the Towers of Hanoi as the number n of potential pieces for selection becomes large.

This is an important problem because it arises when one tries to fit packages optimally into a bin, most efficiently cut pieces of material from raw stock, or find the best design for a series of rooms in a building. It is another example of a problem that cannot be solved perfectly if n is large.

Discovering the Best Choice in a Decision-Making Environment.

Suppose you are playing checkers and wish to make the best possible move.

In the position shown, white has seven possible next moves. If one of these moves is made, the opponent typically will have about seven responses. This means the decision sequence forms a tree similar to those studied in chapter 1.

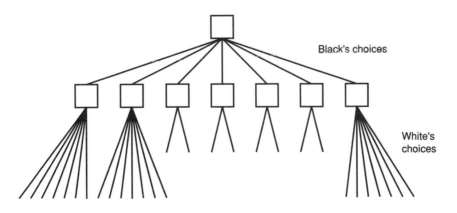

Black's choices

White's choices

This tree could possibly extend to cover all choice sequences of length n for some substantial n. The problem is to determine which sequence of n moves leads to the best ultimate situation.

The details of the problem will not be discussed here; more will be given in chapter 14. But we will note that the number of positions at the bottom of this tree is 7^n assuming there are seven branches below each node. Thus trees of depth one, two, three, etc., will have 7, 49, 343, etc. positions across the bottom level. If a computer program is to examine all of those positions, clearly it will have a run time similar to the Towers of Hanoi, and the calculation will again be intractable.

The checkers model is similar to many other decision-making situations that occur in industrial and governmental applications. Any environment where sequences of decisions over time lead to many different end results will have similar characteristics. It is quite common to obtain exorbitant running times for computer programs designed to simulate these situations.

Exercises

1. Classify, as well as you can, each problem as either tractable or intractable.

(a) A column of n numbers is to be added up.

(b) A jigsaw puzzle of n pieces is to be assembled.

(c) All of the duplicate entries in a list of n numbers are to be removed.

(d) A group of n approaching missiles are to be shot down with n antimissile-missiles. An assignment is to be made of one defending missile to each approaching missile such that the distance of approaching missiles to the border before they are destroyed is maximized.

(e) A person's telephone number is to be found in a telephone book of n names.

(f) The paychecks for n employees are to be computed, including deductions.

(g) The number of atoms in n cubic feet of silicon is to be computed

(within an accuracy of 10 percent).

(h) In an economic model, an industrialist is to find the decision

sequence over the next n months that maximizes profits.

2. The *permutation* program in the exercises of the previous section can be modified to solve the traveling salesman problem. Make the appropriate changes, and use your program to determine whether a better solution can be found to the example traveling salesman problem of that section.

Summary (B)

The chapter began by noting three reasons that it may not be possible to do a desired calculation. Then it examined the first of these reasons—that the amount of machine time required to do the calculation may be unrealistically large. Later chapters will examine the other reasons.

The study of execution times leads to the concepts of tractable and intractable computations. The former class encompasses problems with reasonable execution times in most cases, even if large amounts of data are to be processed. Solutions to problems in the latter class usually will result in astronomically large computation times if problems of nontrivial size are attempted. Both kinds of calculations are important in practice.

Some intractable computations are amenable to approximate solutions that can be computed in acceptable time and that are accurate enough for many purposes. Many of these problems and their approximate solutions are the object of recent research in computer science.

It is also possible that a calculation could not be done because some other resource besides time is not sufficiently available. You can imagine that there may be calculations requiring astronomical amounts of memory, for example, and that they could not be completed because of memory limitations. In practice, this is an uncommon situation and will not be discussed further in this book.

Readings

On the analysis of algorithms:

Aho, A. V., Hopcroft, J. E., and Ullman, J. D., *The Design and Analysis of Computer Algorithms,* Addison-Wesley, Menlo Park, California, 1974.

Knuth, D. E., *The Art of Computer Programming,* Vols. 1-3, Addison-Wesley, Menlo Park, California, 1973.

On intractable computations:

Garey, M. R., and Johnson, D. S., *Computers and Intractability: A Guide to NP-Completeness,* W. H. Freeman, San Francisco, 1979.

Lawler, E. L., et al., eds., *The Traveling Salesman Problem: A Guided Tour of Combinatorial Optimization,* John Wiley, New York, 1985.

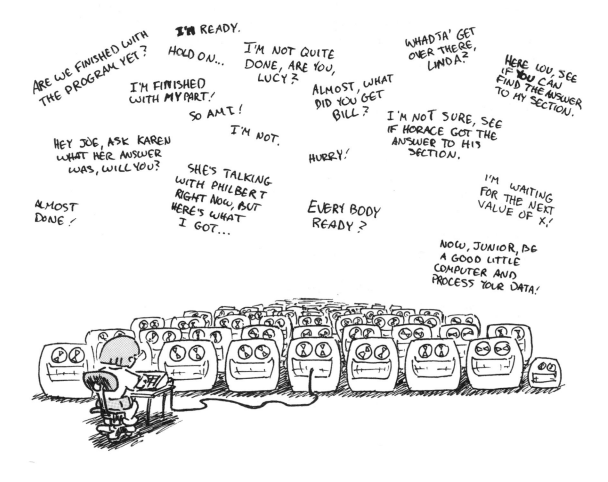

12

Parallel Computation

Using Many Processors Together (A)

The major observation of the previous chapter was that execution time can be a problem. An excessively long computation can cause inconvenience and missed deadlines. Even more seriously, the computation may become useless if it is not completed on time. This is the case, for example, in computing the trajectory for a space vehicle course correction or in calculating inventory requirements for the next day's assembly operations. If the figures are not computed on schedule, the usefulness of the calculation is lost.

Computations must be completed on time, but it is not necessarily easy to build faster machines. A minimum amount of circuitry is needed to do a calculation, and the electricity can travel through the wires no faster than the speed of light. We can make the calculation go faster by shrinking the circuit to smaller and smaller dimensions, but this is a process that cannot go on forever.

The other way to speed up a calculation is to divide it into parts and let several processors work on it together. This becomes a *parallel computation*, and it is the concern of this chapter. In fact, we will study computers that are especially designed to do such computation. They will have many processors, possibly of the kind described in chapter 9, each doing its own part. They will communicate as needed for the purposes of the task, and they will, in most cases, complete their work many times faster than a single processor machine.

The next section will describe a parallel machine and show how it can be used to solve two problems from the previous chapter: the retrieval of individuals with specified height and weight and the Towers of Hanoi problem. Later sections will describe a sorting methodology for parallel machines, problems that arise when the parallelism is of limited degree, communication schemes for parallel machines, and a new type of parallel computer, the connectionist machine.

Parallel Computation (B)

Parallel computation requires a parallel computer, and the first model to be studied here will be composed of 100 machines placed in row. These machines will be nearly identical to the processor studied in all previous chapters. They all will process a version of Pascal that has been slightly modified to account for the parallelism. All will read from a single input source as shown below and simultaneously write to a very fast output device. They are numbered from 0 to 99.

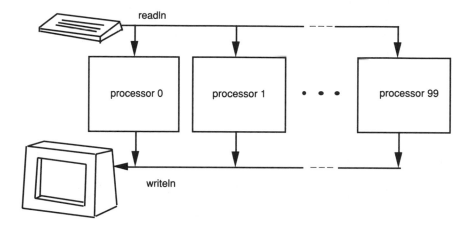

Let us first program this parallel machine to solve the problem of finding all individuals with a given height and weight. We will begin by assuming the number of individuals *n* is 100 or fewer so that one processor can be allocated to each. We will later address the more general problem when *n* may be large.

Here is the program to do the computation. A copy of this code is loaded into every one of the 100 processors. Each processor has its own copy of *targetheight* and *targetweight*, and each processor holds the height, weight, and name of a particular person.

```
program  ParallelPersonSearch;
var
    targetweight, targetheight, weight, height: real;
    name: string;
begin
    {Put code here to enter data into weight, height, and name}
    {for a single individual.}
processor 0 writeln('Give the target height.');
all  readln(targetheight);
processor 0 writeln('Give the target weight.');
all  readln(targetweight);
if (targetheight = height) and (targetweight = weight)
    then this processor writeln(name);
end.
```

The *readln* and *writeln* statements are prefixed to indicate which of the 100 processors do the operation.

The functioning of the 100 processors as they do this computation is clear. First, each processor loads the weight, height, and name of one individual in a sequence of operations that does not interest us here. If there are fewer than 100 individuals, some of the processors will receive null values for height, weight, and name. Then processor 0 prints the message, "Give the target height." Next all processors receive a value from the input, the target height. Then processor 0 prints, "Give the target weight," and all processors receive a second value, the target weight. Finally, each processor compares the target values with the values it stores for one person; if they match, it prints that person's name. The output device will print all the names received from all of the processors.

The timing of this parallel computation is dramatically faster than in the sequential case of the previous chapter. Instead of finding the individuals in time

$$t_{sequential} = 5.1 * 10^{-4} * n$$

as before, the computation runs as fast as if there were only one individual in the database:

$$t_{parallel} = 5.1 * 10^{-4} * 1$$

The dramatic speedup that we were looking for has been obtained:

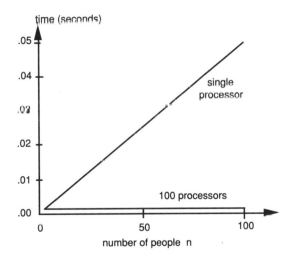

Of course, it is important to remember that these results pertain to a computation where there is a separate processor for each individual. The more general case will be examined later.

The Towers of Hanoi problem provides an interesting second illustration of parallel computation. You might suspect that it cannot be speeded up on a parallel machine because of the sequentiality of the steps. It would seem that one would not be able to decide the second step until the first is completed; one would not be able to decide the third step until the second is done; and so forth. It turns out that because of the special nature of this problem, one can compute all of the steps at once using the parallel machine.

The program for computing a single step of the solution is given at the end of this section. A copy of this program will be placed into every one of the 100 processors, and each processor will calculate a different step of the solution. The first processor computes the first step, the second processor computes the second step, and so forth. All of the steps are computed simultaneously and sent to the system printer, which we assume prints the steps instantaneously and in the order of processor number. We also assume that n is small as in the previous example so that there are enough processors to do the problem. In this problem, we wish to have one processor for every step of the solution, or $2^n - 1$ processors. So n must not have a value greater than 6.

We will not examine immediately the details of this program, but will use the fact that the execution time for calculating one step can be estimated to be about

$$t_{parallel} = 5 * 10^{-3} * n$$

which is enormously faster than the sequential version found in the previous chapter.

$$t_{sequential} = 5.49 * 10^{-3} * 2^n$$

Again, the power of parallel computing is dramatic as is shown on the graph for values of $n = 1, 2, \ldots , 6$:

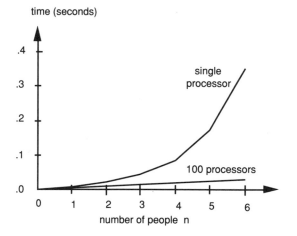

We are tempted to check how long the calculation would be for 65 disks using this parallel computation if we had enough processors. In the previous chapter, we discovered that our sequential machine would not finish the calculation before the sun burns out. Here, we find

$$t_{parallel} = 5 * 10^{-3} * 65 \quad = 0.325 \text{ second}$$

Hurrah! The infamous Towers of Hanoi problem has been crushed by a parallel machine. But let us check further. The parallel machine will need $2^{65}-1$ processors, one for each step in the solution. This can be computed to be around 10^{19} processors. Thus, if we laid our machine out across the face of the earth, including the oceans, we would have to squeeze at least ten processors into every square inch to build a large enough machine.

This section has shown how two computations from the previous chapter can be spread out across a parallel architecture to obtain dramatic improvements in execution time. All of these observations, of course, have assumed that n is small in comparison to the number of processors. The next section will show that not all computations are as easy to speed up as these two examples. The section after that will examine execution times when n is large.

Here is the program that computes one step of the Towers of Hanoi solution. If you do not wish to study this difficult code, jump to the next section. Its method of operation is not easy to explain and is left as an exercise. The code is written in a mixture of English and Pascal for readability. We assume each processor has a location *procnum* that contains a binary version of the processor's number. Thus the first processor will have 00000 in its *procnum*, the second will have 00001, and so forth.

```
program ParallelHanoi;
var
    move:string;
    i,n,mode,one: integer;
begin
all readln(n);
if procnum is greater than 2^n-2 then halt;
if n is odd then
    begin
    move := '1 => 3' ;
    one := 1;
    end
else
    begin
    move :='1 => 2' ;
    one := -1 ;
    end;
mode := 0;
i := 1;
while i <= n do
    begin
    if mode = 0 then
        begin
        if i-th digit counting from right in procnum is 1 then
```

```
            begin
            if move = '1 => 3' then
                move := '1 => 2'
            else
                move := '1 => 3' ;
            end
        else
            mode := 1;
        end
    else
        begin
        if i-th digit from right in procnum is 1 then
            begin
            if i is odd then
                increment move by one
            else
                decrement move by one;
            end;
        end;
    i := i+1;
    end;
this processor writeln(move);
end.
```

One step of the program needs clarification: it is the step where we "increment move by one" or "decrement move by one." Suppose move = "1 —> 2" and one = 1; then incrementing move by one results in move = "2 —> 3." Decrementing move by one yields move = "0 —> 1" but 0 is an illegal peg number; 0 is always converted to 3 so we obtain move = "3 —> 1." A similar procedure is used if we increment a move with a 3 in it. If we increment "3 —> 1" to obtain "4 —> 2", then we convert 4 to 1 to obtain "1 —> 2."

Exercises

1. Show how to program the parallel machine to compute all of the prime numbers between 1 and 100.

2. Show how to program the parallel machine to do the database program of chapter 4.

3. Show how the parallel program for the Towers of Hanoi solves the problem in the case of three disks.

Communicating Processes (B)

The problems of the previous section were special in that they divide across a set of processors in a simple way. Next, we will study a more difficult problem, the sorting of integers when they are distributed across our 100 processor machine. In this case, we will need communication between the processes and the ability to pass the number up and down the line.

Let us assume there are *n* numbers located in processors 0 through *n-1* where *n* is 100 or less. Each processor will have a location *num*, which contains one of the numbers in the list. It will also contain *n*, an index *i*, and its own processor number:

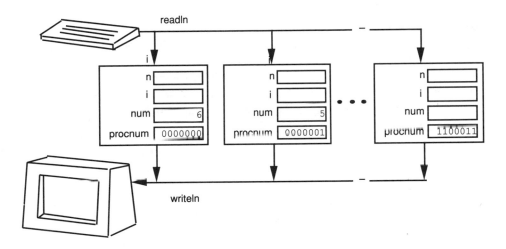

The sorting algorithm will require that each processor, except the first, examine the number in the processor to its left. If the other number is larger than its own, it will exchange them. This operation will be repeated with *n* repetitions, at which time the numbers should become sorted with the lowest in processor 0 and the largest in processor *n-1*. Here is the program:

```
program ParallelSort;
var
    i,num,n,procnum: integer;
begin
{Put code here to read num and n.}
if (procnum > 0) and (procnum <= n-1) then
    begin
    i := 1;
    while i <= n do
        begin
        if num(this processor) < num(left neighbor) then
```

```
        exchange num(this processor) and num(left neighbor);
    i := i + 1;
    end;
  end;
end.
```

Let us examine this program in action. Suppose n is 3, and the first three processors contain 6, 5, and 4:

num	6	5	4
procnum	00	01	10

Program *ParallelSort* will run simultaneously on these three processors. On the first, it will do nothing since $procnum = 00$. The second and third processors will each see their left neighbors have larger numbers, and they will exchange their own numbers with their left neighbors. Thus processor 01 will put 5 into processor 00 and 6 into itself. Processor 10 will put 4 into processor 01 and 5 into itself. Error! Processor 01 has just had both a 6 and a 4 loaded into its *num* location. Also both processors 00 and 10 have 5s. Something is wrong here:

num	5	?	5
procnum	00	01	10

Apparently the computations of one processor confuse those of its neighbor. Each processor looks at its own number and its left neighbor's and decides whether to do an exchange. But by the time it chooses to do the exchange, its own number and its neighbor's may both have changed. It cannot check any value and be sure it will stay that way because other processes may change it. This seemingly straightforward program is fraught with problems.

The solution is to have a set of flags called *semaphores* that guard locations from being changed by any but a selected single processor. That processor will maintain control over the specified locations until its job is done, and then it will change the flags to indicate that it has released the associated locations to other processors. This system of guards can become complicated, but it will restore sanity to the parallel computation.

Let us put a flag with each *num* location; the flag will be a location containing a value of 0 or 1. Then we will follow the rule that a processor will be able to access and change its own *num* only if its flag is 1. If its flag is 0, it will not be allowed to affect its own *num* because that location will be controlled by its neighbor on the right. Of course, a processor will never be able to exchange its *num* value with its left neighbor unless it controls both. Its flag must be 1, and its left neighbor must have a flag that is 0. We indicate in this table the conditions under which processor i can do an exchange. We say its activity is "on" if these conditions are met. Otherwise it is "waiting" or "off" if it is processor 0:

num	-	-
flag	0	1
procnum	i-1	i
activity	*waiting*	*on*

After a process completes a cycle, it should change its own flag and its left neighbor's to release them to other processes. There will be two exceptions to this rule, however: the flag of processor 0 should always be 0 since it never needs to do exchanges with its left neighbor, and the flag of the last processor that holds data should always be set at 1 since it has no right neighbor to take control.

We can examine this strategy by repeating the above sort. We will initialize the first flag at 0, the last flag at 1, all flags of other even-numbered processors at 0 causing them to wait, and all flags of other odd-numbered processors at 1 turning them on:

num	6	5	4
flag	0	1	1
procnum	00	01	10
activity	*off*	*on*	*waiting*

Thus only one of the three processors has the flag configuration to go on; it is processor 01, and it will see that its left neighbor has *num* larger than its own *num* and exchange them. Also, it will change its own flag. (It would change the flag of its left neighbor if that processor were not the left-most one.)

num	5	6	4
flag	0	0	1
procnum	00	01	10
activity	*off*	*waiting*	*on*

This puts processor 01 in the "waiting" state but releases processor 10 to compare its *num* with its left neighbor. Processor 10 then finds the left neighbor's value larger and executes an exchange. Finally, it would change its own flag and its left neighbor's flag, but since it is the right-most processor, it changes its neighbor's flag only:

num	5	4	6
flag	0	1	1
procnum	00	01	10
activity	*off*	*on*	*waiting*

Now process 01 is "on" again, and it can do another compare, an exchange, and a flag change. This completes the sort:

num	4	5	6
flag	0	0	1
procnum	00	01	10
activity	*off*	*waiting*	*on*

Once this flagging strategy is designed, one can revise the parallel sorting program to work properly.

```
program ParallelSortWithFlags;
var
    i,n,num,flag,procnum: integer;
begin
{Put code here to read num and n.}
{We assume that procnum holds the processor number.}
if procnum is even then
    flag := 0
else
    flag := 1;
if (procnum = n-1)   then
    flag := 1;
if (procnum > 0) and (procnum <= n-1) then
    begin
    i := 1;
    while i <= n do
       begin
        wait until flag(this processor)=1 and flag(left neighbor)=0;
        if num(this processor) < num (left neighbor) then
           exchange num(this processor) and num(left neighbor);
        if procnum > 1 then change flag in processor on left;
        if procnum < n-1 then change flag in this processor;
        i := i + 1;
        end;
    end;
end.
```

Finally, we should examine the execution time of this algorithm. The program executes its loop *n* times so the timing formula has the form

$$t_{parallel} = C * n$$

where *C* is some constant value. We noted in chapter 11 that it is possible to sort numbers in time

$$t_{sequential} = C' * n * log_2 n$$

where *C'* is a constant. Since $log_2 n$ is not a very large number, we see that $t_{parallel}$ is not a lot faster than $t_{sequential}$. If we are using *n* processors, we would like to see a speedup by a factor of *n*. There are better parallel sorting methods available that obtain greater speedups, but they are more complex than the one shown here and are beyond the scope of this book.

In this section, we have found that not all computations are as easily divided for parallel execution as those initially presented. Whenever the programming involves interprocess communication, the code can become very complex. Furthermore, the improvements in execution time may not be as large as one would hope.

Exercises

1. Suppose that the list of numbers 7,2,9,6,4,1,5,4 is spread out across processors 000 to 111 in the parallel machine and that they are to be sorted. Show how the program *ParallelSortWithFlags* would complete this sort.

2. Suppose that a programmer codes the sorting program given above but makes one error: the flags are all initialized at zero. How will the program function in this situation? (This is called *deadlock*.)

3. A sequence of *n* characters, where *n* is 100 or less, is spread across the parallel machine with one character in each processor. Show how to program the processors so that a user can type in a short string of characters and find all the places where it appears in the original character sequence. The machine is to type out the numbers of the processors that hold the initial characters of the discovered substrings.

As an example, suppose the initial string is "abcbc" so that it is stored as follows:

character	a	b	c	b	c
procnum	000	001	010	011	100

Then if the user types "bc," the system will find two occurrences of this substring and print the locations of their initial characters: $001, 011$.

Parallel Computation on a Saturated Machine (B)

The previous studies have assumed that *n* is small enough to allow the computation to be divided among the available processors in a convenient manner. For the data retrieval problem, it was assumed that there will be a processor for every individual, and for the Towers of Hanoi problem, it was assumed there would be a processor for every move. In these cases, we say the computation does not *saturate* the machine because there are enough processors to divide the problem optimally.

Realistically, however, we must expect that *n* may be large, that we will not have as many processors as could be used effectively, and that it will be necessary to revise the organization of the code. This is the case when the processors are saturated, and there are two major results: The programming becomes more complicated, and some of the improvement in execution time is lost. This section will investigate both of these effects.

Returning to the retrieval problem, let us now assume that there may be thousands of individuals whose records are spread across the 100 processors. Then we should put 1 percent of the total population on each of the processors. Each processor will search its own 1 percent of the whole, and the results of the 100 separate computations will be a search of the complete population.

Here is the revised program prepared to handle up to 1000 individuals on each processor:

```
program      SaturatedParallelPersonSearch;
type
    stringarray1000 = array [1..1000] of string;
    realarray1000 = array [1..1000] of integer;
var
    name: stringarray1000;
    height, weight: realarray1000;
    m,i: integer;
    targetheight, targetweight: real;
begin
{Put code here to find the number m of                    }
{individuals to be stored in this processor               }
{and then read in the data for those individuals.}
processor 0 writeln('Give the target height.');
all  readln(targetheight);
processor 0 writeln('Give the target weight.');
all  readln(targetweight);
i := 1;
while i <= m do
   begin
   if (targetheight = height [i]) and (targetweight = weight [i]) then
      this processor writeln(name[i]);
   i := i+1;
   end;
end.
```

The execution time for this program can be discovered by carefully considering a series of cases. Suppose there are 100 individuals or fewer. This is the case considered earlier, and the execution time is the same as handling one individual on a sequential machine:

$$t_{1-100} = 5.1 * 10^{-4} * 1$$

If there are between 101 and 200 individuals, they can be distributed among the processors with two on some and one on the others. The execution time is the same as the sequential machine with two individuals:

$$t_{101-200} = 5.1 * 10^{-4} * 2$$

The trend is now clear:

$$t_{201-300} = 5.1 * 10^{-4} * 3$$

etc.

The result gives us a lesson about computing on a saturated machine. The incredible speedup that was apparent when there were enough processors is gone. But the machine is much faster than a sequential computation. At best, a machine with 100 processors will be 100 times faster than one with a single processor:

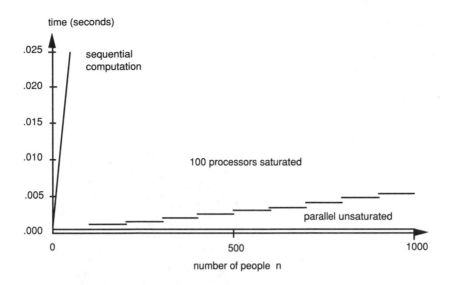

A similar situation occurs with the Towers of Hanoi problem. If n is larger than 6, then we can no longer afford the luxury of putting one disk move on each processor. Instead each processor must compute 1 percent of all the steps, and this could be a large number. The execution time graph rises slowly if n is 6 or less but it rises exponentially for larger n as occurs in the sequential case. It is at best 100 times faster than a single processor. Unfortunately, this is not sufficient improvement to convert an intractable computation into a tractable one.

The sorting algorithm can also be programmed for large lists but with additional complexities. Furthermore, the timing advantage, which was difficult to achieve in the unsaturated case, cannot be maintained.

In summary, parallel computations offer the possibility of huge speedups in computation time, especially in the cases of problems that partition easily into many parts and where high degrees of parallelism are available. However, the introduction of parallelism often results in great increases in program complexity and for many problems does not yield dramatic speed increases.

Exercises

1. Build a chart summarizing the results of this chapter. It should have two columns—one for tractable and one for intractable computations. It should have two rows—one for computations on unsaturated and one for computations on saturated machines. In each cell, describe the degree of speedup that parallel computation can achieve.

2. Carefully analyze the speedup that can be achieved for the Towers of Hanoi problem in the case where n is greater than 6. Draw a graph of execution time, and compare it with the cases of unsaturated parallel execution and sequential execution.

Variations on Architecture (B)

A variety of different interconnection schemes are possible for parallel machines. It is *not* true that all are organized in straight lines, as is the case for the model of the previous sections. The processors can be organized in a ring, a grid, a hypercube, a completely connected set, or any of a multitude of other ways:

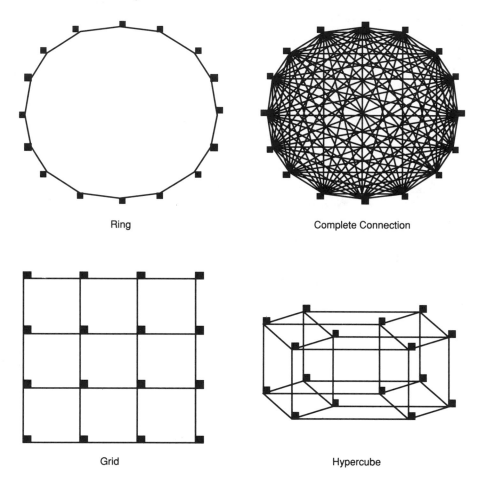

Ring

Complete Connection

Grid

Hypercube

The simpler schemes like the ring and grid are easier to build. The more complicated ones offer greater potential performance.

One simple measure of performance is the number of transfers required for information to reach the most distant points in a network. For example, with 16 processors in a ring connection as shown above, the most widely separated nodes are on the opposite sides of the ring. The transfer of information from one to the other requires 8 movements along communication lines. In general, a ring of n processors will require $n/2$ transfers to move information between the most distant processors. The following table gives distance between the farthest processors for the four configurations shown.

Configuration	16 processors	10,000 processors	n processors
Ring	8	5000	n/2
Grid	6	198	$2n^{(1/2)}-2$
Hypercube	4	14	$\log_2 n$
Complete Connection	1	1	1

The parallel machine described in the previous sections is known as a *Multiple-Instruction Multiple-Data* (*MIMD*) machine. This means that each processor has its own program to manipulate its own data. Thus each processor can have a completely different piece of code, giving total flexibility to the programmer in the organization of the calculation. Another common design is the *Single-Instruction Multiple-Data* (*SIMD*) machine, where one program controls all processors in the array. That single program broadcasts its commands to the complete network, and they all march in lockstep. This architecture is common on designs where there may be many processors, tens of thousands of them, and so there is little possibility of generating individualized code for each one.

This brings up another issue in parallel architectures, the degree of *granularity* in the parallelism. A machine may have *coarse* granularity, with large processors at each node and relatively little communication as in our model. Here there will be few processors, say a few hundred at most, and each will have full instruction sets and large memory—100,000 bytes or more. Or the granularity may be *fine* using as many as hundreds of thousands of tiny processors with very tight communication with each other.

Exercises

1. Suppose a three-dimensional cubical grid is proposed as a machine architecture:

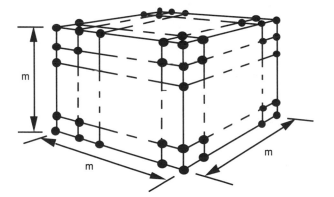

Thus a cube might have m nodes along any edge and m^3 nodes in all. Fill in the table given above for shortest distance between most distant nodes.

2. Could you run the three problems discussed in this chapter on SIMD machines? Discuss each one, and show how it would succeed or fail.

3. Propose a parallel architecture not described in this chapter, and investigate its properties.

Connectionist Architectures (C)

There has been much excitement in recent years over a new kind of computer, the *connectionist* machines. These machines lie at the extreme end of the spectrum in parallel computation with possibly millions of tiny nodes each capable of only very primitive calculation. The connection schemes are massive, with large arrays of nodes communicating wholesale with each other and with other arrays of nodes. These architectures are inspired by studies of the physiology of the human brain, and some researchers believe they carry out computations in a similar way. We will study one simple design for a connectionist machine here, and refer you to a fast-growing literature for additional readings.

Our connectionist architecture is typical of many of those currently under investigation and will be organized as an N by N square grid of nodes where N may be in the hundreds. Each node will receive an input from every other of the N^2 nodes. Thus the network is completely connected. Complete connectivity is not needed for many algorithms, but it is an excellent model for some interesting examples.

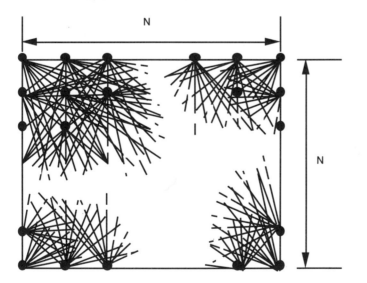

Each node will receive either a 1 or -1 from every other node. It will multiply each of its inputs (1 or -1) by a real value called a *weight* and then add up all of the results. Finally, the node will output 1 if this sum is greater than some constant c, and it will output -1 otherwise. This node will then send its output (1 or -1) to all of the other nodes. All of the nodes will simultaneously be carrying out this computation to recompute their own outputs and broadcast them to their neighbors. If the nodes could all talk as they compute, there would be a tremendous din from their simultaneous chattering.

As an illustration of a single-node computation, consider the following four-node grid and the calculation of the output of its upper left-most node. In this figure, the output of each node is shown on the node. All communication links are omitted except those needed for this example.

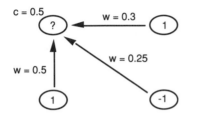

The upper left node will receive the three inputs, multiply them by appropriate weights w, and add them.

$$0.3 * (1) + 0.25 (-1) + 0.5 (1)$$

The sum is 0.55. Since this is larger than $c = 0.5$ for this node, it will output a 1:

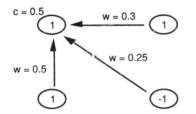

After the upper left output becomes 1, it is transmitted as input to all the other nodes, and they can compute their new outputs.

Consider next a larger version of this machine, a 3 by 3 system. Suppose the upper left node is connected as shown:

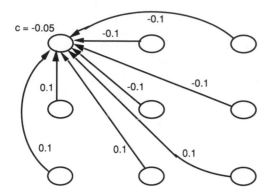

All of this complex information related to the node can be more economically represented in an array.

$$
\begin{array}{ccc}
 & -0.05 & \\
0 & -0.1 & -0.1 \\
0.1 & -0.1 & -0.1 \\
0.1 & 0.1 & 0.1
\end{array}
$$

This array shows the values of all of the arcs from other nodes back to the upper left node. It contains a zero in the upper left corner because it has no transition to itself. The number above the array represents the constant c.

Remember that there are nine nodes, each with transitions coming into it. Thus whole connectionist machine can be represented by nine such arrays. Here they are for this example machine:

-.05		
0	-.1	-.1
.1	-.1	-.1
.1	.1	.1

.05		
-.1	0	.1
-.1	.1	.1
-.1	-.1	-.1

.05		
-.1	.1	0
-.1	.1	.1
-.1	-.1	-.1

-.05		
.1	-.1	-.1
0	-.1	-.1
.1	.1	.1

.05		
-.1	.1	.1
-.1	0	.1
-.1	-.1	-.1

.05		
-.1	.1	.1
-.1	.1	0
-.1	-.1	-.1

-.05		
.1	-.1	-.1
.1	-.1	-.1
0	.1	.1

-.05		
.1	-.1	-.1
.1	-.1	-.1
.1	0	.1

-.05		
.1	-.1	-.1
.1	-.1	-.1
.1	.1	0

This specifies all of the weights and constants for the machine. If you wish to know the weight from node i,j to node k,l, first go to the k,l array and then select the i,j entry in it.

Once the machine is specified, it is now possible to compute with it. Let us set the outputs of all of the nodes and see what happens. (In the following diagrams, all of the details of the connections are omitted.)

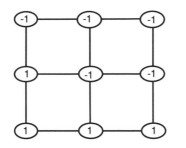

All of the nodes will receive inputs from all of the other nodes, and they will compute new outputs. Examining the upper left corner, the next output can be computed by adding the weights times the inputs on all lines:

$$(-.1)(-1)+(-.1)(-1)+(.1)(1)+(-.1)(-1)+(-.1)(-1)+(1)(1)+(.1)(1)+(.1)(1) = 0.8$$

Since 0.8 is larger than -.05, we see that this node will have a new value of 1·

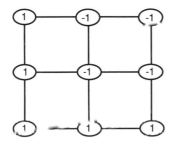

We can compute new values for the other entries also, but in this case, all remain unchanged. Thus they all have reached stable values. If we consider the original configuration to be the input, then this final stable configuration is the output. Thus the input

```
-1  -1   -1
 1  -1   -1
 1   1    1
```

resulted in this output:

$$1 \quad -1 \quad -1$$
$$1 \quad -1 \quad -1$$
$$1 \quad 1 \quad 1$$

Let us think of these nodes as neurons on a visual plane and assume 1 represents black and -1 represents white. Then an input of

has yielded an output of

This will be written as

Now we can experiment with this machine by repeatedly setting the inputs to be some image that interests us and then allowing all the nodes to recompute their values repeatedly until a stable configuration is found:

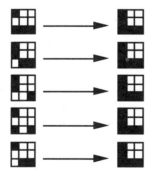

It appears that every pattern that vaguely resembles an L shape will yield an L shape. Also, many patterns that contain mere fragments of the L pattern also yield the L shape:

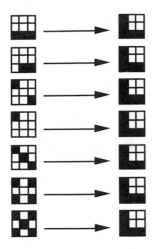

But some configurations lead to something else:

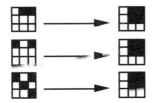

The L shape is much preferred, and all configurations that look vaguely like an L result in an L being formed. In fact, this machine is a recognizer of the L shape, and it attempts to make an L out of anything it encounters.

Summarizing, we began with a nine-node connectionist computer with its weights specified in a set of arrays. We examined its input-output characteristics and determined that there is one particular output configuration that is strongly preferred. Whenever any fragmentary information appears that may be suggestive of that pattern, the machine will generate it as its output. This output may require many iterations of the basic node computation, but the final stable behavior will be that pattern.

This characteristic of bringing forth a total image after having observed only fragmentary evidence is believed by many to be a key aspect of intelligent behavior. Such a system is said to have *associative memory,* and this is clearly a characteristic of human minds. Suppose, as an example, that the stored image is a very complex structure containing information about a particular person. The structure would contain the person's name, an image of his or her face, and remembrances of his or her behaviors. Then if a fragment of that structure appears, say the name, part of the image, or some reminder of the behavior, the rest of the structure comes to mind. The name reminds one of the face, some behavior reminds one of the name, and so forth. The interesting thing about the connectionist studies is that the model was derived as an analog to the brain, and these behaviors seem to be reminiscent of brainlike activities.

Another interesting fact is the way the information about the L is spread across the machine. No particular weight or node is critical to the recognition, and, in fact, the weights can be varied somewhat randomly without greatly affecting behavior. If there are a few small changes, the pattern recognition will degrade relatively little. If large changes are made, more loss of function will occur but it still may not disable the basic behavior. This property of such machines seems again to resemble biological systems and is a desirable characteristic of intelligent machines.

As you study the particular weights given above, you can discern the L shape coded among them. However, as we shall see later, the weights can be revised so that this machine is capable of recognizing many patterns, not simply an L. When this occurs, the weights begin to look like random numbers, yet the L pattern and the other recognizable patterns will still be coded into them.

The final point about the connectionist approach that makes it attractive is that the computer need not be programmed. It can be trained to recognize patterns, and this is the subject of the next section.

Exercises

1. Suppose a 3 by 3 image with all four corners black and all other squares white is presented to the connectionist machine described above. Calculate the new values of all node outputs to determine the output image.

2. Change some of the weights in the 3 by 3 connectionist machine and determine whether its ability to recognize an L has degraded.

Learning the Connectionist Weights (C)

Suppose the 3 by 3 connectionist machine is to recognize some pattern, say L, but that the appropriate values for the weights are not known. Then we can assume that all of the weights are zero and try to find a strategy to compute them. The usual method is to consider each weight individually and to try varying it slightly. If the system performs better when it is slightly larger or smaller, that change is made.

To see how this is done, return to the example of the upper left node, but this time assume all weights are zero:

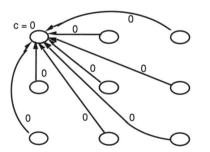

The goal of our procedure is to find values for the weights so that they prefer to output the L shape.
More specifically, the target pattern has this form

$$1 \quad -1 \quad -1$$
$$1 \quad -1 \quad -1$$
$$1 \quad 1 \quad 1$$

and it is necessary to find values for the weights that tend to compute a 1 in the upper left corner when given the other values shown. Assume the first weight to be examined is the one leading from the middle node in the top row to its left neighbor. We will increase it by 0.1 and then decrease it by 0.1, each time checking whether the change of weight helps or hinders the desired result (that the output in the upper left corner is a 1). Summing the eight values from the other nodes, we obtain the following:

If the weight is 0.1 then

$$(.1)(-1)+(0)(-1)+(0)(+1)+(0)(-1)+(0)(-1)+(0)(1)+(0)(1)+(0)(1) = -.1$$

Since -.1 is less than $c = 0$, the output is computed to be -1. This is not the desired output for the upper left corner.

If the weight is -0.1 then

$$(-.1)(-1)+(0)(-1)+(0)(1)+(0)(-1)+(0)(-1)+(0)(1)+(0)(1)+(0)(1) = 0.1$$

Since 0.1 is greater than $c = 0$, the output is computed to be 1, which is the desired result. Of the two values tried, only the second was successful, so it is selected:

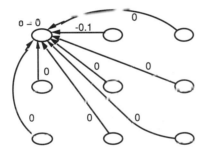

Reexamining this computation, you can see that $w = -0.1$ will be preferred over $w = 0.1$ because the goal is to maximize the summation. Since the weight w is being multiplied by the pattern value at that cell, -1, $w = -0.1$ will do the job better than $w = 0.1$ because -0.1 results in a positive contribution to the sum. This generalizes as follows: When computing weights on arcs leading to a cell with a 1, all weights coming from cells with 1 should be incremented, and all weights coming from cells with -1 should be decremented.

A similar rule can be derived when the arcs lead to a cell with a value of -1. In this case, all weights coming from cells with -1 should be incremented, and all weights coming from cells with 1 should be decremented. Let us see how these rules apply for finding a few more weights.

Consider the weight on the arc from the upper right node. Its pattern value is -1, so its weight should be decremented. Its new value will be -0.1. Consider the weight on the arc from the node just below the upper left corner. This node has pattern value 1 so its arc weight should be increased. Its new value will be 0.1:

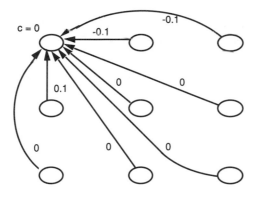

A quantity often computed in these studies is called *energy* because of some analogies that can be made to physical systems. Let us call the sum of the eight products of weight-times-input that was computed above the quantity s. Then energy for this cell is

$$E = c\text{-}s$$

and the weight chosen in each case is the one that minimizes E.

This procedure was carried out for the rest of the weights, and a similar one was used to compute the constants c where variations of +0.05 and -0.05 were used. The result is the set of weights and constants shown in the previous section for the L recognizer. Other more complicated and less intuitive methods are used in computing these weights in some connectionist systems. The method given here is easier to understand and gives satisfactory results for the purposes of our study. Typically in realistic situations where many patterns are to be recognized, this weight computation must be repeated many times before satisfactory values are found. The weights and constants will slowly migrate to acceptable values as the computation is repeated again and again. This process of slowly evolving a satisfactory set of weights and constants is called *learning*. (Other types of learning will be examined in chapter 14.)

Presenting the connectionist machine with many different patterns to learn is called *training* the machine. Now that our machine has "learned" the L pattern, let us train it on a T. If we begin with the values of the weights and constants as shown for the L pattern and modify them again in the same way using the T pattern,

$$
\begin{array}{rrr}
1 & 1 & 1 \\
-1 & 1 & -1 \\
-1 & 1 & -1
\end{array}
$$

then a new set is derived:

c = -0.1

0	0	0
0	0	-.2
0	.2	0

c = 0

0	0	.2
-.2	.2	0
-.2	0	-.2

c = 0

0	.2	0
-.2	.2	0
-.2	0	-.2

c = 0

0	-.2	-.2
0	.2	0
.2	0	.2

c = 0

0	.2	.2
-.2	0	0
-.2	0	-.2

c = 0.1

-.2	0	0
0	0	0
0	-.2	0

c = 0

0	-.2	-.2
.2	-.2	0
0	0	?

c = -0.1

.2	0	0
0	0	-.2
0	0	0

c = 0

0	-.2	-.2
.2	-.2	0
.2	0	0

Presumably after training on both an L and a T, these values code both images. Let us now run the machine on a series of test inputs:

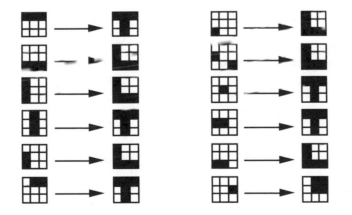

Thus the machine recognizes as an L any image with even the vaguest resemblance to an L. It does the same for a T. Only one of the test inputs yields a non-L, non-T response.

You might examine the weights and constants and ask where the L and the T are stored. The answer is that they are stored everywhere in the sense that each weight contributes in a small way to all decisions. From another point of view, they are nowhere specifically because small perturbations on individual weights will have little effect on total performance.

The examples here are extremely simple and serve only to demonstrate principles. A more realistically sized machine could have a grid with tens of thousands of nodes, as well as auxiliary arrays with more tens of thousands to do background computation. Training could involve thousands of examples, and the learning process could involve thousands of iterations to get the weights to converge to yield acceptable behaviors.

Larger systems are often studied in terms of energy. Given a set of weights and constants, a cell in the pattern is said to have energy c-s if the cell contains a 1 and $-(c$-$s)$ if it contains a -1. If cells can have energies, then a pattern can have energy also; it is the sum of the energies of all of the cells.

The concept of energy is quite useful for the understanding of large systems. Suppose a system has not been trained so that all weights and constants are at initial values. Then all patterns will have the same energy:

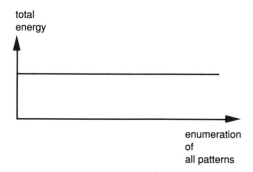

But the effect of training is to lower the energy for training patterns and for patterns similar to them. Thus if the system is trained on two patterns and their variations, there will be two regions of lowered energy:

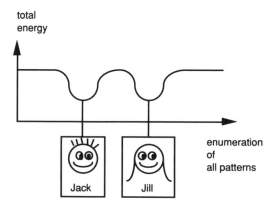

Once training is complete, one can present a fragment of an image to the system as input. This pattern will appear somewhere on the energy curve:

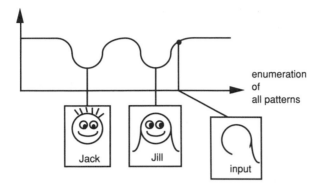

Then we can study the connectionist machine computation algorithm of the previous section to determine what it will do. Careful examination reveals that it always changes cell outputs in the direction of reducing total pattern energy. Thus, in this example, the system will find its output by changing the values of individual cells in the direction of the nearby energy valley. In this case, it would converge on and output the image and name of Jill.

We can return to the previous example of the L-T recognizer and do a similar energy analysis. The L and T will appear in energy valleys, and when the system is started with an input, it will compute interatively until the pattern is reached in the nearest valley. A fragment of an L will migrate on the energy curve downward toward the bottom of the L valley. A fragment of a T will migrate toward the bottom of the T valley. Other fragments will migrate in unpredictable directions.

Connectionist systems are also capable of generalizing from examples. Thus such a system might be presented with images of many people and form a general image of people. They all tend to have a mouth, two eyes, a nose, and so forth. Then being presented with a partial image, the system might conclude that it is a person and be able to fill in all the normal details for people. But it would not necessarily know which person to select. For a discussion of this and other connectionist phenomena, you should to go to the specialized literature.

Exercises

1. Use the set of weights and constants derived from the training set of L and T to determine the output if the input pattern is black in the upper left cell and white otherwise.

2. Vary the weights and constants and repeat the computation of problem 1. How big must the changes be to cause the system to make a different decision?

3. Compute the total energy of the input pattern in problem 1. Compute the energy of the output pattern in problem 1. Notice that the second value should be less than the first.

4. Compute the total energy for patterns identical to and varying from the basic L pattern using the weights and constants computed for the L and T training set. Draw a graph showing total energy for patterns of varying nearness to the basic L shape.

5. Study the values of the constants c for the L recognizer and for the L-T recognizer. Can you discover the algorithm used to learn these values?

6. Train the 3 by 3 connectionist system on two patterns of your choosing and then test their performance.

7. The connectionist computation presented here tends to seek a minimum energy. However, we do not give a proof that this behavior will always occur. J. Hopfield has shown that machine processing is guaranteed to seek minimum total energy if it is built such that the weight from node i,j to node k,l always equals the weight back from node k,l to i,j. Revise the algorithms presented here to adhere to this restriction.

Summary (B)

Parallel computation appears to be the only way to increase machine speed once limits of technology have been reached for traditional machines. Some problems divide rather naturally into parts that can be spread across a parallel architecture, and dramatic speedup is often possible, especially if the number of processors is large compared to the size of the problem. But other problems may be hard to speed up under any conditions. With a limited degree N of parallelism as occurs on realistic machines, the speedup can be no greater than a factor of N, and this is often hard to achieve.

Parallel architectures can vary on many dimensions, including the degree and format of connectivity, the organization of the processors, and the granularity of the parallelism.

A recent trend in computing has been the development of connectionist machines whose architecture has been inspired by studies of the human brain. Large numbers of extremely simple computing devices are assembled in highly interconnected arrays. These machines are trained through the presentation of sample data, and their prominent characteristics include the abilities to do associative retrieval, to complete fragmentary information, and to maintain robust behavior despite perturbations of their mechanisms. The success of these studies shows the importance of research in brain biology for computer science.

Readings

On parallel computation:

Ben-Ari, M., *Principles of Concurrent Programming*, Prentice-Hall International, London, 1982.

Filman, R. E., and Friedman, D. P., *Coordinated Computing: Tools and Techniques for Distributed Software,* McGraw-Hill, New York, 1984.

Harel, D., *Algorithmics, The Spirit of Computing*, Addison-Wesley, Reading, Massachusetts, 1987 (chapter 10).

Hoare, C. A. R., *Communicating Sequential Processes*, Prentice-Hall International, London, 1985.

On connectionism:

Grossberg, S., *Studies of Mind and Brain,* Reidel, Dordrecht, Holland, 1982.

Hopfield, J. J., Neural networks and physical systems with emergent collective computational capabilities, *Proceedings of the National Academy of the Sciences, USA, 79, 2554-2558,* 1982.

McClelland, J. L., Rumelhart, D. E., and the PDP Research Group, *Parallel Distributed Processing,* Volume 2: *Psychological and Biological Models*, The MIT Press, Cambridge, Massachusetts, 1986.

Rumelhart, D. E., McClelland, J. L., and the PDP Research Group, *Parallel Distributed Processing,* Volume 1: *Foundations*, The MIT Press, Cambridge, Massachusetts, 1986.

13

Noncomputability

Speed is Not Enough (A)

Chapter 11 taught us the unpleasant lesson that some important calculations may not be possible because their execution times may be too long. This may lead us to wish for faster and faster machines and for new discoveries that will result in ever greater improvements in performance. Perhaps someday a computer will be built that will do as much work in one second as the combined effort of all the world's current machines could do in a billion years. The sad lesson that we will learn next is that such impressive performance would not be enough to solve many of our problems. There exists a class of problems that are called *noncomputable*, and they have been shown to be unsolvable by any computer within the current paradigm of modern computing. This mystical and elusive class of problems will be the concern of this chapter.

In the next section, we will study an argument that shows that there are functions that cannot be computed by any Pascal program (or by any other known language). This proof will be simple and convincing. It will solidify the main idea of this chapter, but it will have one shortcoming: it will not show us an example of a noncomputable function. The following sections will give a series of ideas that will lead to further understanding of the concept of noncomputability and then will give specific examples of noncomputable problems. The final section will give a proof that one of the examples is, in fact, noncomputable.

On the Existence of Noncomputable Functions (B)

We will call a function *computable* if a Pascal program exists that can compute it. Four examples of computable functions are f_1, f_2, f_3, and f_4 as shown in the tables below:

f_1		f_2		f_3		f_4	
Input	Output	Input	Output	Input	Output	Input	Output
1	2	1	7	1	6	1	100
2	4	2	8	2	6	2	100
3	6	3	9	3	6	3	100
4	8	4	10	4	6	4	4
5	10	5	11	5	6	5	5
6	12	6	12	6	6	6	6

The first function doubles its input and can be computed by this program:

```pascal
program q1;
var
    x:integer;
begin
readln(x);
writeln(2*x);
readln;
end.
```

The second function adds six to its input:

```pascal
program q2;
var
    x:integer;
begin
readln(x);
writeln(x+6);
readln;
end.
```

Similarly, the third and fourth functions are easy to program:

```pascal
program q3;
var
    x:integer;
begin
readln(x);
writeln(6);
readln;
end.
```

```
program q4;
var
    x:integer;
begin
readln(x);
if x < 4 then
    writeln(100)
else
    writeln(x);
readln;
end.
```

Sometimes functions are defined to be computable if they can be programmed in some language other than Pascal, but since any general-purpose programming language can be translated into any other, the definitions are equivalent. The class of computable functions includes all the functions studied thus far in this book and almost every function encountered in high school or early college mathematics.

A *noncomputable* function is any function that cannot be computed by any Pascal program. Initially you might suspect that there is no such thing —that every function can be computed. The fact that there exist noncomputable functions is a profound and fascinating discovery.

The argument that there exist noncomputable functions is straightforward in concept. It states that there are many more functions than there are programs, so it is not possible to have a program for every function. There must be functions that do not have any corresponding programs, and they are the noncomputable functions.

This argument is easy to understand if we propose for the moment the rather extreme assumption that there exist in the world only three programs—P_1, P_2, and P_3 —and the four functions listed above. We may not know which program computes which function, but it is clear that no matter how the programs are paired with the functions, there will always be at least one function left unmatched. These leftover functions are the noncomputable ones since they have no associated programs. For example, if P_1 computes f_4, P_2 computes f_1, and P_3 computes f_2, then f_3 would be a noncomputable function.

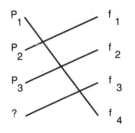

However, in practice there are more than three Pascal programs. There are infinitely many of them, so our argument needs to be improved. Let us begin to list all of the programs that read an integer and print an integer. The first in the list will be a shortest such program. Following the conventions of this book, the shortest possible program that reads an integer and prints an integer is as follows. It has a program name of length one, a variable name of length one and the minimum statements to read and print integer values. (We continue the convention of requiring a *readln* statement just prior to the end.)

```
program p;
var
      x:integer;
begin
readln(x);
writeln(0);
readln;
end.
```

There are other programs that are equally as short as measured by the number of characters:

```
program p;
var
    x:integer;
begin
readln(x);
writeln(1);
readln;
end.

program p;
var
    x:integer;
begin
readln(x);
writeln(2);
readln;
end.
-

-
```

```
program p;
var
    x:integer;
begin
readln(x);
writeln(9);
readln;
end.

program p;
var
    x:integer;
begin
readln(x);
writeln(x);
readln;
end.
```

This is all of the programs of this length (except for the renaming of identifiers), but if an additional character is allowed, more programs can be listed:

```
program p;
var
    x:integer;
begin
readln(x);
writeln(10);
readln;
end.
```

Etc.

We can sequentially list every program of one size, then every one of the next size, then the next, and so forth in an endless chain of programs. Every Pascal program that reads an integer and prints an integer will appear somewhere in the list, although some of them may be long programs and appear very far from the beginning. However, we can, in principle, create such a long list and thus prove that this set of programs is a countable set as defined in chapter 3. These programs can be placed in a row! Let us place these programs in a row and draw a link from each program to the function it computes:

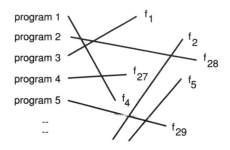

Suppose every function is computable and thus has a link to some program. Then we could move the functions along their links and put the functions in a row also.

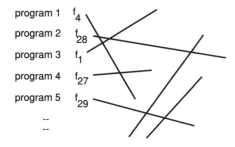

However, we learned in chapter 3 that it is not possible to put all the functions in a row. The set of all functions is not countable. So it must be that we failed to link every function with a program and that some functions do not have programs. Functions must exist that are not computable.

Summarizing once again, not all functions can be computed because there are not enough programs to cover them all. Some functions do not have associated programs that can compute them.

But what is an example of a function that cannot be computed? The next sections will provide background and some very important examples of such functions.

Exercises

1. The set of functions that receive a finite set of binary inputs and compute a single binary output was studied in chapter 6. These are the kind of functions that we can build switching circuits for. Are these functions all computable as defined in this chapter? Give a careful and complete justification for your answer.

2. Consider the set of functions that receive a positive integer and output a binary integer—a 0 or a 1. Are these functions all computable? Give a careful and complete justification for your answer.

Programs That Read Programs (B)

The goal is to find some computations that cannot be done by any Pascal program. It would be interesting to specify a calculation that inputs integers but is noncomputable. While it is possible to do this, the most easily understood examples of noncomputability involve programs that read other programs and print something. These kinds of examples also illustrate some of the most commonly encountered forms of noncomputability. Thus, in this section, we study programs that read other programs:

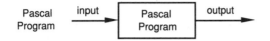

For the purposes of this section, assume that the programs input by other programs are simply sequences of statements separated by spaces. Thus the program called *A* that is usually typed as

```
program A;
var
    x:integer;
begin
readln(x);
writeln(2*x);
readln;
end.
```

will be written on a single line as

```
program A; var x:integer; begin readln(x); writeln(2*x); readln; end.
```

We also will assume that these programs have no subroutine calls.

Let us write a program that can read programs like *A* and do something with them. Let us call the program *B* and specify that *B* will read a program and tell us whether the program it has read has an "if" in it. Thus if *B* were to read *A*, it would type "Has no if." However, if *B* read one of the decision tree programs of chapter 1, it would print "Has an if in it." (We will assume all programs can be typed on a single line. If we attempted to account for multiple-line programs, our programs that read programs would be unnecessarily complex, a distraction worth avoiding.) Here is *B*:

```
program B;
var
    p:string;
begin
writeln('Type in a program.');
readln(p);
```

```
if pos('if',p) > 0 then
   writeln('Has an if in it.')
else
   writeln('Has no if.');
readln;
end.
```

Since the concept of a program reading other programs is strange, it may be helpful to type B into a machine and become comfortable using it. For example, try running B on A and other sample programs. What happens if B is run on B?

We will examine other programs that read programs, but first it is important to introduce the idea of *the halting problem*. As we noticed in chapter 2, some programs have the peculiar behavior that they run forever; they never halt. C is such a program:

```
program C;
var
    x:integer;
begin
readln(x);
while x = x do
   x := x;
writeln(x);
readln;
end.
```

This code will continue looping as long as x equals itself. But x always equals itself, so this program never halts regardless of what input is read.

Some programs may halt in some cases and fail to halt in others. The following code, D, will halt and print the input if it is less than or equal to 10. Otherwise, it will never halt:

```
program D;
var
     x:integer;
begin
readln(x);
while x > 10 do
    x := x;
writeln(x);
readln;
end.
```

Most programs studied in this book halt on all inputs. Failure to halt is usually considered an undesirable property. *The halting problem* for computer programs thus addresses the question of whether those programs halt either on specific inputs or on all inputs.

We might like to write a program that reads other programs and checks whether they halt. Let us call the program *E* and design it to determine, if possible, whether a program will halt on all inputs. If *E* reads a program and finds that it will halt on every input, *E* will type the message "Halts on all inputs." Otherwise *E* will output "Not known whether it halts":

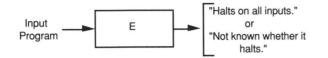

How can we write the program *E*? This could be a complicated undertaking and only a simple version will be attempted here. We could note, as a start, that if a program has no *while* loops (and, by assumption, no subroutine calls), then it can be composed only of input-output statements, assignment statements, and *if* statements. But such a program would surely always halt because each such statement always executes and passes control to the next statement. The program *end* will be reached directly. The only way that nonhalting behavior can occur is if a loop captures control and never terminates, as occurs in *C*. A simple strategy for writing *E* is to have it check whether *while* appears anywhere in the input program. If *E* finds there is no *while* statement in its input program, it can be sure that program will halt on all inputs. If *E* does find *while* statements, it will not be able to guarantee any halting property. Thus *E* can be written as follows:

```
program E;
var
    p:string;
begin
writeln('Type in a program.');
readln(p);
if pos('while',p) > 0 then
    writeln('Not known whether it halts.')
else
    writeln('Halts on all inputs.');
readln;
end.
```

Again, *E* is best understood if it is typed into a machine. It can then be run on various input programs such as *A* through *E* of this section and, in each case, will return the appropriate answer.

Unfortunately E is more simplistic than we might desire. It does not give us any useful information beyond whether the string "while" appears in a given program, and we would actually like a definitive answer for any program. Does it halt on every input or does it not? We wish to create a new program F and require that it be able to read any program and halt after a finite time with the correct answer: either the given input program halts on all inputs or it does not.

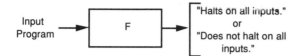

The next section will describe the construction of F.

Exercises

1. Write a program that reads another program and tells whether the program is known never to print anything. If your program cannot determine for sure whether the input program prints anything, it should give a message stating this.

2. Write a program that reads another program and gives its length.

3. Write a program that reads a program and then determines whether every variable declared actually appears in the main part of the program. If a variable is found that never appears after the declaration, your program prints its name.

Solving The Halting Problem (B)

The next task is to see how to write program F. F will have lines of code that can check any input program for its halting characteristics. F will check many features related to halting behavior and if it finds a proof that the given program will or will not always halt, it will print the appropriate message and stop.

The organization of F will be as shown; the input program will be read, and then a series of cases will be examined. When a case is found that applies to the given program indicating its halting or nonhalting behavior, the appropriate message is printed, and all later cases are skipped:

```
program F;
var
    p,solutionfound,case1holds, . . . . :string;
begin
writeln('Type in a program.');
readln(p);
solutionfound := 'false';
```

```
if solutionfound='false' then
   begin
   case 1 code
   if case1holds = 'true' then
      begin
      writeln( put result 1 here  );
      solutionfound := 'true';
      end;
   end;
if solutionfound='false' then
   begin
   case 2 code
   if case2holds = 'true' then
      begin
      writeln( put result 2 here  );
      solutionfound := 'true';
      end;
   end;
-
-
-
if solutionfound='false' then
   begin
   case n code
   if casenholds = 'true' then
      begin
      writeln( put result n here  );
      solutionfound := 'true';
      end;
   end;
end.
```

Thus F can be completed as soon as all of the cases are known. We will now consider them in sequence.

Case 1. The easiest first phenomenon to cover is that addressed by E, the case where "while" does not appear anywhere in the input program. Here we know the message to be printed is "Halts on all inputs," so the case 1 portion of the F program is as follows:

```
if solutionfound='false' then
   begin
   if pos('while',p) > 0 then
      case1holds := 'false'
   else
      case1holds := 'true';
   if case1holds = 'true' then
      begin
      writeln('Halts on all inputs.');
      solutionfound := 'true';
      end;
   end;
```

Case 2. A second easy phenomenon occurs in any program with a *while* loop that has "true" as a test. If the loop is ever entered, it will run forever, and this is a situation where F should print "Does not halt on all inputs." Program G provides an example of this case:

```
program G;
var
   x:integer;
begin
readln(x);
while true do
   x := x;
writeln(x);
readln;
end.
```

The case 2 portion of F should be:

```
if solutionfound = 'false' then
   begin
   Code that checks for a while loop that is
   entered and has  true as a test .
   if case2holds = 'true' then
      begin
      writeln('Does not halt on all inputs.');
      solutionfound := 'true';
      end;
   end;
```

Case 3. A slightly more complicated case is that represented by *C* where a test is made in the loop but the test always produces a true result. If the loop is entered, the repetitions will not terminate. This is another situation in which *F* can return a "no halt" message. The case 3 portion of *F* can be written as follows:

```
if solutionfound = 'false' then
   begin
   Code that checks for a while loop that is
   entered and has a test that is provably
   always true.
   if case3holds = 'true' then
      begin
      writeln('Does not halt on all inputs.');
      solutionfound := 'true';
      end;
   end;
```

Case 4. *D* provides an example of another interesting class of programs. This is similar to case 3 except that it may not be clear whether the loop exit test will pass on the first encounter. In the case of *D*, the exit will occur if the input is not greater than 10. In other examples, more complicated situations may occur, and it is necessary to check whether any input could exist such that the loop exit will fail. Here is an example of a wide variety of constructions that might appear:

```
program H;
var
    x,y:integer;
begin
readln(x);
if x = 1772 then
   y := 1
else
   y := 0;
while y = 1 do
   x   := 1;
writeln(x);
readln;
end.
```

Handling all such examples is a complex undertaking that will not be considered at length here.

Case 5. Another increment in complexity occurs if the loop test includes more than one variable. Here is a program that halts on all inputs, but it is not so easy to discover this:

```
program I;
var
    x,y:integer;
begin
readln(x);
y := 2*x;
while y > x do
    begin
    x := x + 2;
    y := y + 1;
    end;
writeln(x);
readln;
end.
```

This is more complex than case 4 and will not be considered further here.

Other cases need to be considered where three or more variables appear in the test or where very complex tests occur, as in this case:

```
while ((x*z+3) > Z - (Y/(Z1*Z2 + 4 ))) and (X*(YY/Z1) <> YY+Z1+Z2) do
```

Loops may also be nested to two or three or more levels, and there may also be deeply convoluted amalgamations of multiple *if* and *while* constructions. There may also be *while* loops with complicated indexing rules that could be mixed arbitrarily numbers of times with all earlier constructions.

So the job of writing a program *F* that will determine whether other programs halt is very difficult. Perhaps it could be a person's life's work! In fact, mathematicians have shown that no matter how many cases are considered and regardless of how completely each case is handled, the job will never be done. There will always be more cases, and there will always be more code to write on the given cases. *No finite program can be written that will check other programs and halt in a finite time giving a solution to the halting problem.* Thus the goal of finding a noncomputable problem has been achieved. No program can exist that meets the specifications of *F*; this is proved later in this chapter.

In summary, we say that the halting problem is not computable. This does not mean that for a particular program, one cannot discover its halting characteristic. We have determined the halting behavior for many programs in this chapter and others. What it does mean is that there is no single finite program *F* that will answer the halting question for all programs.

As an illustration, if *F* could exist, what would it do if it were given the following program *J*:

```
program J;
var
   x:integer;
begin
readln(x);
while x > 1 do
   begin
   if (x div 2) * 2 = x then
      x := x div 2
   else
      x := 3 * x + 1;
   writeln(x);
   end;
readln;
end.
```

If this program reads 17, it will print 52, 26, 13, 40, 20, 10, 5, 16, 8, 4, 2, 1 and halt. We can give it thousands of other positive integers and probably discover it halts on them also. But will *J* halt on every positive integer? It is not likely that anyone knows, and there is no sure way to find out.

It is possible that someone will discover a way to solve the halting problem for *J*. As with some other programs discussed here, some solution may exist somewhere. Then we will not have to look far to find another program whose halting problem is not understood. There is no single program (or method) for solving all halting problems.

Exercises

1. Find a class of programs, not mentioned above, that halt on all inputs. Show how you have solved the halting problem for this class.

2. Find a class of programs, not mentioned above, each of which fails to halt on some input. Show how you can be sure that it will fail to halt on some input.

3. Run program *J* on a number of inputs and observe its behavior. Do you believe that it halts on all inputs? How can we solve the halting problem for program *J*?

Examples of Noncomputable Problems (B)

Suppose the instructor of a computer programming course wishes to have his or her student's programs checked automatically. A reasonable strategy would be for the instructor to write a master program that solves the assigned problem and then check whether each student's submission is equivalent to the master. In order for two programs to be equivalent, they must print the same result for every input. The checking program would read the two problem solutions: the instructor's master and the student's submission. Then it would print the appropriate answer, either "The two programs are equivalent," or "They are not equivalent."

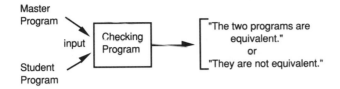

The analysis of this problem proceeds very much as with the halting problem in the previous section. It is often possible to determine that two programs are equivalent, as with

```
program A;
var
    x:integer;
begin
readln(x);
writeln(2*x);
readln;
end.
```

and

```
program A;
var
    x:integer;
begin
readln(x);
writeln(x+x);
readln;
end.
```

So in some cases, equivalence can be discovered. It is also quite common to be able to show that two programs are not equivalent, as with program *A* and the following program:

```
program AA;
var
    x:integer;
begin
readln(x);
```

```
writeln(3*x);
readln;
end.
```

However, there are many cases in which the discovery of equivalence is an exceedingly subtle, if not impossible, matter. Consider these two programs, *K* and *L*, and the difficulty in determining their equivalence assuming that the only inputs are positive integers:

```
program K;
var
   x: integer;
begin
readln(x);
while x > 1 do
   begin
   if (x div 2) * 2 = x then
      x := x div 2
   else
      x := 3 * x + 1;
   end;
writeln(1);
readln;
end.
```

and

```
program L;
var
   x:integer;
begin
readln(x);
writeln(1);
readln;
end.
```

The first program *K* may halt on all inputs and print 1. It seems to do this but we have no way of being sure that it always does. If it does, it is equivalent to *L*; otherwise it is not.

If we attempt to write a checking program as described here, we will run into a series of cases resembling those encountered in the previous section, and we will not be able to complete the task. The *equivalence problem* is another example of a noncomputable calculation.

There are very large numbers of problems related to programs that are noncomputable, as are the halting problem and the equivalence problem. Suppose, you want a program to check whether programs print something on every possible input. For some programs this is easy, but for others, like *K*, it is very difficult. This is a noncomputable problem. Suppose you want a program to determine whether a specific line of code is always executed in other programs for all possible inputs. This is also a noncomputable problem. For example, does *K* execute the instruction *writeln(1)* for every (positive integer) input? Suppose you want a program to determine whether other programs double their input. This again is noncomputable.

In fact, almost every problem related to the behavior of programs is noncomputable in the sense described here. Almost every question related to halting, equivalence, printing, correctness, or any other behavioral property is unanswerable for the class of all programs. Anyone who proposes to write a program to check for property X in the behavior of other programs is probably attempting the impossible:

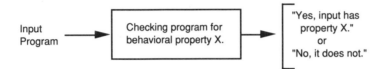

There are also many computations that do not relate to programming languages that are similarly noncomputable. For example, the Post correspondence problem described in chapter 2 is such a computation. There is no program that will read every Post correspondence problem and halt after a finite time, either giving the solution to the problem or giving the message that there is no solution. Another class of noncomputable computations relates to questions about database queries and their answerability.

Are there any questions about programs that are computable? Yes, we can write programs to check almost any syntactic feature of programs. We can write programs that will measure the length of programs, the number of statements, the number of character As, the number of arithmetic expressions, and many other things. We can write a program that will read a sequence of characters and tell whether it is a Pascal program or not. (Your Pascal compiler does this.) We can write a program that will compute almost any property of the sequence of characters that make up the program. But we usually cannot write a program that will discover any general property of the program's execution when it is functioning as a program.

Exercises

1. We will categorize functions in three different ways: noncomputable, computable-tractable, and computable-intractable. Study each proposed computation listed below and classify it, as well as you can, in one of the three ways.

(a) A program is to be written that reads a list of *n* numbers and finds whether any one of those numbers is the sum of any two or more of the others.

(b) A program is to be written that reads a program of length *n*. It then tells the number of characters that will be printed if that other program is run on the input of 17.

(c) A program is to be written that reads a program of length n. If the program that was read computes a tractable computation, it prints "tractable." Otherwise, it prints "intractable."

(d) A program is to be written that reads n numbers and prints the largest one.

(e) A program is to be written that reads a program of length n and translates it into machine language.

(f) A program is to be written that reads a Pascal program of length n. If there is a way to rearrange the characters of this program so that they become a legal P88 assembly language program, the program prints "yes." Otherwise, it prints "no."

(g) A program is to be written that reads a program of length n and tells how many legal Pascal statements are in the program that was read.

2. The Church-Markov-Turing Thesis from chapter 4 states that any computation that we can describe can be computed. In this chapter, we have described some computations that we claim cannot be computed. Contradiction! What is the problem here?

Proving Noncomputability (C)

The above sections have argued that writing programs to solve the halting problem and others would be very hard. In fact, it was asserted that these programs are worse than hard to write; they are impossible to write. However, no proof of this impossibility has yet been given. This section will present a classical proof that the halting problem is not computable. The other examples from the last section can be derived from this basic result.

The method of proof will be by contradiction. We will assume that the halting problem is solvable and that a program has been found that solves it. We will then study the ramifications of this assumption and come across ridiculous conclusions. We will decide that since the assumption that a program exists to solve the halting problem leads to something obviously false, it must be that such a program does not exist.

The proof begins with the assumption that we have a Pascal subroutine called *halt* that reads two things — a program p and its input x. We will assume that *halt* will run for only a finite amount of time, and then it will return its answer in *result*. Either it will return *result* = "Halts." indicating that program p halts on input x or it will return *result* = "Does not halt." indicating that p will run forever if given input x:

```
procedure  halt(var  p,x,result:string);
   var  . . .
   begin
   Body of the halt routine.
   if  . . .  then
      result := 'Halts.'
   else
      result := 'Does not halt.';
   end;
```

(This program is more specific than *F* discussed earlier in that it inputs both a program and that program's input. This program returns "Halts" if *p* halts on input *x* whereas *F* reads only *p* and prints "Halts on all inputs" if *p* halts on all inputs. The subroutine *halt* checks only one input for program *p* while *F* checks all inputs. This difference will be discussed at the end of this section.) We do not know the details of the subroutine *halt*. We assume that someone has filled them in and wonder what the consequences are of having this program.

Next we will write two subroutines that will help with this proof. One is called *selfhalt*, and the other is *contrary*. The former will input a program *p* and then call the subroutine *halt* to find whether *p* halts with itself as an argument:

```
procedure selfhalt(var p,result:string);
   var
      answer:string;
   begin
   halt (p, p, answer);
   if answer = 'Halt.' then
      result := 'Halts on self.'
   else
      result := 'Does not halt on self.';
   end;
```

The second program, *contrary*, is designed to justify its name. It reads a program *p* and runs *selfhalt* to determine whether *p* halts on itself. If *p* does halt on itself, then *contrary* will never halt. If *p* does not halt on itself, then *contrary* will halt immediately:

```
procedure contrary(var p:string);
   var
      answer:string;
   begin
   selfhalt(p, answer);
   if answer = 'Halts on self.' then
      while true do
         answer := 'x';
   end;
```

This is all extremely simple. (It is very strange but simple!) But a real collision with reality occurs when *contrary* is allowed to run with itself as input. Let us analyze very carefully what happens.

Assume that *p* is the subroutine *contrary* listed above. Also assume that this routine *contrary* is executed with input *p*. Thus we are running *contrary* on itself. Let us see what happens. The first statement of *contrary* is *selfhalt (p,answer)*. Consider two cases:

1. Suppose *selfhalt* stops and returns the result *answer* = "Halts on self." Then the second statement of *contrary* will check this and go into an infinite loop. That is, if it is found using *selfhalt* that *contrary* halts on itself, then *contrary* will run forever on itself. The infinite loop *while true do answer := 'x';* ensures this. This is a contradiction. The routine *contrary* cannot both halt on itself and not halt on itself.

2. Suppose *selfhalt* stops and returns the result *answer* = "Does not halt on self." Then the second statement of *contrary* will be a test that fails, and *contrary* will halt immediately. Thus we conclude that if *contrary* does not halt on itself (as determined by routine *selfhalt*), then it will halt on itself. Again, an equally ridiculous conclusion has been found.

This concludes the proof by contradiction. First, it was assumed that the program *halt* could exist as defined. Then the subroutine *contrary* was defined (with its subroutine *selfhalt* which depends on *halt*.) Then it was shown that if *contrary* halts on itself, then it does not halt on itself, and if it does not halt on itself, then it halts on itself. Something is wrong with this argument. But every step is extremely simple and logically sound. The only step lacking justification is the assumption that *halt* can exist. We conclude that it cannot exist.

Therefore we have proved the noncomputability of the *halt* function. This proof may seem like so much mathematical magic because it is so involuted in its structure. It is, however, the classical proof of the mathematical literature translated into the notation and vocabulary of this book.

Once it is clear that *halt* cannot exist, we can prove many other noncomputability results. As an illustration, consider the program *F* discussed earlier. This program, if it could exist, would read a program and tell whether it halts on all inputs. Knowing that *halt* cannot exist, how can we show that *F* also cannot exist?

We can do this proof by contradiction: If *F* did exist, then we could build *halt*, and this result has been shown to be impossible. Assume the program whose halting problem is to be solved has this form:

```
procedure p(var z:string);
   begin
   Pascal code that uses variable z.
   end;
```

Then *halt* can be constructed as follows:

```
procedure halt(var p, x, result:string)
   Code which removes variable z  from the
   argument of p and replaces it with a   new
   variable that appears nowhere  in subroutine
   p. Call the new variable newz.
```

```
Code which inserts a new statement at the
beginning of p: z := (contents of x)
F(p, answer);
if answer = "Halts on all inputs." then
   result := 'Halts.'
else
   result := 'Does not halt.';
end;
```

Here is how *halt* works. Assume it is called with parameter *p* containing the subroutine *p* shown above and with *x* containing the input for *p* . First *halt* modifies *p* so that it has this form:

```
procedure p (var newz:string);
   begin
   Pascal code which uses variable z.
   end;
```

Notice that this new version of *p* acts the same regardless of what its argument is. Variable *newz* is never used in the code. Notice also that this version has a bug in it because *z*, which previously received its input from the argument, now has no value. The next piece of code in *halt* fixes this error; it puts a statement into *p* that properly loads *z*. Now *p* has this form:

```
procedure p(var newz:string);
   begin
   z := The contents of x is placed here.
   Pascal code which uses variable z.
   end;
```

The new subroutine *p* has the properties that it functions the same regardless of its input *newz* because *newz* is never used, and it does exactly what the old *p* would have done using the input in *x*. Thus if the old *p* would have halted on *x*, the new *p* will halt on all inputs. If the old *p* would have run forever on *x*, the new *p* will run forever on all inputs.

Next *halt* calls *F* running on this modified program. According to the specifications of *F*, it will stop after a finite time and return the result "Halts on all inputs," if the revised *p* will halt on all inputs and "Does not halt on all inputs," otherwise. But if the revised *p* halts on all inputs, the original *p* would halt on *x*, so *halt* should return "Halts." If the revised *p* fails to halt on all inputs, the original *p* would not halt on *x*, so *halt* should return "Does not halt." Summarizing, we have seen that if *F* could exist, then *halt* can be constructed, and this is impossible. This concludes the proof that the problem that *F* is specified to solve is noncomputable.

Exercises

1. Do a hand simulation of program *contrary* when it is run with program *B* as an input. Repeat with program *E* as an input.

2. Use the methodology of the section to prove that the following problem is noncomputable: A program is to be read, and after a finite time, the output is to tell whether the input program will ever print anything.

Summary (B)

We began this chapter by asserting that there are numerical functions that cannot be computed by any Pascal program. Then we gave a proof of this assertion. The proof showed that there are noncomputable functions but it failed to provide even one example. We could study some numerical examples but they are both difficult to explain and less important practically.

Our study thus moved to a new domain—programs that read programs. Here it was found that if any proposed program is to read another program and determine almost any property of its execution behaviors, there is a good chance that noncomputability will be encountered; the proposed program will not be constructable using Pascal (or any other language that has been invented or proposed). Thus programs cannot be written to solve the halting, equivalence, printing, correctness, or almost any other behavioral property of programs. This is an extremely important result for computer scientists because one of their main jobs is to write programs that manipulate other programs. Many of the tasks they may set for themselves are not within the realm of possibility.

But it should be noted that problems related to the syntax of programs very often are computable and examples appear throughout this book. Thus, one can write programs that look for character sequences in other programs or that measure their syntactic properties. Also programs can read other programs and translate them into some other language as shown in chapter 10.

This chapter and chapter 11 have shown two types of computations which cannot be done using current or proposed technologies. The next chapter will study another class of very difficult problems.

Readings

On computability and noncomputability:

Cohen, D. I. A., *Introduction to Computer Theory*, John Wiley, New York, 1986.

Harel, D., *Algorithmics, The Spirit of Computing*, Addison-Wesley, Reading, Massachusetts, 1987 (chapter 8).

Hopcroft, J. E., and Ullman, J. D., *Introduction to Automata Theory, Languages, and Computation*, Addison-Wesley, Reading, Massachusetts, 1979.

Manna, Z., *Mathematical Theory of Computation*, McGraw-Hill, New York, 1974.

Minsky, M., *Computation: Finite and Infinite Machines*, Prentice-Hall, Englewood Cliffs, New Jersey, 1967.

14

Artificial Intelligence

The Dream (A)

The final frontier to be examined here concerns our limitations as programmers. As we move toward the next century, it is reasonable to ask how large, how complex, how broad in capabilities, and ultimately, how intelligent our programs will become. Considering any program created earlier in this book, we wonder how many improvements could be made to strengthen its capabilities and increase its usefulness. Could the program be improved to handle a larger class of problems? Could it be revised to do inferences beyond its current capabilities? Could it be designed to create alternative plans and to evaluate them and select the best one? Could the program recognize its own shortcomings and modify itself to give better performance?

As an illustration, consider the database program that was used to help the inspector solve a mystery. We have already noticed its lack of ability to infer new facts from the given information. A method for addressing this problem was suggested near the end of the translation chapter. But how extensive could this inference mechanism actually be? For example, the system could be given the fact that every person must be somewhere at every instant of time, and then it could attempt to infer the whereabouts of every individual at critical times. It could formulate a plan for solving the crime by seeking a proof for each individual's story in relation to the key events. The program no longer would be a passive provider of information but an active developer of theories. Perhaps the program could handle a variety of English syntax instead of simply noun-verb-noun formats. We might, in addition, design mechanisms to remember successful strategies and then use them to improve the system's subsequent performance. Finally, we would want the system to be general enough in its design to manage various information processing problems, not simply household facts.

Such is the dream of *artificial intelligence*: that machines may be programmed to become more and more powerful in the solution of problems until their abilities equal or exceed those of humans. The artificial intelligence researcher looks on the human mind as an example of a very powerful computer, and his or her goal is to write programs so that electronic machines can achieve the abilities of these existing biological machines. Attempts have been made to develop systems that converse in natural language, solve problems, play games, understand visual images, walk on legs and manipulate the environment with hands, compose music, create new mathematics, and long lists of other tasks. If the human mind-computer can do those computations, the argument is that electronic computers should be able to do them also.

Computers already can do some things much better than humans. Certainly they can add numbers faster, millions of them per second, and they can remember facts better, billions of them without making even one error. So the question is not whether computers or humans have better information processing abilities but rather which problems are better handled by machines and which by humans.

The difference between human and machine capabilities seems to depend on the intrinsic complexity of the task. If the complexity is low enough so that efficient programs can be written to do the work, machines will do a superior job. But if the complexity is too great, either the programs are too slow or the code is so complicated that no one knows how to write it.

Putting things into perspective, one can draw a rough graph giving task complexity on the horizontal axis and estimating human and computer capabilities on the vertical axis:

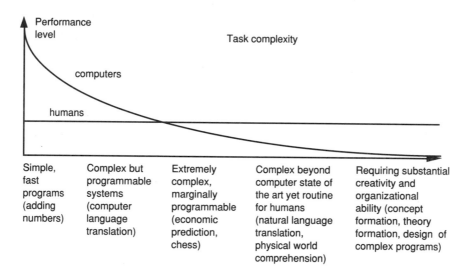

Machines clearly dominate in all situations where moderate-sized programs can be devised that run at acceptable speeds. No sensible person is proposing that standard industrial information processing such as computer language translation or payroll computations would be better done by humans. However, machines are clearly inferior for tasks mentioned on the right half of the graph, such as in natural language translation, concept formation, and any kind of scientific theory formation.

Human performance, in contrast, is much more evenly balanced across the spectrum of possible activities. Humans are moderately competent at simple tasks, such as adding numbers, at all of the intermediate levels of complexity, and even at concept formation and the most profound of tasks. Even the most humble human intellects perform astonishingly well at all levels.

This graph, of course, cannot be taken too seriously since none of the dimensions or terms is well defined. But it does organize our perspective in preparation for a study of artificial intelligence. The usual definition of intelligence roughly refers to the horizontal axis where higher degrees of intelligence correspond to points farther to the right. When humans and machines are being discussed, the definition of "intelligent behavior" typically begins somewhere around the crossover point for the machine and human performance curves. The goal for artificial intelligence researchers is to raise the level of the machine curve as much as possible, especially in the regions on the right.

As researchers attack profoundly more difficult problems, it is appropriate to have corresponding new intellectual paradigms. This chapter will introduce the most important ones—the concepts of *knowledge* and *reasoning* as they relate to intelligent behavior. Instead of dealing with data such as numbers or strings as in the previous chapters, we will discuss larger structures of information, knowledge structures. Of course, these larger structures will be composed of the same primitives as before—numbers and strings—but they will be thought of and manipulated as a whole rather than as one memory unit at a time. Instead of dealing with simple computations as before, such as addition or copy operations, we will be discussing steps in the reasoning process that each may involve many such individual operations. The combination of our abilities to think at the knowledge level and to conceive of computations at the reasoning level enables us to approach more difficult problems. These will provide the starting point for a study of artificial intelligence.

The following sections thus discuss the concepts of knowledge and reasoning at length. The first sequence of topics will examine knowledge as a concept, its representation, the meaning of the word *understand*, the uses of knowledge, and methods for learning knowledge. Then reasoning methodologies will be discussed with applications to game playing and expert system design. Finally, the summary sections will discuss the state of the art in artificial intelligence.

Representing Knowledge (B)

The *knowledge* of an object or event is the set of facts and relationships pertaining to it. For example, one may have knowledge of a particular chair—its position, its material, its color, its size and shape, its owner, its cost, its age, its history, its current use, and many more facts. A particular data item is part of the knowledge of the chair if there are processing tasks related to the chair that reference that item. Thus one might want to use the chair, move it, describe it, copy it, change it, or many other operations, and the data items related to the chair that are required to do these things comprise the knowledge about the chair.

If the computer is to do these and other operations to an object, it must have the required knowledge. The knowledge should be organized in such a way that the machine can use it efficiently to do its job. There are many ways of storing knowledge and here are a few of them:

1. *A Natural Language Description.* You can simply write down in English, for example, all of the facts that are required about the given object for doing the planned tasks. Thus you could give the essential facts about a particular chair as follows:

> The object *a1* is a chair constructed of oak with four legs, a straight back, and a flat seat, all naturally finished. It was purchased for $225.00 new in 1986 and normally resides at position . . .

2. *A Formal Language Description.* You can design a mathematical language especially for the description of objects. Then the knowledge can be expressed in terms of the language. Suppose, as an example, that the following notations have been defined.

```
name(X,Y)        means X has the name  Y
partof(X,Y)      means X is a part of Y
material(X,Y)    means X has the material Y
cost(X,Y)        means X has the cost Y
etc.
```

Then the chair *a1* could be described using this special language instead of English:

```
name(a1,chair)
name(x1,leg)
name(x2,leg)
name(x3,leg)
name(x4,leg)
partof(x1,a1)
partof(x2,a1)
partof(x3,a1)
partof(x4,a1)
material(x1,oak)
-
-
-
cost(a1,225)
-
-
```

3. *A Description Using a Programming Language.* You can write down knowledge using a programming language such as Pascal. For example, the *name* information given above could be represented by a Pascal subroutine *name(X,Y,ANSWER)*, which loads "yes" into *ANSWER* if *X* has the name *Y* and "no" otherwise:

```
procedure name(var X,Y,ANSWER: string);
  begin
  ANSWER := 'no';
  if (X = 'a1') and (Y = 'chair') then
      ANSWER := 'yes' ;
  if (X = 'x1') and (Y = 'leg') then
      ANSWER := 'yes' ;
  if (X = 'x2') and (Y = 'leg') then
      ANSWER := 'yes' ;
  etc.
  end;
```

4. *A Semantic Network Description.* A semantic network is a set of labeled nodes with labeled arcs connecting them. The nodes can be used to represent objects, names, properties, and other entities, and the arcs can show the relationships between these entities. Here is a semantic network that partially describes the chair *a1*:

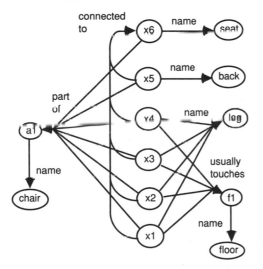

A Semantic Network

Of course, we would like to store this network in the machine. A method for doing it is to notice that every arc can be specified by listing its initial node, its arc label, and its final node:

```
x1    partof    a1
x2    partof    a1
-
-
-
a1    name      chair
-
-
etc.
```

This listing contains all of the information in the network and is suitable for storage in the machine. In fact, we are experts at handling facts in three-tuple form because we studied this format extensively in chapter 4. For the remainder of the chapter, we will continue to draw networks as shown above, assuming you can fill in implementation details if needed by referencing chapter 4.

5. *A Graphical Description*. In this case, a photograph or a pictorial likeness of the object is stored in the computer memory. In the chair example, the machine might store a two- (or three-) dimensional array of characters that indicate the material used. Thus if "O" stands for "oak," the machine might represent chair *a1* as follows:

Many other representations for knowledge have been used, and sometimes combinations of representations are created in particular applications. Rather complex representations are needed to hold the diverse and unpredictable forms encountered in real-world situations.

But how does the designer know which representation to use? The answer is that one should carefully examine the tasks to be performed and employ a representation that readily provides the needed information. This idea can be illustrated by considering specific artificial intelligence problems and ranking each of the five proposed representations on the dimension of appropriateness.

Suppose as a first example that a computer program is to read a photograph and label all of the objects shown. Assume the photograph is stored in "pixel form" as an array of dots that may be either black or white, as is ordinarily done in newspapers:

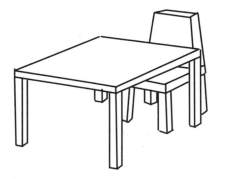

The program is to find all the identifiable objects in the picture and give their locations:

```
Identified objects.
    chair:          coordinates (450,470)
    chair leg:      coordinates (100,120)
    chair leg:      coordinates ( . . . . . )
       -                -
    table;          coordinates ( . . . . . )
```

If the program is to be written, which representation should be used? Consider a natural language representation. This would be a poor choice because the facts given in English would require considerable processing before they could be applied to the pictorial representation. The best representations will offer more direct and easily understandable relationships between the knowledge base and the input data. A specially designed formal language or a programming language would be much more desirable because it could directly implement practical facts needed for the task. Thus in recognition of a chair, the code might look for pictorial regions with smooth edges. It might examine vertical narrow regions near the floor (legs) and look for connections to flat regions about 2 feet above the floor. This kind of processing can be expected to find chairs and other objects as directly and effectively as any known method. A special language might be more desirable than a general-purpose language because it could have features aimed specifically at the problems at hand. But either could be used.

Semantic network descriptions are conceivably as powerful as formal and programming languages and could be used in this problem. However, some of their characteristics are awkward although not impossible to handle. One of their most notable shortcomings is apparent when the designer wishes to group segments of information for one reason or another. For example, in Pascal, if one wishes to collect a series of statements into a single unit, the method is to write them sequentially with the keywords *begin* and *end* surrounding them. This unit of programming information can then be used as a body for a procedure declaration, an *if* statement, a *while* statement, or in many other applications. In semantic nets, such bracketing mechanisms are not as easily implemented.

A graphic description in the example problem might be quite useful because it can provide a template that could be compared directly to the input picture. An unknown object may be identifiable on the evidence that it has a shape similar to that expected for a known class of objects.

The following table summarizes these five representation types and their application to the picture identification problem.

Representation type	Rating for given problem	Justification of rating
Natural language description	Poor	Too much processing is required of natural language source data before it can be applied to a problem
Formal language description	Good	A special language could be designed to represent the important kinds of information
Programming language description	Fairly good	A programming language may be flexible enough to hold the application information
Semantic network description	Fair	Could conceivably work as well as formal languages but encodes some types of knowledge in awkward ways
Graphic description	Good	Can provide a template to be compared to the object being recognized

Next consider another artificial intelligence problem. Suppose a program is to be written which reads English language stories and then answers questions about them. Thus the program might read the story of King Arthur and be expected to respond correctly to these kinds of questions:

1. Who was the central figure of this story?

2. What were the admirable characteristics of this person?

3. What major problem did this individual encounter in the story?

The question again arises: Which representation schemes might be applicable to the problem? The English-language description would be poor in this situation for the same reason as in the previous case. Although the representation of the input and the stored knowledge are in the same language, the relationships between the two are unnecessarily complex and not easily discernable. The formal and programming languages are again applicable for the same reasons. The semantic network representation might be quite good because it makes relationships between the various described entities clear and directly discoverable. Such questions as "Where did King Arthur live?" and "Who are all the people that lived there?" are directly discoverable by following the arcs from the relevant nodes. The graphic description would not necessarily be very useful because the actual shapes of objects in the story are usually not key to its understanding:

Representation type	Rating for given problem	Justification of rating
Natural language description	Poor	Relationships between input and knowledge base are too complicated
Formal language description	Good	A special language could be designed to represent the important kinds of information
Programming language description	Fairly good	A programming language may be flexible enough to hold the application information
Semantic network description	Good	The node and link representation may be quite useful for finding relationships needed in story understanding
Graphic description	Fair	Actual shapes of objects are not ordinarily important in story understanding

The next several sections will discuss the concept of knowledge understanding, a method for learning new knowledge, structures for large knowledge modules, and an example of the usefulness of knowledge in natural language understanding. For the purposes of these discussions, semantic networks will be used because they are easy to visualize in these kinds of processing.

Exercises

1. Draw a semantic network to represent a typical house. It should include each wall, the roof, each window, the doors, a chimney, and so forth. The network should show connectivity, support relationships, and some functional knowledge such as where to enter.

2. Show how the other four representations described in this section can be used to represent the house from problem 1.

Understanding (B)

Suppose the knowledge structure of the chair is stored in the machine (or perhaps the human mind). Suppose also that an image has been perceived from the outside world and is stored in a nearby memory region:

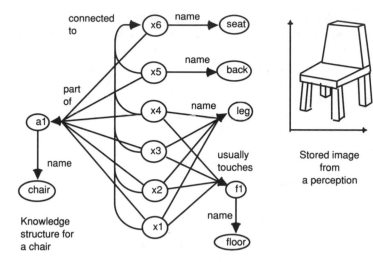

Knowledge
structure for
a chair

Stored image
from
a perception

We would like to be able to use the knowledge to make sense of the image. If the knowledge can be linked in a satisfactory way to the lines and regions in the image, the system would be able to relate the knowledge to the image. In fact, it would be able to identify the object, to name its parts, to explain connectedness relationships of the parts to each other, and to give the uses of this object. It could find all other details that may be stored in its knowledge base (owner, cost, materials, history, etc.). If these linkages can be made, we say that the system *understands* this image with respect to this knowledge. Understanding will involve finding a linkage between these two structures.

Let us follow the process of searching for an understanding of the image with respect to this knowledge. Where, for example, is the seat of the chair? We will link the node *x6* associated with the seat with a randomly selected region in the image:

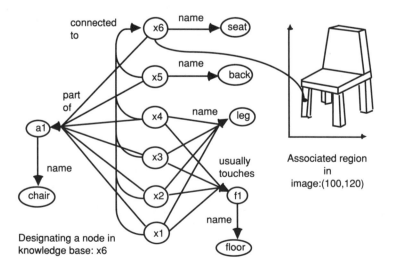

Designating a node in
knowledge base: x6

Associated region
in
image:(100,120)

Assume that the selected region is specified by the coordinates of its central point $(x,y) = (100,120)$. Then we will store this linkage in a table:

Nodes in knowledge base	Associated region in image
x6	(100,120)

Good! We have begun to understand the image as a chair by identifying the seat.

Examining the knowledge structure, we see that five objects are connected to the seat. In order to confirm the linkage that has been made, let us scan the periphery of the selected region in the image and find those five objects. Unfortunately, a search of the surrounding areas yields only one obviously connected part. Perhaps the linkage is incorrect.

Let us break the linkage and try connecting it to other regions. Other attempts may lead to the same result, but eventually the following linkage will be tried:

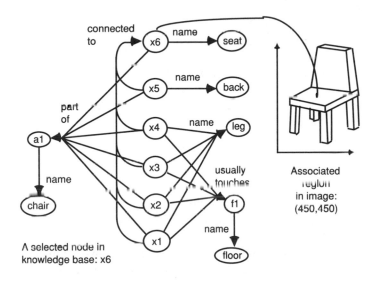

Again, understanding requires continuous confirmation of as many associated relationships as possible. Perhaps the region designated (100,120) can be associated with some other node. Since it touches the floor, we will propose that it is $x3$. Examining $x3$ further, the knowledge base asserts that $x3$ is connected to $x6$. Can this be confirmed in the image? Yes. All linkages thus far appear to be consistent with expectations given by the knowledge base. Carrying this process on, three more objects can be identified as legs, and one can be identified as the back. In fact, a satisfactory linkage has been found between the nodes of the knowledge structure and the regions of the image. The predicted relationships given in the semantic net are confirmed, and the system can assume that the knowledge structure has been correctly related to the image:

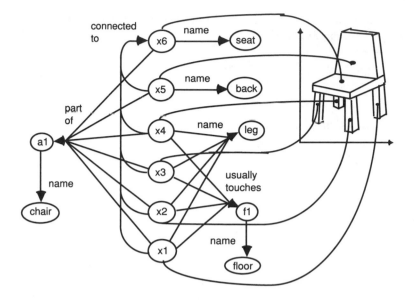

When the system has correctly made these linkages, we say that it *understands* the image. All of its knowledge related to the chair can be used. The system can now find the name of the object of which the identified regions are parts. It follows the *partof* links to *a1* and traces the name link to "chair." The system can now output

```
"This is a chair."
```

Furthermore, it can follow the *name* links for all of the parts and name them. Then it can follow the *use* link, if it exists, to discover the function of this object. It can follow ownership, cost, history, location and other links, if present, to obtain as much additional information about the chair as its knowledge base may hold.

In summary, the understanding of a perception with respect to a body of knowledge involves finding a set of self-consistent links between the parts of the knowledge structure and the parts of the perceived data. After such a linkage is made, the intelligent being can follow arcs in its knowledge base to obtain innumerable useful facts, the name of the perceived object, the names of its many parts, their relationships to each other, the uses of the object, and all other information available in its knowledge base.

Of course, a being seeking understanding may incorrectly set up linkages with a knowledge structure. Then misunderstanding will occur, and incorrect inferences may be made. For example, in the following case, it may incorrectly conclude that an oaken object has been discovered that will be useful for sitting:

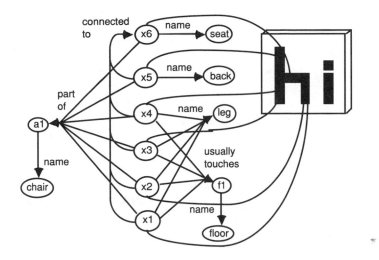

A being may also fail to understand a perception although its knowledge is adequate. The discovery of the proper linkages may involve a calculation outside its repertoire. Either a teacher or additional computational exploration will be necessary to achieve understanding:

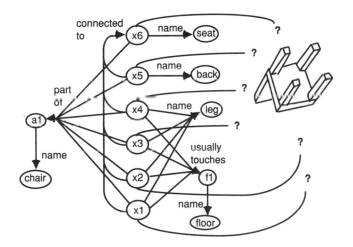

As a philosophical issue, some people have argued about whether computers can truly understand anything. If the above definition of understanding is accepted, then we must certainly agree that computers can understand many things. First, one should ask whether there are domains where significant knowledge can be stored, and second, we should verify that machines are capable of properly relating machine perceptions with such knowledge. On the first issue, it is clear that a computer can store all the relevant information on large sets of objects and their interrelationships. These can include people in organizations, objects in an environment, objects or structures in a mathematical system or in a game, the data structures for computer programs, and an endless list of other examples. On the second issue, we assume the computer "perceptions" are the sequences of characters typed on the keyboard or read from an incoming line. Most certainly computers have been programmed to relate properly the input sequences to the internal structure. The image understanding mechanisms described above provide an example.

As another example of computer understanding, consider the task accomplished by a processor for a computer language such as Pascal. The processor sets up linkages between the language constructs and the string of symbols that comprise the program. On the knowledge side, the machine has representations for such entities as keywords, identifiers, expressions, statements, registers, machine language, and much more. On the perception side, the system receives a string of characters that needs to be understood. The process of understanding involves finding expected objects and relationships in the perceived string as predicted by the knowledge of the language in the processor. This linking of internal structures to the string represents a rather complete understanding of that string as a program.

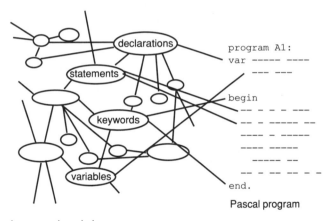

Language knowledge

Pascal program

While the processor will completely understand the input string as a program, it may not understand additional meanings the user has intended. Thus there may be variables, such as X, that have particular meanings to the user, such as dollars earned. These cannot be known to the processor. However, if the machine had this additional knowledge, it could conceivably understand these facts as well.

Other examples of machine understanding will be discussed later in this chapter. In fact, we might begin to believe that machines can understand absolutely everything. After all, is it not reasonable to assume that all knowledge is representable in some kind of computer language? And is it not also reasonable to assume that if there is a linkage possible between that knowledge and perceptions, a computer could eventually find it? The discovery of the linkage might require much time, but the computer should be able to find it.

Careful reflection will lead us to another conclusion: there are kinds of knowledge that probably can never be satisfactorily represented in machines. The most important example is the knowledge of our own humanity—the knowledge that comes from being born human, growing up, and surviving in the world. We all have had parents, friends and loved ones, and we have shared experiences with them over the years. We have struggled hard, suffered anguish, cared for people and for our values, celebrated successes, and wept over our failures. All of these experiences build cumulatively in our psychobiological selves into an immense complex of memories and feelings. These experiences are unique to each of us but also shared to a great extent between us. This vast array of emotions and remembrances has been earned by each of us in a multitude of events that cannot be repeated or simulated. These are the kinds of knowledge that cannot be satisfactorily stored in a machine.

When a fellow human being says, "My baby just spoke her first word," or "My cousin died yesterday," we, as human beings, can link these observances into our human memories and understand them. We have plenty of representations for the emotions and ramifications of the statements, and our understanding involves our linking to them.

We could attempt to build a simulation of human experience and emotion into a machine and claim that it also understands these uniquely human utterances. We could have nodes for pain, hope, fear, love, and stored remembrances of associated events. All of these could be connected in complex ways, and the system might seem to understand and to respond, "Wonderful!" or "I am sorry" at the appropriate times. But the simulation will probably lack authenticity, and at best, it will never be more than a simulation. It is not likely that humans will ever agree that machines can understand the human experience.

In summary, this section gives a definition for the concept of understanding and indicates that machines are capable of this behavior in many domains. However, it argues that machines will probably never be able to understand some things, such as human emotion, in any satisfactory way.

Exercises

1. Draw a picture of a typical house and its associated semantic net. Explain the process a machine would go through in using the network to "understand" the image of the house.

2. Suppose the chair network of this section were used to try to understand your house image of exercise 1. What processing would take place, and what mechanism would prevent the machine from recognizing your house as a chair?

3. Suppose a computer program is designed to receive digitized versions of paintings by the masters. Then it is supposed to "understand" these paintings and comment on them. What will the machine possibly be able to do and what will it probably fail to do?

4. A computer program has been designed to write music. Comment on the nature of music as a human endeavor and the role that music written by machines may play.

5. Discuss the replaceability of humans by machines. Does the use of automated bank tellers foreshadow a day when most interactions between businesses and the public will be done by machine? Could teachers, counselors, or judges be replaced by machines? What are the situations when a machine is preferred and when is a human preferred?

Learning (B)

Once the fundamental issues of knowledge are understood, the next problem is to discover how to build adequate stores of knowledge for the many purposes of intelligence. One way to build a knowledge base in a machine is to prepare it in an appropriate form and read it directly as data. Another way is to have the system *learn* the knowledge; that is, it uses its own mechanisms to acquire and properly format its knowledge. This latter method is highly desirable if it can be achieved because the task of assembling knowledge is difficult.

We will study two kinds of learning in this chapter: *rote learning* and *concept learning*. *Rote learning* refers to the most primitive kind of knowledge acquisition; information from the outside world is coded into internal formats and stored in a relatively raw form. The amount of memory space used is roughly proportional to the amount of information acquired. *Concept learning* is a much more profound type of knowledge acquisition because it attempts to build a small construction to represent a large amount of data. It attempts to find a summary that properly describes a multiplicity of data items. A learned concept may use relatively little memory in comparison to the amount of data it represents.

Chapter 12 examined connectionist networks that theoretically can achieve both kinds of learning. However, we will use more conventional models of computing in this chapter because they are better understood and more well developed for the purposes of the current study. This section will begin with an examination of rote learning and then show improvements in a basic mechanism that will lead to concept learning.

Suppose that a being has no concept of a "chair." The being has never seen one and has never encountered the term *chair*. Suppose further that the being is presented with this image:

We must assume, however, that the being can distinguish some primitive elements in the scene, if not the chair. Let us say that it distinguishes a group of oaken boards but does not recognize the configuration to be anything special. Then its internal representation would indicate little more than the existence of the recognized objects:

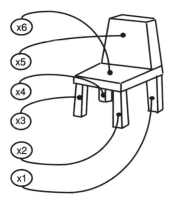

Initial understanding of the image.

Next we assume that someone says, "This is a chair." This utterance asks the intelligent being to comprehend the image as something more than a pile of wood. It is a very special assembly of wood that has enough importance to have been given a name. The being thus notes more carefully exactly the nature of the set of objects, assigns them a representation as a group, and attaches the name "chair":

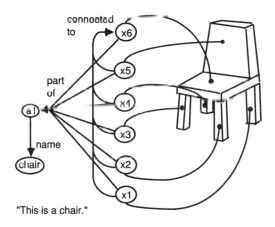

"This is a chair."

For further comprehension, we will assume the teacher also names the components of the chair and demonstrates its use for sitting. Then the system would increase its knowledge structure to account for these additional data:

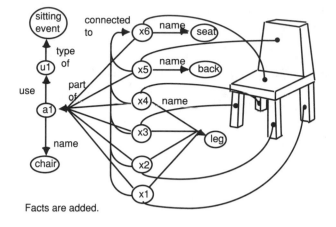

Facts are added.

Thereafter, the being should be able to see this object and recognize it as a "chair." This is an example of what we will call *rote learning*. A single data item has been observed, and a memory representation has been created for it. The system could similarly be given other objects to learn and name, such as a table, a lamp, a stool, a puppy dog, and so forth. Each new object has its own configuration and its own memorized structure. If a thousand such objects were so learned, a thousand such representations would be created.

Suppose next the system is given the following image and asked to identify it:

It would clearly fail because there is no way to build a correspondence between the image and any internal representation. It does not match the description of a table, a lamp, a puppy dog, or any other object in memory. It is not a chair because a chair must have six major components, and this has only five. The system could not understand this image with respect to its current knowledge base.

Let us now indicate to the system that this new image is also a "chair." Let us similarly name its parts and demonstrate it as a useful auxiliary for sitting. The system now has two representations for "chair":

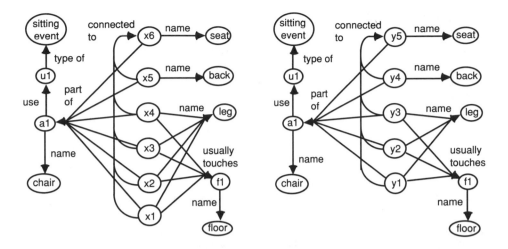

At this point, the system has two choices: it could continue its rote memory strategy for learning and store both of these representations, or it could attempt to combine them and perhaps generalize to some extent. Let us pursue this second strategy and note that these two diagrams are identical except for the number of legs. So they can be merged if the difference between numbers of legs can be accounted for:

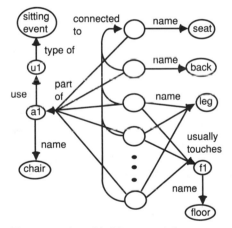

The merge of two "chair" representations.

The new representation asserts that something is a chair if it has a seat, a back, is useful for sitting, and has any number of legs.

A merger of this kind is called *concept formation*, and it has a number of advantages. First, it saves memory space because it enables the system to store information for more than one data item. In fact, an unlimited number of data items can have a single representation, as is the case with a human's concept of chair. Second, the merged representation allows the learner to deal with new situations that have never before been encountered. Thus the system can recognize objects as chairs with, perhaps, one leg or no legs or a thousand legs if they meet the other prerequisites that chairs must have. The general concept has much greater usefulness than individual rote memory instances.

Concept formation of this type also has some dangers. It may be that an attribute may be observed to appear in a few examples and falsely generalized to be expected in all examples. For example, a being might observe that the winners of several U. S. presidential elections were taller than their major adversaries. On this basis, the system might conclude that the tallest candidate will always win, a typical but not necessarily reliable observation.

This section has described the acquisition of knowledge through rote memory and concept formation processes that enable a system to generalize from instances. The result of a lot of learning can be some large knowledge structures as will be described in the next section.

Exercise
1. Draw semantic networks for two kinds of vehicles, say a car and a truck. Show how to merge the two networks to obtain a more general description of a vehicle.

Frames (B)

If one carries out extensive learning, rather large knowledge structures will evolve. These structures are called *frames*, and they are hypothesized to be of central importance in intelligent thought. They necessarily will be complicated and will include a variety of notations, indicating, for example, which relationships are obligatory, which are typical, which are possible although unusual, and which strange collections of relationships may occur. In realistic situations, frames may be built up over the years through a process of hundreds or thousands of concept learning merges. These merges result in huge numbers of auxiliary and extraneous connections that may include variations on the original template, as well as seemingly unlimited numbers of related facts—history, associations, usages, special relationships, and long lists of other facts.

As an illustration, consider how much most people can say about their own knowledge of chairs. They can talk in considerable detail about a variety of chairs they have seen. They can probably give endless descriptions of chairs that are in their home, chairs they remember from schools or museums or theaters, chairs that were comfortable or not, chairs in stories, chairs that were broken, and other chairs. They can probably tell innumerable stories about chairs in their lives, chairs in literature or movies, and chairs in history. They probably can describe in detail the construction of chairs, their materials, their finish, where they are built and sold, how much they cost, and much more.

Therefore, a semantic network that represents something close to a human's knowledge of the concept "chair" will be a very large structure. It will include tens of thousands of nodes and arcs. Whenever the being needs information related to chairs, this frame will be called upon for understanding and for guiding correct action.

Researchers hypothesize that intelligent beings must have hundreds or even thousands of such modules and that thinking involves sequentially activating them as they are needed. This leads to the view of the intelligent being as a kind of frame-shuffling machine. Perceptions from the world impinge on numerous frames, and a few of those frames become successful in understanding those perceptions. Those activated frames prompt the being to appropriate action, and simultaneously additional changes may be observed. This leads to new perceptions, possible confirmation of current frame activity, and conceivably the activation of additional frames. The being is seen as perpetually grabbing frames that enable understanding, responding as dictated by those frames, receiving new perceptions, activating additional frames as needed, responding further, and so forth.

Consider the actions of a person walking down a hall. The theory might account for the sequence of actions as follows: A walking frame is activated to coordinate the eyes and muscular activities to achieve the walking behavior. A hall frame enables understanding of the visual images. Suppose the person turns into an office. The turning and visual door frames are activated to enable this movement. Suppose another person is encountered. Then a frame for that person is activated along with the frame for friendly conversation. "Hi; how are you? ... " The weather is mentioned, and the weather frame is activated. The appropriate words can now be understood: rain, snow, cold, slippery, and others. A newspaper is noticed on a nearby desk with the headline "Commission Appointed to Study Deficit." The politics and deficit frames come into action to permit relevant conversation: presidential proclamations, the appearance of positive actions, the requirements for large annual interest payments. The friendly conversation frame interrupts to indicate that the interaction should end. The person leaves the office, moving through the door frame and returning again to the walking and hall frames.

The frames system is called a *memory-rich* theory because it emphasizes the importance of memory and access to complex structures. It proposes that humans depend primarily on remembrance in perceiving the world and in responding. It places less faith in inference or reasoning mechanisms as bases for typical behaviors. It asserts that the actions and thoughts of the person walking down the hall, meeting another person, conversing, and leaving are primarily governed by fast, efficient memory access methods. The claim is that the person did not calculate much to get the legs to move, to understand the visual images, or to converse.

One of the main arguments for memory-rich theories is that the elements of the human mind-computer are too slow to do a large amount of sequential computation. The neurons of the brain respond in a time on the order of milliseconds, and the actions of a human are too fast to allow for much more than memory access. For example, a tennis player observing a ball at a distance of 30 feet approaching at 30 miles per hour will have a fraction of a second to respond. This means that the player's mind has, at best, time for a few hundred sequential neural cycles. Yet the amount of computation for appropriate response includes the need to perceive the ball, calculate its trajectory, and properly activate a myriad of muscular responses throughout the body. It would seem that this is too much computation to complete in so few cycles even with tremendous parallelism. The memory-rich theory proposes that the player amalgamates the experiences of thousands of incoming balls perceived and properly answered into a massive frame for hitting balls. When the next tennis ball approaches, this huge structure comes into action to monitor the perceptions, to predict the trajectory, and to drive the body to hit the ball back. The player depends heavily on remembrance rather than on calculation to return the ball properly.

This section and previous sections have concentrated on concepts in knowledge representation and learning. The next sections will show applications of some of these ideas to the problems of processing natural language, general problem solving, and game playing.

Exercises

1. Specify as well as you can remember all of the details of the outside of some particular building. Then go and observe the building and check the accuracy of your memory. How many of the details did you correctly remember? How many details were supplied by your general frames for all buildings? Did you "remember" some details that were not actually there but were filled in by your general frame for buildings?

2. Explain the meaning of the sentence "Make a wish." Then describe in some detail a frame for the events of a typical American birthday party. Suppose events have occurred that bring to the speaker's and hearer's mind the birthday party frame, and then the sentence "Make a wish" is uttered. What new meaning does this sentence have in the context of the party frame? What knowledge will the hearer associate with this sentence that could not have been possible without the party frame? Who spoke the sentence? Who was it directed to? Why was it spoken? What other events are associated with this action? What other sentences might be uttered in this environment, and how would the frame aid in their understanding? Is it possible to understand these sentences without the associated frame?

An Application: Natural Language Processing (B)

In order to show an application of the above ideas, we will examine methods for processing English-language sentences in the presence of a knowledge base. We will suppose that the machine is in a place called *room1* and that it has a full representation of the objects in the room as well as other objects in its world. Our examples will continue to be built around the chair example, and we will list three chairs explicitly in the knowledge base:

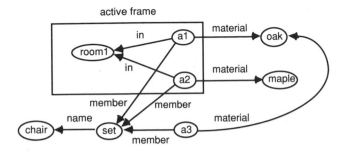

We will assume the only active frame contains the set of objects in *room1*, but we list one object outside the frame to remind ourselves that there are other objects. A node is included, called *set*, which stands for the set of all chairs. Objects *a1*, *a2*, and *a3* are members of that set.

We will study methods for handling three kinds of sentences: (1) declarative sentences, (2) questions, and (3) imperative sentences. The function of a declarative sentence is to transmit information to the hearer, in this example, the machine. The declarative sentence will enable the machine to add new nodes and/or transitions to its knowledge base. The purpose of the question is to solicit information from the knowledge base. The question specifies what information is to be retrieved, and the machine's task is to find it and generate a proper answer. An imperative sentence causes the machine to find the objects in the knowledge base that are referenced in the sentence and then to carry out the specified actions on those objects. This may also involve making some associated changes in the knowledge.

Considering declarative sentences first, assume someone speaks the utterance, "Nancy owns the oak chair," in the context of our knowledge base. The following is a small grammar in the style of chapter 10 that is capable of generating this sentence:

Syntax	Semantics
S—>NP VP.	M(S) = glue(M(NP),M(VP))
NP—>PROPN	M(NP) = M(PROPN)
VP—>V NP	M(VP) = glue(M(V),M(NP))
NP—>ART NP1	M(NP) = M(NP1)
NP1—>ADJ NP1	M(NP1) = gluc(M(ADJ),M(NP1))
NP1—>N	M(NP1) = M(N)
PROPN—>Nancy	M(PROPN) = (Nancy) ←name (p) →member (set) →name (person)
V—>owns	M(V) = (n) →owner (p) →member (set) →name (person)
ADJ—>oak	M(ADJ) = (n) →material (oak)
N—>chair	M(N) = (n) →member (set) →name (chair)
ART—>the	

The *glue* function in the semantics rules will be used to join separate graphs together.

The declarative sentence will be processed as follows:

Declarative Sentence Processor.

1. The grammar rules with their semantic components are used to create a semantic network representing the sentence meaning. This network will be called *M(S)* where *S* stands for the sentence.

2. The active frame for the sentence processing is selected. This is called the *focus*. It specifies the portion of the knowledge base that will be used in the processing.

3. A match is found between objects specified in *M(S)* and objects in the knowledge base.

4. Additional nodes and linkages specified by the sentence are added to the knowledge base.

In our example, the sentence "Nancy owns the oak chair" will result in the addition of several nodes and linkages to the knowledge base. These will specify that a person named Nancy is associated with chair *a1* by the "owns" relationship. We will now examine these steps in detail.

Consider step (1) first. Beginning with *S*, a generation of the target sentence must be found. Associated with each rule application is its semantic function that will be used in creating the meaning representation *M(S)*.

Generation	Syntactic rule	Semantic Rule
S	S—>NP VP.	M(S) = glue(M(NP),M(VP))
NP VP.	NP—>PROPN	M(NP) = M(PROPN)
PROPN VP.	VP—>V NP	M(VP) = glue(M(V),M(NP))
PROPN V NP.	NP—>ART NP1	M(NP) = M(NP1)
PROPN V ART NP1.	NP1—>ADJ NP1	M(NP1) = glue(M(ADJ),M(NP1))
PROPN V ART ADJ NP1.	NP1—>N	M(NP1) = M(N)
PROPN V ART ADJ N.	PROPN—>Nancy	M(PROPN) = (Nancy) ←name— (p) —member→ (set) —name→ (person)
Nancy V ART ADJ N.	V—>owns	M(V) = (n) —owner→ (p) —member→ (set) —name→ (person)
Nancy owns ART ADJ N.	ART—>the	
Nancy owns the ADJ N.	ADJ—>oak	M(ADJ) = (n) —material→ (oak)
Nancy owns the oak N.	N—>chair	M(N) = (n) —member→ (set) —name→ (chair)
Nancy owns the oak chair.		

Following the methodology of chapter 10, the semantic portions of the above rules can be applied:

M(S) = glue(M(NP),M(VP))

    = glue(M(PROPN),M(VP))

    = glue(M(PROPN),glue (M(V),M(NP)))

    = glue(M(PROPN),glue (M(V),M(NP1)))

    = glue(M(PROPN),glue (M(V),glue(M(ADJ),M(NP1))))

    = glue(M(PROPN),glue (M(V),glue(M(ADJ),M(N))))

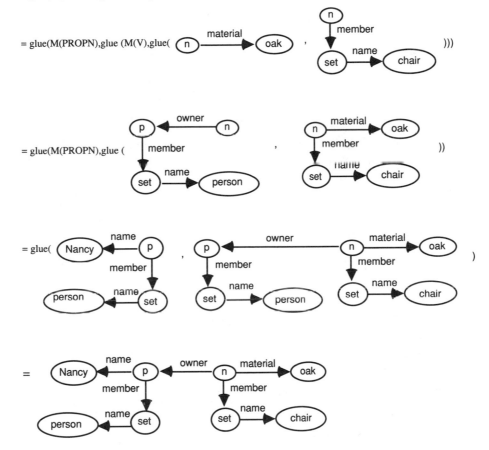

M(S) is a graph that represents the meaning of the original sentence. It states, with nodes and arcs, that Nancy is an entity p that is a member of a set of entities each with the name "person"; that is, Nancy is a person. Furthermore, this person is the owner of object n, which is a member of the set of chairs and is made of oak.

    Step (2) of the processing procedure selects the active frame in the knowledge base, the set of objects in *room1*. Then step (3) attempts to match parts of the M(S) graph with parts of the active portion of the knowledge base:

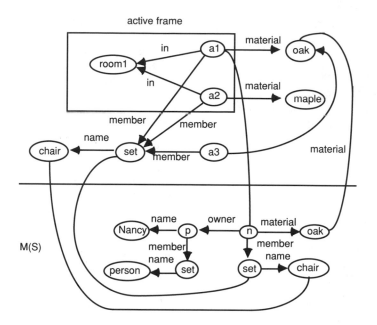

This match seems to imply that *n* in the sentence meaning corresponds to *a1* in the knowledge base. Notice that *n* does not match *a2* because the associated material is wrong. It does not match *a3* because *a3* is not in the active frame.

Once the correspondence has been found between some nodes in *M(S)* and nodes in the knowledge base, the new information in *M(S)* can be accounted for. Step (4) does this by gluing the nodes in *M(S)* that are not found in the knowledge base to the appropriate nodes in the knowledge base:

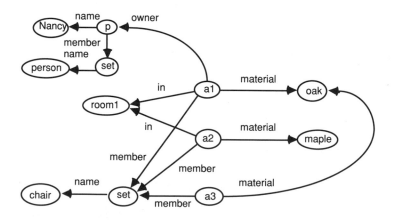

Summarizing, the knowledge base at the beginning of this section listed three chairs: *a1*, *a2* and *a3*. In the context of *room1*, the sentence "Nancy owns the oak chair" was spoken. The meaning graph *M(S)* was generated and matched against the active knowledge base nodes, those in *room1*. It was determined that *a1* is the object referenced by the noun phrase "the oak chair"; but the portion of *M(S)* corresponding to "Nancy owns" was not found in the knowledge base, so it was added. The result of processing the sentence "Nancy owns the oak chair" is the addition of the nodes indicating that Nancy owns *a1*.

In a modern natural language processing system, a large variety of additional mechanisms are included that cannot be discussed here. Such systems must handle, for example, relative clauses, pronouns, ellipses, complex syntactic constructions, and a long list of other language behaviors. Furthermore, many contemporary systems use representations other than semantic nets. Thus, while the flavor of the kinds of processing needed to handle natural language utterances is conveyed by the description given here, the details of systems actually being built will often be quite different.

Relatively few additions to these mechanisms are needed to enable the system to handle questions. First, we need more rules to handle question syntax:

Q—>WH VP   M(Q) = glue(M(WH),M(VP))

WH—>who   M(WH) =

Then an algorithm for question processing is needed:

Question Processor:

1. Find the meaning graph *M(Q)* for the question.
2. Select the active frame in the knowledge base, the focus.
3. Find a match between parts of *M(Q)* and the active portion of the knowledge base.
4. The question mark in *M(Q)* should match some node in the knowledge base. The system should return as an answer the contents of that matching node.

Using these added rules and the question handling strategy, you should be able to carry out the processing of "Who owns the oak chair?" You should use the database that exists after the assertion "Nancy owns the oak chair." Most of the steps are similar to those for the previous example. But in the final step, the node with "?" will match the node with "Nancy," indicating that the answer to the question is "Nancy." This processing has some resemblances to the methodology of the database retrieval system in chapter 4.

Finally, we can examine a methodology for processing imperative sentences. Here the system is being asked to find certain objects in the active frame and do something to them. Some additional rules and an imperative sentence handler are needed:

I—>IMPV NP   M(I) = glue(M(IMPV),M(NP))

IMPV = pick up   M(IMPV) =

Imperative Sentence Processor.

1. Find $M(I)$.

2. Select the active frame.

3. Match $M(I)$ to the active frame.

4. Apply the action indicated by the imperative verb to the object referenced in the sentence.

You should be able to complete the details for an example sentence. Suppose the machine is a robot capable of navigating in the room and picking up objects. Then the command "Pick up the oak chair" will reference *a1*, and proper processing will cause the machine to "pick up *a1*."

This completes our discussion of mechanisms for processing natural language input to a computer. Many other topics in natural language processing must be omitted for lack of space. We have not, for example, considered the problem of how the system might generate natural language instead of recognize it. We might like to have the system be able to respond to "Tell me everything you know about the oak chair." The system would then find the object *a1* and create sentences from its associated arcs:

"This chair is in *room1*. It is owned by Nancy . . . "

We also have not examined mechanisms for handling indirect requests. Thus if a person is carrying *a1* out of the room, the sentence "Nancy owns the oak chair" may not mean that the hearer should store this ownership fact in memory. It may really mean, "Put that chair back! It belongs to Nancy."

Exercises

1. Carry out the details for the processing of "Who owns the oak chair?"

2. Carry out the details for the processing of "Pick up the oak chair."

3. Design grammar rules to enable the processing of the following sentences:

Nancy owns what?

What is in this room?

Don owns the maple chair.

The oak chair is brown.

4. How would you build a mechanism to respond to the request, "Tell me about the oak chair."

Reasoning (B)

Reasoning is the process of finding or building a linkage from one entity in memory to another. There must be an initial entity, a target entity, and a way of choosing paths from the initial entity toward the target. For example, if the system holds facts about family relationships, it might wish to determine the relationships between one member and a second. If it follows a parent link, a sibling link, and a child link, then it will *reason* that the second individual is a cousin of the first.

Rather than discovering existing links, reasoning often involves constructing links from the initial entity to the goal. If the being observes the state of the world, it may select some new goal state that it wishes to achieve and then reason a strategy for achieving it. Here it tries to discover a sequence of actions for going from the initial state to the goal. This sequence of actions is the desired linkage between the entities.

An illustration of this more complex type of reasoning comes from the monkey and bananas problem. Suppose the following are in a room: a monkey, a chair, and some bananas hanging from the ceiling. If the goal is for the monkey to get the bananas, it is necessary to find a sequence of actions that begins at the current state and reaches the goal state. In terms of semantic nets, the initial state is represented as follows:

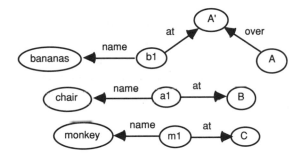

Here A, B, and C represent positions on the floor below the bananas, the chair, and the monkey, respectively. A' represents a position well above A, which is reachable only by standing on the chair. The goal is represented by the following subnet:

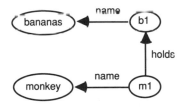

It is desired to achieve a state of the world such that the monkey can hold the bananas (and presumably eat them).

The path from one state to another is a sequence of state-changing operations that will convert the initial state to the target state. Five operations will be available for this problem:

Operation	Meaning	Preconditions
go X	monkey goes to X	monkey is not at any Y' (not standing on chair) and monkey is not at X
push X	the monkey pushes the chair to X	monkey and chair are at Y and Y is not equal to X
climbup	the monkey climbs from current position X to X'	monkey and chair are at same location X
grasp	the monkey grasps the bananas	the monkey and bananas are at X'
climbdown	monkey climbs from current position X' to X	monkey is at some X'

The first operation *go X* takes the monkey from its current position to position *X*. We will consider only three possible values for *X*: *A*, *B*, and *C*. But this operation cannot be applied if the monkey is already at *X* or if it is standing on the chair (at some *Y'*). As an illustration, suppose the monkey is at *C* and proposes to apply operation *go X* to go to *A* or *B*. Then we can construct the resulting states achieved in each case:

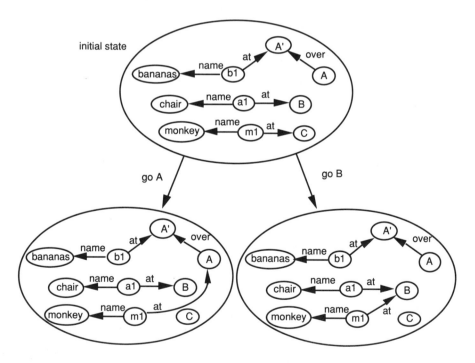

The monkey and bananas problem thus requires that one find the correct sequence of actions from the initial state to any state having the condition that the monkey holds bananas:

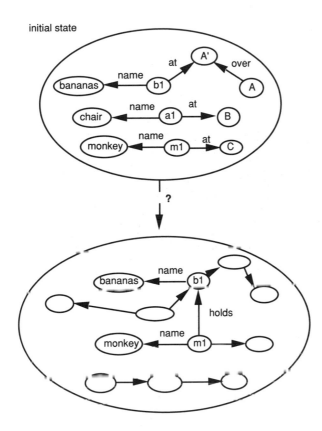

This is not necessarily an easy problem. If you consider the set of all possible action sequences, there are many things the monkey could do, and only a few of the possible sequences lead to success:

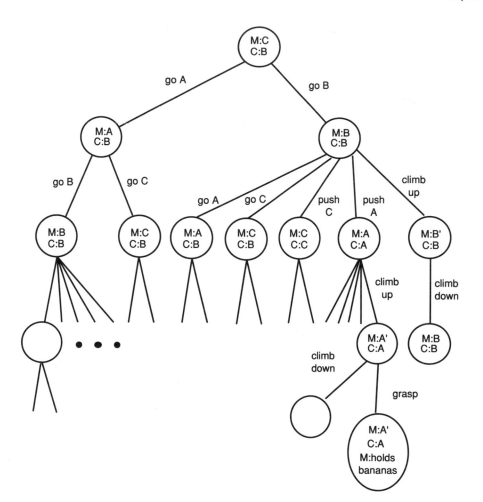

(The semantic net notation is abbreviated here: M: and C: indicate, respectively, the positions of the monkey and chair.) If the monkey visualizes every possible sequence of actions, it will think for a long time before it finds a successful sequence.

Fortunately, humans have a broad repertoire of remembered tool-using frames, so there is no need to do much reasoning in this problem. If the target is not instantly reachable, the human has remembrances of successful quests on previous occasions. He or she will immediately search for "tools" to help achieve the goal. Is there a rock or a stick nearby? Or the human might remember receiving help from a comrade if there is one available. In the current case, the chair is the only hope for help. Perhaps it could be thrown at the bananas or used as a stick. But if the human had no experience using tools and had never before seen one used, he or she would probably have considerable difficulty reasoning a solution from first principles.

There are many methods for doing reasoning. You can start at the top of the tree of all possible actions and search down the branches for a goal. You also can attempt to reason backwards from the goal toward the initial state. You thus might argue that the goal cannot be achieved until a certain subgoal is reached, but that subgoal requires some previous achievement, and so forth. Or you might use a kind of distance measure as a guide toward the target: "If I can reach state S, I know I will be closer to success. I will do that first and then see what I should do next to reduce further the distance to the goal."

We will examine a search algorithm that tries to find a path by searching downward from an initial node toward the goal. It will work by examining nodes farther and farther down the tree until the goal is found. Nodes that are about to be examined are called *active* nodes; those that have been examined and found not to be goals are called *closed* nodes.

Suppose this tree is about to be searched:

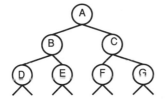

The procedure will begin by marking the top node *active*:

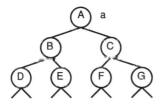

Then this node (A) is examined to see if it is a goal. If it is, the search halts. Otherwise its two successors are marked active, and it is marked *closed*:

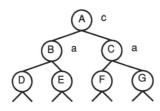

Then one of the active nodes is examined; assume the left-most one is chosen in this case. If it is not a goal, its successors are marked active, and it is marked closed:

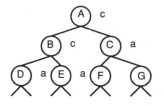

This process continues either until a goal is found or until all nodes of the tree have been examined.

Here is an algorithm for doing this search task. It searches a tree of possible actions until a goal is found. It uses a list, called *ACTIVE*, that stores the set of nodes that need to be examined next. It has a second list, called *CLOSED*, that stores the set of all nodes that have been examined:

```
     begin
(a)  put the initial node on ACTIVE list;
     the CLOSED list begins empty;
     while there are nodes on ACTIVE do
       begin
(b)      remove a node from ACTIVE using criterion C and call it N;
(c)      if N is a goal then
           begin
           print "success";
           print the list of actions on arcs from initial node to N;
           halt;
           end.
(d)      find all children nodes of N that are not on ACTIVE or CLOSED
             and add them to the ACTIVE list;
(e)      add N to CLOSED;
       end;
     print "failure";
     end.
```

Criterion C is the strategy for guiding the search. If no helpful strategy is available, C may choose the next node from *ACTIVE* randomly. But if there is a way to gauge the direction that the choice should take, C is the mechanism or subroutine that makes the decision.

The monkey and bananas problem can be solved with this search algorithm. We will not discuss immediately how C makes selections except to assume that it usually makes good decisions. Here is a trace of the computation:

(a)   ACTIVE = { (M:C, C:B) }, CLOSED = { }.

(b)   Criterion C selects N = (M:C, C:B).   ACTIVE becomes empty.

(c)   N is not a goal.

(d)   Children of N are added to ACTIVE. ACTIVE = { (M:A, C:B),(M:B, C:B) }

(e)   CLOSED = { (M:C, C:B) }.

(b)   Criterion C selects N = (M:A, C:B). ACTIVE is reduced to { (M:B, C:B) }

(c)   N is not a goal.

(d)   The children of N = (M:A, C:B) are   (M:B, C:B) and (M:C, C:B). But one is
       on ACTIVE and the other is on CLOSED.

(e)   CLOSED = { (M:C, C:B), (M:A, C:B) }

(b)   Criterion C selects N = (M:B, C:B). Active is reduced to { }.

(c)   N is not a goal.

(d)   The children of N are added to ACTIVE (except for those already on
       CLOSED) ACTIVE = { (M:A, C:A),(M:C, C:C),(M:B', C:B) }

(e)   CLOSED = { (M:C, C:B),(M:A, C:B),(M:B, C:B) }

(b)   Criterion C selects N = (M:A, C:A) from ACTIVE.
       ACTIVE = { (M:C, C:C), (M:B', C:B) }

(c)   N is not a goal.

(d)   The children of N not already on ACTIVE or CLOSED are (M:B, C:A),
       (M:C, C:A), (M:A', C:A). These are added ACTIVE,
       ACTIVE = { (M:C, C:C), (M:B', C:B), (M:B, C:A), (M:C, C:A),(M:A', C:A) }

(e)   CLOSED = { (M:C, C:B), (M:A, C:B), (M:B, C:B), (M:A, C:A) }

(b)   Criterion C selects N = (M:A', C:A).
       ACTIVE = { (M:C, C:C), (M:B', C:B), (M:B, C:A), (M:C, C:A) }

(c)   N is not a goal.

(d)   There is only one child of N not already on ACTIVE or CLOSED:
       (M:A', C:A,M holds bananas)
       ACTIVE = { (M:C, C:C), (M:B', C:B), (M:B, C:A), (M:C, C:A),
       (M:A', C:A, M holds bananas) }

(e)   CLOSED = { (M:C, C:B), (M:A, C:B), (M:B, C:B), (M:A, C:A),(M:A', C:A) }

(b)   Criterion C selects N = (M:A', C:A, M holds bananas).

(c)   N is a goal.
       Print "success".
       Print: go B, push A, climbup, grasp.
       Halt.

The selection criterion *C* greatly affects the operation of this algorithm. You can observe its
effects by searching the same tree with different *C*:

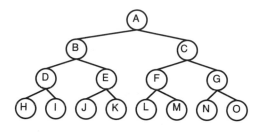

Suppose *C* always chooses the node on *ACTIVE*, which is shallowest (nearest *A*) and on the left when there are ties. Then the nodes will be selected in the order *A,B,C,D,E,F,G,H,I,J,K,L,M,N,O*. This is called a *breadth-first* search and results in a flat frontier of newly examined nodes that progresses downward on the tree:

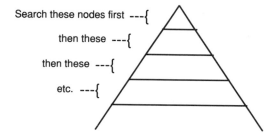

A different strategy is to have *C* select the deepest node on *ACTIVE*, preferring those on the left if there is a tie. This results in an order that goes to the bottom of the tree very quickly and then moves across the tree: *A,B,D,H,I,E,J,K,C,F,L,M,G,N,O*. This is called a *depth-first* search, and it gives a sideways movement for the frontier of new nodes.

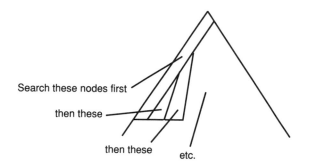

Both strategies are common in applications because they exhaustively cover the whole tree. If a goal is to be found, they will find it. The only restriction is that for a depth-first search, the tree must be finite.

But a third strategy is often preferred over both. It assumes the system has some knowledge about how to find the goal, and node selections are made in the direction of the earliest possible achievement of the goal. For example, in the monkey and bananas problem, if there were many positions for the monkey to select, it might prefer to move to those near the bananas. If it were frustrated in its attempts to reach its goal, it might look for objects that could be used and bring them also near the bananas. Reexamining the example tree, if L is a goal node, criterion C might select $A,C,F,$ and L in sequence and immediately solve the problem. If the information were weaker, the algorithm might choose A,B,C,F,G,M,L solving the problem quickly but with a small number of superfluous excursions. The design of the C function attempts to build in information that will enable the search to go as directly as possible toward the goal:

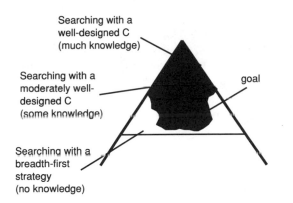

Many times when the C function is constructed, the designer is not sure whether the information being programmed will help. If it does help, the system will quickly converge to its solution. If not, the system will wander somewhat before finding the goal. In the worst case, the system might never find the goal. When the C function is programmed with knowledge that may or may not help find the solution, it is called a *heuristic* function. Examples of heuristic functions are those that suggest that in a navigational situation going toward the goal is usually helpful, in a manipulative system trying a tool often helps if the task is not immediately solvable, in a building situation constructing the foundation is typically a good first step, and so forth. These heuristics often lead effectively toward solutions, but sometimes they fail, and a wider search is needed to solve a problem.

Exercises

1. Consider a grid of streets, with numbered streets going north and south (First Street, Second Street, etc.) and lettered streets going east and west (A Street, B Street, etc.). Assume one is at the corner of Fifth Street and G Street and wishes to go to the corner of Seventh Street and H Street. Further assume there are four operations E,W,N,S meaning go east one block, go west one block, go north one block, and go south one block, respectively. Show the decision tree with the initial

node at the top (the corner of Fifth and G Streets). Show all possible decision sequences of length three. Show the operation of the above search algorithm in the cases where

(a) *C* chooses a breadth-first search,

(b) *C* chooses a depth-first search limited to depth three, and

(c) *C* selects the node closest to the direction of the goal.

2. Draw the complete tree of allowable moves to depth three for the Towers of Hanoi problem with two disks. Show how the search algorithm finds the solution using a breadth-first strategy *C*. Can you invent a better *C* function?

Game Playing (B)

We next consider reasoning processes when an adversary is trying to defeat our efforts. In a game-playing situation, one searches down the tree of alternative moves in a similar manner to the previous section, but it is necessary to account for the opponent's actions. The nature of the search can be seen by examining the tree for the game of Nim with 5 squares:

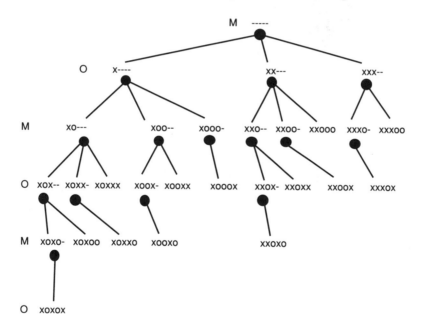

This tree needs to be searched with the goal of finding a winning position. But the problem is made more difficult by the knowledge that the opponent will attempt to choose paths that avoid a win for the machine.

The tree has two kinds of nodes: those labeled M where the machine is to make the move and those labeled O where the opponent is to move. Nodes will be marked W if they are known, by one means or another, to lead to a win for the machine. If the machine is at a node where it sees a win for itself anywhere among the child nodes, it will move toward that child node:

In fact, we can mark the parent node as a winning node since the machine is capable of making the move:

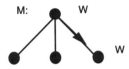

But if the opponent is in the same situation, the move will usually be made away from the position W where the machine would win.

For an 0 node, the position cannot be marked W as a win for the machine unless *all* of the children nodes are marked W:

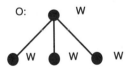

That is, the opponent is not in a position where the machine is guaranteed to win unless all of its choices are positions where the machine will win.

These observations lead to a method for analyzing a game. Begin at the bottom of the tree and mark all terminating positions where the machine will win with Ws. Then consider all nodes just above terminating positions. Nodes where the machine is to move that have at least one W-marked child are marked W. Nodes where the opponent is to move are marked W only if all of their child nodes are marked W. This process is repeated for layer after layer of nodes up the tree until the top node is reached. If the top node is labeled W, the machine will be able to win the game, and its strategy is to move in the direction of the W at each decision point. If the top node is not labeled W, the machine will not win unless the opponent blunders.

Carrying out this procedure on the 5-Nim game tree, you can discover that the machine will win, and its first move should be a single X:

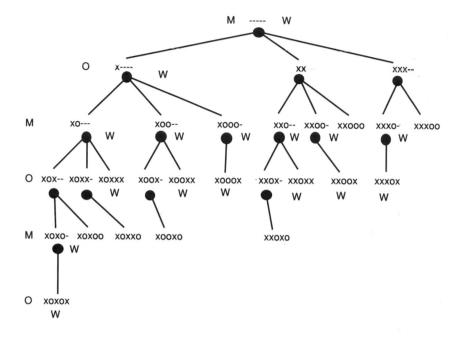

Regardless of what response the opponent gives, the machine will be able to win on the next move.

After some study, we realize that the Nim game of size 5 is not very interesting. The first player always wins, and the moves are so obvious that no one can remain interested in it very long. As soon as we have decided who will play first, we know the winner even before the game begins.

We can then move on to larger Nim games, but they also can be solved in the same way. If we have a computer fast enough to build the tree and pass the Ws to the top, those games will be solved as completely as 5-Nim. For those games also, it will be known before play begins who will win (although it will not always be the first player).

Generalizing even further, we can say that any game with the characteristics of Nim can be solved completely by building the tree and passing Ws up from the bottom. But what are those characteristics? First, the game tree must be finite so that it can be completely searched. Second, it should be deterministic with no throw of the dice or other random process. It is not possible to analyze the tree so simply if the move outcomes are not known. Finally, the game must offer both players complete information about the state. If the opposition holds cards not known to the machine or if other state information is not available, the machine will not know where it is on the tree. *In summary, any deterministic finite game of complete information can be solved by the procedure given here.* Before play begins, we can use the above procedure to determine the winner. (Some games allow for the possibility of a draw. This is easy to account for and is left as an exercise.)

The final interesting observation is that many common games fit the specification given. For example, chess and checkers are deterministic, finite games of complete information. If we had a machine fast enough to build their complete trees, we could determine who will be the winner of these games before the first move is played and how to make each move to achieve the guaranteed win. However, these game trees are so large that no one has been able to build them, and so their solutions remain unknown. (These games might seem to be infinite since two players could simply alternate their pieces back and forth forever to achieve unending play. However, there is no need to analyze a game that loops back on its own previous states since such play results in neither a win nor a loss for the machine.)

The tree search methodology can still be used to play large games if a technique can be found to avoid following paths to the end of the game. The usual method is to have an *evaluation function* that can compute a number that estimates the value of a given game state. Then the decision procedure can attempt to reach states of high value. In the game of chess, for example, the procedure could add up the pieces on each side giving greater weight to the stronger pieces such as the rooks and queens. The value of a position would be the weighted value of the machine's pieces minus the weighted value of the opponent's. The machine would then seek positions with greater piece advantages. Typical chess programs also allot points for positional advantage — such things as a castled king or a good pawn structure.

The search tree in this case would look more like the following. The system has constructed move sequences to a constant depth   four in this case   instead of going to the game's end. The game state evaluation is given at each node reached along the bottom.

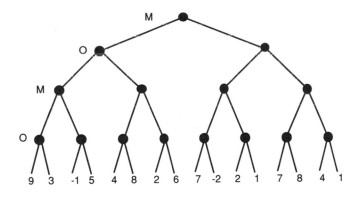

Next you can compute a value for every other node of the tree. The value of the node at any machine move M is the maximum of the values of its children. This assumes it will always try to obtain the best position as scored by the evaluation function. The value of any node at an opponent's move is chosen to be the minimum of its children on the assumption that the opponent will harm the machine's position as much as possible. Using these two rules, the values can be passed up from the bottom to obtain a score at the initial node of the tree. This is a process called *minimaxing*:

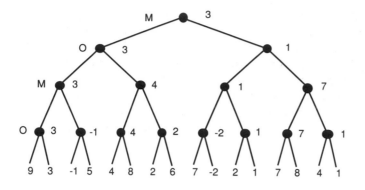

As before, the marker at the tree top shows the best achievable state reachable at the bottom of the tree. The nodes with this same value show the machine which move to make at each point to achieve this best value.

The tree search can be shortened by using *tree pruning* strategies that make it possible to omit parts of the calculation. The most powerful known technique is *alpha-beta* tree pruning, which uses partial results from the search to prove the uselessness of other portions of the search. An illustration of this is shown in the following tree where the program has evaluated three board positions below the O nodes:

The first O node will have value 3, and the second 0 node will have value 1 or less. Then the top node, which chooses the maximum of its children, will have value 3. Although one node (marked with ?) has not been evaluated, we know the value of the top node. So we can avoid the cost of generating that last node and evaluating its quality. This type of pruning can result in huge savings in realistic games.

Game-playing programs that use limited search with evaluation functions as described here completely depend on the accuracy of the evaluations for their quality of play. Precise accuracy will lead to excellent play, and moderate accuracy will lead to rambling play. Much recent research in game playing has been centered on the improvement of board evaluations.

Exercises

1. At the beginning of this section, a method was described for backing Ws up from the bottom of a game tree to determine whether the first player can force a win. Show how to modify this theory in the case where a game can have three outcomes: win W, loss L, or draw D.

2. Analyze the game of tic-tac-toe and determine whether it is a win, a draw, or a loss for the first player.

3. Assume that the minimax tree shown above has the following values across its nodes at the bottom: 6,-10,4,7,2,19,-7,4,8,-2,-8,3,3,11,4,-4. Do a minimax back up to determine the best value that the first player can achieve.

4. Repeat the minimax search shown in this chapter but show that some of the values at the bottom of the tree are not needed to find the value at the tree root. The alpha-beta procedure enables a system to avoid computing some of these values.

Game Playing: Historical Remarks (C)

The history of game playing has gone through three rather interesting phases. The first stage came in the very early days of computing, during the 1940s. Many individuals at that time believed that computers would win as resoundingly at chess and checkers as they do at adding numbers. It was believed that computers could search and evaluate thousands of moves in these games while humans looked at only a few dozen. With such a remarkable advantage, the machines would clearly outsearch any human and take over the world championships.

However, when the first programs began to work, their authors were shocked at their incredible incompetence. Even the most bumbling amateurs could beat them, and researchers scrambled to determine why. The answer lay in a combination of two factors, the first related to the nature of the game trees and the second related to the power of the human mind. Chess and checkers have average branching factors around 35 and 7, respectively, so that the number of nodes at depth i is 35^i and 7^i. Even with substantial pruning, the programs could examine trees of depth no more than three or four. Humans, on the other hand, seem to have a magical instinct to look at the "right" moves, and they were examining lines of play far deeper than the machines:

Game tree:

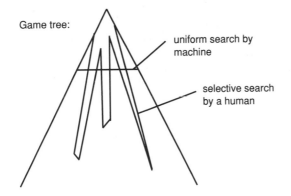

uniform search by machine

selective search by a human

The machines were wasting their computation time on huge numbers of positions that humans ignore. The humans were discovering the strong moves with their deeper well-guided searches.

This led to the second phase of game-playing research—a period of about two decades when researchers attempted to capitalize on the early lessons learned. The common wisdom was that the combinatorics of the game tree made uniform search a ridiculous undertaking. Only selective search of the type that humans do could succeed. Thus, a variety of heuristic tree search methods were developed, including ways to find "hot spots" on the board, play standard tricks on the opponent, and plan long sequences of offensive moves. The resulting programs improved over the years and occasionally exhibited spectacular play. But against competent human players, they remained poor competitors. The programs were able to see many lines of play to a deep level, but they were not finding moves of the quality that humans can find.

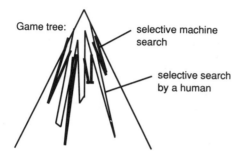

Humans continued to have an instinct for the game that mystified the scholars.

In about 1970, the community had another surprise. A group of researchers at Northwestern University rejected the accepted theory that selective search is the only reasonable approach to game playing. They brought a uniform search chess program to a national computer championship and defeated all other machines. And they continued to defeat all comers for some years after that. They also played better against humans than any previous program, achieving a good record against amateur but not master-level players. The analysis in this case was that for the best total game performance, conservative error-free tactical play is more important than occasional spectacular play. The faster machines of the 1970s made search depth good enough, about 5 or 6 in chess, to achieve solid play, and, within that depth, the machine never made a mistake. If the opponent program ever missed even one key move during the game, the uniform search program would discover it and crush its opponent.

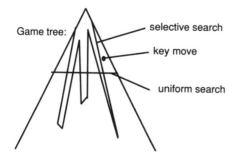

The best chess and checker game programs have continued to use this same strategy. They examine millions of positions before each move over a relatively uniform tree and use a variety of methods to speed up search and improve evaluation. Despite this huge computational effort and despite four decades of research, they still cannot win the world championship. However, chess and checker programs are finally able to play at the master level, and they continue to improve each year.

Computer game playing has provided a fascinating study in computer and human intelligence, giving insights on the nature of each. Computers continue to excel at doing simple activities millions of times, and their best performance is achieved when one is able to organize this activity to obtain useful results. Humans continue to have astonishing, almost mystical abilities to recognize significant patterns and to use them effectively. In game playing, computers and humans have achieved substantial levels of intelligence, but they use profoundly different methods.

Exercise

1. Assume the company you work for is proposing to build an automatic decision maker for corporate decisions. It will receive information about economic conditions, the current corporate status, projected trends for the future, and so forth. The program is to search the tree of possible decisions for the coming years and decide which sequence of decisions will lead to the best long-term well-being for the firm. Is there any information that comes from the history of game playing that will affect your judgment on the current project?

Expert Systems (B)

During the 1970's artificial intelligence researchers became interested in the reasoning processes of so-called "experts." These people work at specialized jobs over many years and develop apparently well-formulated routines for functioning effectively. Such a person begins a problem-solving task by looking for key factors and then selects some initial action perhaps to gather some information. This may result in a decision and additional actions until the task is complete. At each stage, the expert seems to use an established formula for action: looking for certain facts, making appropriate conclusions, searching for other needed information, and so forth. The behaviors seem well formulated, predictable, rule based, and perhaps within the range of computer simulation.

Some examples of the kinds of experts that have been studied are doctors in the performance of routine diagnosis and prescription, repairmen in the test and diagnosis of equipment failures, geologists in the search for minerals, and agricultural experts in the task of giving advice on the care and nurture of crops. These people have been interviewed at length to discover their knowledge and how their decision-making processes work. They are led by the interviewer through innumerable typical scenarios and asked to explain in detail every thought that helps them reach their conclusions. Then the interviewer, sometimes called a *knowledge engineer*, attempts to construct a model of their expert knowledge and reasoning processes.

A common observation of many researchers in this field is that experts often express their knowledge in terms of if-then rules: "If I observe that X and Y are true, I know that condition Z is occurring. If condition Z occurs and A and B are true, I usually prescribe $Q \ldots$ " In fact, the if-then form of knowledge representation is so common that it has become the basis for many computer programs that attempt to emulate expert behaviors. We will now examine a portion of such a program to try to gain a feeling for this work.

Suppose the Internal Revenue Service of the U.S. Government employs experts to decide when to audit income tax forms. Further suppose that our task is to build a program to do this job automatically. We will first interview an expert in this field and then attempt to code his or her knowledge in the form of if-then rules. Finally, we will examine a processor of such rules, and observe its actions in mimicking the expert.

First, we will pretend that the following interview takes place:

Interviewer:	When do you prescribe an audit?
Expert:	I often look for something unusual either in the income declarations or in the deductions.
Interviewer:	What kinds of peculiarities are likely to appear in income?
Expert:	First, the income may be ridiculously low when you consider the person's profession. The other thing I look for is poorly documented income.
Interviewer:	What do you expect in terms of income documentation?
Expert:	The person should either have a W-2 form or a systematic method for writing receipts for all funds received.
Interviewer:	Let's go back to deductions. What do you look for there?
Expert:	If I see the person claiming deductions that exceed 20 percent of their income, I become suspicious.

The interview may be complex and go on for many hours. However, we will limit ourselves to analyzing only these few sentences.

Specifically, we wish to code the knowledge from the interview into a set of if-then rules. The first exchange between the interviewer and expert yields this rule.

"If the income is unusual

or

the deductions are unusual, then

prescribe an audit."

In abbreviated notation, this rule will be written as

```
IncomeUnusual or DeductionsUnusual -> Audit
```

The second interaction leads to another such rule, which can also be written in concise notation:

```
IncomeNotDoc or IncomeTooLow  ->  IncomeUnusual
```

We will assume that *IncomeTooLow* is easy to check. One notes the person's profession and then looks up in a table the minimum expected income for that profession. Let us assume that a function called *CheckData* exists to examine the income tax form and related tables. Then this rule will be written as

```
IncomeNotDoc or CheckData(Income < MinIncome(Profession))—>
                                        IncomeUnusual
```

The last part of the listed interview yields two more rules:

```
CheckData (No W2) and CheckData (No Receipts) —> IncomeNotDoc
CheckData (Deduction > 0.2 * Income) —> DeductionsUnusual
```

Next we need an algorithm that will execute these rules like a kind of computer program. The algorithm resembles the search algorithm given above in that it builds a tree beginning at the root node. The function of the computation, however, will not be to find a goal at the bottom of the tree but rather to *achieve* a goal at the root of the tree.

The algorithm uses several ideas that need to be defined. We say a node is *achieved* if a rule leading to it is *satisfied* or if it is a *Checkdata* call that yields "yes." The rules are of two kinds: those that have left-side parts connected by *and* and those with left-side parts connected by *or*. If the left-side parts are connected by *and*, the rule is *satisfied* when all its left-side parts are achieved. If the left parts are connected by *or*, the rule is *satisfied* when at least one of its left parts is achieved. A node is said to be *fully explored* if it is a *Datacheck* node and the check has been made or if there are no more rules with this node as a right side that have not been selected and added to the tree. The purpose of the search is to find enough facts to achieve the goal at the root. A list called *ACTIVE* is used as before to store the tree nodes that need to be examined:

```
put the goal node on ACTIVE (For the tax example, this is Audit.)
begin building a tree by creating a root node that contains the goal
while ACTIVE has nodes not fully explored do
   begin
   select an unachieved node on ACTIVE that is not fully explored
   if the node uses CheckData then
      begin
      execute CheckData
      if CheckData returns "yes" then
         mark this node as achieved and mark nodes above
         this node achieved if they are also achieved.
      if the root level goal is achieved then
         halt with success.
      end
   else
      begin
      select a rule for achieving this node
      add it to the tree to give a new set of child nodes
      put the tokens on the left side of the rule on ACTIVE
      end
   end
halt with failure
```

Each step of the tree-building process begins by selecting a node on the existing tree (from the *ACTIVE* list). For example, suppose *IncomeNotDoc* is chosen:

Then a rule is selected that is capable of achieving that node:

```
CheckData (No W2) and CheckData(No Receipts) -> IncomeNotDoc
```

The rule provides the basis for adding more nodes on the tree; each item on the left side of the rule becomes a new node:

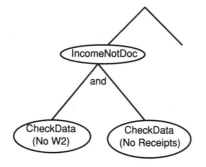

If the algorithm selects a node that is a *Datacheck*, it does the data check rather than building more nodes on the tree.

This algorithm can now be illustrated by observing its actions on the income tax problem. Suppose the following simplified form has been submitted:

Name:	John Smith
Profession:	Professor
Income:	$60,000 (no W2 or receipts)
Deductions:	$10,000

The algorithm begins by placing *Audit* on the *ACTIVE* list:

```
ACTIVE = {Audit}
```

And it initializes the tree by constructing the root node:

It then enters the loop, selects a node on *ACTIVE*, and selects a rule for achieving this node:

```
IncomeUnusual or DeductionsUnusual -> Audit
```

This rule is used as the basis for growing two child nodes on the tree:

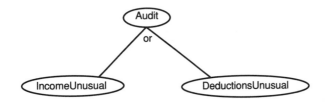

The *ACTIVE* list also receives these terms:

```
ACTIVE = {Audit, IncomeUnusual, DeductionsUnusual}
```

Repeating the loop, suppose the algorithm next chooses *IncomeUnusual* and finds a rule for achieving this node:

```
IncomeNotDoc or CheckData (Income < MinIncome (Profession))
                                               —> IncomeUnusual
```

Then more nodes can be grown on the tree, and the appropriate additions can be made to *ACTIVE*:

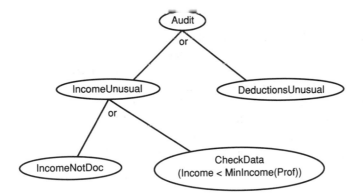

```
ACTIVE = {Audit, IncomeUnusual, DeductionsUnsual, IncomeNotDoc,
          CheckData (Income < MinIncome (Profession))}
```

The third repetition of the loop results in the following change if the *IncomeNotDoc* node is chosen:

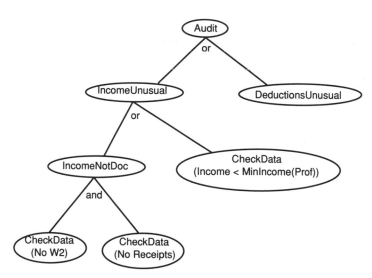

Additional repetitions will eventually result in the *CheckData* nodes at the tree bottom being selected. These will each reference the income tax form, and, for our example, return "yes." So they will be achieved. Their parent nodes will also be achieved; so also will each ancestor node to the top. In fact, the algorithm will halt with success; the *Audit* node has been achieved. The program recommends that this income tax form be audited.

The nodes on *ACTIVE* are not removed, because there may be many rules that lead to any given conclusion. If one rule is not successful in achieving a node, perhaps some other one will be.

The tremendous value of such a program is clear. Instead of having a person perusing forms at whatever rate is comfortable, a machine can apply the same procedures to thousands of forms. If the knowledge engineer has correctly encoded the expert's methodology, the system will do the same job, and the effectiveness of the expert will be multiplied manyfold. Furthermore, the automatic system offers many other advantages. It can be studied for accuracy and improved possibly beyond the original expert's procedures, and it can be changed easily if the tax law changes. A new employee working in the area could also study the system and thereby learn the methodologies of the profession.

The type of system described here is called an *expert system*. Such systems usually have rules resembling those of our example and a similar execution algorithm. They often have complex node and rule selection heuristics of the kind described in the game playing section. They also may enable the user to input facts with less than perfect confidence, and they may yield answers with less than perfect confidence as a human would do. Thus a confidence factor with a value somewhere from 0 to 1 is associated with each fact where 0 indicates no confidence, 1 indicates complete confidence, and fractions indicate intermediate levels. Finally, expert systems usually include an ability to print their own reasoning chain, the tree, so that the user can see what conclusion has been derived and what steps led to this conclusion.

Exercises

1. Show how the tax audit expert system would handle the following case:

Name:	John Smith
Profession:	Professor
Income:	$60,000 (W2 included)
Deductions:	$20,000

2. Show how the tax audit expert system would handle the following case:

Name:	John Smith
Profession:	Professor
Income:	$60,000 (W2 included)
Deductions:	$5,000

3. Design a set of rules that indicate the prerequisites to your favorite university level course. The top level goal should be *CourseRecommended*, and the rules should be designed to achieve this goal if a person meets the criteria that you specify. Demonstrate the use of these rules on typical cases by employing the algorithm for rule execution.

4. Interview an expert in some field, and design a set of rules to emulate the person's behavior when addressing some particular problem.

Perspective (B)

Now we have learned how to store knowledge in a computer and how a computer can learn, reason, and understand. It would seem that the fundamental mechanisms are at hand and that it should be possible to build intelligent machines. If we want to build a machine to understand natural language, it would appear that we need only to store sufficient knowledge and have some linguists compile a set of rules for the portion of the language of interest. If we wish to build an image-understanding system, apparently we need only to build a knowledge base for that domain and construct the needed reasoning capabilities. If we want to build machines to invent jokes, compose music, analyze scientific data, interview job applicants, write stories, or create mathematics, we can hope that there will be knowledge bases large enough and reasoning systems powerful enough to do any of these jobs. Humans are capable of all of these behaviors, and we have reason to believe that they follow principled methodologies. Computers seem to have ample memory size and speed, so there does not appear to be a lack of computational power.

In fact, computer programs have been written that demonstrate almost every imaginable intelligent behavior. As an example, a volume was published in 1963 with eighteen extremely exciting papers describing such systems. It is called *Computers and Thought* and was edited by E. Feigenbaum and J. Feldman. Here is a brief description of some of the reported results.

"Some Studies in Machine Learning Using the Game of Checkers," A. L. Samuel: A checker playing program is described which used a tree search and board evaluation methodology similar to the one explained in this chapter. The board evaluation function had the form $f = C_1 X_1 + C_2 X_2 + \ldots\ldots + C_{16} X_{16}$ where the C_is were constants to be determined and the X_is were features of the board such as the king advantage, number of pieces in the king row, or number of pieces in the board center squares. The C_is were numbers "learned" during actual play by slowly varying their values until best possible behaviors were achieved. The paper describes a game with "a former Connecticut checkers champion, and one of the nation's foremost players" which the program won by making "several star moves." (The quotations are from a journal that Samuel references.)

"Empirical Explorations of the Geometry Theorem Proving Machine," H. Gelernter, J. R. Hansen, and D. W. Loveland: The paper describes a program for solving plane geometry problems typical of those taught at the high school level. This program used a diagram of the geometry problem to heuristically guide the search for long proofs. The use of the diagram reduced the number of child nodes below a typical node from about 1000 to about 5 and thus greatly increased the program efficiency. This program was able to find some proofs that would be difficult for high school students - some with as many as 20 or more sequential steps.

"BASEBALL: An Automatic Question Answerer," B. F. Green, Jr., A. K. Wolf, C. Chomsky, and K. Laughery: A program is described that answered questions about baseball such as "Who did the Red Sox lose to on July 5?" or "Did every team play at least once in each park in each month?" The program stored data on baseball games in a tree structure giving for each month a list of all places, for each place a list of all days, and for each day a list of all games. Answers were obtained by translating the question into a standardized form and then matching it to the tree of data.

"GPS, a Program That Simulates Human Thought," A. Newell and H. A. Simon: The General Problem Solver, GPS, was a general search program for finding goals using sequences of operators. It utilized heuristic information to help choose the correct operator at each point and solved a variety of classical problems. The GPS was studied both as an exercise in artificial intelligence and as a possible model for human intelligence.

With such impressive results in the early 1960s, one surely would expect profound machine intelligence within a decade or two of that time. In fact, in 1957, Herbert Simon and Allen Newell had already predicted that within ten years, computer programs (1) would be able to win the world chess championship, (2) would find and prove some important new mathematical theorem, (3) would write music possessing aesthetic value, and (4) would be the models for most studies in psychology. (See reference by Simon and Newell in the readings.) The power of the new computers was clear, and the early results were encouraging. Many wise people were predicting a major revolution in the capabilities of machines. (Simon later received a Nobel Prize for his work in economics.)

Unfortunately, the original optimism proved to be unfounded. None of the early projects matured to astound the world. None of the Simon-Newell predictions came true in a decade, and most people will agree that they still have not been reached. Thirty years after the original period of great optimism, artificial intelligence remains a science in its infancy with relatively few results applicable to real-world problems. All of the systems described are examples of interesting laboratory studies, and large numbers more of them have been undertaken in recent years. But researchers have had great difficulties expanding initial narrowly defined projects, which in principle demonstrate exciting behaviors, into large, practical systems capable of what people are willing to call "intelligent."

The problem of building intelligent systems turned out to be much more difficult than the early researchers realized. People would begin projects, achieve a fraction of their goals in six months, and then predict that they could achieve all of their goals in a few years. They never dreamed that barely more than their original results would be achieved in their whole lifetimes. Again and again projects were begun in the many fields of artificial intelligence with great early optimism but were never able to achieve more than limited success on small problems.

Of course, all of these efforts have been newsworthy and well published over the years. Articles were common in the media in the early days predicting a new age when computers would achieve or surpass human abilities in various fields. Those articles continue to the present day, though we are not much closer to the goal now than we thought we were then.

Why has the field of artificial intelligence failed to produce intelligent machines? We do not know, but we are finally aware that real intelligence involves far more complexity than was ever predicted. It involves vast amounts of knowledge that we do not yet know how to acquire or organize or use. It involves complex reasoning of a kind that we cannot yet comprehend. It probably involves many other mechanisms that we do not even realize are needed. We simply do not understand intelligence.

But some progress has been made. Programs being written as we enter the 1990s are better than those written in the 1960s. The failures of the early decades have demonstrated what will not work, and able people are applying the best-known methodologies to create better systems for the future. At the risk of oversimplifying a rather complex picture, a few brief comments are included here about several subfields of artificial intelligence to give a feeling for the current state of the art.

Automatic Programming. This research area attempts to build systems that will automatically write programs. It assumes the user will give examples of the desired program behavior or will specify with a formal or natural language what the desired program is to do. The system will then write a program to satisfy the user's requirements. Automatic programming systems have been built that reliably create some small LISP programs, three or four lines long, from examples of the target behavior. Systems have also been created that enable a user to specify a program in an interactive session with a formal language, which then will create the target program. However, for general-purpose programming, such systems are usually not as convenient for serious programming as traditional programming languages.

Expert Systems. Hundreds of these systems have been programmed for industrial and governmental applications. They usually have from a few hundred to a few thousand rules, and if they are properly designed, they can be depended upon to carry out their narrowly defined tasks with some reliability.

Game Playing. Chess and checker programs have been developed to the point that they can challenge master-level players, and they are improving every year. Many other games have been programmed with varying levels of success.

Image Understanding. Computer systems have been built that are aimed at specific domains such as aerial photographs or pictures of human faces and which correctly find and label the significant features a high percentage of the time.

Mathematical Theory Formation. At least one system built (by Douglas Lenat) can derive new mathematical concepts from more primitive ones. This system was demonstrated in a series of computations where it derived the rudiments of number theory from concepts of set theory. However, it is not clear that the approach is applicable to broader classes of problems.

Natural Language Understanding. A number of systems have been built that are aimed at specific domains such as personnel databases or equipment repair tasks and that deliver proper responses a high percentage of the time. Such systems usually have limited vocabularies, fewer than a thousand words, and limited syntactic capabilities.

Natural Language Translation. If a system is constructed to understand natural language in a limited domain, it is within the state of the art to convert the system into a translator to some other natural language. Therefore, we can say that natural language translation can be achieved with high accuracy in limited domains where small vocabulary and narrow syntactic variety are needed. In an application where wide vocabulary and syntactic variety are needed, completely automatic natural language translation is far beyond the state of the art. However, computers are still useful in these translation tasks by parsing input sentences, by displaying word alternatives in the object language that can be selected by a human translator, and by providing convenient editing.

Learning. The performance of a few systems has been improved by the use of learning mechanisms that optimize parameters as described in the sections of chapter 12 on connectionist networks. The Arthur Samuel checker program used this scheme. Also, concept learning mechanisms have been applied to analyzing complex scientific data with the result, in a few cases, that trends or relationships in the data were automatically discovered.

Speech Recognition. Many systems have been built that enable a user to speak rather than type inputs to the machine. These systems often require a user to speak samples of the application vocabulary so that the machine can be tuned to the individual's voice. They also may require that the user speak sentences leaving a short pause (of about 1/3 second) after each word. Vocabulary sizes are usually limited to fewer than 2000 words, and the recognition rates on individual words may be highly dependent on the tuning of the system, the clarity of the user's speech, the quality and placement of the microphone, and other factors.

In summary, researchers have found that computers can be programmed to exhibit to a small extent almost any intelligent behavior - perception, learning, problem solving, language processing, and others. Numerous projects have demonstrated these kinds of behaviors. But to achieve any of these phenomena to a large extent or to integrate them to obtain moderately intelligent behavior is very difficult and in most cases, far beyond the state of the art. The best results have occurred in the environment of narrow domains where only limited kinds of behaviors are needed and usually where there has been tolerance for error.

Some researchers believe that most artificial intelligence subfields face the same central problem of complex representation and reasoning and that if the problem can be solved in one field, it will be solved for all of them. For example, if one could solve properly the natural language problem to the point that a machine can process language as well as humans, then the methodology that makes this possible will be the key to solving many diverse problems such as those related to vision, problem solving, theorem proving, automatic programming, and many others. Thomas Truscott has called this hypothesis the *Thesis of AI Completeness,* and it is likely to remain a controversial idea for years to come.

In the commercial world, artificial intelligence has had some important successes. In the field of expert systems, large numbers of useful programs have been developed, and they are being operated regularly in many enterprises. In natural language processing, some commercial systems have become available, and thousands of people are now able to do some standard tasks such as access databases with typed natural language input. Game-playing programs have become commercially profitable and are widely available. Perhaps a lesser noticed but extremely important product of artificial intelligence research has been the series of computer languages that have been created to do the research. These include LISP, which is widely used as a symbolic programming language, Prolog, which is becoming popular and has even served as a prototype language for the Japanese fifth-generation computer series, and a long list of languages for programming expert systems.

Finally, we have noticed that there are aspects of human intelligence that seem to be completely out of reach for the foreseeable future. First, there is the ability to understand the human condition —an ability that we propose one must be a human to have. Second, there is the astounding pattern recognition ability that humans exhibit in game playing, for example. People are able to see in a single position things not visible to a machine in a search of a millions of positions. Last, there is the huge knowledge base that humans have and the incredible flexibility with which it is used in achieving intelligent behavior.

Exercises

1. Assume that you are asked to prepare the specifications for a robot vision and audio output system. The robot is to roam an area too dangerous for humans (because of radiation or other hazards) and report verbally its observations. The vision and audio output system will have three main subsystems: an image processor to find the important features in the scene, a problem-solving system to decide which features are significant enough to describe, and a language planning and output system to enunciate the needed utterances. Prepare specifications for each of the three subsystems that you believe are within the current state-of-the-art.

2. Present arguments for and against the Thesis of AI Completeness.

Summary (A)

Artificial intelligence is a field of study where researchers attempt to build or program machines with capabilities more complex than have been possible traditionally. These include the abilities to perceive and understand incoming data, to learn, to process natural language, and to reason. The fundamental paradigm for such studies includes the concepts of knowledge and reasoning, and these were examined in this chapter.

The knowledge of an object is the set of all information required to deal with it in related processing. Knowledge can be stored in various forms and is used in understanding perception or in reasoning processes. Knowledge can be input to a machine by being formatted and read in directly, or it can be acquired by the machine through learning.

Reasoning is the process of finding a sequence of linkages that will lead from one object in memory to another. Often, the goal of reasoning is to find a way to change the current state of the world into some desired state. Reasoning is done by selectively searching the tree of possible action sequences until the desired one is found. Many artificial intelligence systems have been built over the years using these ideas, and some of them are described here.

This section concludes this book, which is a study of what computers are, what they can do, and what they cannot do. The early chapters introduced programming and are primarily a study of what computers can do. A variety of example problems and their solutions were given, and the culmination was the Church-Markov-Turing Thesis, that any process that we can describe precisely can be programmed on a machine.

The second part of the book examined what computers are so that they may be understood in a deeper way. Specifically, they are simply boxes capable of executing the fetch-execute cycle at very high speed. Their usefulness comes primarily from the fact that convenient languages can be translated into a form that is amenable to the fetch-execute style of computation. They are made up of millions of tiny switches etched into silicon crystals and organized to store information and compute.

The last part of the book examined advanced topics in computer science. These included the study of execution time and the division of computations into tractable and intractable classes. Then parallel computing was introduced as a means for reducing execution time, and some example problems were studied within this paradigm. One fascinating type of parallel machine is the connectionist network that spreads information and computation across an array of tiny processors and programs itself through learning. Next we studied noncomputability and attempted to gain intuition for a class of functions that, as far as we know, cannot be programmed. Finally, we studied artificial intelligence and the attempts of researchers to build machines that can know, understand, learn, and reason in ways that are reminiscent of human thinking.

Readings

On artificial intelligence in general:

Charniak, E., and McDermott, D., *Introduction to Artificial Intelligence*, Addison-Wesley, Reading, Massachusetts, 1985.

Feigenbaum, E. A. and Feldman, J. (eds.), *Computers and Thought*, McGraw-Hill, New York, 1963.

Nilsson, N. J., *Principles of Artificial Intelligence*, Tioga Press, Palo Alto, California, 1980.

Rich, E. A., *Artificial Intelligence*, McGraw-Hill, New York, 1983.

Shapiro, S. C. (ed.), *Encyclopedia of Artificial Intelligence*, John Wiley, New York, 1987.

Simon, H. A. and Newell, A., "Heuristic Problem Solving: The Next Advance in Operations Research", *Operations Research* , January-February, 1958.

Winston, P., *Artificial Intelligence*, Addison-Wesley, Reading, Massachusetts, 1985.

On knowledge representation:

Brachman, R. J., and Levesque, H. J. (eds.), *Readings in Knowledge Representation,* Morgan-Kaufmann, Los Altos, California, 1985.

Findler, N. V. (ed.), *Associative Networks, Representation and Use of Knowledge by a Computer,* Academic Press, New York, 1979.

Sowa, J. F., *Conceptual Structures,* Addison-Wesley, Reading, Massachusetts, 1984.

Winston, P., *The Psychology of Computer Vision,* McGraw-Hill, New York, 1975.

On learning and automatic programming:

Biermann, A. W., Guiho, G., and Kodratoff, Y., *Automatic Program Construction Techniques,* Macmillan, New York, 1984.

Michalski, R. S., Carbonell, J. G., and Mitchell, T. M., *Machine Learning,* Springer-Verlag, Berlin, 1983.

Michalski, R. S., Carbonell, J. G., and Mitchell, T. M., *Machine Learning,* vol. 2, Morgan Kaufmann Publishers, Los Altos, California, 1986.

Minsky, M., and Papert, S., *Perceptrons,* The MIT Press, Cambridge, Massachusetts, 1969.

Mitchell, T. M., Carbonell, J. G., and Michalski, R. S., *Machine Learning. A Guide to Current Research,* Kluwer Academic Publishers, Boston, 1986.

On natural language processing:

Allen, J., *Natural Language Understanding,* Benjamin/Cummings Publishing Company, Menlo Park, California, 1987.

Grishman, R., *Computational Linguistics,* Cambridge University Press, Cambridge, England, 1986.

Sager, N., *Natural Language Information Processing,* Addison-Wesley, Reading, Massachusetts, 1981.

Simmons, R. F., *Computations from the English,* Prentice-Hall, Englewood Cliffs, New Jersey, 1984.

On reasoning:

Ernst, G. W., and Newell, A., *GPS, A Case Study in Generality and Problem Solving,* Academic Press, New York, 1969.

Kowalski, R. A., *Logic for Problem Solving,* North-Holland, Amsterdam, 1979.

Pearl, J., *Heuristics,* Addison-Wesley, Reading, Massachusetts, 1984.

Wos, L., Overbeek, R., Lusk, W., and Boyle, J., *Automated Reasoning: Introduction and Applications,* Prentice-Hall, Englewood Cliffs, New Jersey, 1984.

On game playing:

Levy, D., *Computer Gamesmanship,* Simon and Schuster, New York, 1983.

On expert systems:

Hayes-Roth, F., Waterman, D. A. and Lenat, D. B., *Building Expert Systems*, Addison-Wesley, Reading, Massachusetts, 1983.

Shortliffe, E. H., *Computer-Based Medical Consultations: MYCIN*, American Elsevier Publishing Company, Inc., New York, 1976.

On perspectives:

Dreyfus, H. L., *What Computers Can't Do: A Critique of Artificial Reason*, Harper & Row, New York, 1972.

Hofstadter, D. R., *Godel, Escher, Bach: An Eternal Golden Braid*, Basic Books, New York, 1979.

McCorduck, P., *Machines Who Think*, W. H. Freeman and Company, San Francisco, California, 1979.

Weizenbaum, J., *Computer Power and Human Reason*, W. H. Freeman and Company, San Francisco, California, 1976.

Appendix

The Rules for the Subset of Pascal Used in this Book

Here are the rules that generate the Turbo Pascal programs in this book. The rules leave out a few details such as parentheses in arithmetic expressions, two-dimensional arrays, nested Boolean expressions, and the formatting that one can include in a *writeln* statement to specify field widths.

Although these rules specify legal syntax for programs, they also can generate some programs that are illegal semantically, such as programs that do not declare variables. You must write code that follows the syntactic constraints given here and also follows the other rules of the language.

A manual on Pascal will include all the syntactic rules for the language, a much larger set than is given here. Usually such rules are given in the form of flowcharts.

Program:

```
<program>   -> program  <identifier>;
                  <type declaration>
                  <variable declaration>
                  <multiple procedures>
                  <compound statement>.
```

Type Declaration:

```
<type declaration> ->  nothing
<type declaration> ->  type
                          <identifier> = array[<int>..<int>] of <type>;
<int>  ->  any integer
```

Variable declaration:

```
<variable declaration> ->  nothing
<variable declaration>  ->  var
                              a sequence of  <identifier:type>'s
                              each  followed by a semicolon
<identifier:type> -> <identifier list> : <type>
<identifier list>->  a list of  <identifier>'s separated by commas
```

Type:

```
<type> -> string
<type> -> integer
<type> -> real
<type> -> <identifier>
```

Procedure declaration:

```
<multiple procedures> ->   nothing
<multiple procedures> ->   a sequence of  <procedure declaration>'s
<procedure declaration> -> procedure  <identifier> <parameter list>;
                               <variable declaration>
                               <compound statement>;
<parameter list> -> nothing
<parameter list> -> (a list of <var declaration>'s separated by
                               semicolons)
<var declaration> -> var <identifier:type>
```

Compound statement:

```
<compound statement>   ->  begin
                           a sequence of <statement>'s
                               each followed by a semicolon
                           end
```

Statement:

```
<statement>  ->  <compound statement>
<statement>  ->  writeln(list of  <expression>'s separated by
                                                commas)
<statement>  ->  readln(<identifier[]>)
<statement>  ->  readln
<statement>  ->  if  <boolean expression> then
                        <statement>
                 else
                        <statement>
<statement> ->  if  <boolean expression>  then
                        <statement>
<statement> ->  <identifier[]> := <expression>
<statement> ->  while <boolean expression> do
                        <statement>
<statement> ->  <identifier> <argument list>
```

Expression:

```
<expression> -> <string expression>
<expression> -> <integer expression>
<expression> -> <real expression>
```

String   expression:

```
<string expression> -> <identifier []>
<string expression> -> 'any string of printable characters  '
<string expression> -> <string expression> + <string expression>
<string expression>  ->
            copy(<string expression>,<integer expression>,<integer
                                                  expression>)
```

Integer expression:

```
<integer expression>  ->  any integer
<integer expression>  -> <identifier[]>
<integer expression> ->  <integer expression> <intop>  <integer
                                            expression>
<integer expression>  -> length(<string expression>)
<integer expression> -> pos(<string expression>,<string expression>)
<intop>  -> one of +, *, -, or  div
```

Real expression:

```
<real expression>  )  any real number
<real expression> -> <identifier[]>
<real expression> -> <real expression> <realop> <real expression>
<realop> -> one of +, *, -, or  /
```

Boolean expression:

```
<boolean expression>  ->  <identifier[]> <comp> <expression>
<boolean expression>  ->  true
<comp>  -> one of >, <, >-, <-, =, or  <>
```

Identifier and identifier-index:

```
<identifier[]> -> <identifier> possibly followed by an
                            <integer expression> in square brackets
<identifier>  ->  a sequence of letters and/or digits
                        that begins with a letter
```

Argument list:

```
<argument list> -> nothing
<argument list> -> (a list of  <identifier[]>'s separated by commas )
```

Index

Boldface numbers indicate pages where terms are defined or are treated in an important way.

Errata for

Great Ideas in Computer Science
by Alan W. Biermann

Most of the illustrations in this book were drawn with the assistance of a computer graphics program. In the very last stage of typesetting, a computer problem resulted in some unexpected and undetected errors which make some illustrations undecipherable. Correct versions follow.

The illustration on page 222
should look like this:

The illustrations on page 236
should look like this:

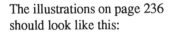

The illustrations on page 235
should look like this:

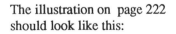

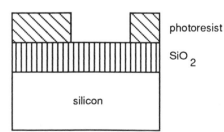

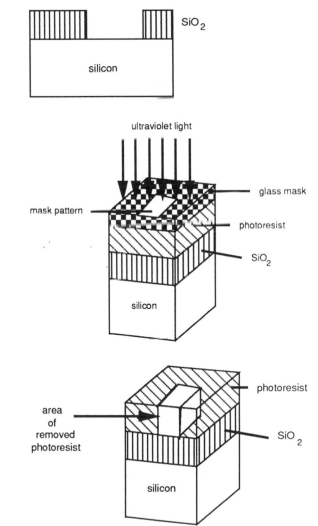

The illustrations on page 237
should look like this:

area of removed
SiO$_2$

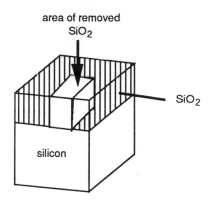

silicon

SiO$_2$

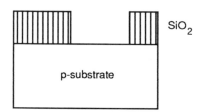

SiO$_2$

p-substrate

The illustrations on page 238
should look like this:

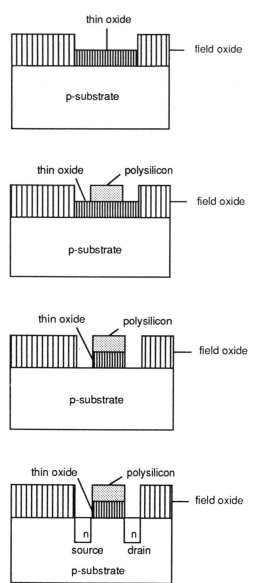

thin oxide

field oxide

p-substrate

thin oxide   polysilicon

field oxide

p-substrate

thin oxide   polysilicon

field oxide

p-substrate

thin oxide   polysilicon

field oxide

n   n

source   drain

p-substrate

The illustrations on page 239
should look like this:

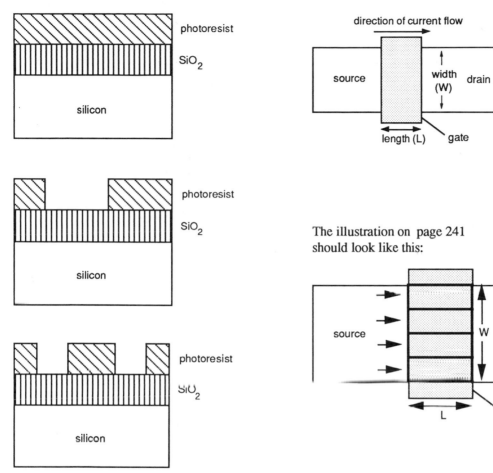

The illustration on page 240
should look like this:

The illustration on page 241
should look like this:

The illustrations on page 242 should look like this:

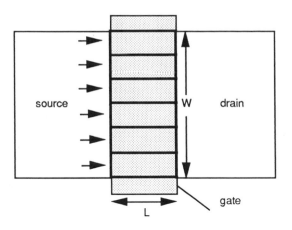

source W drain

gate

L

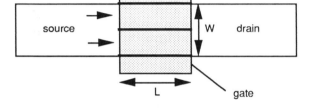

source W drain

gate

L

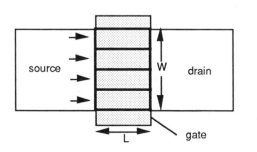

source W drain

gate

L

The illustration on page 245 should look like this:

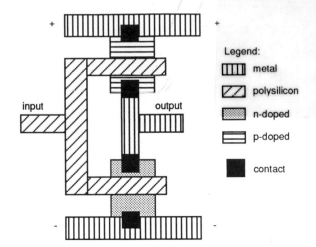

+   +

input   output

-                    -

Legend:

| | | | metal

polysilicon

n-doped

p-doped

contact

The illustration on page 247 should look like this:

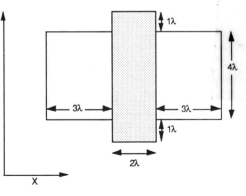

1λ

4λ

3λ 3λ

1λ

2λ

X

The illustration on page 411 should look like this:

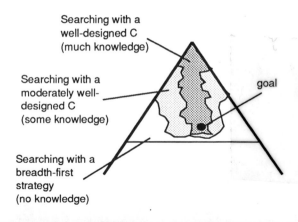

Searching with a
well-designed C
(much knowledge)

Searching with a
moderately well-
designed C
(some knowledge)

goal

Searching with a
breadth-first
strategy
(no knowledge)